Critical Theory and the Critique of Antisemitism

Critical Theory and the Critique of Society Series

In a time marked by crises and the rise of right-wing authoritarian populism, **Critical Theory and the Critique of Society** intends to renew the critical theory of capitalist society exemplified by the Frankfurt School and critical Marxism's critiques of social domination, authoritarianism, and social regression by expounding the development of such a notion of critical theory, from its founding thinkers, through its subterranean and parallel strands of development, to its contemporary formulations.

Series editors:
Werner Bonefeld, *University of York, UK and* **Chris O'Kane**, *John Jay College of Criminal Justice, City University of New York, USA*

Editorial Board:
Bev Best, Sociology, Concordia University
John Abromeit, History, SUNY, Buffalo State, USA
Samir Gandesha, Humanities, Simon Fraser University
Christian Lotz, Philosophy, Michigan State University
Patrick Murray, Philosophy, Creighton University
José Antonio Zamora Zaragoza, Philosophy, Spain
Dirk Braunstein, Institute of Social Research, Frankfurt
Matthias Rothe, German, University of Minnesota
Marina Vishmidt, Cultural Studies, Goldsmiths University
Verena Erlenbusch, Philosophy, University of Memphis
Elena Louisa Lange, Japanese Studies/Philology and Philosophy, University of Zurich
Marcel Stoetzler, Sociology, University of Bangor
Moishe Postone ז״ל, History, University of Chicago
Mathias Nilges, Literature, St Xavier University
Charlotte Baumann, Philosophy, Sussex/TU Berlin
Amy De'ath, Contemporary Literature and Culture, King's College London
Rochelle Duford, Philosophy, University of Hartford
Edith Gonzalez, Humanities, Universidad Intercultural del Estado de Puebla, México
Sami Khatib, Art, Leuphana University
Dimitra Kotouza, Education, University of Lincoln
Claudia Leeb, Political Science, Washington State University
Jordi Maiso, Philosophy, Complutense University of Madrid
Cat Moir, Germanic Studies, University of Sydney

Kirstin Munro, Political Science, University of Texas, Rio Grande
Duy Nyugen, English, University of Houston

Available titles:
Right-wing Culture in Contemporary Capitalism, Mathias Nilges
Adorno and Neoliberalism, Charles Andrew Prusik
Toward a Critical Theory of Nature, Carl Cassegård
Spectacular Logic in Hegel and Debord, Eric-John Russell
Adorno and Marx, Werner Bonefeld and Chris O'Kane

Critical Theory and the Critique of Antisemitism

Edited by
Marcel Stoetzler

BLOOMSBURY ACADEMIC
LONDON • NEW YORK • OXFORD • NEW DELHI • SYDNEY

BLOOMSBURY ACADEMIC
Bloomsbury Publishing Plc, 50 Bedford Square, London, WC1B 3DP, UK
Bloomsbury Publishing Inc, 1385 Broadway, New York, NY 10018, USA
Bloomsbury Publishing Ireland, 29 Earlsfort Terrace, Dublin 2, D02 AY28, Ireland

BLOOMSBURY, BLOOMSBURY ACADEMIC and the Diana logo
are trademarks of Bloomsbury Publishing Plc

First published in Great Britain 2023
Paperback edition published 2025

Copyright © Marcel Stoetzler and Contributors, 2023

Marcel Stoetzler has asserted his right under the Copyright, Designs
and Patents Act, 1988, to be identified as Editor of this work.

Series design by Ben Anslow

All rights reserved. No part of this publication may be: i) reproduced or
transmitted in any form, electronic or mechanical, including photocopying,
recording or by means of any information storage or retrieval system without
prior permission in writing from the publishers; or ii) used or reproduced
in any way for the training, development or operation of artificial intelligence (AI)
technologies, including generative AI technologies. The rights holders expressly
reserve this publication from the text and data mining exception
as per Article 4(3) of the Digital Single Market Directive (EU) 2019/790.

Bloomsbury Publishing Inc does not have any control over, or responsibility for,
any third-party websites referred to or in this book. All internet addresses given
in this book were correct at the time of going to press. The author and publisher
regret any inconvenience caused if addresses have changed or sites have
ceased to exist, but can accept no responsibility for any such changes.

A catalogue record for this book is available from the British Library.

A catalog record for this book is available from the Library of Congress.

ISBN: HB: 978-1-3502-8137-0
PB: 978-1-3502-8141-7
ePDF: 978-1-3502-8138-7
eBook: 978-1-3502-8139-4

Series: Critical Theory and the Critique of Society

Typeset by Newgen KnowledgeWorks Pvt. Ltd., Chennai, India

For product safety related questions contact productsafety@bloomsbury.com.

To find out more about our authors and books visit www.bloomsbury.com
and sign up for our newsletters.

Contents

List of contributors ix

Introduction: Critical Theory's critique of antisemitism 1
   Marcel Stoetzler

Part 1 Elements

1   The Critical Theory of antisemitism and the limits of enlightenment   29
   Jordi Maiso, translated by Alex Álvarez Taylor

2   Antisemitism in the British 'New Liberalism' movement: J. A. Hobson on capitalism and imperialism   51
   Matthew Bolton

3   Antisemitism and the critique of society as economic object   75
   Werner Bonefeld

4   Jews and other 'others': Identity and constellation in intersectional and Critical Theory   91
   Christine Achinger

5   Antisemitism, anti-capitalism, community: (Con)fusing reft and light   111
   Marcel Stoetzler

Part 2 Extensions

6   'Pathic' identification in populist movements: The spectre of antisemitism in right and left protest   143
   Patrick Ahern

7   Ancient aliens down to earth: Conspiracy theories, antisemitism and 'anonymous authority'   155
   Joan Braune

8   Antisemitism, antiblackness and the nation in the storming of the US Capitol   175
   Christopher D. Wright

9 Antisemitism and racism 'after Auschwitz': Adorno on the 'hellish unity' of 'permanent catastrophe' 203
   Jonathon Catlin

10 Antisemitism, centre-periphery dynamics and anti-Zionism in Poland today 231
   Anna Zawadzka, translated by Maja Jaros

11 Labour, antisemitism and the critique of political economy 253
   Matthew Bolton and Frederick Harry Pitts

Index 275

Contributors

Christine Achinger is Associate Professor of German Studies at the University of Warwick, UK. Her research interests are in critical social theory, literary studies, Jewish Studies, history and theories of antisemitism, and constructions of gender, race and national identity. Her publications include *Distorted Faces of Modernity: Racism, Antisemitism and Islamophobia* (co-edited with Robert Fine; 2015), 'German Modernity, Barbarous Slavs and Profit-Seeking Jews: The Cultural Racism of Nationalist Liberals' (with Marcel Stoetzler; 2013), 'Allegories of Destruction: "The Woman" and "the Jew" in Otto Weininger's *Geschlecht und Charakter*' (2013) and *Gespaltene Moderne. Gustav Freytags Soll und Haben – Nation, Geschlecht und Judenbild* (2007).

Patrick Ahern, PhD, is a political and ethical philosopher whose research focuses on themes of Critical Theory, early modern thought, human rights theory and critical social justice. His previous publications include 'The Possibilities of a Failed Promise: Placing Walter Benjamin and Theodor Adorno in Dialogue with Rights' and 'Empowered Peace: Spinoza's Defense of Dynamic and Inclusive Democracy'. He is currently serving as a senior lecturer in the Department of Philosophy at the University of Dayton in Dayton, Ohio.

Matthew Bolton, PhD, is a researcher at the Zentrum für Antisemitismusforschung at Technische Universität Berlin. He is a fellow of the London Centre for the Study of Contemporary Antisemitism and has authored *Corbynism: A Critical Approach* (with Harry Pitts; 2018). His work has appeared in journals such as *Philosophy and Social Criticism*, *Political Quarterly*, *British Politics*, *Journal of Contemporary Antisemitism* and *Fathom*. He is currently writing a book on the concept of justice and the historical process of capitalist state formation.

Werner Bonefeld is Professor Emeritus of Politics, University of York, UK, and Adjunct Professor at Postgraduate School ZRC SAZU, Slovenia. Book publications include *Critical Theory and the Critique of Political Economy* (2014), *The Strong State and the Free Economy* (2017) and *A Critical Theory of Economic Compulsion* (2023). With Beverley Best and Chris O'Kane, he is co-editor of the three-volume *Sage Handbook of Frankfurt School Critical Theory* (2018); and with Chris O'Kane, he is co-editor of *Adorno and Marx* (2022).

Joan Braune, PhD, teaches Philosophy and Leadership Studies at Gonzaga University and works in Critical Theory and Critical Hate Studies. She is author of *Erich Fromm's Revolutionary Hope: Prophetic Messianism as a Critical Theory of the Future* (2014), co-editor with Kieran Durkin of *Erich Fromm's Critical Theory: Hope, Humanism and* the *Future* (2020) and author of *Understanding and Countering Fascist Movements: From Void to Hope* (forthcoming in 2024). She also serves on the editorial board of the *Journal of Hate Studies* and has published numerous articles, chapters and reviews.

Jonathon Catlin is an intellectual historian working on German and Jewish thought, Critical Theory, Holocaust history and memory, and the politics of climate catastrophe. He earned his PhD in History and the Interdisciplinary Doctoral Program in the Humanities at Princeton University, where his dissertation investigated the concept of catastrophe in twentieth-century European thought. His writings have appeared in *Antisemitism Studies*, *Memory Studies*, *History and Theory*, *European Journal of Cultural and Political Sociology* and *Journal of the History of Ideas Blog*, where he is also a contributing editor. In 2023, he began a postdoctoral research fellowship at the University of Rochester Humanities Center, New York.

Jordi Maiso is Professor at the Department of Philosophy and Society at Universidad Complutense de Madrid. He has published *Desde la vida dañada. La teoría crítica de Theodor W. Adorno* (From Damaged Life: Theodor W. Adorno's Critical Theory) (2022) and several essays on Critical Theory, aesthetics and social theory. He is Director of the Iberoamerican review of critical theory *Constelaciones. Revista de Teoría Crítica*, and President of the Spanish Society of Critical Theory Studies. His work addresses the critique of modern capitalist society, chiefly focusing on issues such as the culture industry today, antisemitism and the politics of resentment, and the social constitution of subjectivity.

Frederick Harry Pitts is Senior Lecturer in Politics at the Department of Humanities and Social Sciences, University of Exeter Cornwall. He is a co-investigator at the ESRC Centre for Sociodigital Futures, a fellow of the Institute for the Future of Work and Secretary of the British Universities Industrial Relations Association. He is the author of five books, including *Value* (2020).

Marcel Stoetzler is Senior Lecturer in Sociology at Bangor University, UK. He is a sociologist and historian working on social theory, in particular the Critical Theory of the Frankfurt School, as well as antisemitism, nationalism, race and gender. His publications include *Beginning Classical Social Theory* (2017), *Antisemitism and the Constitution of Sociology* (2014) and *The State, the Nation and the Jews: Liberalism and the Antisemitism Dispute in Bismarck's Germany* (2008). He is a member of the editorial board of *Patterns of Prejudice*, an associate research fellow at the Birkbeck Institute for the study of Antisemitism, London, and an honorary research fellow at the Centre for Jewish Studies, the University of Manchester.

Christopher D. Wright is an independent intellectual and IT worker in Baltimore, Maryland, United States, who has addressed urbanism and revanchist politics, Marxism and racism, and the underappreciated implications of the transformation of labour processes on the constitution of class struggle. His contributions have been published in five countries and in four languages.

Anna Zawadzka, PhD, is a sociologist working at the Polish Academy of Sciences, Institute of Slavic Studies (Warsaw), and as a gardener's assistant. In her research, she most often uses a socio-graphic qualitative approach and discourse analysis. She is the author of *The First Time: Constructing Heterosexuality* (2015), a monograph based on interviews with women and girls about the experiences of virginity and virginity loss. Her current research focuses on correlations of antisemitism and anti-communism within the framework of post-communist cultures of Eastern European countries.

Introduction: Critical Theory's critique of antisemitism

Marcel Stoetzler

This volume hopes to make a contribution to the literature on the Critical Theory of the 'Frankfurt School' and to that on contemporary antisemitism by exploring what specific contribution the former has to make to the latter. Although in the 'golden age' of antisemitism research, the 1940s and 1950s, Critical Theory's contribution was as central as it was obvious and widely acknowledged, the last decades' academic literature on Critical Theory did not dwell on the subject of antisemitism very much, while antisemitism research (leaving aside the more journalistic-descriptive and the more polemical literature) has now become predominantly the domain of historians. In the process, the *theory* of antisemitism became mostly an object of intellectual history. When contemporary analysis of antisemitism invokes social theory at all, it tends to be blinded by the glory Critical Theory once enjoyed: 'Oh, we did that already, way back, didn't we?' Meanwhile, empirical research slumps back into the lazy habits of concept-less empiricism. The fact that the mainstream of the academic industry moved on from a once-celebrated paradigm suggests, of course, to contemporary observers that this probably happened for good reasons: academics in the social sciences and humanities are profoundly critical of the concept of progress except within their own bubble, where the necessities of self-preservation on the job market suggest that new is good. Regrettably, this is not necessarily so. Against the condescension of 'cutting-edge research' and its supposedly ever-progressing 'excellence', this proudly old-fashioned volume suggests 'bringing Critical Theory back in' and see what difference it still makes.

The 'Frankfurt School' Critical Theory of antisemitism reflects and undergirds the struggle against antisemitism from a theoretical position that is critical also of liberal social and political thought. Critical Theory rejects the capitalist mode of production and its social and political forms from a Marxian perspective fortified by Freudian psychoanalysis and shaped by the historical experience of the limits and reversals of 'enlightenment' – the process in which human civilization edges towards becoming (more) humane – that marked the twentieth century: fascism, Stalinism, National Socialism (NS), the Holocaust and their various echoes and iterations. Critical Theory differs from more mainstream socialist or liberal critiques of antisemitism in framing its anti-antisemitism in the sustained critique of categories of thought and practice central to modern liberal, bourgeois, capitalist society that more traditional theories tend to accept as given, or critique only superficially, such as identity, nation, state, race, sexual identity and central planks of twentieth-century 'new' or 'left liberalism' such as nationalism, nationalist social democracy and nation state-centric anti-imperialism.[1] One way of describing the difference between Critical Theory's critique of antisemitism and broadly liberal critiques is that the former treats antisemitism as a symptom, or an aspect, of the structures of a society that the theorist rejects and aims to overcome, rather than seeing it as a flaw in those of a society that the theorist is fundamentally in agreement with but wishes should better live up to its professed ideals. For Critical Theory, antisemitism is not a bug but a feature. It aims not to remove the bug but the system that features it.

Critical Theory as discussed in the present volume develops in the critique of antisemitism elements of a critique of capitalist modernity that resists the fallacy of antisemitism. It asks why modern capitalist society, even in some of the critiques and oppositions that it produces of and to itself, seems bound to produce antisemitism. It asks how the critique of antisemitism is linked to and grounded in other aspects of the critique of society, including capitalism, racism, patriarchy and heterosexism. It asks how antisemitism can appear to be anti-hegemonic or even liberatory, and how it functions as a bridge linking right-wing and left-wing oppositions to contemporary liberal, capitalist, bourgeois society.

However, this is neither a book about 'left-wing antisemitism' nor one about 'right-wing antisemitism'. Several chapters discuss antisemitism's presence in left-wing and right-wing contexts at the same time, sometimes comparatively, and reflect on what the concepts 'left-wing' and 'right-wing' can actually mean in the present context. Given that the Critical Theory perspective has a vested interest in the cause of social emancipation, it is uniquely placed, though, to provide the critical analysis needed to explore elements of antisemitism also in the social movements devoted to notions of liberty, humanity, emancipation, solidarity and equality. It is uniquely positioned to understand and explain why antisemitism poses particular problems for emancipatory movements by frequently using, unlike most other forms of racism, a rhetoric of liberation. Authors included in this collection make the case that modern antisemitism can best be understood as a modern, deeply reactionary ideology that presents itself as anti-hegemonic (which may but does not necessarily mean 'left-wing').

The volume is in two parts, titled 'Elements' and 'Extensions': the chapters in the first part offer a general overview of the Frankfurt School's Critical Theory of antisemitism whereby most focus on particular concepts and elements, including aspects of the historical and philosophical contexts of its emergence; those in the second part extend

---

[1] An early reference point for the critique of 'identity politics' is Marx's critique of his comrades in his 1852 'Enthüllungen über den Kommunistenprozess zu Köln' when he chastised them for fetishizing class as much as democrats did 'people': 'Just like the democrats turn the word *people* into some holy being, so you do the word *proletariat*' (qtd in Claussen 1994: 133; emphases in the original). In a similar vein, Adorno rejected nationalism in any form, including its allegedly benign forms, when he wrote that 'supposedly healthy national feeling' inevitably becomes 'excessive' because 'the identification of the person with the irrational connection between nature and society which the person happens to be part of' is the root of its 'untruth' (in Adorno's essay 'Meinung Wahn Gesellschaft'; qtd in Claussen 1994: 150).

the Frankfurt School–inspired perspective to a range of contemporary matters.² The distinction is not strict, of course: the first bunch of chapters is somewhat more exegetical, aiming to break down key concepts, while the second is somewhat more geared towards contemporary debates, contexts and concerns. For several contributions, the relationship between the concepts 'race' and 'antisemitism' is a central theme. Some readers might be disappointed not to find a 'definition' of antisemitism, though, not even a 'working' one: in our defence, we might say that theorists and historians can do without 'definitions' because they enjoy the luxury of not having to formulate policies or issue court orders. As Critical Theory considers concepts to be 'shorthand for process' (Adorno 1989: 267), and process to be infinite and undefinable, it engages in the unfolding of concepts instead of the fetishism of definitions.³

Before briefly introducing the chapters of this volume, I will in the following survey some of the key writings that provide the horizon out of which the perspective of this volume may best be understood, that is, some of the writings that constitute the links or mediations between the original Frankfurt School writings and most of the contributions to the present volume.⁴ More detailed knowledge of those intermediaries may help readers who do not share this rather specific background to understand better the spirit and trajectory of this volume. I will begin with the undisputed, most

---

² This volume in many ways continues and complements an earlier edited volume, *Antisemitism and the Constitution of Sociology* (Stoetzler 2014), and the *Sage Handbook of Frankfurt School Critical Theory* (Best, Bonefeld and O'Kane 2018), which is the only one of several handbooks on Critical Theory published in recent years that pays detailed attention to the subject of antisemitism. The idea to the present volume was first suggested by Werner Bonefeld and initially developed together with Christine Achinger in the context of the preparation of the 2014 volume.

³ This does not mean, of course, that it would not be convenient to have an agreed definition, but even a definition would probably best take the form of a history of all those many attempts at defining. Even a bare-bones, sensible definition of antisemitism as 'hatred of Jews *as Jews*' is destabilized by the classic question who or what *are* 'the Jews' (and, with a nod to Isaac Deutscher, how Jewish are they?): one's answer to this question obviously shapes one's understanding of any definition of antisemitism as the definition presupposes an identification. There's the rub: the politics of definition shade into identity politics. The difficulties with and anxieties about such identification and definition may stem largely from the fact that the group category 'the Jews' escapes all the categories with which we usually disaggregate and define group identities in the modern period: the firm conviction that 'religion', 'ethnicity', 'culture' and 'nation' are clearly definable, distinct concepts is hardly two centuries old, which means that a referent that preexisted these differentiations by millennia must escape their grasp. It is therefore impossible to find any consensus on whether 'the Jews' are a nation, an ethnicity or a religion, or all of the above, although most people lack the courage to admit and live with this undecidability. It seems to me that the more any pundit is convinced that 'the Jews' are for example, 'a religion' but not 'a nation', or vice versa, the firmer their view on what best defines antisemitism. The most pragmatic response to this conundrum is therefore the most theoretical one: to assert the non-identity.

⁴ Large parts of the academic literature on the Frankfurt School come either from a Habermasian perspective, which means that they are in the same ball park as liberal, pragmatist or Arendtian republicanism (often interesting but different from *Frankfurt School* Critical Theory), or from a Marcusean one, which (unlike Marcuse himself) tends to be hardly distinguishable from a generic New Left perspective (i.e. Gramscian-Althusserian, 'anti-imperialist', post-colonial-nationalist etc. – again, often interesting and valuable but different from Critical Theory), or even a Heideggerian perspective, where the difference between right-wing and left-wing versions of *Kulturkritik* (critique of civilization) does not seem to register. By contrast, in this introduction I emphasize interpretations of Critical Theory that stick to what I hold to be its core conception, the critical interpenetration of non-traditional readings of Marx (i.e. differing from the traditions of the Second, Third and Fourth Internationals), Freudian psychoanalysis and modern empirical social research methods.

frequently referenced classic of this literature whose principal proposition is written all over the present volume, as is the memory of its author.

Moishe Postone's 'Anti-Semitism and National Socialism'

Moishe Postone's now canonical 'Anti-Semitism and National Socialism: Notes on the German Reaction to "Holocaust"' (1980) was written as a reflection on the reception of the TV series 'Holocaust', four feature-length films first aired in the United States in April 1978, then in West Germany in January 1979.[5] It is rare that a film actually changes a societal reality, but this was one such occasion. The airing in the Federal Republic was an extraordinary historical event also because of the panels of historians taking phone calls from viewers that followed the broadcasts of the films. Those of us who grew up in the world of 'social media' will struggle to imagine the impact of television phone-ins in those days of old. Equally unimaginable will be the fact that back then in West Germany some of the tenets of the 'Frankfurt School' were fairly common talking points in the public sphere. 'Holocaust' was central to the concerns of Critical Theory in at least two respects: one, the central role the analysis of antisemitism and NS played in it; two, the dialectical role that 'culture industry' plays in capitalist society for the progress of enlightenment. 'Holocaust' is a prime example of the ambiguities of that role: it is TV drama at its best, star-studded (Meryl Streep!!), extremely watchable (all-round great acting), narratively simplified to elicit maximum emotional impact, using empathy to make viewers identify and get hooked and allowing for just enough shades of grey to follow a psychologically realistic aesthetic in a subject that fundamentally could not be more black and white. According to the laws of its genre, it is a masterpiece.[6] The production values that allowed it to put the Holocaust into the forefront of public discourse in late-capitalist society[7] obviously have their price – and so the film series was strongly disliked by a range of commentators at the time for a variety of reasons, such as 'trivializing' the issue. Postone's piece, published in the prestigiously hip *New German Critique* in the first of three (!) special issues on 'Germans and Jews', all of 1980 (issues 19, 20 and 21, featuring a roster of big names), tapped into this extraordinary trans-Atlantic situation.

Although the hint in the title is clear enough, it is often overlooked that Postone's article does not so much reflect on antisemitism as such but on the relationship between antisemitism and NS: its argument is very much historically specific in character. It begins with a critique of post–Second World War liberal and conservative as well as socialist discourses on antisemitism and NS: when talking about 'the Nazi past', 'liberals and conservatives have focused attention on the persecution and extermination of the Jews' (Postone 1980: 97) and have used it to emphasize its discontinuity with the

---

[5] A German translation of the article had already been published twice in 1979 (Postone 1979a and b).
[6] The films are easy to find on the internet. The German director Alice Agneskirchner released a documentary on 'How "Holocaust" Came to TV' in 2019 (https://www.imdb.com/title/tt10912168/?ref_=nm_knf_i20), that is, forty years after.
[7] 'Holocaust', until then a very rare word, was voted German 'Word of the Year' for 1979 (https://gfds.de/aktionen/wort-des-jahres/). For context, the second to fifth places that year were taken by 'boat people', 'Nachrüstung', 'Ölschock' and 'alternativ', respectively.

present, to the effect that 'what happened to the Jews has been instrumentalized and transformed into an ideology of legitimation for the present system', that is, that of the Federal Republic (98): the latter may employ a lot of old Nazis, but surely they now refrain from killing Jews. For that purpose, the 'intrinsic relationship between anti-Semitism and other aspects of National Socialism' was ignored. The left, by contrast, 'has tended to concentrate on the function of National Socialism for capitalism' and therewith also 'elements of continuity between the Third Reich and the Federal Republic' (98) in order to critique the latter's authoritarian and patriarchal capitalism. Crucially, both the right and the left subsumed the extermination of the Jews under 'the general categories of prejudice, discrimination and persecution', as well as 'racism in general' (98), which they treated separately from the 'socio-economic examination of National Socialism'. Overcoming this separation is what Postone attempted to do in the second half of the essay (104–15), by implication trying to fetishize neither continuity nor discontinuity post-1945 by integrating the analysis of antisemitism and the Holocaust into a general theory of the particular form of the NS version of capitalist society.

Postone discusses in the first section (97–100) the reactions to the airings of the film series, reflecting on the historical constellation that made this event possible, and moves in part two (100–4) to a discussion of how the post-1968 generation of the German New Left's understanding of antisemitism and the Holocaust (or lack thereof) differed from that of those politicized earlier. Based on his own experiences as a student in Frankfurt/Main, this section has elements of an ethnography and contains psychoanalytically inspired interpretations of Postone's own observations. Postone noted that the younger comrades, different from their older peers, were able to be shocked by 'Holocaust' because they had never studied the concrete details of the Holocaust: they were more familiar, though, with pre-NS working-class history and the anti-fascist resistance. Postone links this – in a text now more than forty years old – to a shift to what we discuss today, in similar contexts, as 'identity politics': for the younger New Leftists, 'the need for identification led to an emphasis on resistance to Hitler which avoided coming to terms with the popularity of the Nazi regime' and 'also served to block an understanding of the situation of the Jews in Europe' (101). Postone suggests that 'theory itself became a form of psychic repression' (102), something that may have a familiar ring to many of us theorists (and to which the study of history is such an important antidote). Another interesting observation that resonates with the present is that any number of political struggles at the time, including against 'the appalling mistreatment of political prisoners (of all prisoners, in fact), discrimination of foreign workers, racism, and atomic energy in its political as well as ecological consequences' were 'presented in terms of "learning from the past"', when learning from 'the past', that is, the NS (National Socialist) past, was really not required for being opposed to any of these matters (103).[8]

---

[8] Even today, pieties about learning 'the lessons' (as if there was a set of generally agreed-upon lessons) indicate in fact the refusal to study, let alone understand 'the past'. This is also nowadays the case when every other Sunday-speech endorsement of even the most vanilla form of multiculturalism claims direct descent from 'learning the lessons' from the Holocaust: the same tepid and conflicted liberalism that miserably failed to prevent the catastrophe now claims to be its sole logical conclusion.

The shift in attitude (and knowledge) between the older and younger New Leftists in Germany may be related to Postone's observation that 'no western Left was as philosemitic and pro-Zionist prior to 1967. Probably none subsequently identified so strongly with the Palestinian cause' (103). Postone hints that identification, which always involves projection, is the key concept here. Postone came to believe that a psychological explanation (quite rare in his overall work) was required here because the reversal from philosemitic pro-Zionism to anti-Zionism with sometimes manifest antisemitic undertones was triggered not by the suffering of the Palestinians, which had begun much earlier, but by the 1967 war: 'Philo-Semitism revealed its other side' (104). Jews who fail to be 'victims and therefore virtuous' are replaced by more suitable objects of identification.[9]

After the first two sections of the text set the scene in this way, Postone begins, in section three, his attempt to theorize the Holocaust as a concrete, determinate event by discussing antisemitism specifically in its relation to NS.[10] His starting point is that 'attempts at an explanation which deal with capitalism, racism, bureaucracy, sexual repression or the authoritarian personality, remain far too general' (106). In particular, there was no functionality to the Holocaust, which sets it apart from most if not all other genocides. This, as opposed to victim numbers as such, is its 'qualitative specificity'. Saying that the Holocaust was 'its own goal' (105) rather than a means to anything else is saying that the Nazis took their antisemitism seriously: implausible as this must seem to non-Nazis, antisemitism actually directed their actions. *They meant it.* The point here is that the Nazis did not see themselves as a regular party amongst others but as a radical movement of revolt committed to the mission of fighting a peculiar, all-determining power.

> Probably all forms of racism attribute potential power to the other. This power, however, is usually concrete – material or sexual – the power of the oppressed (as repressed), of the 'Untermenschen'. The power attributed to the Jews is not only much greater and 'real', as opposed to potential, it is different. In *modern* anti-Semitism it is mysteriously intangible, abstract and universal. (106; emphasis in the original)

---

[9] In extension of Postone's argument, it could be said that Palestinians and others at the bottom ranks of the world system's hierarchy may want to pay attention to Zionism's fall from grace in this context: treat with suspicion overenthusiastic proclamations of solidarity by metropolitan Westerners as they may sometimes turn out to be the kind of narcissistic love that drops its object when it stops paying the desired emotional dividends in the business cycles of political discourse. Antisemitic undertones in some of the anti-Zionist proclamations of those, or descendants of those, who once were 'the most pro-Zionist', may serve as a warning sign, being the signature of unacknowledged libidinal charge.

[10] Postone's essay is therewith also an early instance of the more recent trend in Holocaust Studies to restore antisemitism, and thus questions of ideology, as central to the analysis of NS and the Holocaust. Postone explicitly brackets out the question why 'Nazism and modern anti-Semitism . . . became hegemonic *in Germany*' (1908: 105; emphasis added): his question is exclusively *what it was* that became hegemonic, as opposed to why it became so *in a particular place*. By 'modern antisemitism', it is important to note, he means specifically the type of antisemitism that culminated in Nazism, not, as would be more common usage, any form of antisemitism in the modern period.

This abstract power can take various bodily material forms and is therefore difficult to check. It is not identical to its forms of appearance but hidden and conspiratorial: 'The Jews represent an immensely powerful, intangible, international conspiracy' (106).

Up to this point, Postone provides a *description* of Nazi antisemitism that does not yet, as he writes, do the job he set out to do: to *explain* modern (i.e. Nazi) antisemitism in terms of NS. This requires the 'historical-epistemological frame of reference' (107), developed on mere five pages (107–12), which are the ones for which the article is most famous.

The 'socio-historical epistemology' (107) that Postone looks for takes as its starting point the fact that 'modern antisemitism' personifies in the Jews the effects of rapid capitalist industrialization, as it was experienced, for example, in Germany, without, though, attacking or critiquing modern industry (or industrial modernity) (108). The required epistemology needs to allow, so Postone suggests, 'for a distinction between what modern capitalism is and the way it appears, between its essence and appearance' (108). Here follows what is probably the only really new idea ever formulated in the field of antisemitism studies after their 1940s/1950s heyday: 'These considerations lead us to Marx's concept of the fetish, the strategic intent of which was to provide a social and historical theory of knowledge grounded in the difference between the essence of capitalist social relations and their manifest form.' The 'specific characteristics of the power attributed to the Jews by modern anti-Semitism – abstractness, intangibility, universality, mobility . . . are all characteristics of the value dimension of the social forms analyzed by Marx' (108). In a footnote, Postone expands on how in Marx the 'commodity as a form . . . represents a duality of social dimensions [value and use-value] which interact such that the category *simultaneously* expresses particular "reified" social relations and forms of thought' (108, fn. 13; emphasis added). This is what is meant by a 'socio-historical epistemology': there is no real split between how reality 'actually' is and how we perceive and think about it, but rather a dialectical, mutually constitutive relationship. Philosophically, this is perhaps the most important Marxian inheritance within Critical Theory.

The point here is that we are trained and conditioned through daily practice in capitalist society to handle commodities, and the way the commodities structure how we do this shapes at the same time how our thinking is organized. The aspect of this permanently ongoing process picked up by Postone is that under capitalist social relations, the *reality of an abstraction* (value) that is materialized in a concrete thing (money) produces as its opposite the *illusion of the naturalness* of a concretely useful thing (the commodity) although that useful thing is a commodity only in a specific social form (a historically specific societal interrelationship), the commodity form. If a particular concrete commodity (say, an umbrella) did not have the social form called 'commodity form', it would not be a commodity (and vice versa). In everyday life, though, we tend to think of money as capitalist (abstract, powerful, 'the root of all evil' etc.) but of umbrellas as concrete and useful things. We naturalize and thingify the commodities, ignoring their social character. Capitalist everyday ideology ('common sense') may prompt us to blame the umbrellas' typical flimsiness on a deplorable loss of artisanal savoir-faire, deflecting from the fact that their capitalist *social* form all but determines their concrete, *material* form. (They are flimsy because they are produced as commodities for a mass market under conditions that require the capitalist to make a profit at least at the average rate, not because umbrella-makers suddenly forgot how to make decent umbrellas.) On top of all this, also the materializations of the abstract appear as natural: for example, whatever material thing society uses as money (gold, pearls, shells) we come to think of as naturally *being* money, although money of any description is obviously an entirely social thing (109). Capitalist everyday common sense (i.e. 'fetishized thought') fetishizes both, the supposed naturalness of in fact historically specific institutions and their laws (say, 'the market') and the supposed naturalness of the concrete and the human, such as 'concrete labour' that 'is understood as the non-capitalist moment which is opposed to the abstractness of money' (110). (Such supposed naturalness is, with the rise of racism in the late nineteenth century, increasingly biologized.) In this perspective, industrial production must appear as 'mere creativity', whereas 'capitalism' is something to do with money, greed and finance. (A critique of 'capitalism' on this basis is of course entirely different from Marx's perspective who formulated a critique of the 'capitalist *mode of production*' and rarely ever used the word 'capitalism', perhaps just to avoid this kind of muddled thinking.)

The salience of this argument is that it demonstrates that the Hitlerite form of (ostensible) anti-capitalism that celebrates blood, soil, concrete labour, nature, 'the machine' and community derives from the worldview normally and spontaneously produced by capitalist everyday life (110). The latter does not *necessarily* produce it, though: this is where the argument turns to the specific relation between antisemitism and NS advertised in the title of the piece. Postone asserts that

> the hypostatization of the concrete and the identification of capital with the manifest abstract . . . renders this ideology so functional for the development of industrial capitalism in crisis. National Socialist ideology was in the interests of capital not only for the very obvious reason that it was virulently anti-Marxist and that the Nazis destroyed the organizations of the German working class. It was also in the interests of capital in the transition from liberal to quasi-state capitalism. The identification of capital with the manifest abstract overlaps, in part, with its identification with the market. The attack on the liberal state, as abstract, can further the development of the interventionist state, as concrete. This form of 'anti-capitalism', then . . . is an aid to capitalism in the transition to quasi-state capitalism in a situation of structural crisis. (111)

The fact that NS ideology is a 'quasi-state capitalist' response to capitalist crisis makes modern antisemitism a perfectly logical and – pardon the pun – organic fit, like hand in glove. It also implies that antisemitism is a fitting element in any other quasi- or fully state-capitalist projects that attack abstract law, abstract reasoning, the market, liberalism, finance capital and so on.

Postone's brilliant intuition (probably inspired by the critique of 'false immediacy' that is a leitmotif of many of Adorno's writings) was to detect the very same thought pattern in modern antisemitism and in the way how capitalist society 'ordinarily' understands itself, radicalized and racialized by Nazism in a specific situation of crisis:

The opposition of the concrete material and the abstract becomes the racial opposition of the Aryans and the Jews. Modern anti-Semitism involves a biologization of capitalism – which itself is only understood in terms of its manifest abstract dimension – as International Jewry . . . The Jews were not seen merely as *representatives* of capital (in which case anti-Semitic attacks would have been much more class-specific). They became the *personifications* of the intangible, destructive, immensely powerful, and international domination of capital as a social form. (112; emphases in the original)

In the short fourth section (112–13), Postone states that many factors made the Jews the obvious target of an ideology that attacked the abstract while celebrating the concrete side of capitalism, and briefly discusses one of them with an argument that replicates his principal argument at the level of the political forms of state and nation:

Just as the commodity, understood as a social form, expresses its 'double character' in the externalized opposition between the abstract (money) and the concrete (the commodity), so is bourgeois society characterized by the split between the state and civil society. The split is that between the individual as citizen and as person. As a citizen, the individual is abstract. This is expressed, for example, in the notion of equality before the (abstract) law or in that of one person, one vote (at least in theory). As a person, the individual is concrete, embedded in real class relations which are considered to be 'private'. (113)

Although Postone does not develop this very clearly, the analogy seems to suggest that in the form of the modern nation-state, the state's constituents are both, citizens and private persons (*citoyen* and *bourgeois*), that is, abstract and concrete *at the same time*. In the eyes of many nationalists, though, there was one notable exception:

In this sense, the only group in Europe which fulfilled the determination of citizenship as a pure political abstraction, were the Jews following their political emancipation. They were German or French citizens, but not really Germans or Frenchmen. They were of the nation abstractly, but rarely concretely. They were, in addition, citizens of most European countries. The quality of abstractness, characteristic not only of the value dimension in its immediacy, but also, mediately, of the bourgeois state and law, became closely identified with the Jews. In a period when the concrete became glorified against the abstract, against 'capitalism' and the bourgeois state, this became a fatal association. (113)

In the concluding fifth section, from page 113, Postone wraps up his argument by referring to Auschwitz as a factory to 'destroy value' (114), the negation of a capitalist factory, and warns that the left should not (again) be fooled into thinking 'that all forms of anti-capitalism are, at least potentially, progressive' (115).

Detlev Claussen's *Grenzen der Aufklärung*

For readers of German, studying Critical Theory and the critique of antisemitism beyond the core texts by Horkheimer, Adorno and other 'Frankfurt School' authors has (or perhaps rather, used to have) a rather obvious and convenient starting point in two volumes, originally published in 1987 and 1988, respectively, that mark the high point of the intense re-appropriation of the classic texts from the 1940s and 1950s by theorists and historians in West Germany, Israel and the United States during the 1980s: Detlev Claussen's monograph *Limits of Enlightenment: On the Societal Genesis of Modern Antisemitism* and the edited volume *Civilizational Caesura: Thinking after Auschwitz* by Dan Diner.[11] Certainly in German, there were many other related studies to follow, but none will have had the same impact. I will try in the following to give a rough outline of what these two volumes contain and then much more briefly point to some relevant later publications. I will focus on Claussen's monograph for two reasons: one, it has been of great influence in the German- but is virtually unknown in the English-language context; two, discussing it allows me to address many of the things that are central to much of the subsequent literature that I will only summarily point to. As was (still) common at the time, antisemitism in its various forms is discussed in these publications in relation to an analysis of the much more specific subject matter of Auschwitz, or the Holocaust.

Claussen's monograph is an exasperatedly angry book, furious about the post-Nazi world's failure to have taken Auschwitz seriously at all. It takes its lead from *Dialectic of Enlightenment* not only in terms of the central themes (and the title, 'Limits of enlightenment', of course, which is borrowed from the chapter 'Elements of Antisemitism' in *Dialectic of Enlightenment*) but also in terms of the style which eschews the linear, transparent, analytical logic of more respectable and digestible academic writing. Its six chapters are iterations more than steps in an argument, circling around a number of ideas much like (or perhaps even more than) the chapters of *Dialectic of Enlightenment* do. Where Claussen deliberately differs is in the use of history: he seems to aim at making explicit the history of which the concepts of Critical Theory are condensed crystallizations. Theory's shorthand is translated back into fragments of narrative, that is, historicized.[12] Without much signposting or the convenience of smooth transitions and summaries, Claussen's text switches from explication of theoretical and philosophical texts (Horkheimer, Adorno, Marcuse, Freud, Marx, Heine, Börne, Hegel, Kant, Arendt, Sartre) to the history that produced them, in particular that of the French Revolution and its aftermath. The text is fragmentary,

---

[11] Claussen's monograph was titled *Grenzen der Aufklärung. Zur gesellschaftlichen Geschichte des modernen Antisemitismus* in 1987 but *Grenzen der Aufklärung. Die gesellschaftliche Genese des modernen Antisemitismus* in its second edition from 1994. There has also been a third edition from 2005 with an added preface. Diner's edited volume is titled *Zivilisationsbruch. Denken nach Auschwitz*.

[12] 'In order to understand the societal dynamics that led to Auschwitz, the dialectic of enlightenment needs to be comprehended in a more historically determinate manner than Horkheimer and Adorno did' (Claussen 1994: 43). This could serve as a motto also for most chapters in the present volume.

demanding and unpredictable but also rather unitary and densely textured, which explains both why it influenced many of its (German) readers (at least those open and favourable to this style that is typical of Critical Theory) but also failed to have any impact at all on English-language academia.

Claussen's principal proposition is that the history of antisemitism and Auschwitz is essentially about the failure of emancipation in modern society, and that Critical Theory attempts to reflect on this failure and the 'limits of Enlightenment'. It aims to de-reify the concept of 'the Holocaust' which had only become the generally accepted signifier for what had before then not yet been a presumably clearly defined object through the 1978 television series 'Holocaust'. Claussen sees 'the Holocaust' in this specific sense as an artefact of the culture industry ('Holocaust'), that is, of the falsification of memory, the loss of experience and the rationalization of the total destruction of meaning.[13] The point of theory is not to explain and subsume Auschwitz under this or that general category but to expose it as the image of the 'exterminatory negation' of thinking (Claussen 1994: 29). If antisemitism and Auschwitz are about the ultimate destruction of the hope for emancipation, which is bound up with the ability to think and critique (hence 'the Enlightenment'), then the 'working through' of the memory of Auschwitz must aim at the restoration of that ability, aiming at enlightenment's breaking through its own limitations. Forms of remembrance and commemoration that fail to do so are on the wrong side of that divide. Channelling Adorno, Claussen argues against the 'pedagogization' (Pädagogisierung) of Auschwitz: 'the more the public is treated as the target of instruction' by 'enlightened officials', the more resentment will build up against the lessons (38). The pedagogy must itself be emancipatory, and sociology, rather than allowing itself to be reduced to a mere content provider, must reflect on the forms of its delivery and distribution.

Following Horkheimer and Adorno's arguments in *Dialectic of Enlightenment*, Auschwitz means not merely that 'a singular people' was destroyed but a type of society (Claussen 1994: 41–2): the Nazis' attempt to 'perpetuate violence' had as its target the type of society that allowed the hope for emancipation: modern bourgeois society, as a reality that contained in itself the potential of something better, destroyed itself in Auschwitz. The same is not true of any other antisemitic atrocity in history: the Nazi excess of systematic rationalized violence destroyed the emancipatory-utopian potential also inherent in modern bourgeois society. Their killing machine ('Tötungsmaschinerie') (49) resulted from this society's *history* of violence, though: Claussen mentions colonial violence but also the June massacres in Paris in 1848 and the mass shootings of guerrillas in the Franco-Prussian war (209). Although the rule of the law of value and the contract-based exchange of equivalent portions of value depend on the suspension and tabooing of direct violence, bourgeois society has never been remotely as non-violent as it believes itself to be.

National Socialism escalated, perpetuated and institutionalized the kind of violence that refuses to acknowledge the humanity of the enemy who becomes 'unworthy of

---

[13] Claussen insists on using 'Auschwitz', a specific, concrete place name that works as a *pars pro toto*, rather than 'Holocaust' or 'Shoah', which are words that have more generic primary meanings: a 'sacrificial burning'; 'the disaster'.

life'. This change in the logic of violence determines the change of form of antisemitism from ordinary pogromism to the 'antisemitism of reason' (the famous phrase Hitler used in a letter from 1919) (Claussen 1994: 214). Even though the 'aryanisations' of Jewish-owned businesses could still be interpreted in terms of instrumental-rational logic (exploitation and plunder), this changed with the start of the exterminatory campaign against the Soviet Union (215). Nevertheless, the genocide depended as much on the coldness and indifference of 'calculating commodity owners' who kept a low profile as on others' furious participation in 'murderous excesses' (49). In this sense, Claussen writes that 'Auschwitz continues to exist because societal conditions continue to reproduce indifference against social oppression, present and past suffering' (50).

If Critical Theory's most central concern is with how emancipation is both made possible and thwarted by modern capitalist society, this also shapes its theory of antisemitism. Post-French Revolution society both provided emancipation and turned it into 'the compulsion to assimilate to an unfree society' (Claussen 1994: 52). The form of emancipation that the bourgeois revolution created, and that subsequently failed so catastrophically in Auschwitz, was linked to the sphere of circulation that the French Revolution had opened up by taking it away from the mercantilist-absolutist state. It was based on the possibility of (relatively) many to own, buy and sell property. In that sphere, though, also the space had opened that allowed the articulation of the possibility of emancipation beyond the failed emancipation of the bourgeois revolution that created this sphere. The theory of that emancipation was formulated by Marx not incidentally in London, the capital of circulation, in what contemporaries mocked as the 'Jewish-Hegelian jargon' (59). The sphere of circulation became ubiquitous, though, and thereby was abolished as a separate sphere (58): in totalized capitalism, everything becomes the sphere of circulation, and hence, nothing. Claussen suggests that Horkheimer thought that crushing that sphere, and 'the Jews' who supposedly represented it, meant crushing the very idea of emancipation. He also asserts that Horkheimer and Adorno 'thoroughly mistrusted the restoration of liberalism in the Western hemisphere' after the Second World War (67). When in the world before Auschwitz, economic rationality had set limits to antisemitic violence, after 'the de-bourgeoisification of capitalist society' (70) all that was left from the characteristics of bourgeois society was 'the coldness of the bourgeois subject'. (In this context, it is important to reflect on the ambiguity of the 'culture industry': against bourgeois coldness, it brought back *pity*, which Nietzsche had ridiculed and the Nazis had abolished, in the form of sentimentality, a heavy dose of which can trigger critical thinking in rare cases such as that of the film 'Holocaust' [70].)

Although Critical Theory rejects the notion of 'eternal antisemitism', its increased pessimism concerning the possibility of emancipation can be used as an argument in favour of Jewish nationalism (as is the case among some contemporary students of Critical Theory especially in Germany): the argument would be that although a Jewish national state can of course not operate outside the totality of the world system of nation-states, bourgeois society and the capitalist mode of production (the root causes of the impossibility of emancipation), a nation-state might at least provide as much protection from violence as is immanently possible within that system (to which end it would of course have to do what all states do, namely project and exert violence). The diminishing belief in the possibility of emancipation and equality in the diaspora must affect Critical Theory's view of the Jewish nation-state. On this issue, Claussen develops a nuanced position based on a comment by Horkheimer that is neither pro- nor anti-Zionist and seems to illustrate well what a Critical Theory position on this thorny issue could look like, as opposed to the left-liberal or 'traditionally-Marxist' ones that tend to assert identity one way or the other. Claussen begins from the historical starting point that the social changes that occurred in the period around the French Revolution destabilized 'the traditional, in pre-capitalist society seemingly solid Jewish sense of self' (87) but did not in its place produce a similarly solid sense of 'Jewish-national identity': it created non-identity, rather, which is neither definable as a new positivity nor simply the negation of an identity.[14] It is a term of ambiguity and ambivalence that must remain at a tension with any attempt at defining and affirming an identity, such as in nationalism. Importantly, 'non-identity' is first of all an experience, a positively given, a reality, a product of history and society, a fact of modernity that will always undermine any attempts at asserting identity no matter what. Auschwitz, though, suggests that emancipation was (and perhaps is) pointless, even a trap: also this *perception* is a fact. As the hope and drive for emancipation based on the assertion of non-identity are central tenets of Critical Theory, Auschwitz might even be said to be its undoing (which is perhaps another reason for Auschwitz's centrality to Critical Theory). At this point of the argument, Claussen quotes a statement by Horkheimer that is worth repeating at length:

> The Jews in the diaspora had professed justice, God the Just, as the highest, and were persecuted. Then they had to flee to Israel to escape that injustice, and founded a state there. Who could blame the Jews for something that was a necessary consequence of world-wide nationalism, the uniformization of competing states. Just as the individual once had to become a citizen in order to partake in the affairs of the country, it is now necessary to become a nation if one is to exist in the world. Except that Israel the fatherland now supplants justice, and a particular patriotism the hazy expectation for mankind. An Israeli might point out to me in good Hegelian manner that their brave soldiers, kibbutzim and pioneers were the determinate negation of the ghetto, without which that hope was but abstract talk, and the waiting for the Messiah the spurious infinite. I cannot deny this. But neither can I ward off the sadness that a repetition of the exodus into the Holy Land was necessary though the right day had not dawned yet, and I cannot overcome the fear that the contradiction will prove to be as seductive as it was in the case of Prussia by which Hegel demonstrated it. (Horkheimer 1978: 215; translation amended)[15]

---

[14] In a generic sense, modernity turned *all* pre-modern identities into ambiguities, but nineteenth-century nationalisms managed (to varying degrees) to contain the fluidities and ambiguities of modernity (where 'all that is solid melts into air') quite well by re-reifying populations as nations. In the twentieth century, with the world system of capitalist states more solidly in place than in the nineteenth, narrowing the wiggle room for constructing new societies by articulating nation-building as modernization, nation-builders and -rebuilders had a more difficult time of it. This is ever more so the case in the twenty-first.

[15] See also Neubauer (2012), and Catlin in this volume.

Claussen comments, 'It is the thing itself that entangles us in the contradiction' (1994: 88): therefore, there is no way around it. Horkheimer asserts that the irresolvable contradiction induces sadness as it is not possible for Critical Theory to either give up the hope for emancipation or acknowledge the crude fact that Auschwitz has dealt it a (near) fatal blow. Sadness must translate into the soft-spoken nuanced acceptance of ambiguity, as opposed to the macho bravado of either the committed Jewish nationalist or the full-throated rationalist defender of the universalism that has always had, and will always have, the correct answer, whatever the circumstances, whatever the question. Horkheimer ingeniously pours cold water on the Hegelian defence of the Jewish nation-state, without actually arguing against it, by comparing it with Hegel's likening of Prussia to the working of reason in the world: the comparison to modernizing Prussia is a kind of compliment (Prussia/Israel being the state that represents bourgeois rationality in a sea of semi-feudal backwaters), but with an obvious sting. Even rule by the most enlightened state officials is still rule by the state with all the reversals and excesses to be expected and, in the case of Prussia, demonstrated by the very history that created not the necessity but the possibility of Auschwitz. However powerful the case made by Auschwitz, Israel, too, cannot escape the logic of the nation-state. Horkheimer's invocation of his sadness seems to suggest that he thought this was still as good as it gets, under the circumstances.

Horkheimer's point that the Jews having to become a nation-state repeats and echoes Jewish individuals having had to become citizens to be emancipated indicates the centrality of the demand for assimilation to the history of (failed) emancipation: both are processes of assimilation to the bourgeois order, to modern capitalist society and the world system of nation-states, respectively. Most of Claussen's historical discussions are focused on the link between emancipation and assimilation.[16] Nevertheless, the quest for emancipation remains central to Critical Theory, along with its critique: 'Only out of the unhappy consciousness that the basic constitution of society has not changed and all attempts at emancipation have only produced variations of the same dynamics can the emancipatory dimension [of Critical Theory] be reconstructed after Auschwitz' (Claussen 1994: 108).

Dan Diner's *Zivilisationsbruch. Denken nach Auschwitz*

For generations of students, myself included, *Zivilisationsbruch. Denken nach Auschwitz* (*Civilizational Cesura: Thinking after Auschwitz*), a volume of essays edited by Dan Diner in 1988, would have been the first port of call as a textbook on how various Frankfurt School writers thought about Auschwitz. Much more than Claussen,

---

[16] Central to his argument is a richly historicizing but critical discussion of Marx's 1843 double essay 'On the Jewish Question' (Claussen 1994: 89–108; also 46–48 and 173–5). Claussen underlines two decisive weaknesses of Marx's position in 1843: 'fixation on [the sphere of] circulation distorts the critique of society', and 'identification of circulation with Jews' creates an abstract and unhistorical notion of 'the Jew' (98). He asserts that Marx in 1843 had not yet developed the critique of political economy and missed therefore the decisive difference between pre-bourgeois and bourgeois society (99) and therefore treats the oppressed unhistorically (108).

though, Diner has also been read internationally, not least perhaps because his own approach owes more to Arendt and Habermas than Horkheimer and Adorno, whose global impact does not quite compare.

Diner explains his inspired neologism *Zivilisationsbruch* on the first three pages of the book's preface: Auschwitz 'affects [some of] the basic preconditions of human interaction', constituting 'something like the refutation of a civilization whose thinking and acting' is based on 'anticipatory trust' in a generally utilitarian attitude: violence and murder only happen when they benefit the perpetrator in a utilitarian manner (Diner 1988: 7). This argument is essentially psychological (members of society trust that no irrational violence will take place) and has little in common with Horkheimer and Adorno's critique of civilization in *Dialectic of Enlightenment*, for example, although the notion of a caesura certainly reverberates with Adorno's many references to the radically changed condition of society 'after Auschwitz'.[17] Diner's explanation of the concept of 'Zivilisationsbruch', though, seems to suggest that Auschwitz was the moment when a previously utilitarian, rational, predictable and trustworthy civilization suddenly broke down, whereas Critical Theory asserts that irrational, self-destructive violence is – and has always been – very much part of our civilization, which is why it sees Auschwitz as a lens through which to study the fault lines and limitations of civilization and enlightenment *as such*, not just after a certain breaking point in its history.[18]

In spite of being framed in this way, the volume was (and remains) an important source of key positions of Critical Theory authors on antisemitism and the Holocaust. It also contains instructive texts on authors not related to the Frankfurt School – Anders, Arendt, Bloch – and texts that discuss why some Frankfurt School authors (Kracauer, Marcuse, Benjamin) did *not* say very much on those topics.[19] The volume opens with Leo Lowenthal's seminal short text 'Individual and Terror' (initially published in English in 1946)[20] that is a key text on the relationship of the experience of the concentration camps and the concept of totalitarianism (and, perhaps tellingly, mentions antisemitism only once, in passing) and contains a comprehensive discussion of Horkheimer by Diner, an essay on Adorno by Claussen (complementary to Claussen's 1987 book), an interview with Raul Hilberg on his teacher Franz Neumann and closes with the republication of a translation of Postone's 'National Socialism and

---

[17] The concept 'Zivilisationsbruch' is explained by Diner in detail in an essay published in 2003. Diner explains his approach here as different from that of the Frankfurt School. For Critical Theory as expressed in *Dialectic of Enlightenment*, the analysis of Auschwitz, and antisemitism in general, drives towards and necessitates asking questions about the meaning of reason, rationality, enlightenment and civilization (be it human, 'Western' or capitalist civilization). This is different from asserting that the deed of Auschwitz has *in fact* ruptured, or broken, civilization; the latter, much more than the former, seems to me somewhat Eurocentric. Freyenhagen (2020) takes a similar position on this, arguing that Diner presupposes in his concept of 'Zivilisationsbruch' a completely different, and uncritical, understanding of civilization than do Adorno and Horkheimer.

[18] This is evident on the first page of the first chapter of the volume by Lowenthal, who asserts that 'fascist terror' was 'rooted deeply in the dynamics of modern civilization' (Löwenthal 1988: 15).

[19] More recent literature offers different perspectives, such as Müller's (2002) piece on Marcuse.

[20] The title of the English publication of 1946, based on a lecture given in 1945 titled 'The Aftermath of Totalitarian Terror', is 'Terror's atomization of man'. This is a classic of totalitarianism theory. The German translation was first published in 1982 (Dubiel 1988: 26–7).

Antisemitism'.²¹ Apart from Lowenthal's classic text, Postone's is the only one in Diner's volume that is not *about* a theorist but is a primary source in its own right, indicating that already by that time it must have been widely recognized as such.

The ISF pamphlet 'Ulrike Meinhof, Stalin and the Jews'

In the Federal Republic of Germany, a lot of Frankfurt School–influenced discussion of antisemitism, NS, anti-Zionism and related topics has in the past taken place (and continues to do so) in a vital public sphere of (often academically highly trained) intellectuals who do not work in academia, though, and who publish in social movement–related as well as in academic outlets, and some that are both. An influential case in point is the text 'Ulrike Meinhof, Stalin and the Jews: The (New) Left as Tragic Drama' published in May 1988 by Initiative Socialist Forum (ISF), a group based in Freiburg/Br. in southwest Germany (ISF 1990: 119–66). The ISF is part of a varied range of non-university-affiliated small organizations in Germany, often stemming from the 1960s/1970s student movement, that are influenced by Critical Theory. The text links a critique of antisemitic (in this context, Stalinist) anti-Zionism to a discussion of the (authoritarian, Maoist-Stalinist) degeneration of the anti-authoritarian movement of 1968 grounded in a discussion of the positions of the anti-Bolshevik Marxist left of the 1920s and various references to authors it had influenced such as Horkheimer, Marcuse and Adorno. The text deals with German left-wing anti-Zionists at the time calling Israel 'fascist', denying the legitimacy of its existence as a state, equating it, or its policies, with Nazi Germany and, in the name of anti-imperialism, failing to formulate any criticism at all of even the most authoritarian forms of Palestinian nationalism.

The ISF make two central arguments concerning the extreme anti-Israel position held by some on the contemporary Left: for one (ISF 1990: 128–48), they argue it derives from the Leninist doctrine of the right of nations to self-determination, its proposition of a 'revolutionary' form of nationalism that rests on the fusion of class and nation, and the idealist notion that the ('revolutionary') state could be the actual expression of the will of its constituents (128–9). Secondly, it derives from the left's failure to develop a theory of fascism and NS, and in particular the centrality of antisemitism to it (148–61): they argue that the left never really superseded the 1935 definition by Dimitroff of 'fascism in power' as the dictatorship of 'the most reactionary, chauvinist, imperialist elements of finance capital' (148). From a position of seeing antisemitism as a merely accidental element of fascism, and fascism in turn as the dictatorship of 'finance capital', it is not a very long journey to calling Israel 'fascist' while failing to critique the actually fascist demagoguery against the power of (supposedly Jewish) finance capital and its imperialism. While the second strand of the argument is broadly similar to the now canonical critique of a fetishized (mis-)understanding of the concept of capital, as

---

[21] I follow Jacobs (2015) in spelling Lowenthal without Umlaut (except in direct quotations) as this is how he spelt his name after moving to the United States. He was born Löwenthal which is sometimes also rendered Loewenthal. In German-language publications, he is commonly spelt Löwenthal. The title of Postone's essay differs in this version from all others, reversing the two concepts.

proposed by Postone, the first strand concerns the classical Marxist discussions of the concepts of nation and state. It is quite unique within the range of left-wing critiques of antisemitism for its straightforward rejection of nationalism. The ISF assert that the Leninist definition of the nation (as formulated by Stalin in 1913) was explicitly developed against the idea of Jewish nationality (as the latter lacked two necessary criteria, territoriality and shared language) (1990: 134). According to this ideology, legitimate states have to be expressions of the rights of historical subjects called nations (130), which means that a 'Jewish nation state' is illegitimate (and probably a malicious ruse) as no 'Jewish nation' exists.[22] The ISF assert against this notion (in the manner of political realism) that 'the history of the founding of states' is not 'the history of the realization of rights' but rather that of successful *violence*. 'The question whether Israel is a legitimate state has been answered through its foundation and is hence redundant' (131). This state's 'right to exist' can only be questioned from a position of romantic, '*völkische* speculation' about 'organic nations' and their 'souls'. (Critical Theorists usually assert the validity, or at least logical necessity, of the concept of human and other rights of individuals, whereas nations and states, not being individuals, cannot themselves 'have' rights; at most they can act on behalf of right-bearing individuals.) At the same time, Leninism presupposes a (rather mechanical) dialectic of national and social revolution (141): only centralized and homogenized territorial nation-states can produce (capitalist social relations and hence) socialism, a progressivist position challenged by more recent Marxist discussions on the link between capitalism and modernity. Furthermore, Leninists tend to posit that only through the mediation of the nation-state can the (national) individuals be internationalists: those who seem (or pretend) to be non-national or international *individuals* are denounced as rootless cosmopolitans and not part of the internationalism of nations.

US and UK reworkings: Jack Jacobs and Robert Fine/Philip Spencer

From the English-language world, I would like to point to two recent publications only that are of central importance and are closely connected to the material discussed so far. Jack Jacobs's book of 2015, *The Frankfurt School, Jewish Lives, and Antisemitism*, an intellectual history of enormous erudition,[23] consists of three chapters. The first describes the varying degrees to which key Frankfurt School scholars can be said to have been influenced by their Jewish backgrounds, whereby Jacobs rejects the (now somewhat fashionable) idea to regard Critical Theory a kind of Jewish philosophy. He points instead to specific areas where awareness of the Jewish context and its traces in

---

[22] It is telling that it had not occurred to the 'anti-imperialists' that if not a 'Jewish nation' then surely an '*Israeli* nation' did in fact become a reality in the post-colonial space left behind by the vanishing British Empire, a process not entirely different from the way Pakistan, India, Bangladesh and other nations were formed in the same period, and did in this sense acquire what they would normally think of as the right to national self-determination. Not perceiving this obvious parallel speaks to their reactionary fixation on 'the Jewish question'.
[23] Of 250 pages, 100 are endnotes and bibliography.

fact helps understanding it. The second chapter gives a detailed account of the various contributions Critical Theorists made to the study of antisemitism in the 1930s and 1940s, arguably the best survey available on these matters, highly recommended as a next step for readers whose appetites have been whetted by the present volume. The third chapter is the most original and deals with the thorny issue of left-wing takes on Israel, Zionism and anti-Zionism: similar to but in more detail than Claussen, Jacobs discusses with great subtlety the complicated ways in which some of the key members of the Frankfurt School related to these matters. Jacobs compares here the attitudes and views of Horkheimer, Lowenthal, Fromm and Marcuse. (Others such as Adorno, who grew up a Catholic, only get a few mentions in this chapter.) None of them were 'sympathetic to Zionism' before the foundation of the state of Israel (Jacobs 2015: 111). Subsequently, their views became more varied, and here Jacobs observes 'an inverse relationship between knowledge of Judaism and positive attitudes towards Israel' (148). Only Fromm was profoundly immersed in Jewish religious traditions, and only he came pretty close to being an anti-Zionist all but in name: Jacobs writes that he 'clearly would have preferred to see the Jewish state replaced by a bi-national state' (148) in the Magnes/Buber vein. 'Marcuse, the *least* Jewishly knowledgeable, was least inclined to continue to raise fundamental questions about the state' after its foundation. He would have never questioned its legitimacy as such but was most vocal in critiquing Israeli policies (148; emphasis in the original). Horkheimer and Lowenthal were privately more ambivalent but publicly more reluctant to voice any critical views than was Marcuse, not least out of fear inadvertently to play into the hands of neo-Nazi or Stalinist antisemites.

Marcuse supported the notion that Israel exists because of the need for 'a sovereign state which is able to accept and protect Jews who are persecuted or live under the threat of persecution' (Jacobs 2015: 120). At the same time, he held that its foundation took place 'without due regard to the rights and interests of the native population', but that similar things could be said about 'practically all states in history' (120). He 'publicly proclaimed solidarity with Israel at the time of the 1967 war' but was critical of subsequent Israeli policies (123).

Fromm who had been a Zionist until the mid-1920s subsequently rejected the idea of a Jewish state and was also 'considerably harsher' in his criticisms of Israeli policies (Jacobs 2015: 123). From 'at least 1950', Fromm was involved in the Freeland League, an organization that found Palestine unsuitable and too small for a Jewish state (124). The philosophical-theological (or, from a different angle perhaps, poetical) reasoning behind Fromm's rejection of Jewish statehood is well expressed in this extract from a letter written in 1972:

> As long as the world is as it is each individual – whether Jewish or not – is, I believe, an exile, and from the traditional standpoint the Jewish people must be an exile too. To want to abolish 'exile' in its spiritual meaning is to deny the discrepancy between what man is and what man could be. (Qtd in Jacobs 2015: 128)

Although Fromm had at this point ceased to be a member of the Frankfurt School for decades, he restates here a crucial element of Critical Theory: 'exile' means non-identity and the need to embrace and assert one's alienation in order to maintain the expectation that things could be better. As the Messiah could come any moment through any old little door, *false* messiahs must be refuted: Jewish, or any other, nationalism's banal positivity – making oneself at home in the false state of things – cannot but kill the utopia of transcendence. It is easy to see how this position leads to a more emphatically critical position than Marcuse's who wants to fight imperialism (amongst other things) but acknowledges the need for statehood, false Messiah or not, in a genocidal world order. (Like Horkheimer, Fromm never visited Israel; Marcuse and Lowenthal did.)

Lowenthal and Horkheimer stand somewhere in between these two poles. Horkheimer accepted, like Marcuse, the necessity of Israel as a refuge for Jews but, like Fromm, did not accept Zionism because it meant that the Jews gave up on being 'a people and its opposite, a rebuke to all peoples' (qtd in Jacobs 2015: 140), a becoming positive, a surfeit of assimilation to the ways of the world as it is. *Unlike* Fromm and Marcuse, though, he 'rarely criticized Israeli policies' (142). Lowenthal's position was quite close to Horkheimer's: 'There was no other possibility than to make a pact with the devil, with normality' (qtd in Jacobs 2015: 146); utopian messianism, though, did remain his life's 'background music'. This sums up the – happily contradictory – Frankfurt School position on these matters very well.

From among the increasingly huge number of recent publications on antisemitism, perhaps the one that is most explicitly written from a Critical Theory perspective is the small co-authored volume of 2017 by Robert Fine and Philip Spencer, *Antisemitism and the Left: On the Return of the Jewish Question*. It covers similarly broad grounds as Claussen's book, which it refers to, and, very usefully, is comprehensively referenced. It is as it were the politely cool British equivalent of Claussen's book. Its sections on Marx (Fine and Spencer 2017: 30–43) and the Frankfurt School (53–63) are amongst the most useful short texts available in English on these matters. The book's principal target is antisemitism that represents 'the Jews' as the enemy of universalism: 'a universalism that creates its own "other" ends up as no universalism at all', Fine and Spencer argue (44). It takes as its guiding question how 'the ambiguities of enlightenment universalism', an aspect of the dialectic of enlightenment, were reflected in the thinking of a number of left-wing theorists and movements. They assert that 'it was a great strength of critical theory both to re-affirm the validity of universalism as a principle, and to insist that it loses all meaning when set in opposition to the particular' (62).

The most original part of their argument is perhaps the critique of Habermas whose notion of 'postnationalism', an iteration of Enlightenment universalism, 'can be abused to label others "nationalist" or stigmatise others as its enemies' (100). This is an instance of their argument that universalism can become exclusionary, which is especially pertinent as Habermas presented 'postnationalism' as a particular achievement of – wait for it – the Germans, or else, of 'Europe' as Habermas argued subsequently. And indeed, as Fine and Spencer describe, a whole range of liberal opinion leaders attack Israel for being nationalist (101–5) when the world supposedly has moved on from, and has overcome, nationalism. Sadly, the latter does very much look like wishful thinking (not to say utter delusion). They mention the philosopher Alain Badiou who 'aligns himself to the tradition of universalism he traces back to St Paul's disconnection of Christianity from established Judaism, and from this "universalistic" vantage point denounces "Israel" as the placeholder for all that is hostile to the modern cosmopolitan and non-identitarian state' (102). Fine and Spencer refer to the example of Badiou as a kind of ironic and perverted late blossom of the Enlightenment, but the reference to St Paul suggests rather that this very particular universalism-cum-antisemitism is in fact the very old one of the church against which the Enlightenment rebelled.[24] Then again, perhaps, in a dialectical manner, it is both of these at the same time.[25]

[24] Whereas Habermas's attempt to find this cosmopolitan state in Germany, out of all places, had at the time something counterintuitive and utopian to it, Badiou is simply reproducing a traditional topos of French nationalism (whether or not he thinks that France actually *is* such a non-nationalist nation-state, or perhaps assumes that all the world, bar Israel, now has become revolutionary France). Both master thinkers might or might not, at various moments, have imagined Europe, birthplace and launching pad of any number of genocidal imperialisms, was this enlightened place that stands in such stark contrast to old-fashioned nationalist Israel.

[25] Among the further literature on the topic of the present volume, the most important and useful in English is Lars Rensmann's monograph *The Politics of Unreason* (2017), written from a different perspective on the general social-theoretical framework of Frankfurt School Critical Theory than the one pursued here; for a review, see Stoetzler (2020). Mark P. Worrell (2008) has produced a book-length study of 'Antisemitism among American Labor', a large-scale empirical study of antisemitic attitudes among US workers conducted by the Institute of Social Research in 1944–5 that remained unpublished. Worrell's interpretation is limited by his view that Horkheimer and Adorno had since the early 1940s abandoned dialectical thinking, Marxism and critique in general, a view for which *Dialectic of Enlightenment* serves (without being examined) as the chief exhibit and which leads Worrell to dub Franz L. Neumann, Paul Massing and A. R. L. Gurland 'the other Frankfurt School': he suggests they continued, as if in opposition to the institute's leadership, the programme of Critical Theory as set out by Horkheimer in the 1930s. Worrell implausibly presents the Labor Study, which these three produced together with the core institute members Lowenthal, Pollock and Adorno, as the product of 'the other Frankfurt School', and provides detailed interpretations of the empirical material that are framed by his own (Marxist as much as Durkheimian and Weberian) perspective. The book provides, though, a valuable detailed overview of this crucial empirical study, including large chunks of hugely interesting primary material in the original English. Eva-Maria Ziege's (2009) elegant and comprehensive monograph on the same subject (in German) demonstrates convincingly the complementary character of the theoretical and empirical works of the institute in the 1940s, and its continuity with the programmatic essays published by Horkheimer and others in the 1930s. Broad outlines of her perspective (in English) can be gleaned from Ziege (2012) and (2014). A good short survey of this topic in English is by Collomp (2011) (who mentions neither Worrell nor Ziege). Jacobs (2015: 78–82) confirms Ziege's perspective; see also Wheatland (2009). On Ziege (2009), see Stoetzler (2011). The literature on the infinitely more famous younger sibling of the Labour Study, *The Authoritarian Personality*, also keeps growing in interesting ways, such as most recently through an essay by Kranebitter (2022) who looks at the interviews conducted with prisoners at San Quentin: although *The Authoritarian Personality* has a reputation for having been conducted in a middle-class context (university students), this was not entirely the case, and difficult methodological issues arose precisely from the institute's attempt to broaden the study's base. An interesting new perspective on the Critical Theory of antisemitism is sketched out in a short essay by Joni Alizah Cohen (2018), who points to contemporary neo-Nazis' hostility to transgender women and to 'transgenderism' as a kind of sexual cosmopolitanism understood as part of a Jewish plot: they link 'Jewish sexology' as represented by Magnus Hirschfeld (not unreasonably) to the Frankfurt School, and see (very unreasonably) the notion of 'the fluid nature of gender and sex' as a 'Talmudic abstraction'; pace Postone, Cohen thus suggests that 'just as the Jew becomes the concrete manifestation of the abstraction of capitalism and the law of value, the trans woman becomes the concrete manifestation of the abstraction and denaturalisation of gender'. An important recent volume on populism (Abromeit et al. 2017) contains a chapter by Mark Loeffler on the role of antisemitism in this context, taking up central motives from Postone. Apart from the literature referenced in the chapters of the present volume, other important and useful contributions include Achinger (2013), Agger (1983), Bonefeld (2014), Braune (2019), Buchstein (2018), Catlin (2020), Claussen (1987, 2014), Fine (2016), Fischer (2016, 2017, 2018a

The contributions to this volume

Despite being anything but encyclopaedic or conclusive, my hope is that this volume will fulfil the function of a general survey and introduction to the field, covering the essentials, as well as going beyond and across its confines. Several of the chapters relate to a particular country but none are intended as case or country studies: the volume assembles variations on a few central theoretical themes which should, if the approach works, emerge from the constellation of the pieces that rehearse them. Similar arguments are made from different angles, producing repetitions that I hope readers will find helpful: chapters should explain each other, while the missing dimensions will have to be filled in by the readers (more like in a radio play than a television show, no effort is made to show it all).

Jordi Maiso, opening the first part, 'Elements', demonstrates how the contributions of the Critical Theory of the Frankfurt School researched and theorized modern antisemitism in the framework of the theory of modern, capitalist society and its evolution, but also that of the social constitution of the self: antisemitism has to do with objective and subjective elements of social constitution and reveals the 'limits of enlightenment' as well as the scars of failed emancipation. Matthew Bolton explores some of the background against which Critical Theory's critique of antisemitism emerged, using the often-discussed antisemitism of the British 'New Liberal' J. A. Hobson as an example for how 'left-wing' conceptualizations of capitalism produced the 'elements of antisemitism' Horkheimer and Adorno theorized. Hobson argued for state intervention to rebalance the societal distribution of wealth and remove the drivers for imperialist expansion. Restoration of the 'natural' balance between capital and labour, he thought, was prevented by the influence of international finance – not least the 'active financial race' of Jewish financiers. Werner Bonefeld makes the case for seeing antisemitism as innate to capitalist society rather than a social pathology: modern antisemitism articulates a personalized critique of the crisis-ridden dynamic of real economic abstractions, of price and profit, and their regulation by 'the invisible hand'. Christine Achinger explores the contributions of Critical Theory to an analysis of the relationship of constructions of Jewishness to those of other groups defined along the lines of gender and race. Such constructions of different 'others' are interconnected and historically changing responses to the challenges generated by the rise of capitalist modernity. She argues that 'politics of identity' have to become self-reflexive and have to be if not replaced, then at least supplemented by a 'politics of non-identity'. In this

---

and 2018b), Forrestier (1999), Geller (2020), König (2016), Krebbers and Schoenmaker (1999), Krebbers (2000), Müller (2002), Murphy (2018), Postone (2017), Rensmann and Salzborn (2021), Schechter (1999), Spencer (2016), Stoetzler (2018, 2019, 2021), Stögner (2017), Wheeler (2001), Worrell (1998), Ziege (2019). Adorjan (2014) only mentions antisemitism in passing but is very helpful in illustrating the Marxian side of the theory. Also issue (2012) of the journal *Constelaciones*, a special issue titled *Antisemitismo: Clave civilizatoria y funcionalidad social* (mostly in Spanish, some articles in English or in Portuguese), and issue 7.1 (2020) of the journal *Critical Historical Studies*, a special issue on Moishe Postone, are to be mentioned. The journal *New German Critique* has published too much relevant material to be listed here, including the above-mentioned triple special issue of 1980.

context, she relates Adorno's concept of the 'constellation' to that of 'intersectionality'. Marcel Stoetzler argues that the dialectic of capitalism and emancipation is central to understanding antisemitism. He uses a discussion of the concepts 'left' and 'right', dating from the period of the French Revolution, in terms of *liberté, fraternité* and *égalité* to distinguish elements of antisemitism that accuse 'the Jews' of either promoting or obstructing (liberal or socialist) progress that in turn is linked in contradictory ways to the capitalist mode of production and the nation-state.

The second part, 'Extensions', begins with Patrick Ahern's discussion of 'pathic' conspiratorial paranoia and projection in both right-wing and left-wing movements, and asks how a movement can develop a critical form of solidarity without making use of self-defeating, 'pathic' forms of identification like those that contain elements of antisemitism. Joan Braune draws, like Ahern, on Adorno in her discussion of 'conspirituality', the mixture of New Age spirituality with far-right conspiracy theories that has recently become a recruiting ground for fascist organizations. Again, conspiracy thinking that gives (false) names to the 'anonymous authority' that governs our lives plays a central role in this and is often antisemitic. Christopher D. Wright walks the discourse on 'the abstract' and 'the concrete' which is central to many of the arguments on antisemitism in this book back to its Hegelian root and invites us to rethink these categories in terms of 'the infinite' and 'the finite'. Taking the 6 January 2021 attack on the US Capitol as his jumping-off point, he argues that the revanchist populism that drove this event is fully in favour of the military, police and pro-business aspects of the state (finite) but against the broadly social and universalistic elements of the state typically thought of as egalitarian and democratic (infinite). Its antisemitism, like its anti-blackness, is an anti-globalist, anti-universalist sentiment that fears and resents the declining value of racial and national privilege. Jonathon Catlin explores the chronotope ('time-place') 'after Auschwitz' in several of Adorno's writings. He argues that Adorno on the one hand used it as the representation of a metaphysical rupture after which morality, education and life itself can never be the same, but on the other hand insisted that 'Auschwitz' must be understood as an outgrowth or symptom of the more fundamental pathology of the 'permanent catastrophe' of modern history writ large, which thus forms 'a kind of coherence, a hellish unity' with the atom bomb and 'torture as a permanent institution' from the Third Reich to the Vietnam War. Anna Zawadzka frames her analysis of antisemitic forms of anti-Zionism in contemporary Poland in two dimensions: one, the Stalinist legacy of anti-Zionism, which itself rests on a 'regular', European-Christian antisemitic tradition; and two, the influence of the anti-Zionism of the 'Western' left that is adopted by many Polish citizens. She argues that Poland's status as a semi-peripheral country within Europe leads modern-minded activists with pro-Western attitudes, somewhat ironically, to embrace and reproduce Poland's tradition of antisemitic anti-Zionism. Focusing on a country that must (still, although, at the point of writing, with decreasing plausibility) be counted as one of the 'core' areas of the world system, Matthew Bolton and Frederick Harry Pitts relate the antisemitism in the British Labour Party that was hotly debated in the Corbyn era to the 'truncated' or 'foreshortened' critique of capitalism that has dominated the Labour party since its formation, viewing capitalism as a conspiracy imposed on an otherwise benign form of productive society by a small group of capitalists motivated by greed, corruption and personal immorality. The nation-state counts in this worldview as the first line of defence of the community of productive workers against the rapacious cabal of global capitalists. Elements of antisemitism are latently present in such a perspective, cutting across factional divisions and the left-right spectrum, awaiting political activation. In the Corbyn years (2015–20), such activation came from, on the one hand, the left's focus on the machinations of global 'bankers' in the wake of the 2008 financial crisis, and on the other hand, the Manichean anti-imperialism and absolutist anti-Zionism which Corbyn had long been personally associated with.

References

Abromeit, J., B. M. Chesterton, G. Marotta and Y. Norman (eds) (2017), *Transformations of Populism in Europe and the Americas, History and Recent Tendencies*, London: Bloomsbury.

Achinger, C. (2013), 'Allegories of Destruction: "Woman" and "the Jew" in Otto Weininger's Sex and Character', *Germanic Review: Literature, Culture, Theory*, 88 (2): 121–49.

Adorjan, I. (2014), 'The Fetish of Finance: Metatheoretical Reflections on Understandings of the 2008 Crisis', *Critical Historical Studies*, 1 (2): 285–313.

Adorno, T. W. ([1965] 1989), 'Society', in S. E. Bronner and D. M. Kellner (eds), *Critical Theory and Society: A Reader*, 267–75, New York: Routledge.

Agger, B. (1983), 'The Dialectic of Desire: The Holocaust, Monopoly Capitalism and Radical Anamnesis', *Dialectical Anthropology*, 8 (1/2): 75–86.

Best, B., W. Bonefeld and C. O'Kane (eds) (2018), *The Sage Handbook of Frankfurt School Critical Theory*, London: Sage.

Bonefeld, W. (2014), 'Antisemitism and the Power of Abstraction: From Political Economy to Critical Theory', in M. Stoetzler (ed.), *Antisemitism and the Constitution of Sociology*, 314–32, Lincoln: University of Nebraska Press.

Braune, J. (2019), 'Who's Afraid of the Frankfurt School? "Cultural Marxism" as an Antisemitic Conspiracy Theory', *Journal of Social Justice*, 9: 1–25, available at: https://transformativestudies.org/wp-content/uploads/Joan-Braune.pdf (accessed 28 June 2023).

Buchstein, H. (2018a), 'Otto Kirchheimer's *The Policy of the Catholic Church toward the Jews* (1943): A Forgotten Chapter of the Frankfurt School's Research on Antisemitism', *Antisemitism Studies*, 2 (2): 254–71.

Catlin, J. (2020), 'Review Essay: The Frankfurt School on Antisemitism, Authoritarianism, and Right-Wing Radicalism', *European Journal of Cultural and Political Sociology*, 7 (2): 198–214.

Claussen, D. (1987), *Vom Judenhaß zum Antisemitismus. Materialien einer verleugneten Geschichte*, Darmstadt: Luchterhand

Claussen, D. ([1987] 1994), *Grenzen der Aufklärung. Die gesellschaftliche Genese des modernen Antisemitismus*, Frankfurt/M: Fischer.

Claussen, D. (2014), 'Conclusion: The Dialectic of Social Science and Worldview. Translated by Marcel Stoetzler', in M. Stoetzler (ed.), *Antisemitism and the Constitution of Sociology*, 333–41, Lincoln: University of Nebraska Press.

Cohen, J. A. (2018), 'The Eradication of "Talmudic Abstractions": Anti-Semitism, Transmisogyny and the National Socialist Project', available at: www.versobooks.com/blogs/4188-the-eradication-of-talmudic-abstractions-anti-semitism-transmisogyny-and-the-national-socialist-project (accessed 28 June 2023).

Collomp, C. (2011), '"Anti-Semitism among American Labor": A Study by the Refugee Scholars of the Frankfurt School of Sociology at the End of World War II', *Labor History*, 52 (4): 417–39.

Constelaciones 4 (2012). Special issue on *Antisemitismo: Clave civilizatoria y funcionalidad social*.

Critical Historical Studies 7.1 (2020). Special issue on Moishe Postone.

Diner, D. (ed.) (1988), *Zivilisationsbruch. Denken nach Auschwitz*, Frankfurt/M.: Fischer.

Diner, D. (2003), 'Den Zivilisationsbruch erinnern. Über Entstehung und Geltung eines Begriffes', in H. Uhl (ed.), *Zivilisationsbruch und Gedächtniskultur. Das 20. Jahrhundert in der Erinnerung des beginnenden 21. Jahrhunderts*, 17–34, Innsbruck: Studienverlag.

Dubiel, H. (1988), 'Kommentar zu Leo Löwenthals "Individuum und Terror"', in D. Diner (ed.), *Zivilisationsbruch. Denken nach Auschwitz*, 26–9, Frankfurt/M.: Fischer.

Fine, R. (2016), 'Cosmopolitanism and the Critique of Antisemitism: Two Faces of Universality', *European Review of history: Revue européenne d'histoire*, 23 (5–6): 769–83.

Fine, R., and P. Spencer (2017), *Antisemitism and the Left: On the Return of the Jewish Question*, Manchester: Manchester University Press.

Fischer, L. (2016), *'A Difference in the Texture of Prejudice'. Historisch-konzeptionelle Überlegungen zum Verhältnis von Antisemitismus, Rassismus und Gemeinschaft*, Graz: Leykam Buchverlagsgesellschaft.

Fischer, L. (2017), 'Marxism's Other Jewish Questions', in J. Jacobs (ed.), *Jews and Leftist Politics: Judaism, Israel, Antisemitism, and Gender*, 67–83, Cambridge: Cambridge University Press.

Fischer, L. (2018a), 'The Frankfurt School and Fascism', in B. Beverley, W. Bonefeld and C. O'Kane (eds), *The Sage Handbook of Frankfurt School Critical Theory*, vol. 2, 799–815, London: Sage.

Fischer, L. (2018b), 'Antisemitism and the Critique of Capitalism', in B. Beverley, W. Bonefeld and C. O'Kane (eds), *The Sage Handbook of Frankfurt School Critical Theory*, vol. 2, 916–31, London: Sage.

Forrestier, G. (1999), 'Wrong Direction: On Reclaiming a One-Way Street', [anonymous] *Reflections on June 18*, available at: http://apples-underground.blogspot.com/2009/02/apples-from-underground-trip-into.html. (This article was originally published in a brochure titled *Reflections on June 18, Contributions on the Politics behind the Events That Occurred in the City of London on June 18, 1999*, London, October 1999, pp. 16–21. All other contributions to this brochure, except the one by Forrestier, can be found here: https://libcom.org/article/reflections-june-18-1999.) (accessed 28 June 2023)

Freyenhagen, F. (2020), 'Adorno and Horkheimer on Anti-Semitism', in E. Hammer, P. Gordon and M. Pensky (eds), *Blackwell Companion to Adorno*, 103–22, Oxford: Blackwell.

Geller, J. (2020), 'Splitting the Difference: Freud's Disavowed Theory of Antisemitism', *Antisemitism Studies*, 4 (2): 216–36.

Horkheimer, M. (1978), *Dawn and Decline: Notes 1926–1931 and 1950–1969* (trans. M Shaw, with an afterword by E. Gebhardt), New York: Seabury.

Initiative Socialist Forum (ISF) ([1988] 1990), 'Ulrike Meinhof, Stalin und die Juden: die (neue) Linke als Trauerspiel', in *Das Ende des Sozialismus, die Zukunft der Revolution. Analysen und Polemiken*, 119–66, Freiburg: ça ira.

Jacobs, J. (2015), *The Frankfurt School, Jewish Lives, and Antisemitism*, New York: Cambridge University Press.

König, H. (2016), *Elemente des Antisemitismus. Kommentare und Interpretationen zu einem Kapitel der* Dialektik der Aufklärung *von Max Horkheimer und Theodor W. Adorno*, Weilerswist: Velbrueck.

Kranebitter, A. (2022), 'Rebels without a Cause? "Criminals" and Fascism in *The Authoritarian Personality*', *Journal of Classical Sociology*, 22 (3): 257–81.

Krebbers, E., M. Schoenmaker (1999), 'Campaign against the MAI potentially antisemitic' https://www.doorbraak.eu/gebladerte/30012v02.htm (last accessed 23 July 2023).

Krebbers, E. (2000), 'ATTAC's open flank'. https://www.doorbraak.eu/gebladerte/30004v02.htm (last accessed 23 July 2023; more materials by the group 'De fabel van de illegaal' in a range of languages can be found here: https://www.doorbraak.eu/gebladerte/v01.htm).

Loeffler, M. (2017), 'Populists and Parasites: On Producerist Reason', in J. Abromeit, B. M. Chesterton, G. Marotta and Y. Norman (eds), *Transformations of Populism in Europe and the Americas, History and Recent Tendencies*, 265–92, London: Bloomsbury.

Lowenthal, L. (1946), 'Terror's Atomization of Man', *Commentary* (January), available at: www.commentary.org/articles/leo-lowenthal/the-crisis-of-the-individual-ii-terrors-atomization-of-man/ (accessed 28 June 2023).

Löwenthal, L. (1988), 'Individuum und Terror', in D. Diner (ed.), *Zivilisationsbruch. Denken nach Auschwitz*, 15–25, Frankfurt: Fischer.

Müller, T. B. (2002), 'Bearing Witness to the Liquidation of Western Dasein: Herbert Marcuse and the Holocaust, 1941–1948', *New German Critique*, no. 85: 133–64.

Murphy, J. (2018), 'On the Authoritarian Personality', in B. Best, W. Bonefeld, C. O'Kane (eds), *The Sage Handbook of Frankfurt School Critical Theory*, vol. 2, 899–915, London: Sage.

Neubauer, S. (2012), 'Elements of a Critical Theory of Zionism: The Jewish State, the Disastrous History and the Changing Functionality of Antisemitism in the Late Thought of Max Horkheimer', *Constelaciones*, 4: 119–32, available at: https://constelaciones-rtc.net/article/view/784.

Postone, M. (1979a), *Antisemitismus und Nationalsozialismus* (trans. R. Schumacher), in *Diskus, Frankfurter Studentenzeitung*, issue 3–4, 37–47.

Postone, M. (1979b), *Antisemitismus und Nationalsozialismus* (trans. R. Schumacher), in *Autonomie*, 14: 58–67.

Postone, M. (1980), 'Anti-Semitism and National Socialism: Notes on the German Reaction to "Holocaust"', *New German Critique*, no. 19: 97–115.

Postone, M. (2017), 'The Dualisms of Capitalist Modernity: Reflections on History, the Holocaust, and Antisemitism', in J. Jacobs (ed.), *Jews and Leftist Politics. Judaism, Israel, Antisemitism, and Gender*, 43–66, Cambridge: Cambridge University Press.

Rensmann, L. (2017), *The Politics of Unreason: The Frankfurt School and the Origins of Modern Antisemitism*, Albany, NY: SUNY Press.

Rensmann, L., and S. Salzborn (2021), 'Modern Antisemitism as Fetishized Anti-Capitalism: Moishe Postone's Theory and Its Historical and Contemporary Relevance', *Antisemitism Studies*, 5 (1): 44–99.

Schechter, R. (1999), 'Rationalizing the Enlightenment: Postmodernism and Theories of Anti-Semitism', *Historical Reflections/Réflexions Historiques*, 25 (2): 279–306.

Spencer, P. (2016), 'Marxism, Cosmopolitanism and "the" Jews', *European Review of History: Revue européenne d'histoire*, 23 (5–6): 828–46.

Stoetzler, M. (2011), 'Review of *Antisemitismus und Gesellschaftstheorie, Die Frankfurter Schule im amerikanischen Exil*, Eva-Maria Ziege 2009 (Suhrkamp)', *Patterns of Prejudice*, 45 (3): 263–6; also in *East European Jewish Affairs*, 41 (1–2): 100–2.

Stoetzler, M. (ed.) (2014), *Antisemitism and the Constitution of Sociology*, Lincoln: University of Nebraska Press.

Stoetzler, M. (2018), 'Dialectic of Enlightenment. Philosophical Fragments', in B. Best, W. Bonefeld and C. O'Kane (eds), *The Sage Handbook of Frankfurt School Critical Theory*, vol. 1, 142–60, London: Sage.

Stoetzler, M. (2019), 'Capitalism, the Nation and Societal Corrosion: Notes on "Left-Wing Antisemitism"', *Journal of Social Justice*, 9: 1–45.

Stoetzler, M. (2020), 'Loving to Hate the Jews: Antisemitism according to the Frankfurt School. Review of *The Politics of Unreason: The Frankfurt School and the Origins of Modern Antisemitism*, by Lars Rensmann, SUNY Press, New York, 2017', *Patterns of Prejudice*, 54 (3): 287–93.

Stoetzler, M. (2021), 'Anti-liberal Liberals, the Nation and Liberal Antisemitism', *Constelaciones, Revista de Teoría Crítica*, 13: 203–37.

Stögner, K. (2017), 'Nature and Anti-nature: Constellations of Antisemitism and Sexism', in U. Brunotte, J. Mohn and C. Späti (eds), *Internal Outsiders – Imagined Orientals? Antisemitism, Colonialism and Modern Constructions of Jewish Identity*, 157–70, Würzburg: Ergon Verlag.

Wheatland, T. (2009), *The Frankfurt School in Exile*, Minneapolis: University of Minnesota Press.

Wheeler, B. R. (2001), 'Antisemitism as Distorted Politics: Adorno on the Public Sphere', *Jewish Social Studies*, 7 (2): 114–48.

Worrell, M. P. (1998), 'Authoritarianism, Critical Theory, and Political Psychology: Past, Present, Future', *Social Thought & Research*, 21 (1/2): 3–33.

Worrell, M. P. (2008), *Dialectic of Solidarity: Labor, Antisemitism, and the Frankfurt School*, Leiden: Brill.

Ziege, E.-M. (2009), *Antisemitismus und Gesellschaftstheorie, Die Frankfurter Schule im amerikanischen Exil*, Frankfurt: Suhrkamp.

Ziege, E.-M. (2012), 'Patterns within Prejudice: Antisemitism in the United States in the 1940s', *Patterns of Prejudice*, 46 (2): 93–127.

Ziege, E.-M. (2014), 'The Irrationality of the Rational: The Frankfurt School and Its Theory of Society in the 1940s', in M. Stoetzler (ed.), *Antisemitism and the Constitution of Sociology*, 274–95, Lincoln: University of Nebraska Press.

Ziege, E.-M. (2019), 'Das "jüdische Problem" und die *Dialektik der Aufklärung*', in S. Noerr, Gunzelin, E.-M. Ziege (eds), *Zur Kritik der regressiven Vernunft. Beiträge zur Dialektik der Aufklärung*, 123–48, Wiesbaden: Springer.

Part 1

Elements

1

The Critical Theory of antisemitism and the limits of enlightenment

Jordi Maiso, translated by Alex Álvarez Taylor

An awareness of the significance and reach of modern antisemitism is central to the process of development of Adorno and Horkheimer's Critical Theory.[1] Reflecting on the persecution of Jews and its social consequences was of fundamental importance to the reformulation of their theoretical project in the early 1940s, the first tangible results of which were visible in *Dialectic of Enlightenment*. Rather than an isolated phenomenon, Critical Theory regards antisemitism as the product of a determinate socio-historical constellation. Instead of focusing attention on the phenomenon as such, understanding antisemitism requires consideration of the whole social nexus within which it proliferates. In this sense, antisemitism played a key intellectual role, allowing Critical Theory to keep its finger on the pulse of a modern society that had left the bourgeois-liberal world behind. It offered a sophisticated and comprehensive perspective on the ways in which a specific tension between domination and emancipation had emerged historically. In practice, the increasingly virulent persecution of Jews, not only in Nazi Germany, became a yardstick for gauging the currency of modernity's emancipatory expectations and for recalibrating the priorities of a Critical Theory of society. The reality of antisemitism demands that one take stock of the 'limits of enlightenment' (Claussen 2005), as indicated by the title of the fifth chapter of *Dialectic of Enlightenment*, the iconic key text of the Critical Theory of antisemitism: 'Elements of antisemitism. Limits of enlightenment'.

Indeed, the persecution of the Jews, which many considered a residue from the dark Middle Ages, did not disappear in the so-called Age of Enlightenment. It revealed an undercurrent of irrationality and violence that had never been fully addressed

---

[1] The present text is deeply indebted to the work of José Antonio Zamora and to our collaboration over the past fifteen years. I am also grateful to Alex Álvarez Taylor for translating the text into English.
 This chapter was written with support of the following research projects funded by the Spanish government: 'Constelaciones del autoritarismo: Memoria y actualidad de una amenaza a la democracia desde una perspectiva filosófica e interdisciplinar' (PID2019-104617GB-I00) and 'La contemporaneidad clásica y su dislocación: de Weber a Foucault' (PID2020-113413RB-C31).

in modern societies and which could flare up again at any time. Even the darkest prognoses of the time paled in comparison with the news of the planned and systematic extermination of the European Jews, which Adorno came to associate with a place name – 'Auschwitz', the German name for a town in Poland that simultaneously implies an entire process and infrastructure of annihilation. In Adorno's words, the events at Auschwitz shed 'a deathly-livid light' (1951a: 268) on the history of civilization as a whole. The Nazi policy of extermination, conceived as the 'final solution of the Jewish question', appeared as the culmination of the history of modern antisemitism and forced Critical Theory to reflect on the failed promises of assimilation, on the intensification of forms of violence and their escalation at the heart of modern European civilization itself. For antisemitism was not something that plagued Western democracies as if from without: the extermination of the Jews had been planned and tolerated in the countries of Central Europe in a culture that supposedly upheld the principles of law, reason and order.

This epochal constellation led Horkheimer and Adorno to assume that 'the Jews are today the group which, in practice and in theory, draws to itself the destructive urge which the wrong social order spontaneously produces' ([1947] 2003: 192; 2002: 137). Accompanying the rise of fascism, the recrudescence of antisemitism demanded a renewed awareness of the need to rethink Critical Theory's position on the course of history. As early as August 1940, at the outset of the collaborative effort that culminated in *Dialectic of Enlightenment*, Adorno wrote to Horkheimer:

> I often have the feeling that everything we were used to seeing from the standpoint of the proletariat would today have been conferred on the Jews in a terribly concentrated form. I wonder . . . whether we should not speak of the things we really want to say in relation to the Jews, who today represent the polar opposite of the concentration of power. (2004: 84)

Naturally, this does not have to imply that Jews ought to replace the proletariat as those to whom the theory is addressed or as the privileged subject of history. It is not a question of attributing to the category of 'the Jews' the power that would be needed to constitute a political subject capable of articulating the promise of an emancipated society. What the Jewish perspective allows for is a corrective to the understanding of history held by some more 'traditional' currents of Marxism (cf. Zamora 2004: 117). Such a perspective aims to act against the triumphal bias that causes social movements to cling to the radiant promise of a 'final victory', always shining in the distant future, instead of attending to the devastation wrought by the failures of the present. This means doing justice to the categorical imperative of a young Marx who demanded 'the overthrow of all social relations that reduce the human being to the condition of a degraded, enslaved, helpless and despised creature' (1843: 385). Nevertheless, under the new historical conditions, 'overthrowing social relations' seems to have become a distant goal. For this reason, Adorno's later formulation of the imperative is far more modest: 'Hitler has imposed a new categorical imperative upon the human beings in the state of their unfreedom: to arrange their thinking and action so that Auschwitz never repeats itself, so that nothing similar ever happens again' (1966: 358).

Occasionally it has been alleged that the Critical Theory of antisemitism is incapable of accounting for the specificity of the violence and discrimination to which Jews are subjected in comparison with other forms of 'prejudice' (Rensmann 2017; Ziege 2009). However, this criticism overlooks that Critical Theory enables not only the identification of affinities between antisemitism and other forms of discriminatory violence but also allows for their integration within a social theory that accounts for the social and psychic constitution of subjects, and *thereby* seeks to account for the specificity of persecution of Jews. The figure of the Jew appears as the scapegoat par excellence: for fascism, Jews are not merely a minority but 'the negative principle as such' (Horkheimer and Adorno 2003: 192 [2002: 137]), the destruction of which salvation depends on. This calls for an analysis of the ways in which National-Socialist antisemitism – which culminates in extermination – emerges out of the modern form of antisemitism. This modern iteration is itself informed by a thousand-year-long tradition of persecuting Jews on a religious basis; hence the need to consider the social context in which the modern form of antisemitism appears and reproduces itself. Throughout much of European (and before that, Mediterranean) history, Jews have been the social group most associated with the issue of hatred towards 'the other' or 'the stranger'. Nevertheless, the idea of an 'eternal antisemitism' is misleading. Rather than positing it as an ahistorical constant, the task of any social theory worth its salt is to explain how antisemitism takes root, ever anew and differently, within concrete socio-historical situations (Claussen 1987: 66–7). For this reason, Critical Theory recognizes that an adequate understanding of antisemitism demands a theory capable of relating the analysis of the objective constitution *of society* with the ways in which subjects are constituted within and *by society*, taking into consideration the pressures that cause subjects – despite all the advances made by civilization – to continue maintaining an 'archaic disposition towards violence' (Adorno 1967: 680). Only such *general* framing can produce a meaningful social theory of antisemitism as a *specific* phenomenon.

Antisemitism and the dialectic of the process of civilization

Firstly, for Critical Theory antisemitism plays a key role in accounting for the dialectic of the civilizational process. 'As a rebellion against civilization fascism is not simply the reoccurrence of the archaic but its reproduction in and by civilization itself' (Adorno 1951b: 414). For this reason, antisemitism is not to be viewed as a marginal phenomenon. Rather, analysis of antisemitism can reveal substantive elements within the constitution of the social order: it implies the eruption of the latent potentials of oppression and repression accumulated in its history. According to Horkheimer and Adorno, antisemitic violence expresses the revolt of a repressed, deformed and prohibited mimetic impulse against domination. What is peculiar about this form of violence is that such a rebellion of oppressed nature finally ends up serving to perpetuate domination itself (Horkheimer and Adorno 2003: 210 [2002: 172]). How is this to be explained? Antisemites often justify their hostility towards Jews in idiosyncratic terms: as a spontaneous, almost somatic, irrepressible kind of aversion, one that in the face of specific triggers can result in a violent and defensive response. Nevertheless, Adorno and Horkheimer's analysis inverts the argument. Instead of regarding the specific characteristics or behaviour of Jews as the cause of idiosyncratic reactions – as the logic of victim-blaming mentality would have one infer – one ought to locate the root of the problem in the wounds and deformations that the civilizational logic produces in specific subjects, ones that predispose them to have strongly adverse reactions when confronted with certain stimuli. Notable here is the severity of the reaction when the behaviour or characteristics exhibited resemble living nature, a nature not completely subdued, since such a nature recalls the painful memory of everything that had to be repressed throughout the process of adaptation. This explains the repulsion felt by antisemites when confronted with the attributes they impute to Jews: mimetic behaviour, undisciplined gesturality, unrestrained expressiveness, a corporality that evokes the animal element, something primary and partially beyond dominant hygiene norms, definitively 'whatever is not quite assimilated, or infringes the commands in which the progress of centuries has been sedimented, is felt as intrusive and arouses a compulsive aversion' (2003: 204 [2002: 147–8]). The memory of such elements reveals the coercive quality of a civilizational process that demands that subjects submit to a lamentable logic of hardening and discipline. The fictive projections of antisemites, the perverse fantasies with which they represent their victims, allow one to recognize everything that has been proscribed and excluded from civilization: 'Those blinded by civilization have contact with their own tabooed mimetic traits only through certain gestures and forms of behavior they encounter in others, as isolated, shameful residues in their rationalized environment' (2003: 206 [2002: 149]). By this token, the idiosyncratic rejection of Jews helps to indicate, as it were, the 'sore' spots of modernity, where the failed promises of civilization become evident.

The rage that is discharged in antisemitic aggression functions by projecting hatred onto that which is repressed. Its strength derives from tapping into a deep well of frustration. Such frustration progressively accumulated under the weight of civilizational coercion, which imposed discipline and restrictions upon subjects but never managed to fulfil any of its promises to them. For this reason, it is argued that 'antisemitism is a well-rehearsed pattern, indeed, a ritual of civilization, and the pogroms are the true ritual murders' (2003: 195 [2002: 140]). Anything that seems to have escaped coercion, anything that recalls cheated happiness must fall under the same repressive yoke as that suffered by 'civilized' subjects, the same yoke that gives the lie to the claim of having arrived at a truly civilized state. Deep down, repressed subjects 'always go short, economically and sexually' and therefore 'hate without end; they find relaxation unbearable because they do not know fulfilment' (2003: 195 [2002: 140]). In this sense, domination can only subsist insofar as the dominated 'turn what they yearn for into an object of hate' (2003: 225 [2002: 154]). The precarious position of the Jews, who, in spite of their outsider status, seem to embody the image of powerless happiness, undermines the tiresome task of adapting to the world as it is, turning them into ideal targets for resentment. Nietzsche's influence is felt in such analyses. He writes of how accumulated frustration can turn into an aggressive impulse that seeks to 'sanctify *revenge* with the term *justice*' (Nietzsche 1887: 309–10; emphases in the original). Ultimately the persistence of antisemitism reveals that the current social order 'really cannot exist without defiguring human beings. The persecution of the Jews, like persecution as such, cannot be separated from that order. Its essence, however it may hide itself at times, is the violence which today is openly revealed' (Horkheimer and Adorno 2003: 194 [2002: 139]).

Adopting Freudian (1919) terms one might argue that for the antisemite the figure of the Jew embodies the ambivalence of the *Unheimliche*,[2] that is, to the extent that he embodies the picture of repulsion before a strangeness that is nevertheless perturbingly familiar. This representation indicates all that has been repressed in the name of establishing the 'identical, purpose-directed, masculine character' of the subject, which requires every other individual 'to inflict terrible injuries' on him- or herself (Horkheimer and Adorno 2003: 50). The dynamic of antisemitic reaction shows that civilizational control has proven incapable of mastery. There remain instinctual forms of reaction before the menacing forces of nature, for example, the spasms of skin, muscles and members, as well as gestures and forms of mimetic behaviour that imply 'touching, nestling, soothing, coaxing' (206).

The advance of civilization implies a certain distancing from such behavioural logics. In *Dialectic of Enlightenment*, magic is characterized as the conscious use of mimesis. Thus, it is through mimesis itself that rationality paves its own way, culminating in exclusively objectifying forms of behaviour: work, rational action. For this is required a discipline that seeks to harden the self to prevent it from dissolving back into surrounding nature. Consequently, the promise of happiness announced in every conscious relationship with nature must be repressed, for it implies sacrificing the distance upon which the strong self is based. An increasingly rigid subject is established through opposition to any form of gentle adaptation towards nature. Thus, the blind and coercive attributes of mimetic behaviour are prolonged by the social domination of nature. 'All that remains of the adaptation to nature is the hardening against it' (Horkheimer and Adorno 2003: 206 [2002: 149]). Since there exists the desire to forget the horror against which mimesis was originally reacting and which rational praxis seems to have successfully escaped, both mimetic behaviour and anything that might remind us of horror become taboo. Yet such a repressive dynamic proves fatal for rationality, since it prevents itself from becoming conscious of the regressive elements that persist in it.

Everything that is archaic, backward and anachronistic, everything that recalls the old domination and primitive forms of defensive response, arouses derision and anger. All these things are living reminders of the enduring violence that continues to hold sway over the relations of production; yet it is a violence to which civilized beings must submit and which they must try to forget in order to live. Rationalized

---

[2] Regarding the use of this Freudian concept, see Horkheimer and Adorno (2003: 206 [2002: 271]) and Fenichel (1946: 373).

idiosyncrasy is thus directed against the unmastered mimetic impulse. The repressed returns in its image. The forbidden desire to let go, to lose oneself in a state of nature, is given free rein in the controlled anarchy of the pogrom, in violence towards the vulnerable and stigmatized, particularly since such violence serves to eliminate this same desire. The lure of the forbidden turns into rage and violence against weakness in those who struggle to achieve awareness of their own renunciations and sacrifice, since such an awareness would threaten the coercive adaptation that ensures survival. Persecution, however, is unleashed not only against those in a vulnerable position but in particular against those who are perceived to have eluded the social norm from which the majority proved unable to escape (Adorno 1967: 677). The idiosyncratic aversion that may give way to the violent response is underpinned by a mechanism of projection. Hence Horkheimer and Adorno's conclusion (2003: 210 [2002: 152]):

> This mechanism needs the Jews. Their artificially heightened visibility acts on the legitimate son of Gentile civilization like a kind of magnetic field. In being made aware, through his very difference from the Jew, of the humanity they have in common, the rooted Gentile is overcome by a feeling of something antithetical and alien ... It makes little difference whether the Jews as individuals really display the mimetic traits which cause the malign infection or whether those traits are merely imputed.

The only thing that matters is that their position may serve as a suitable and functional screen for such projection.

According to this line of reasoning, for antisemites, the figure of the Jew is little more than a screen onto which to project repressed psychic material. All the excesses and crimes attributed to 'the Jews' since time immemorial – from infanticide to conspiracies and well-poisonings – are nothing but the projection of the taboo desires that populate the dark night of repressive civilization: the craving for 'exclusive ownership, appropriation, unlimited power, and at any price' (Horkheimer and Adorno 2003: 192 [2002: 137–8]). They attribute to their victims what they must restrain in themselves. This false projection is 'the antithesis of genuine mimesis' (2003: 211 [2002: 154]). Instead of doing justice to the reconciliatory dimension of mimesis in the subject, the false projection is fed by the repression of mimesis, which is put at the service of paranoid delusion. 'The person chosen as foe is already perceived as foe' (2003: 212 [2002: 154]). But the mechanisms of repression and paranoid projection are not simply the internal mechanisms of the psychic economy but those of civilization. The totalitarian order does nothing more than put them at its service. The insanity of the paranoid type reduces the external world to a reflection of his delusions of grandeur and persecution, and his fear imagines a gigantic danger that corresponds to these delusions (2003: 215–23 [2002: 157–63]). Thus, his dreamed omnipotence is a surrogate, the repetition of an empty scheme, for which all objects are equal and interchangeable. Since self-perception and reflection are absent, reality is degraded to a sphere for applying schemas. Fascism's destructive impulse is nothing but a developed form of its own inability to deal with difference.

Antisemitism and the dialectic of bourgeois emancipation

At the outset of modernity, Jews found themselves in an uncomfortable situation. On the one hand, they were subject to the protection of 'emperors, princes, or the absolutist state' (Horkheimer and Adorno 2003: 199). As Horkheimer indicated (1942: 333), protection is the original form of domination, though, since it leaves the protected at the mercy of the arbitrary goodwill of the protector. On the other hand, Jews were the group on which the anger and frustrations of the population were vented. Persecution obliged them to seek positions from which they could gain influence in order to survive and improve their economic situation. This led some Jewish individuals into highly visible roles in an increasingly monetarized economy that would ultimately make way for the logic of capitalism, creating a perception of 'the Jews' as economic modernizers and turning them into objects of increased hatred: they were perceived to be, and accused of being, beneficiaries of 'the economic progress which today is their downfall', by the 'craftsmen and farmers whose status capitalism undermined' (Horkheimer and Adorno 2003: 199 [2002: 143]). Dominant groups benefited from their position as alleged 'colonizers of progress', reaping the fruits of the modernization process and accepting that the fury of the population that bore its brunt would periodically flare up and address itself towards 'the Jews'.

Pogroms represented a break with taboo, 'a permitted, or rather ordered, excess, the festive transgression of a prohibition' (Freud 1913: 170). If they were tolerated, it was because they served to internalize the violence of domination. Hence Adorno and Horkheimer speak of antisemitism as 'a luxury for the common people' (2003: 194 [2002: 139]). The Christian tradition, which presented Jews as 'Christ-killers', offered a justificatory narrative for such assaults, basing itself on a long tradition of animosity and recriminations. As Horkheimer and Adorno pointed out, this was conducive even in the secularized societies of the twentieth century:

> To accuse the Jews of being obdurate unbelievers is no longer enough to incite the masses. But the religious hostility which motivated the prosecution of the Jews for two millennia is far from completely extinguished. Rather, antisemitism's eagerness to deny its religious tradition indicates that that tradition is secretly no less deeply embedded in it as secular idiosyncrasy once was in religious zealotry. (2003: 200; 2002: 144)

But if the Jews become the primary object of resentment, it is above all because of their perception as representatives of the sphere of economic circulation or exchange. 'Trade was not their vocation, but their destiny' (2003: 200 [2002: 144]), a destiny to which a centuries long tradition of persecution had consigned them. It was this aspect that, from the nineteenth century onwards, allowed them to appear as the great beneficiaries of incipient capitalism. The expansion of the spheres of circulation, commerce and the liberal professions were perceived by many as an expansion of the Jewish sphere of influence.

But while some Jews seemed to gain from the new social order, in collective terms they remained vulnerable. In this sense, it is the Enlightenment promise of emancipation that allows antisemitism to become a key to understanding the contradictions of liberal bourgeois society. From the very beginning the promise of emancipation was regarded as being conditional on the requirement of assimilation: the Jews had to renounce their own history to participate in abstract equality as citizen-subjects with rights and obligations. Already in 1789 Clermont-Tonnerre pointed out that 'Jews as a nation must be denied everything, Jews as human beings must be granted everything' (see Claussen 1987: 68). To the extent that assimilation required them to renounce their history and the specificity that distinguished them in an embrace of the bourgeois subject's abstract universality, the ideals of freedom, equality and humanity to which they aspired proved to be empty husks. Adorno himself would also point out the 'totalitarian and particularistic' character of bourgeois universality (1964: 620). In fact, pre-bourgeois forms of domination were characterized by a relatively overt character, legitimized as they were according to the division of the estates and a religious world view. Within this order, Jews occupied an extraterritorial position in which they figured either as objects of protection or persecution, depending on the case in question. In contrast, the abstract forms of domination that arise with capitalist social relations depend for their legitimation upon an abstract universality that is to be extended to every human being, a schema in which freedom and equality are understood in purely formal terms. According to the aforementioned logic, hoping for emancipation meant accepting an assimilatory requirement that was not without consequences: 'The enlightened self-control with which adapted Jews effaced within themselves the painful scars of domination by others, a kind of second circumcision, made them forsake their own dilapidated community and wholeheartedly embrace the life of the modern bourgeoisie, which was already advancing ineluctably toward a reversion to pure oppression' (Horkheimer and Adorno 2003: 193 [2002: 138]). Such a process leads to Jews becoming the ideal target for the frustrations generated under the novel forms of abstract domination. Paradoxically, in the end Jews were charged with paying the price of failure: failure to make good on the promises of the bourgeois revolutions in which a large part of the population had placed their hopes.

Expropriated of their history and reduced to mere owners of commodities, Jews became objects of hate – and so, modern antisemitism was born. In Detlev Claussen's terms (1987: 74), its emergence stems from the failure to achieve emancipation in the wake of the revolution and subsequent Napoleonic wars. Its rise ought to be understood as a response to the French Revolution and its socioeconomic consequences. As Jews left the ghettos and began ascending socially in the emerging capitalist order, especially within the so-called liberal professions, and particularly if baptized, they became the targets of widespread resentment. This took place within the aggravating context of the capitalist valorization process, in which relations of domination and servitude could no longer be explained in terms of direct personal relations, but in terms of the process of abstract universal mediation based on the production and exchange of commodities. No longer overt, social domination manifested itself in anonymous and objectified imperatives, in what Marx called the 'mute compulsion of economic relations' ([1867] 1981: 765).

One issue with the impersonal character of capitalist domination is that underlying the apparent, outward rationality of the exchange mediation lie coercive and violent social relations that increasingly exacerbate conditions of inequality. Jews, as the only recognizable representatives of the sphere of circulation, were identified with the everyday mechanism of exchange and the frustrations resulting from it, which affected the vast majority of the population. Since they were identified with money, Jews as a whole came to be regarded as personifications of the abstract mechanisms of valorization. They came to be perceived as being responsible for the preponderance of impersonal forms of social power. In this respect, 'antisemitism becomes abstract' (Claussen 2005: 45). Nevertheless, this development never spared Jews from being scapegoated for the implacable injustices of the economic system. They were depicted as being as destructive, powerful and international as capitalism itself; Richard Wagner in a text from 1850 called 'Judaism in Music' would even go so far as to name them as the real 'dominators'.[3] The practical function such an argument serves in reproducing new forms of domination is obvious: 'That is why people shout "Stop thief!" – and point at the Jew. He is indeed the scapegoat, not only for the individual manoeuvres and machinations, but in the wider sense that the economic injustice of the whole class is attributed to him' (Horkheimer and Adorno 2003: 198 [2002: 142]).

Antisemitism and the dialectic of the commodity form

The specificity of capitalism's social constitution is owed to the fact that, within it, domination takes the form of a process of social mediation, in which it assumes an increasingly abstract and anonymous appearance. While its coercive moment is indeed tangible, the logic that governs the social system is not easily identifiable; there is no palpable embodiment of what Marx defined as the 'automatic subject' (1867: 169). What the social constitution generates is an ensemble of deceptive appearances that prevent us from unravelling the web of social mediations. According to Marx's analysis of the commodity form, individuals perceive the social relation they establish with one another in exchange as a 'natural characteristic' of the commodities traded. In other words, what makes commodities exchangeable appears to be an inherent quality of the commodities themselves. However, as Marx makes clear, this interchangeability derives from the social structure and the specific form taken by social relations in commodity-producing society. And it is within this structure that an inversion takes place, one between social relations and the manifest attributes or qualities of things.

---

[3] Just like that, the *creditor of kings* [Gläubiger der Könige] has become the king of the pious [König der Gläubigen], and we cannot regard the emancipatory claim of this king as anything but enormously naïve, for it is we who find ourselves in need of emancipation from the Jews. In the current state of affairs, the Jew is already more than emancipated: he *dominates*, and will continue to dominate as long as money remains the moment before which our activity loses all its strength. (Wagner, qtd in Claussen 1987: 89–90)

This, in turn, means that the 'suprasensible' and social dimension of the commodity comes to present itself as an inherent attribute of the commodity itself (87).

For Adorno there is no doubt that social objectivity, as an antagonistic totality, constitutes a real unity that embraces everything. It is characterized, above all, by a dynamic of quid pro quo, in which social objectivity is constituted as an autonomous entity vis-à-vis the individuals who keep it ticking over. The world of capital is an inverted world. It is constituted thanks to the actions with which individuals ensure its reproduction. Yet as it grows increasingly independent from the individuals that constitute it, it develops its own dynamic. Such a dynamic obeys laws that operate, as it were, 'behind the backs' of individuals, weighing on them as an 'alien' and 'autonomous' force. Both Marx and Adorno note that this description ought to be understood in ironic terms, especially since their theorizations of society are, above all, designed to *criticize* and *challenge* the autonomization of the social synthesis, revealing the sore spot of persisting heteronomy in the capitalist social system.

Such heteronomy stems from the fact that individuals are, simultaneously, both subjects and objects. The system is indeed constituted by their actions; however it crystallizes in a pseudo-objectified logic that coercively confronts them and turns them into mere executors and appendages of the social dynamic they have set in motion (Adorno 1969: 316). In this way, Critical Theory avoids either falling back into a form of positivism that renders a reified objectivity absolute by obscuring its genesis, or turning into a sociology of (inter)action that hypostatizes and takes at face value the form of appearance of individuals in existing society: acting but atomized individuals. The existing social organization prevents, though, the individuals' constitution as true subjects. Traditional (i.e. 'non-critical') sociology in either its positivist or action-theoretical versions posits the autonomized form of social objectivity as both external and opposed to the subjects, as a fixed reality whose genesis has become almost impenetrable and impossible for individuals to grasp. The individuals tend not to take for granted the process of societal structures' – the capital relation's – autonomization, even if the real abstraction of the sum of exchange values is nothing other than the autonomized reification of their labour as a whole.

Marx's value theory intended to lay bare the reasons why individuals act the way they do without knowing what they do. By exchanging the products of their labour as equivalent values, they are in fact equating different labours with one another, however in a non-conscious manner. The money-form makes possible the reconstruction of a real abstraction or a *really-existing-universal*. However, since the genesis of this universal is no longer visible, it is perceived as something existing in itself, as a quality or attribute of the object and not as the result of the subject's activity. Adorno denounces the logical connection between value, money and capital as indicative of the growing irrationalization of society: 'society, that which has become autonomous, is no longer comprehensible; only the law of its autonomisation is comprehensible. Incomprehensibility refers not only to its essential structure, but also to ideology' (1969: 296). The sum of value amounts to a 'real abstraction', but this is nothing less than the autonomization of abstract labour.

In the capital-form, fetishized cognition introduces a split between the natural materiality of labour and its products on the one hand, and money and interest on the other. Since money and interest come to be perceived by participants as abstract and separate, they become the sole target of denunciation. For Marx, interest originates in the surplus value wrested from living labour, yet this connection is concealed by the fetish-character of commodities, money and capital: 'It is in interest-producing capital that the automatic fetish, as self-valorising value, as money that begets more money, becomes visible in all its purity, and, in this form, no longer shows any scar of how it was generated' (1894: 405). Marx's critique of the fetishism of capital is thus directed towards the exploitative core of the ensemble of social relations subjected to its form. Its aim is to unmask the imposed subject-object inversion. Enlisting the Marxian critique of fetishism, in 'Elements of Antisemitism', Horkheimer and Adorno use the term 'the true Shylock', '*der wahre Shylock*', to describe the capitalist proprietor of the means of production as the 'true' usurer. In contrast to the merchant and the banker,

> he grabbed not merely from the market but from the source: as a functionary of the class system, he took care not to go short of the fruits of his workers' labour. The workers had to deliver as much as possible. As the true Shylock he insisted on his banknote [*Schein*]. By virtue of owning the machines and materials, he forced the others to produce. He called himself the producer, but he and everyone secretly knew the truth. The productive work of the capitalist, whether he justified his profit as the reward of the enterprise, as under liberalism, or as the director's salary, as today, was the ideology which concealed the nature of the labor contract and the rapacity of the economic system. (Horkheimer and Adorno 2003: 198 [2002: 142])

Like those who, cheated out of receiving fair compensation for their labour-power, are unable to locate the source of deceit other than in the sphere of circulation, in the distribution of commodities, the illusory belief arises that the source of injustice is to be located in the sphere of exchange rather than in surplus-value extraction. Making the sphere of circulation responsible for exploitation is thus a socially (almost) necessary illusion. Hatred of the Jews and hatred of the sphere of circulation participate in the same obfuscation that is necessarily generated by the system (Claussen 2005: 109–39). This is taken advantage of by antisemites who distinguish between 'productive' (*schaffendes*) and 'usurious' (*raffendes*) capital, that is, between capital invested in the industrial sector of production and capital invested in the credit system of the commercial and financial sector. 'Bourgeois antisemitism', Adorno and Horkheimer argue, 'has a specific economic purpose: to conceal domination in production' (2003: 197 [2002: 142]).

Antisemitism and the dialectic of the process of subjectivation

The Critical Theory of antisemitism is based on an assumption that may appear to clash with 'healthy' common sense: namely that antisemitism, a scandalous thing to diligent liberals, in the end proved to function perfectly within an increasingly total form of capitalism. Here, Freud's diagnosis of the malaise or discontent in civilization is pertinent: 'One might speak of the claustrophobia of humanity in the administered world, of a feeling of being trapped in a completely socialised nexus, like a net. The thicker the net, the greater the desire to escape, but the more difficult it becomes. This reinforces the sense of anger felt towards civilisation. The struggle against it becomes violent and irrational' (Adorno 1967: 676–7). At this point the theorization of antisemitism becomes crucial, since it helps to explain the increasingly impersonal and coercive character of sociality in terms that are relatively easy to assimilate. Believing s/he has identified the causes of social domination – personified in clearly recognizable figures – the antisemite assumes s/he can eliminate them by participating in the powerful antisemitic community. However, at the same time as naming and blaming alleged culprits, antisemitism repeats the operation by which oppressive structures underpinning practices of domination and exclusion are obfuscated or masked. For disadvantaged subjects, however, this does not diminish antisemitism's functional value. Having an explanation and a scapegoat makes the anguish of subjects at the mercy of all-pervasive and anonymous social forces more tolerable;[4] after all, antisemitic frustration already has a target. Nevertheless, it ought to be pointed out that the social processes of integration, atomization, subjugation and coercion affect not only antisemites but extend to everyone in society. Ultimately, antisemitic tendencies are rooted in the inertial forces of socialization.

In attempting to elucidate the causes of antisemitism, critical theorists found their main ally in Freudian psychoanalysis.[5] Their use of psychoanalysis, however, did not consist in directly analysing the contents of antisemitism in the manner of Rudolf Löwenstein (1952) or in speculation regarding the specific traits of the 'Jewish psyche'. Inevitably, such uses of psychoanalysis lead into the trap of psychologism. Such analyses regard antisemitism merely as an outcome, failing to take into account its psychodynamic basis in the individual subject, which is what makes analysis of its social dimension possible. A collaborator of Adorno and Horkheimer during the period of Californian exile, the psychoanalyst Otto Fenichel struck at the heart of the matter: 'Since psychoanalysis is a method for the study and treatment of the psychic life of individuals, strictly speaking there can only be a psychology of antisemites, not of antisemitism' (1946: 373). Accordingly, Critical Theory and psychoanalysis converge in their analyses of processes of violence-internalization, examining what it is that makes individuals more or less likely to identify with groups, actively participate in antisemitic offences or tacitly and passively condone such acts (Claussen 1988).

---

[4] Nietzsche had already observed the importance of being able to project blame upon a concrete agent:

> For every sufferer instinctively looks for a cause of his distress; more exactly, for a culprit, even more precisely for a guilty culprit who is receptive to distress, in short, for a living being upon whom he can release his emotions, actually or in effigy, on some pretext or other: because the release of emotions is the greatest attempt at relief, or should I say, at anaesthetizing on the part of the sufferer, his involuntarily longed-for narcotic against pain of any kind. (1887: 373–4)

[5] For a more detailed analysis of the relation between social theory and psychoanalysis, see: Bock (2018), Claussen (1988), Dahmer (2019), Maiso (2013), Safatle (2017) and Zamora (2007).

The antisemitism of the fascist era thus appears to result from the coercive character of socialization in post-liberal societies, where the social apparatus weighs inexorably upon the individual, demanding the total subordination of internal and external life to social constraints. In these modes of socialization, weakened or damaged individuals are characterized by the experience of *harm*: society imposes itself on the individual with such a degree of coercive violence that one can no longer speak of coherent personalities but of individuals constituted as 'systems of scars' (Adorno 1952: 24). Individuals sense that their lives are totally subordinate to a logic that they do not understand and before which they remain prostrate. The disproportionate gap between social power and individual impotence increases the volatility of the libidinal economy, leading to an all-pervasive anxiety and marked desire for security that crystallizes in what Fenichel termed 'narcissistic neediness' (1939: 177). Such neediness encourages a search for 'phantasms and personifications with which dependent individuals attempt to rearticulate the abstract and impenetrable aspect of social relations in terms of lived experience' (Adorno and Jaerisch 1968: 186). Hatred of the Jew as the cause of all misfortune is thus one example of a magical formula designed to create an appearance of meaning or sense in an otherwise inexorable reality. Not only does it offer a concrete explanation of abstract harm and an escape valve for frustration but it also helps to further reinforce the subject's social dependency and further mystify the causes of social coercion.

In this context, the value of psychoanalysis is that it helps explain the mechanisms and performative role of the 'antisemitic illusion' in a psychic economy subordinate to the reality principle. Freud had shown that the ego, as the point at which internal and external reality converge, was not only the organ of knowledge but also the organ of repression and censorship and the defence mechanisms of the psyche. Freud's theory made it possible to access the 'dark, subterranean side of history' that flourished in the destructive thirst for violence that National Socialism had normalized – a case of the fate of human instinct and passion when it is repressed and disfigured by civilization (Horkheimer and Adorno 2003: 265 [2002: 192]). Accordingly, Adorno states that Critical Theory is uninterested in psychoanalysis either as a form of ego-psychology or social psychology. Instead, it regards psychoanalysis as the psychology of the libido that always follows the path of least resistance in the struggle between the drives and the imperative of adaptation (Adorno 1955: 72–3). The psychological mechanism of antisemitism is to be interpreted from this standpoint. Having said this, for Adorno the mechanism exceeds the psyche, since 'antisemitism is not a matter of individual psychology'; rather, it is an attitude, a feeling that is

> linked to a contemporaneous awareness of power. Antisemitic situations are always those in which a demonstration of power must be addressed towards a weaker individual; they themselves arise under the pressure of power. In every respect, German antisemitism conveys the quality of having been induced in the subject, of threatening from on high that power may well turn against the subject should he not also become an antisemite. (2003: 84)

'Antisemitic behaviour is unleashed in situations in which blinded people, deprived of subjectivity, are let loose as subjects' (Horkheimer and Adorno 2003: 195 [2002: 140]). At this point the theme of 'tolerated excess' arises once more. In 'tolerated excess' the possibility of giving in to one's instincts and indulging in aggressive behaviour not only does *not* endanger the subject who transgresses the norm, it may even perform a useful function for him. Expressing antisemitic attitudes helps compensate the wounded narcissism of weakened and impotent subjects, enabling them to feel that they are at once established and rebellious, both part of a majority and members of an elite. Their invective amounts to a perversion of the ideal of civil liberty (2003: 226 [2002: 165–6]). The psychoanalyst Otto Fenichel gave the idea consistency:

> Human beings find themselves caught in the conflict between the inclination to rebel and the respect for authority for which they have been educated. Antisemitism offers them the means of satisfying these two contradictory tendencies at the same time: the rebellious tendency through destructive actions against defenceless people, and the respectful tendency towards authority through obedient action in accordance with the preferences of the established powers. (1946: 375)

By this token, it is significant that research on the authoritarian personality revealed that the type of people most likely to engage in 'conformist rebellion' were precisely those who felt most aggrieved by the logic of society (Adorno 1950: 302). It is the experience of injustice, the feeling of having been cheated, that leads such subjects to demand that others should also swallow the same bitter pill. Formulating a physiognomy of their 'type', Adorno presented antisemites as

> people who suffer injustice in the social struggle for survival, but who, in their own way, identify with said competition. They are Darwinists. They believe in the survival of the fittest, feel they are 'fitter' than the Jews, and believe that the Jews are naturally doomed to go under. When nature does not work as expected, they lend it a hand. (2003: 85–6)

Certainly, such reflections do not apply exclusively to antisemitism; they might also be applied to cases of violence against other social groups. This, however, stems from the fact the psychodynamics of what has come to be known as 'racial prejudice' is not based on the specific characteristics of the object against which hatred is directed, but on the realization that having such an object can serve as a useful outlet for the destructive impulses of some subjects, enabling them to vent frustration without calling into question the primacy of the reality principle. Jews perform this function due to their ambivalent status, one that enables them to embody a figure both of power and of pure impotence. Such ambivalence also encourages the projection of arguments that legitimize violence against Jews.[6] Thus, the supposed contents of 'antisemitic

---

[6] Some of these features, such as 'clanishness' aid rationalization; others, such as the expression of weakness and masochism, provide psychologically adequate stimuli for destructiveness. There can be hardly any doubt that all these requirements are fulfilled by the phenomenon of the Jew. This is not

ideology' – whether in allegations of natural inferiority or as shadowy architects of a global conspiracy – are pure rationalizations that have no intention of establishing any kind of truth content. They serve, rather, a psychic function whose main concern is to legitimize violence. Operating here is a mechanism of projection, for 'those impelled by blind murderous lust have always seen in the victim the pursuer who has driven them to desperate self-defence, and the mightiest of the rich have experienced their weakest neighbour as an intolerable threat before falling upon him' (Horkheimer and Adorno 2003: 212 [2002: 154]). This is the rationality that justifies allowing subjects to suspend self-control and give free rein to their destructive, violent and even sadistic impulses.

Understanding the logic of antisemitic violence means remaining conscious of the fact that, as Horkheimer (1996: 464) pointed out, 'the tendencies in people which make them susceptible to propaganda for terror are themselves the result of terror, physical and spiritual, actual and potential oppression'. It is this situation of pressure and menace that leads aggressors, as if by a fatal mechanism, to unleash on their victims what they themselves unconsciously fear above all else:

> No one who seeks shelter shall find it; those who express what everyone craves – peace, homeland, freedom – will be denied it, just as nomads and travelling players have always been refused rights of domicile. Whatever someone fears, that is done to him . . . The evicted compulsively arouse the lust to evict them even [from the graveyards where they are buried]. The marks left on them by violence endlessly inflame violence. (Horkheimer and Adorno 2003: 208 [2002: 150])

If the social mechanism has branded them with the stigma of exclusion, then, so the thinking goes, it is likely that the victims are not so innocent: this, even today, is the legitimating rationality behind calls for bloodshed by antisemites and xenophobes of all stripes. Pulsating in the background is the desire for self-assertion and the exercise of force. In this respect, antisemitism is not an anomalous deviation from the existing social order but a demonstration of how social pressure negatively affects human beings and ensures the continual reproduction of persecution and violence. In a society characterized by blind and relentless coercion, marked by vast levels of discontent, individuals sense that violence is the governing principle of the existing order. Antisemitic denunciations are thus calls to aggression that allow dispossessed and resentful subjects to participate in actively inflicting the same social violence that they are normally obliged to endure (Lowenthal and Guterman 1949: 114). This is how the penultimate finishers in the race endow their position of privilege with a

---

to say that Jews must draw hatred upon themselves, or that there is an absolute historical necessity which makes them, rather than others, the ideal target of social aggressiveness. Suffice it to say that they can perform this function in the psychological households of many people. The problem of the 'uniqueness' of the Jewish phenomenon and hence of antisemitism could be approached only by recourse to a theory . . . of modern society as a whole. (Adorno 1950: 269)

sense of reality vis-à-vis those finishing last. Indeed, 'rage is vented on those who are both conspicuous and unprotected. And just as, depending on the constellation, the victims are interchangeable: vagrants, Jews, Protestants, Catholics, so each of them can replace the murderer, in the same blind lust for killing, as soon as he feels the power of representing the norm' (Horkheimer and Adorno 2003: 195 [2002: 140]). Leaving of course the roots of the problem intact, it does allow for the externalization of accumulated aggression.

In this way antisemitism appears as a mobilization of the unconscious dynamics of the subject. These dynamics are subsequently channelled and adjusted to the imperatives of the reproduction of social power, wherein the latter takes advantage and exploits the demands of the libidinal economy. In Adorno's words, 'Antisemitism is a mass medium; in the sense in which it appeals to emotions, conflicts, preferences and unconscious tendencies, which it reinforces and manipulates, instead of rendering them conscious and clarifying them' (1962a: 366). It generates a cohesive power strong enough to bring together subjects who frequently feel isolated and misunderstood, offering them the longed-for feeling of 'community'. Since it appeals to emotional needs, conflicts and often primary and irrational dispositions, Adorno and Leo Lowenthal regard antisemitism as a kind of 'inverted psychoanalysis'. But in doing so, it 'incessantly reinforces the defence mechanisms instead of working towards their dissolution, it plays capriciously with unconscious and preconscious elements instead of raising them to consciousness' (Adorno 1962b: 155). Antisemitism appeals to the wounded aspect of subjectivity and is seemingly assimilated to what Freud called a *Schiefheilung* (1921: 139), a 'crooked cure' for psychic conflicts that re-establishes a superficial equilibrium between the reality principle and the pleasure principle – often at the price of a flight from reality.[7] In fact, antisemitic behaviour may mitigate discontent and anxiety by reducing the collateral friction within one's own psyche and finding an outlet for accumulated grievance. Nevertheless, it certainly does nothing to reduce the subject's position of weakness and dependence within the social order. In the words of Wolfram Stender (1996: 79), in the 'pseudo-logic' of antisemitism, 'objective obfuscation and individual scarring come to constitute a stable short-circuit'. From this arises the need to specify the precise sense in which one can speak of antisemitism in terms of 'pathology' (paranoia, perversion, etc.). If it amounts to a 'crooked cure', then that obtains because instead of resulting in the social ostracization of antisemitic individuals, it allows them to become more attuned to the prevailing norm, functioning as a kind of 'delusion' that makes it easier for them to meet the demands of adaptation and to internalize its costs.[8]

---

[7] If antisemitism is a 'symptom' which fulfils an 'economic' function within the subject's psychology, one is led to postulate that this symptom is not simply 'there', as a mere expression of what the subject happens to be, but that it is the outcome of a conflict. It owes its very irrationality to psychological dynamics which force the individual, at least in certain areas, to abandon the reality principle. (Adorno 1950, 295)

[8] This means that further reflection is needed on the relationship between individual and collective pathology, as well as on the latter's normalizing effect on the former, which would explain why only some subjects develop clinical symptoms. The 'pathic' projection is

This is how antisemitism, charged with a destructive and violent pathos, can have a stabilizing function for the social order. For 'with false culprits, not only does real social conflict disappear, libidinal conflicts in adapted 'healthy' individuals also disappear' (Stender 1996: 75).

Ultimately, insofar as antisemitism is regarded as a 'prejudice' it would be unwise to assume that it can be defeated by superior argumentation or the refutation of its premises. The crux of the matter lies in the way antisemitism – like racism, nationalism or superstition – takes root in the psyche of its subjects. Conscious of the obviously irrational nature of their prejudice, subjects state that they are simply expressing an 'opinion'. This view of 'opinion' is symptomatic of a late-liberal relativism that has renounced any concept of binding truth, 'insofar as everyone is allowed to think whatever they like regardless of whether it is true, for each individual thinks only of that which helps them to affirm themselves and gain a competitive advantage' (Adorno 1954: 470). In this respect, antisemitism can help to orient individuals in a world perceived as alien and hostile, helping to relieve the subject of the arduous task of actually having to confront reality in a critical way. The claim is often made that Jews *must have done something* to have attracted so much hate over the years. Here, having an 'opinion' no longer represents an initial step towards independent knowledge but plays a primarily psychological role. 'Here, rather than restrict the hypothetical judgement, the "opinion of the I" emphasises it' (Adorno 1961: 574). In this context, 'opinion' functions as an affectively charged means of self-affirmation. The subject thus resists anything that might disprove his or her 'opinions' by way of facts. Recognition of error would also mean inflicting a narcissistic injury upon the subject, something he or she could hardly tolerate. Combating antisemitic opinion means addressing the social logic that both debilitates subjects and encourages the psychic internalization of 'crooked cures'. For 'what the subject attributes to himself in the name of opinion as a private prerogative is nothing other than the imprint of the objective situation in which the subject finds himself' (591). As such, the complacent liberal conviction that 'normal' and considered opinions will always prevail over 'insane' or 'pathological' ones can no longer be taken for granted. The problem is that the very need to resort to 'opinions' – holding Jews responsible for every kind of evil, redressing grievances through collective narcissism, asserting the inferiority of certain ethnic or cultural characteristics – expresses precisely what is normal about the social logic; it is simply a normal way of processing its conflicts. Hence Adorno's conclusion: 'If there really is no right life in the false, then there can be no right consciousness in it either' (591).

---

systematically mobilized by politics in such a way that 'the object of illness is determined in a way that conforms to reality' and 'the system of delirium becomes a rational norm in the world' (Horkheimer and Adorno 2003: 212 [2002: 154]). This is probably why Adorno and Horkheimer call the psychosocial mechanism of paranoid antisemitic projection *pathic* rather than pathological. Since the object is a social ailment that responds to the Freudian schema of 'culture and its discontents' it should not be interpreted according to the criteria of psychiatric doctrine. In Adorno's view, the pathic designates the 'illness of the normal (people)', of those adapted to their times (Pohl 2010: 63–4).

Antisemitism after Auschwitz

Critical Theory's main argument is that individuals hope to find in antisemitism a palliative cure for the 'suffering generated by rationalised civilisation' (Adorno 2019: 29). Clearly, the 'manifest contents' of antisemitic proclamations are absurd. Yet what determines their plausibility is not whether they correspond to the facts, but the extent to which they help a wide array of subjects internalize the social imperatives of the day. As such, 'what is considered "pathological" today can become the dominant tendency tomorrow with a change in social conditions' (Adorno 1950: 157). It only takes one U-turn in the socio-political climate to make what was hitherto taboo admissible once again. In the post-Nazi constellation, hatred of Jews could no longer be openly expressed once fascism's military defeat and news of the extermination of European Jewry re-established the taboo on voicing such sentiment. Hence the bitter irony with which Adorno and Horkheimer begin their reflection: 'But there are no longer any antisemites. They were just liberals who wanted to express their antiliberal opinions' (2003: 226 [2002: 145]). Under the new order regulating what can and cannot be said, antisemitism becomes crypto-antisemitism, a 'rumour about the Jews' (Adorno 1951a: 125) that can no longer be explicitly discussed. In this sense, Adorno points out how

> gossip, rumour . . . the opinion that is not openly expressed, has always been the means of expression of the various kinds of discontent that dare not come to light in any given social order. Whoever expresses him- or herself in the forms of opinion and rumour, right away gives the impression of belonging to a secret community of truth-speakers whom the official institutions of society routinely oppress. (1962a: 363)[9]

Whoever violates the social taboo is entitled to feel like a rebel: here is someone with the courage to openly express the 'truth' that no one else dares to address. Undergirding such courage, however, is the certainty, the knowledge that freely expressing one's own 'opinion' will earn one the support of a compact social majority. After the Second World War, the re-establishment of the taboo had been designed to protect the vulnerable and tackle the indifference of a population that had acquiesced in extermination. For this reason, the rumour that revolts against the taboo vindicates both the harm inflicted and the very right to persecute, but without articulating itself openly. Hence Adorno's claim that the veiled insinuation, the allusion, 'can often be more dangerous than the frank manifestation' (1962a: 378). The initiated will get the reference. From this results a climate of hostility perpetuated under the guise of 'democratic normality' – one that clings to the expectation that a change in the balance of power may one day make open aggression fully 'respectable' again.

---

[9] The difficult second sentence in this quotation, beginning with 'whoever', reads in German like this: 'Wer sich derart der Meinung, dem Gerücht zuwendet, wirkt von vornherein so, als ob er einer heimlichen, wahrhaften und durch die Oberflächenformen der Gesellschaft nur unterdrückten Gemeinschaft angehörte'.

Even in the 1950s and 1960s, precisely during the time of the 'economic miracles', critical theorists were well aware of the enormous fragility of the democratic regimes. In the social forms of advanced capitalism, democracy had barely managed to articulate itself at the formal level. At the material level, it failed completely. Proper democracy would presuppose and be based on a truly autonomous individual, one prepared to be the subject of his or her own life. However, the social logic posed an obstacle to the possibility of making such progress from the outset. Added to this was the fact that the defeat of fascism in 1945 had only been achieved in military terms. The conditions that had made the rise of authoritarian and antisemitic dynamics possible were still very much in place, at least at the societal level. First, the tendency towards greater concentrations of capital persisted. This entailed not only further polarization between those who possessed social power and those who did not but also the threat that many of the well-off – clinging to their status and privileges – would be declassed. Furthermore, despite rising levels of prosperity and full employment, an increase in the powers of production meant that increasing numbers of individuals were made to feel that they were not indispensable employees but always potentially *unemployed* persons, that is, virtually superfluous to the social system. Hence Adorno's warning:

> The more strongly our society becomes 'integral', a completely organised whole, the greater the pressure it exerts on the relatively powerless individual. And it is precisely this process that reinforces the defensive mechanisms associated with prejudice. It is conceivable that even the most appalling form of discrimination, the Nazi policy of genocide, is closely linked to the fact that the present form of economic organisation proves incapable of guaranteeing the reproduction of the population living under such conditions. (2019: 47–8)

For as long as this sort of pressure and latent anguish persist, social life will retain a destructive potential that can detonate at any moment. This is what informs Adorno's view, stated as late as 1967, that 'as far as the state of consciousness and unconsciousness of human beings is concerned', the possibility that an event like Auschwitz might repeat itself could not be ruled out. For 'barbarism endures to the extent that the conditions that gave rise to the collapse remain in place. That is the entire horror. Despite the invisibility of the danger today, social pressure continues to exert its gravitational pull, dragging humans towards the unspeakable that culminated in Auschwitz at the level of universal history' (674). Auschwitz is understood here as the culmination of a process rather than an isolated event. The roots of extermination are to be found in specific social and historical conditions that pave the way for the various forms of violence, exclusion and barbarism that reach their most inhumane and brutal expression in Auschwitz. Socialized individuals suffer under such conditions; however, they also learn to live with them. Hence the need to understand how the current conditions of socialization produce 'normal monsters' (Adorno 1966: 282): that is, not only frustrated subjects seeking an outlet for aggressive impulses but also those who are fully integrated within their social environment, those who have hardened, become cold, who divide the world into friends and enemies and are willing to do anything to achieve their goals. As long as this logic of subjectivation endures, the impotence of the only thing capable of stopping the excesses of antisemitic aggression or the baleful logic of prejudice will persist: 'reflection, meaning, ultimately truth. The infantile hobby of murder confirms the closed life to which one must adapt oneself' (Horkheimer and Adorno 2003: 195 [2002: 140]). Until this situation changes, all genuine solidarity with the persecuted, outsiders and misfits will have to be articulated against the grain.

References

Adorno, Th. W. ([1950] 2003), *The Authoritarian Personality*, *Gesammelte Schriften*, vol. 9.1, 143–509, Frankfurt: Suhrkamp.
Adorno, Th. W. ([1951a] 2003), *Minima Moralia. Reflexionen aus dem beschädigten Leben*, *Gesammelte Schriften*, vol. 4, Frankfurt: Suhrkamp.
Adorno, Th. W. ([1951b] 2003), 'Freudian Theory and the Pattern of Fascist Propaganda', *Gesammelte Schriften*, vol. 8, 408–33, Frankfurt: Suhrkamp.
Adorno, Th. W. ([1952] 2003), 'Die revidierte Psychoanalyse', *Gesammelte Schriften*, vol. 8, 20–41, Frankfurt: Suhrkamp.
Adorno, Th. W. ([1954] 2003), 'Beitrag zur Ideologienlehre', *Gesammelte Schriften*, vol. 8, 457–77, Frankfurt: Suhrkamp.
Adorno, Th. W. ([1955] 2003), 'Zum Verhältnis von Soziologie und Psychologie', *Gesammelte Schriften*, vol. 8, 42–85, Frankfurt: Suhrkamp.
Adorno, Th. W. ([1961] 2003), 'Meinung Wahn Gesellschaft', *Gesammelte Schriften*, vol. 10.2, 573–94, Frankfurt: Suhrkamp.
Adorno, Th. W. ([1962a] 2003), 'Zur Bekämpfung des Antisemitismus heute', *Gesammelte Schriften*, vol. 20.1, 360–83, Frankfurt: Suhrkamp.
Adorno, Th. W. ([1962b] 2003), 'Aberglaube aus zweiter Hand', *Gesammelte Schriften*, vol. 8, 147–76, Frankfurt: Suhrkamp.
Adorno, Th. W. ([1964] 2003), 'Fortschritt', *Gesammelte Schriften*, vol. 10.2, 617–38, Frankfurt: Suhrkamp.
Adorno, Th. W. ([1966] 2003), *Negative Dialektik*, *Gesammelte Schriften*, vol. 6, Frankfurt: Suhrkamp.
Adorno, Th. W. ([1967] 2003), 'Erziehung nach Auschwitz', *Gesammelte Schriften*, vol. 10.2, 674–90, Frankfurt: Suhrkamp.
Adorno, Th. W. ([1969] 2003), 'Einleitung zum 'Positivismusstreit in der deutschen Soziologie', *Gesammelte Schriften*, vol. 8, 280–353, Frankfurt: Suhrkamp.
Adorno, Th. W. (2003), 'Individuum und Gesellschaft. Fragmente und Skizzen', in R. Tiedemann (ed.), *Frankfurter Adorno Blätter VIII*, 60–84, Munich: Text+Kritik.
Adorno, Th. W. (2019), *Bemerkungen zu 'The Authoritarian Personality'*, Berlin: Suhrkamp.
Adorno, Th. W., and M. Horkheimer (2004), *Briefwechsel*, vol. II, edición de Ch. Gödde y H. Lonitz, Frankfurt: Suhrkamp.
Adorno, Th. W., and U. Jaerisch ([1968] 2008), 'Anmerkungen zum sozialen Konflikt heute', *Gesammelte Schriften*, vol. 8, 177–95, Frankfurt: Suhrkamp.
Bock, W. (2018), *Dialektische Psychologie. Adornos Rezeption der Psychoanalyse*, Wiesbaden: Springer.
Claussen, D. ([1987] 2000), 'Vom Judenhass zum Antisemitismus', in D. Claussen, *Aspekte der Alltagsreligion*, 65–105, Frankfurt: Neue Kritik.
Claussen, D. (1988), *Unterm Konformitätszwang. Zum Verhältnis zur Kritischen Theorie und Psychoanalyse*, Bremen: Wassmann.

Claussen, D. (2005), *Grenzen der Aufklärung. Zur gesellschaftlichen Genese des modernen Antisemitismus*, Frankfurt: Fischer.
Dahmer, H. (2019), 'Kritische Theorie und Psychoanalyse', in U. H. Bittlingmayer, A. Demirovic and T. Freytag (eds), *Handbuch Kritische Theorie*, 235–75, Wiesbaden: Springer.
Fenichel, O. ([1939] 1985), 'Trophäe und Triumph', *Aufsätze 2*, 159–82, Frankfurt: Ullstein.
Fenichel, O. ([1946] 1985), 'Elemente einer psychoanalytischen Theorie des Antisemitismus', *Aufsätze 2*, 373–89, Frankfurt: Ullstein.
Freud, S. ([1913] 1961), *Totem und Tabu, Gesammelte Werke IX*, Frankfurt: Fischer.
Freud, S. ([1919] 1994), 'Das Unheimliche', *Studienausgabe*, vol. IV, 242–74, Frankfurt: Fischer.
Freud, S. ([1921] 2009), *Massenpsychologie und Ich-Analyse, Studienausgabe*, vol. 9, 61–134, Frankfurt: Fischer.
Horkheimer, M. ([1942] 1987), 'Vernunft und Selbsterhaltung', *Gesammelte Schriften*, vol. 5, 320–50, Frankfurt: Fischer.
Horkheimer, M. (1996), *Briefwechsel 1941–1948. Gesammelte Schriften*, vol. 17, Frankfurt: Fischer.
Horkheimer, M., and Th. W. Adorno ([1947] 2003), *Dialektik der Aufklärung*, in Th. W. Adorno, *Gesammelte Schriften*, vol. 3, 7–296, Frankfurt: Suhrkamp.
Horkheimer, M., and Th. W. Adorno (2002), *Dialectic of Enlightenment* (trans. E. Jephcott), Stanford, CA: Stanford University Press.
Löwenstein, R. (1952), *Psychoanalyse de l'antisemitisme*, Paris: Presses Universitaires de la France.
Lowenthal, L., and N. Guterman (1949), *Prophets of Deceit*, New York: Harper.
Maiso, J. (2013), 'La subjetividad dañada. Teoría crítica y psicoanálisis', Constelaciones. *Revista de Teoría Crítica*, 5: 132–50.
Marx, K. ([1843] 1981), 'Zur Kritik der hegelschen Rechtsphilosophie. Einleitung', *Marx Engels Werke*, 1: 378–91, Berlin: Dietz.
Marx, K. ([1867] 1981), *Das Kapital. Band I, Marx Engels Werke*, vol. 23, Berlin: Dietz.
Marx, K. ([1894] 1981), *Das Kapital. Band III, Marx Engels Werke*, vol. 25, Berlin: Dietz.
Nietzsche, F. ([1887] 1988), *Zur Genealogie der Moral*, in *Sämtliche Werke. Kritische Studienausgabe*, vol. 5, Munich: DTV/de Gruyter.
Pohl, R. (2010), 'Der antisemitische Wahn. Aktuelle Ansätze zur Psychoanalyse einer sozialen Pathologie', in W. Stender, G. Follert and M. Özdogan (eds), *Konstellationen des Antisemitismus*, 41–68, Wiesbaden: Springer.
Rensmann, L. (2017), *The Politics of Unreason: The Frankfurt School and the Origins of Modern Antisemitism*, New York: SUNY Press.
Safatle, V. (2017), 'Freud em Frankfurt: a funçao da psicanálise no pensamento de Theodor Adorno', in D. Kuperman (ed.), *Por que Freud hoje*, 63–89, Sao Paulo: Zagodini.
Stender, W. (1996), *Kritik und Vernunft. Studien zu Horkheimer, Habermas und Freud*, Lüneburg: zu Klampen.
Zamora, J. A. (2004), *Th. W. Adorno: Pensar contra la barbarie*, Madrid: Trotta.
Zamora, J. A. (2007), 'El enigma de la docilidad: Teoría de la sociedad y psicoanálisis en Th. W. Adorno', in M. Cabot (ed.), *El pensamiento de Th. W. Adorno. Balance y perspectivas*, 27–42, Palma: Universitat de les Illes Balears.
Ziege, E. M. (2009), *Antisemitismus und Gesellschaftstheorie. Die Frankfurter Schule im amerikanischen Exil*, Frankfurt: Suhrkamp.

2

Antisemitism in the British 'New Liberalism' movement: J. A. Hobson on capitalism and imperialism

Matthew Bolton

The 'New Liberalism' movement emerged in the last decades of the nineteenth century as an attempt to reformulate the British liberal political and intellectual tradition to meet the new demands of modern industrial capitalist society. Led primarily by 'radical' journalists and intellectuals – some acknowledged today to be among the founders of British sociology – the New Liberalism deemed inadequate the ideas of 'individualism' and 'negative freedom' that had hitherto dominated British liberalism. Leading New Liberal figures such as Leonard Trelawny Hobhouse and John Atkinson Hobson argued that the new conditions of industrial capitalism called for a systemic programme of positive state intervention in order to remedy social ills and provide the conditions through which individuals could realize their self-development. Hobson extended his 'productivist' analysis of domestic capitalism to the international sphere, formulating one of the first economic analyses of imperialism. The result was a novel form of 'progressivism' (Emy 1973: xiii): a radical strain of thought that placed the question of 'the social' at the centre of the liberal project.

The influence of New Liberalism's reorientation of the liberal approach to the state and capitalism has been profound. Its central theme – that the nation-state should actively intervene in market relations to secure the social and moral harmony of the productive community living within its borders, constructing a protective barrier against the threats posed by unproductive or parasitical elements both at home and abroad – lay the groundwork for the moralistic critique of capitalism, centred on the nation-state, that has dominated much of the liberal and socialist left ever since. The development of the British welfare state by the Liberal and Labour parties across the 1930s and 1940s owed much to the framework established by Hobhouse, Hobson and their followers. As such, leading Labour politicians and left intellectuals have regularly paid homage to their New Liberal forebears across the party's history: Tony Blair extolled Hobhouse and Hobson's 'bridge' between liberalism and socialism as prefiguring New Labour's 'Third Way' (1996: 15); Anthony Crosland praised Hobson as an 'early prophet' (2006: 58) of pre-Keynesian state planning in his influential 1956 *The Future of Socialism*; for the communitarian 'Blue Labour' MP Jon Cruddas, 'New Liberal thinkers are rightly considered to be pioneers of the British tradition of ethical socialism' (2010: 19) that Labour should reclaim. But Hobson's influence in particular stretches beyond the limits of parliamentary politics – his 'underconsumptionist' theory of imperialism, outlined in his seminal 1902 *Imperialism: A Study*, was a formative influence on theories of imperialism produced by revolutionary figures such as Vladimir Ilyich Lenin and Rosa Luxemburg. Lenin liberally cited Hobson's book in his own *Imperialism, the Highest State of Capitalism*, describing it as 'a very good and comprehensive description of the principal specific economic and political features of imperialism' (1988: 19). The political theorist Hannah Arendt too drew heavily on Hobson's work in her *The Origins of Totalitarianism*, describing *Imperialism* as a 'masterly analysis' (1979: 148).

In 2019, nearly eighty years after his death, Hobson made a brief return to the centre of British politics when it was reported (Finkelstein 2019) that Jeremy Corbyn, then leader of the Labour Party, had penned a glowing introduction to a 2011 re-publication of *Imperialism*.[1] Corbyn praised the book as 'brilliant', 'correct' and 'prescient' in its analysis of the inner workings of imperialist economics. What Corbyn, like Lenin, failed to mention was the handful of blatantly antisemitic remarks contained within the book's pages. In *Imperialism*, Hobson claimed that 'men of a single and peculiar race' – Jews – had taken control of international financial houses and urged on imperialist war in South Africa, and that 'no great war could be undertaken by any European state, or a great state loan subscribed, if the House of Rothschild and its connexions set their face against it' (1902: 57). In the context of the crisis of antisemitism within Corbyn's Labour Party, his silence on these passages of Hobson's book – which, as shall be shown, were both empirically wrong and drew on a long history of antisemitic associations among Jews, finance and disproportionate political power – was taken as further evidence of, at best, his 'blindness' towards antisemitism.[2] But the debate quickly broadened out to a consideration of Hobson's own antisemitism and the extent to which it was related to his general economic analysis. Some sought to defend him (e.g. Sassoon 2019) by arguing that his depiction of Jewish power and influence was marginal to the overall argument laid out in *Imperialism*, and thus a minor aberration unrelated to the thrust and continued value of his work. But others (e.g. Feldman 2019) pointed to multiple instances of antisemitism and 'race thinking' across his oeuvre, not just in relation to the Boer War (which was the immediate context in which Hobson wrote *Imperialism*) but also in relation to his earlier analyses of the causes of poverty and other social ills.

In this chapter, I will seek to show how, far from being an unfortunate accident with no connection to, or perhaps contradicting, the rest of the New Liberal

---

[1] Corbyn's introduction appears in the 2011 Spokesman Books edition of *Imperialism*.
[2] It might seem somewhat ironic, but in fact is perhaps rather more revealing, that an avowedly socialist leftist like Corbyn was caught celebrating a liberal with antisemitic leanings: this constellation invites reflection on how the terms 'left-wing', 'socialist' and 'liberal' relate to each other. On this, see the chapters by Bolton and Pitts, and Stoetzler in this volume.

programme, Hobson's antisemitism is intrinsically connected to his broader theory of domestic and global capitalism. Founded on an opposition between 'social utility' and 'parasitism' – the latter a concept happily adopted by Lenin (1988: chapter VIII) – Hobson's depiction of industrial society lends itself rather easily, albeit by no means inevitably, to antisemitic interpretations. Thus rather than merely listing all of the antisemitic statements in Hobson's prodigious output, the first half of the chapter sets out the general philosophical and theoretical framework of Hobson's critique of late nineteenth-century capitalism. By setting out the overall context of his work in this way, it thus becomes possible to recognize the significance of what might, at first glance, seem like trivial or accidental asides. The second half of the chapter turns to Hobson's theory of imperialism, which he developed in response to his experiences working in South Africa as a journalist during the Boer War. In *Imperialism* itself, the antisemitic undertones are less overt than in some of his earlier writings, and can, without a broader knowledge of his theoretical presuppositions and intellectual trajectory, indeed seem like inexplicable outliers. But once the general framework and the more overt antisemitism of the earlier works is understood, and the relation between his earlier and later work established, the retention of the antisemitic remarks which are in *Imperialism*, however toned down, is more easily explained. Moreover, by situating Hobson's antisemitism within the wider New Liberal world view, it becomes possible to recognize the latent potential for antisemitism which lies within its modern variants on the contemporary liberal-left.

British Idealism and 'old Liberalism'

The ideological roots of the New Liberalism can be traced back to the philosopher Thomas Hill (T. H.) Green's peculiarly English form of Hegel-inspired idealism in the mid-nineteenth century. British Idealism emerged in the face of the tremendous upheavals wrought by the development of industrial capitalism, opposing itself to the 'laissez faire' individualism which had hitherto dominated the liberal tradition. The main tenet of this 'classical liberalism' was a 'monadic account of social relations' (Allet 1981: 15–16), whereby individuals were regarded as having inalienable 'natural rights' *prior* to any social interaction. The first priority for classical liberals was the protection of those rights *from* the 'excessive and unjust powers of state and church', in the name of 'negative liberty' (Bell 2009: 187). This world view was expressed in economic terms by a steadfast commitment to free trade and opposition to state-led protectionism. For William Gladstone, the talismanic mid-century leader of the Liberal Party, inequality and poverty were the result of an ineradicable 'original sin' present within every individual, and thus ultimately unalterable by state activity. The 'old Liberalism' translated its 'strict adherence to the doctrine of nonintervention' in the economic sphere to a general 'skepticism' about interventionist 'international entanglements' on the global stage, producing 'a long line of radical critics of empire'. This anti-imperialist impulse was motivated by the belief that imperialism abroad 'threatened to undermine Britain from within, infecting both political institutions and public morality' (Bell 2009: 188).

The practical effect of the 'orthodox liberal' approach to the domestic economy was to legitimize vast economic inequality as the natural state of things. This was the point of departure for T. H. Green's formulation of a new mode of liberal thought able to compete with Burkean forms of conservative traditionalism on the one side, and the socialism of the incipient labour movement on the other – the latter, in Green's view, threatening to place the individual under 'the control of society'. For Green, the amorality of a purely negative liberalism could end up *reducing* the liberty of individuals – for example, by doing nothing to prevent drunkenness. Liberal theory 'needed an infusion of publicly oriented thinking, a new perspective that would simultaneously champion individual responsibility and transcend class politics' (Morefield 2005: 30–1).

This 'new perspective' was outlined in Green's 1866 lectures on the 'Principles of Political Obligation', in which the individualist world view of natural right and negative freedom was countered by a depiction of society as a single, interconnected living organism. Green argued that the 'organic' unity of society appears in the form of 'an absolute and common good . . . common to the person conceiving it with others, and good for him and them, whether at any moment it answers their likings or not' (Green 1986, §202). The common good exists prior to the individualist 'conception of both moral duty and legal right' and is the shared *social* foundation upon which custom, duty and political-legal structures rest. The recognition and development of that pre-political common interest or good is an ethical imperative – indeed, it 'constitutes the moral progress of mankind' (§6) – and is the only way to ensure that society does not descend into a battleground of conflict, coercion and dominance.

Such a holistic conception of society was distinct from previous modes of liberal thought by virtue of the fact that it was a conception of society at all. From the traditional liberal perspective, there had been – to coin a phrase – 'no such thing as society', merely the aggregate of individual rational preferences. For Green, as for Hobhouse in his 1911 book *Liberalism* (1994) – widely regarded as the most 'authoritative statement of New Liberal political theory' (Collini 1979: 121) – the social 'common good' exists above and beyond individual preferences. The influence of Hegel's *Philosophy of Right* is evident here but as one which sees the relation of individual and totality as one of the primacy of the latter, rather than the contradictory mediation of one by the other. For Hobhouse, unlike Hegel, it is not possible for an individual right to come into 'conflict with the common good', as no right 'can exist apart from the common good' (1994: 61).[3] Any disharmony between individual right and the common good thus betrays a deficient understanding of the latter. For all its invocation of organic unity, however, Green's theory was resistant to the kinds of state intervention advocated by the later New Liberals, particularly when it came to limitations on private property. To this extent, New Liberalism represented a break with British Idealism, rather than its continuation.

The New Liberal use of biological terms such as 'organism' and, increasingly, 'evolution' to conceptualize social life derived not just from Green but also from the

---

[3] As Collini points out, despite downgrading individual rights in theory, when it came to concrete political debates Hobhouse was steadfast in defending the rights of the individual, often opposing Hobson's more strident claims to the priority of society over the individual (1979: 126).

work of Herbert Spencer, with his *The Study of Sociology* being a 'prime influence on the shaping of Hobson's mind' in particular (Freeden 1978: 79). This was despite the fact that when it came to state intervention, Spencer's position was diametrically opposed to that of the New Liberals. Spencer's evolutionary theory was founded upon a faith in the spontaneous development of society into 'a harmonic body of cooperating individuals' (78). Any active attempt to solve social problems risked disturbing this delicate natural balance. Nevertheless, his assumption that there was a 'unifying principle which could explain, give meaning to and ultimately direct human progress' (78) and which could be studied through scientific methods was a crucial stepping stone in the development of New Liberalism. Hobhouse critiqued the non-interventionist 'mechanicalism' of Spencer's theory of social evolution by arguing that consciousness (or *Geist*, to use the Hegelian term) was itself an expression of nature, and thus attempts to rationally guide social development through reform were part of the 'natural', evolutionary process.

Social utility and parasitism

There was thus no automatic relationship between an organic theory of society and support for active state intervention. Two further concepts were crucial to the development of the New Liberal world view – 'social utility' and 'parasitism'. Tracing the provenance of each of these terms again reveals the debt New Liberalism owed to the English 'Radical' liberal tradition of earlier decades – but also, perhaps more surprisingly, to utilitarianism.

The utilitarian influence (Weinstein 2007) rested on the latter's impetus for state-led social reform on the basis of rational planning and, crucially, John Stuart Mill's development of a utilitarian calculus based on a *qualitative*, rather than merely quantitative, notion of 'the greatest happiness'. This cleared the path for New Liberalism to develop the notion of 'social utility', grounded within a qualitative conception of the common good, and more than the sum of individual goods. The notion of social utility was given particular prominence in the work of Hobson, sometimes presented in Rousseauist style as a form of 'general will', and understood as the expression of the 'psycho-physical structure' of an organic social community (Freeden 1978: 107–8). For Hobson (1909: 217), 'every well-ordered reform of the economic structure is an expression of the moral force of the community, the "general will" finding embodiment in some stable and serviceable form of social support'. Again, the presupposition built into this conception is that there could be no *objective* tension, or legitimate contradiction, between 'social' and individual wills. The 'social will' was for Hobson an 'empirical fact' expressing in political form the 'natural harmony' of society.

The influence of the Romantic art critic John Ruskin can be discerned in Hobson's efforts to establish (or discover) a qualitative, ethical and general standard of utility against which society should be judged. During the 1890s, Hobson (2013a) adapted Ruskin's notion of 'illth' – that which is 'inherently and eternally incapable' of its opposite, wealth, causing only 'devastation', 'trouble' and 'delay' (Ruskin 1985: 211) – as he sought to develop a contrast between the supposedly 'objective' economic wealth that is the principal object of classical political economy – measured in money and linked to the figure of the so-called economic man, who cared about nothing but his immediate financial interests – and 'subjective' wealth, namely the welfare of society as a whole, including happiness, moral standards and aesthetic beauty. In his 1894 book *Evolution of Modern Capitalism*, Hobson criticized the ill effects of 'machine civilization' in a style similar to Ruskin, calling for its replacement by a new economy in which there was 'adequate social control over machine production' coupled with 'education in the arts of consumption such as may assign proper limits to the sphere of machine-production' (1906: 406). Consumers educated in the art of cultivating 'subjective wealth' would temper machine society's drive to produce for the sake of production, leading to 'fewer machines, less monopoly, and less [economic] instability' (Cain 2002: 33).

However, Hobson, unlike Ruskin, was not opposed to industrial production as such. Like virtually all New Liberals, he looked upon the Industrial Revolution as progressive development, drawing on the opposition between 'industry' and 'militancy' that had been central to the previous generation of liberals. From this perspective, '"industry" reflected the moral and intellectual qualities of the skilled artisan and the small entrepreneur' as opposed to the 'unskilled mass of labourers, casuals, and "loafers" whose ignorance and moral frailty made them easy prey for the "classes"' (Cain 2002: 126), that is, the aristocracy whose dominance was the result of war and violence rather than productive activity (a notion also central to Spencer's thinking). The new generation of liberals had developed this affirmative perspective to take account of the growth of modern industrial processes. In a 1900 article on the 'ethics of industrialism', Hobson argued that 'modern industrialism' meant 'close co-operation' between large numbers of people, 'with instruments which they utilize in common, for the production of commodities in which they have a common interest' (Hobson, qtd in Cain 2002: 127). The industrial world, Hobson argued, amounted to 'a vast mutual benefit society, a continual education in the paths of peace and practical brotherhood' (127).

Hobson's critique of modern capitalism was thus centred upon its perceived *abuse*, or over-extension, of industrial society, and the monopolization of its benefits, rather than its essential character. The 'ethic of industrialisation' was being gradually deformed by vast inequalities in wealth and power, with big businesses using their monopoly power to impose machine production far beyond what was necessitated by the ethical standard of social utility. This perversion of industry was made manifest in the form of waste, which he regarded as 'the other side of the coin from wealth' (Freeden 1978: 131). Hobson identified three key sources of waste in late-nineteenth-century capitalism: the un- or underemployment of economic resources, whether labour (through unemployment and the 'idleness' of the aristocratic rich), undeveloped land or hoarded capital; the waste of energy used in economic competition rather than cooperation; and poor consumption, both the wasteful expenditure of the rich and the inability of consumers to make good use of what was distributed to them (Freeden 1973: 430–1). In each case, actual production, distribution and consumption fell woefully short of the objective standard of social utility.

The parasitical poor

The concept of 'parasitism' was in many ways the logical result of a world view founded on the idea of society as an organism whose health was to be judged against a standard of 'social utility' or, in negative terms, wastefulness. The figure of the parasite, a non-productive being feeding off the endeavour of others, is the personalization of the 'waste' that is preventing society from achieving its productive harmony. As a biological concept, 'parasite' is politically and economically polyvalent – anyone or anything deemed to be unproductive or inefficient could be its target. Hobson would thus use this idea at different times to describe both the idle rich and the 'unproductive' London poor (Cain 2002: 40).

As David Feldman (1994: 263) notes, the question of what should be done with the 'socially unfit' – 'those who will or cannot contribute to the common good' – marks the dark underbelly of the concept of the 'common good', raising the possibility that 'there might be limits to how "common" the "common good" might be'. In *The Social Problem*, Hobson argued that the 'rejection of the unfittest is essential to all progress', and thus the state should not leave the 'production of children' to 'unrestricted private enterprise' (1919: 214) – in short that the state should prevent the 'unproductive' from reproducing for the common good of the race. In *Imperialism*, he would argue that 'prevent[ing] reproduction from bad stock, however difficult and dangerous it may be, is obviously the first duty of an organised society' (1902: 163–4). Hobson was by no means an outlier in flirting with this kind of language: the idea that social misery was at least in part due to the physical and mental deficiencies of parts of the population, which could be cured through the curtailing of individual rights, was widely held.[4]

Few liberals – with Hobhouse a notable exception (see Ray 1983: 214) – offered much resistance to this line of thought. Indeed, the practical implication of Hobson's notion of an organically grounded 'social will', founded on the denial of any conflict between social and individual interests, was that any curtailing of individual rights could ultimately be justified on the grounds that the interests they represented were not a true expression of that organic unity. This brought to the fore the possible contradiction between the New Liberal ideas of organic 'community', and individual democratic freedoms. Democracy might get in the way of achieving the perfect social utility of the organic whole. Hobson squared this circle by using biological language to argue that 'the body politic will become diseased and suffer if any of its members is deprived of all participation in government' (qtd in Freeden 1978: 113). Thus 'social utility' necessitates the protection of individual liberty, not for its own sake but for the health of the social whole itself.

---

[4] Those in Hobson's liberal-socialist milieu who gave their explicit support for eugenicist policies included Sidney and Beatrice Webb (the founders of the Fabian Society), the economist John Maynard Keynes, William Beveridge – whose 1942 report *Social Insurance and Allied Services* was pivotal to the creation of the postwar welfare state – and the playwright George Bernard Shaw, who even advocated the use of a 'lethal chamber' to kill those whose care 'wastes other people's time' (Bernard Shaw 1910). For an account of the intertwining of eugenics with 'Fabian socialism', see Ray (1983).

Hobson's brand of biological 'race thinking', tied to notions of 'social efficiency' and 'parasitism', should not be ahistorically equated with the exterminatory modes of political thought and practice that would later emerge from this paradigm. In *Imperialism*, he fiercely attacked the so-called scientific defence of imperialism based on white supremacist notions of 'race struggle' expounded by Social Darwinists such as Karl Pearson, arguing that as civilizations develop racial struggles are 'shifted on to higher planes', namely 'skill, knowledge, character and even higher levels of self-expression' (1902: 172). Nevertheless, racial categories remained at work in Hobson's theories. After all, the idea of the evolutionary transmutation of biological struggle to an intellectual level is premised on the recognition of biological struggle as a factor in the development of civilization in the first place. Moreover, in his examination of the 'parasitic' existence of London's poor, Hobson's critical eye had been drawn to particular characteristics he ascribed to the large Jewish immigrant presence in the East End. His writings on this topic will be discussed in the 'Antisemitism' section below.

The parasitical rich

By the mid-1890s, Hobson 'was more likely to use the language of biology as a weapon against the rich and their unearned incomes', rather than the parasitical poor (Cain 2002: 40). In this, he was at one with socialist-inclined groups such as the Fabians, for whom the notion of a parasitical class of non-workers feeding off the labour of others was a common rhetorical device. This critique of the 'parasitical' sectors of industrial capitalism extended the classical radical liberal condemnation of 'Old Corruption', which had pitched the 'classes' – an alliance of land, finance and the Bank of England – against the productive 'masses'. This dualistic opposition lay behind Hobson's deep 'suspicion' of the unproductive 'dealing' and 'trading' that comprised the increasingly dominant service economy in Britain, as opposed to the active, energetic 'making' of the industrial sector. Whether rich or poor, for Hobson the end result of a parasitical existence was biological degeneration. Without productivity, without the expansion of energy, 'one by one the higher activities are debilitated, and cease to work; the attempt to consume without producing, to enjoy without effort' leads to a 'physical decay' which is the '"natural" consequence of attempted evasions of the physical law which imposes exercise as the condition of digestion' (Hobson 1919: 122).

The answer to such 'wasteful' deformations of the spirit of industrialism for Hobson was not the overthrowal or even systemic transformation of capitalist society. His aim was not the abolition of private property or of 'the competitive system', nor the socialization of 'all instruments of production, distribution and exchange', but that the state should provide workers with the economic and educational resources needed to employ 'their personal powers for their personal advantage and enjoyment' within the organic structures of a harmonious social community (Hobson 1909: 172–3). In 1899, Hobson made clear his opposition to the stoking of 'class division' as a response to social ills, writing that the emergent labour movement 'is distinctively a class movement . . . and, as such, must simply be regarded as the largest form of individualism' (Hobson, qtd in Freeden 1978: 152). Focusing on the demands of labour alone represented a form of partialism which merely inverted the monopolistic power of big business that had deformed the social whole (whereas individuals looking to their individual advantage *individually* did not threaten the harmony of the whole).

Hobson thus called for 'concrete reforms' which would encourage a 'spirit of ethical democracy... bind[ing] individuals and classes by a conscious bond of moral fellowship' (Hobson, qtd in Freeden 1978: 74). The end result would be a 'social harmony which entailed self-sacrifice and altruism' on the part of each of its members, whatever their social position (93). In this, his perspective crossed over with that of his imperial protectionist opponent, Joseph Chamberlain, who too advocated for 'an alliance of producers, of combining industrial capitalists and workers against landlords and rentiers' (Cain 2002: 43). Chamberlain's 'Tariff Reform' movement – which sought to end global free trade and establish a protectionist trading bloc within the British Empire – argued that Britain had lost its 'primary' (agriculture) and 'secondary' (manufacturing) industry to foreign competition and had been reduced to 'tertiary' pursuits – commerce, finance, services (Semmel 1960: 145). The domestic shift to 'unproductive' employment was held responsible for British economic crises, with the blame pinned on 'cosmopolitan' capitalists, whose interests were opposed to those of the nation (148). This argument provided a crucial plank in Hobson's first attempts to theorize imperialism.

Underconsumption and the 'organic theory of surplus value'

That 'underconsumption' lies at the root of social problems in modern industrial society – and is also the main driver of imperialism – is perhaps the idea most associated with Hobson, and the New Liberalism in general. Hobson himself regarded underconsumption as the principle source of his self-styled 'economic heresy' (Hobson 2011). The main heresy involved was the rejection of the principle hitherto at the heart of liberal political economy – that 'thrift' and 'abstinence' were the keys to a thriving capitalist economy (Freeden 1978: 130). For Hobson, the problem with contemporary capitalism was *too much* thrift, not too little – leading to 'oversaving', a glut of unused and thus 'wasted' capital in the hands of business owners (Hobson 1906: 314). The flipside of the 'oversaving' of one section of the community was 'underconsumption' by another. A lack of spending power amongst workers leads to a general lack of demand across society. This results in a corresponding reduction in production, with economic depression and unemployment the final outcome. The solution to the crisis-ridden condition of modern industrial society, and the only 'guarantee of social progress', was therefore for the state to actively seek to improve the 'quality and character of consumption' across society, redistributing the power to consume and supplying the moral education required to ensure that that consumption was socially beneficial (424).

The idea of underconsumption was a logical development of Hobson's biological-social paradigm (see Allet 1981: chapter 4). At its heart is the idea that there is, as Hobson put it in his 1896 book *The Problem of the Unemployed*, 'a natural relation between production and consumption, between effort and satisfaction' (88). This was in effect a reiteration of the famous 'Say's Law', one of the founding tenets of classical political economy (Say 2001), which stated that production creates its own demand – in short, that, left to its own devices, there would be a natural balance between production and consumption within any domestic economy. Underconsumption, a lack of demand in the economy, must therefore be the result of external interference in this natural harmony.

At the core of Hobson's theory was an idea whose origins, once again, lay in the previous era of liberal thought: John Stuart Mill's notion of the 'unearned increment', itself based on David Ricardo's theory of rent (Allet 1981: 16). Ricardo had argued that landowners accrued rents from the happenstance of having inherited fertile land, rather than any productive endeavour. Mill extended Ricardo's analysis to the industrial city, arguing that 'unearned incomes' were now also being derived 'from the growth of towns' (Mill, qtd in Allet 1981: 16). This move allowed New Liberals to repurpose 'traditional liberal arguments against monopoly and privilege' to win support for new taxes on property to pay for social reforms (Freeden 1978: 44).

Hobson developed Mill's insights further, arguing that cooperative activity, both within the act of production itself and the wider economy, made a 'distinctive' contribution to the total sum of economic wealth that was 'different both in quantity and in character from that which the unorganised activities of the individual participants could compass' (Hobson 1930: 27). A portion (although by no means all) of the economic value produced by society was generated through the productive power inherent in cooperation, and thus exceeded the total contributed by land, labour and capital, classical political economy's 'factors of production'. For Hobson, 'this was a difference which could not be comprehended except in organic terms' (Allet 1981: 75). Surplus value above and beyond the contribution of each economic 'factor' is the material manifestation of the organic unity of society. Given its social origins, this 'social surplus' should be claimed by the community as a whole, via taxation and the limitation of private property.

Hobson did not identify one particular economic 'factor' or the social group associated with it – rentiers, capitalists, workers – as the permanent recipient of this 'unearned income'. What decided which factor did, when it came down to it, accrue the social surplus was not inherent in the structure of the economy, but rather relied on the relative bargaining power and institutional resources of each group *after* the moment of production. Hobson was clear that in the capitalist society of his day, capital did indeed claim the lion's share of the social surplus, with labour losing out. But this, he argued, was not 'a theoretical necessity' but a mere 'empirical fact' based on the current balance of institutional power between capital, labour, landowners and the state (Clarke 1978: 51).

Although Hobson's focus on 'the intrusion of force into the bargaining process' between economic factors competing to claim the social surplus carries resonances of Marxian theories of class struggle, he regarded his work as fundamentally distinct: for Hobson, Marxists recognized the existence of a social surplus, but they did 'not correctly appreciate its organic nature and thus erred in assigning it to the proletariat rather than the public' (Allet 1981: 87, 95).[5] Nor did Marxists 'give credence

---

[5] For his efforts, Hobson was labelled a 'social fascist' by the British Communist Party.

to the full economy of costs involved in production' (95). Hobson regarded abstinence to be the ultimate origin of capital, and capital as being productive of wealth, in that capital-intensive machinery saved more labour time than the cost of producing the machines (81). He therefore rejected the classical Marxian understanding of capital as 'crystallised labour' – meaning that the creation of labour-saving machinery is itself the result of previously exploited labour – and insisted that any surplus from labour-saving machinery belonged to capital by right (Hobson 1909a: 71).

Thus the New Liberals were by no means making a claim that 'all value is social' – as Hobhouse put it, the task was rather to 'distinguish the individual from the social factors in wealth' (qtd in Freeden 1978: 46). The question of where the line was to be drawn was not to be answered with demands for workers to receive the full fruits of the productive process – popularly taken to be Marx's position, although in truth closer to that of Ferdinand Lassalle, and indeed explicitly rejected by Marx in his 'Critique of the Gotha Programme' (1974: 341–5) – but rather on the grounds of social utility. In Hobson's view, appropriation of the social surplus by particular interests was another manifestation of socially destructive waste. It stripped the surplus of its economic functionality, necessarily leading to oversaving and underconsumption by severing the connection between 'effort and reward' that lay at the heart of an efficient social system (Clarke 1978: 52). This effort could come in the form of abstinence or the act of labour itself. Hobson applied here a peculiar, somewhat naïve, set of psychological ideal types: those who had worked hard and sacrificed to save would not oversave, as they would reward themselves for that sacrifice once it had come to fruition. By contrast, those accruing a social surplus towards which they had contributed nothing had no motivation to expand their consumption: Hobson believed that the rich man may have 'the power to consume' but not 'the desire' (1896a: 74). It was here – at the supposed natural limit of desire, at the point of equilibrium between effort and reward – that he drew the line between legitimate accumulation and 'parasitism'.

It is clear that for Hobson an unequal distribution of resources was not *inherent* in the system of capitalist production. It was the result of a *choice*. If capitalists were behaving in a parasitical manner, appropriating surplus that was owed to the whole of society, then this was because the state had not recognized the organic nature of the surplus and acted accordingly. It is this insistence on the element of choice in the maldistribution of social wealth, a kind of moralistic voluntarism, that separates Hobson and the New Liberals from classical Marxian critiques of capitalist appropriation, according to which surplus value automatically and, within capitalist society, 'rightfully' accrues to the capitalist by virtue of ownership of the means of production and the commodification of labour power – a process which the state can temporally ameliorate but not halt. But beyond this, the distinction between Hobson's analysis and most traditional forms of Marxism is less clear than either side supposed. Both traditions ultimately rest on a 'distributive' critique of capitalism, in which what is problematized is the distribution of resources and control of production rather than capitalism as a historically specific form of social reproduction (see Postone 1993: chapter 1). Neither makes any distinction between 'wealth' and the form that wealth takes under capitalism, namely value – precisely that which lay behind Marx's rejection of the Gotha Programme. As such, while Hobson and traditional Marxists may disagree on which part of capitalist society 'deserves' the 'social surplus' and control of the productive process, both take a positivist, uncritical attitude to the core components of that process. Both critiques thus leave the core dynamics of capitalist society untouched. It is this shared focus on distribution of the resources of capitalist production, rather than the social form of that production, which explains the continued appeal of Hobson's world view for contemporary leftist movements.

Imperialism

Hobson's theory of imperialism, developed during the campaign against the 1899–1902 Boer War between Britain and the South African Republic/Transvaal and the Orange Free State, was intimately connected to these ideas. As noted earlier, anti-imperialism in one form or another had a long and storied history within the British liberal movement, albeit one matched by an equally important tradition of liberal imperialism. Hobson's pioneering work on imperialism drew on both traditions in different ways. But his attempt to systematize his anti-imperialism within a broader theory of economic and political rationality undoubtedly represented a radically new approach to the question, and its long-term influence has been profound.

The anti-imperialism of the classical liberal tradition depicted the expansion of overseas territory as another means for 'the aristocratic Few' to enhance their power and prestige at the expense of 'the Many', increasing the power of the military and presenting endless justifications for higher taxation (Cain 2002: 47). Great importance was again attached to 'the City of London and metropolitan finance' within 'the complex of interests behind colonialism and aggression overseas' (48). This position was closely linked to opposition to any rise in national debt, regarded as a ploy by financial and landed interests to amass 'unproductive wealth' and stymie industry and free trade (48). The focus of critique was thus more on the deleterious consequences of imperialism for the British political and economic system rather than concern for the rights or welfare of the colonized peoples themselves.

By the 1880s, a new strand of 'liberal internationalism' extended the classical critique, insisting 'on both the possibility and the moral necessity of progressive change in the structures and norms of world order' (Bell 2009: 184). Conflict between 'civilised' states should be replaced by cooperation, through international trade and law. However, as Duncan Bell notes, while for some 'empire was inimical to progress, for others it was, if enacted properly, a virtuous agent of it' (184). Those in the latter camp founded this belief on what Hobson himself called a 'radical distinction' between 'colonialism' and 'imperialism' (1902: 36). In the opening section of *Imperialism*, Hobson writes that colonialism – consisting of 'the migration of part of a nation to vacant or sparsely peopled foreign lands' – can be 'considered a genuine expansion of nationality, a territorial enlargement of the stock, language and institutions of the nation', and thus broadly positive (6). Imperialism, by contrast, describes the wielding of political power by a minority of whites – 'the majority' of which 'are not descended from British settlers' – over a 'vast preponderance' of 'subject or "inferior" races', within the 'alien climatic and other natural conditions' which 'mark out a civilization distinct from that of the "mother country"' (6–7).

This distinction again rests upon biologically influenced ideas of organic communities and parasitism. As Cain puts it, Hobson believed that 'nations have ends or ideals' of their own, and that 'places like North America', founded through 'emigration and colonization . . . were extensions of [British] civilization and thus organic growths' (2002: 64–5). This led Hobson to propose – in a manner strikingly similar to Carl Schmitt's (2003) later concept of *Großraum* – the idea of multiple imperialist 'federations' between those 'states most closely related by ties of common blood, language, and institutions' (Bell 2009: 195). Unlike colonialism, imperialism was the implantation of an alien community upon a racially, culturally, environmentally and psychologically distinct other, and thus a form of biological malfunction. In *The Social Problem* – published a year before *Imperialism* – Hobson drew on the psychologist Gustave Le Bon's idea that different races have a 'common character' formed by deep-lying psychological structures, which 'mould the destiny of nations' and cannot tolerate 'attempts at grafting alien sentiments and ideas' from an alien racial-psychological structure (1919: 286). Thus British rule in India, and increasingly Africa, was a form of 'parasitism' (Hobson, qtd in Porter 1976: 184), born of a lack of organic connection between the 'physical and psychical' character of the British and Indian peoples (Cain 2002: 65). The maintenance of such parasitism led to the 'mental and even physical degeneracy' of both peoples (Hobson 1900: 294). Moreover, the struggle to enforce imperial rule on 'alien peoples' through autocratic means raised the prospect of such techniques being re-imported back home. Imperialism for Hobson was thus 'the enemy of democracy, both at home and abroad' (Allet 1981: 143). The question this raised was what, or who, was driving the imperialist charge.

The economic theory of imperialism

The origins of Hobson's theory can be traced to an 1898 article on 'Free Trade and Foreign Policy' (2013b) in which he pushed back against calls to solve Britain's domestic economic problems through the forcible opening of new markets abroad. Arguing that the benefits accrued for British industry from foreign trade had been substantially overestimated, he suggested that domestic trade was 'a more solid and substantial basis of industrial prosperity' than foreign trade – less susceptible to international politics, and ensuring the 'full advantage' of any exchange remained within Britain, rather than being sent abroad (2013b). The root cause of the decline of British industry, he suggested, was not a lack of foreign markets but rather domestic oversaving and underconsumption. Resources that could otherwise be used to raise consumption and thus production levels at home were instead being exported abroad. It was this dynamic which underpinned what he called the 'new imperialism'.

The logical conclusion was that boosting demand at home through state redistribution would remove the need for capital investment abroad, and thus imperialism would be eradicated. There was an inverse relation between imperialism and social reform at home – the more of the latter, the less of the former, and vice versa. Hobson thus writes that 'it is not industrial progress' or capitalism itself 'that demands the opening up of new markets and areas of investment, but mal-distribution of consuming power which prevents the absorption of commodities and capital within the country' (1902: 85). Again the question of *choice* is crucial here: the increasing levels of inter-imperialist competition signalled by the 'scramble for Africa' were the result of a deliberate decision to favour 'a militant imperialism animated by the lust for quantitative growth' over 'a peaceful democracy engaged upon the [qualitative] development of its natural resources' (Hobson 2013b). Unlike Lenin or Rosa Luxemburg, for whom a critique of imperialism necessitated an attack on the fundamental principles of capital accumulation itself, for Hobson both oversaving and imperialist expansion were the contingent result of an irrational abuse of the capitalist system – something that could, and should, be fixed within the terms of the current social organization. In his view, even in purely capitalist terms, choosing to carve out new imperial territory rather than redistributing the social surplus and raise demand at home was economically irrational – at least from the perspective of the *national* economy. Arguing that imperialism ran against the national economic interest set Hobson apart from later Marxist theorists, for whom imperialist expansion was necessary to stabilize the domestic economy, and provided additional benefit to the workers of the home country.

The Boer War

The Boer War provided the immediate trigger for Hobson's 'economic theory' of imperialism. For the New Liberals, the war in South Africa represented the pinnacle of the 'New Imperialism' invading Africa, a debased form of 'stock-jobbing imperialism' (Fieldhouse 1961: 188) directly driven by economic, and especially financial, interests rather than the 'natural' expansion of a 'national race'. In 1899, as he was beginning to flesh out these links between underconsumption and imperialism, Hobson was asked by the *Manchester Guardian* to go to South Africa and report on the growing tensions between the British and Boer settlers, focused on control of the Transvaal goldmines. These articles were then published in book form as *The War in South Africa* (Hobson 1900). The British government justified the declaration of war as a defence of the political rights of British immigrants and fears that the Boers were seeking to challenge regional British control. Hobson rejected this account, instead viewing the war 'as a capitalist plot organized by investors in South African mines', driven by the financiers who controlled the mines and wanted greater control over the black labour force (Allet 1981: 27).

Hobson's experience in South Africa added two new elements to his developing theory of imperialism. The first was 'a strong sense of the international, cosmopolitan nature of financial capitalism' (Cain 2002: 92). Hobson argued that the level of French and German investment in the goldmines of the Rand 'largely outweigh[ed] the English interest' (1900: 193). He drew attention to the supposedly Jewish background of these foreign financiers, writing that 'the economic resources of the country' have been

> thrown ... more and more into the hands of a small group of international financiers, chiefly German in origin and Jewish in race. By superior ability, enterprise, and organisation these men ... have attained a practical supremacy ... the stress which my analysis lays upon the Jew has reference to the class of foreign capitalists of which the foreign Jew must be taken as the leading type. (189)

The prime architects of the war were those 'whose trade is finance, and whose trade interest is not British', and who sought to 'add to their other businesses the business of politics' (196–7). It was 'not Hamburg, not Vienna, not Frankfurt, but Johannesburg [that was] the New Jerusalem' (190). In highlighting the role of Jewish financiers, Hobson hoped to demonstrate that the interests behind the war were not those of the British nation, but sectional and cosmopolitan (Clarke 1978: 92). This idea of unproductive international financial interests being both counter to, and more powerful than, those of productive national 'industry' thus reproduces the dichotomy between 'industry' and 'parasitism' on the global stage.

The second novel aspect built on the same dichotomy, namely the perversion of public discourse by the financial interests responsible for the war. The war had huge public support at home, despite being, in Hobson's view, counter to British interests. This lapse into 'jingoism' was explained by Jewish control of the international press agencies whipping up support for the war. The 'Rand mining magnates', he wrote, 'are chief owners of at least two important London daily newspapers, and of several considerable weekly papers, while the wider and ever-growing Jewish control of other organs of the press warrants a suspicion that the direct economic nexus between the English press and Rand finance is far stronger than is actually known' (Hobson, qtd in Allet 1987: 105). As far back as 1892, Hobson had warned of the growing prominence of 'Jewish financiers' in the 'increasingly commercialized [news] ... syndicates' such as Reuters, cautioning that 'the press [was] falling into the hands of "this active financial race"', who were using their power to '[direct] foreign policy along lines favourable to the bond holding faction of the commercial community' (Hobson, qtd in Holmes 1979: 136).

Some commentators (e.g. Porter 1976: 215) have noted a contradiction between Hobson's focus on the voluntarist conspiratorial machinations of individual international (Jewish) financiers underpinning imperialism and his structural (and thus impersonal) underconsumption thesis. But the central contention of the latter is that 'oversaving' was the result of disproportionate institutional power and organization of different interest groups. The stronger that institutional power, the greater the distribution of resources that group can expect from the overall product. Without a deeper critique of the mechanisms of capital accumulation as such, the theory remains at the level of conspiracy, in the sense that inequality is not systemic but the contingent product of efforts by different social groups to organize themselves in such a way as to maximize their returns. That an international finance-media nexus could conspire to claim for themselves an oversized portion of the social value thus runs with the grain of the theory as a whole. That that nexus should be specifically categorized as Jewish, however, requires further explanation.

Antisemitism

Hobson's antisemitism, evident in both his work on imperialism and, as we shall see, his analysis of poverty in London, was not merely an unfortunate personal quirk but had deep roots within the broader British liberal-left tradition. Unlike other European countries, where antisemitism was grounded in questions of civil society – about legal emancipation, universal political rights – in Britain, 'the Victorian engagement with race had an imperial complexion', with antisemitism tending to emerge in relation to foreign policy (Julius 2010: 397). Thus the antisemitic 'agitations' that appeared in the 1870s were focused on the influence of 'foreign Jews' on both imperial policy and the domestic economy. Traces of the antisemitic association of Jews with 'warmongering' and imperialism that would later play such a central role in Hobson's assessment of the Boer War can be found in 1870s controversy over the foreign policy of Benjamin Disraeli – still the sole British prime minister of Jewish background. Mindful of the need to defend the concept of empire, Disraeli had refused to support Bulgarian Christian nationalists against the Ottoman Empire and floated the possibility of military action in response to Russia's subsequent war on the Ottomans. This position was framed by opponents, including William Gladstone, as promoting 'Asiatic' or 'Hebraic' interests at the expense of the British national interest and of those of liberalism in general (266). Disraeli was accused of seeking to 'imperialize' the British constitution, on the basis that, 'being of Jewish descent', he had 'no sympathy with English political life' (Koebner and Schmidt 1964: 156). Richard Koebner and Helmut Dan Schmidt suggest the new concept of 'imperialism' first became 'a popular word in the English language as an anti-Disraeli slogan' (143). The 'first revulsions against imperialism . . . carried mild anti-Jewish overtones' from the outset, they suggest, so that the reappearance of many of the same anti-Jewish themes in the opposition to the Boer War twenty years later should come as no surprise (227).

In the intervening period, the question of Jewish immigration became the main vector for antisemitism in Britain. In the four decades prior to the First World War, 'between 120,000 and 150,000 Jews settled in Britain', mostly Russian and Eastern European Jews fleeing a wave of pogroms. Many settled in London's East End, during a period where it was badly hit by recurrent economic crises. The combination of economic crisis, social distress and immigration made the presence of Russian Jews a widespread topic for public debate, with an 'anti-Alien' movement drawing support from across the political spectrum. This constituted a shift in the terrain of the so-called Jewish question in Britain, moving from a political or constitutional framing to a 'social problem' (Feldman 1994: 262). This was part of the general shift, in which the New Liberals were integral, towards redefining the role of the state in the light of novel conceptions of the 'common good' – and thus also the question of whether that good should include the Jewish immigrants (269).

For Hobson, it was the possible 'social cost' imposed by the arrival of the migrants in one of the poorest areas of the country that attracted his attention. His various journalistic articles on the 'Jewish Question' in London, later reworked for his 1881 book *Problems of Poverty*, was not primarily concerned with the absolute numbers of migrants, but rather 'the *quality* of these immigrants' (Allet 1987: 103; emphasis added). By this he did not mean the supposed uncleanliness or physical weakness that had alarmed some. Indeed, Hobson wrote that the Jews were 'steady, industrious, quiet, sober, thrifty, quick to learn, and tolerably honest' (1896b: 59). This evaluation was one widely shared by liberals, with Jews seen as the admirable epitome of hardwork, self-reliance and abstinence. But in Hobson's view it was precisely these traits which made 'the foreign Jew' such a terrible competitor. He is the nearest approach to the ideal ' "economic" man . . . Admirable in domestic morality, and an orderly citizen, he is almost void of social morality. No compunction or consideration for his fellow-worker will keep him from underselling and overreaching them' (60).

We have already seen how Hobson adopted John Ruskin's romantic critique of the 'economic man' – the man with no interest in 'subjective wealth' of beauty, art and morality, who cares only for the 'objective wealth' of money. For Hobson, the 'foreign Jew' personified this 'economic man' to a degree hitherto unknown in Britain, and it was therefore the arrival of competition from *this particular source*, Eastern European Jewry, rather than competition in itself, that gave him alarm. For Hobson, and for other observers such as the Fabian, Beatrice Webb, Jews lacked the 'capacity for combination' (in the sense of striking or building trade unions) and were 'unchecked by social feeling of class loyalty and trade integrity' (Holmes 2016: 16). Jewish migrants were willing to 'work at any level of wages', driving down 'the rate of wages even below what represents starvation point for the native worker' and leading to the persistence of 'sweating workshops' (Hobson 1896b: 61).

This antisocial tendency was compounded by the financial support offered to Jewish immigrants by the Jewish Board of Guardians. While the board argued that they prevented Jewish migrants from becoming an economic burden to Britain, for Hobson such grants were counterproductive – not only attracting more migrants but exacerbating the 'sweating' problem by encouraging Jewish immigrants to become 'masters' of their own sweatshop, even if this meant forfeiting a labourer's wage. Hobson argued that 'most men will contentedly receive less as master than as servant, but especially the Jew . . . The Jew craves the position of a sweating-master, because that is the lowest step in a ladder which may lead to a life of magnificence, supported out of usury' (1896b: 98). The direct link Hobson makes here between 'sweating mastery' and 'usury' is particularly telling – whether in the squalor of the East End or the splendour of the financial houses, the Jew is irredeemably cast in the role of the unproductive 'parasite', living off the labour of others. Here again Jews as a collective are ascribed innate characteristics which makes them prone to the sectionalism and self-interested activity that Hobson made it his life's work to oppose.

The 'rich Jew'

Long before his trip to South Africa, Hobson's attitude to 'rich Jews' mirrored that towards poorer migrants. In one article, he referred to the antisemitic Liberal journalist Arnold White's idea that Jews might be 'weaned away' from finance and 'restored' by being brought 'back into contact with the land' through agricultural activity. Hobson rejected White's thesis, arguing that the 'nature and intellectual character of the Jew everywhere makes him averse to manual labour' (Hobson, qtd in Holmes 1979: 135). This supposed inherent aversion to manual and 'productive' labour provided the connection between the poor Jew who set up as a 'sweating master' in the East End and the financial plutocrat who had 'gravitat[ed] . . . to that least productive form of trade from the public point of view, money-lending' (135). In 1892, Hobson had warned that the British press was falling into the hands of 'this active financial race', and he raised concerns about the leader of the Liberal Party, Lord Roseberry, meeting certain leading 'financial Jews' at the races (136).

Hobson's later writing on the war sought to provide concrete evidence of what he had long suspected about the nefarious influence of Jews on British policy. The first chapter of *The War on South Africa* carried the title 'For whom are we fighting?': the answer was the 'rich and ably organised syndicate' of Jewish interests in the Transvaal (Hobson 1900: 193). This supposed communal interest not only grew 'out of [Jewish] exploitation of the goldfields' but also the Jews' control of dynamite companies, the Stock Exchange, loans and mortgages, alcohol trade and the press – with all conflicts of interest between these various fields brushed aside (Holmes 1979: 138). John Allet suggests that for Hobson there was thus capitalism, and then a distinct 'Jewish capitalism' (1987: 107). The same is true for imperialism itself – a Jewish materialism had deformed the noble, if misguided, aims of British colonial expansion, using international connections to whip up support for a war against the national interest. In one extraordinary section of his essay 'Capitalism and Imperialism in South Africa', Hobson warned of Jewish financiers leaving 'economic fangs in the carcas[s]e of their prey' and forcing British foreign policy to dance to their 'diabolical tune' (Hobson, qtd in Allet 1987: 106).

This kind of anti-Jewish antiwar rhetoric was by no means limited to Hobson alone, but was central to much of the antiwar movement as a whole (see Hirshfield 1980). Figures such as the leftists William Morris and Eleanor Marx, as well as Liberal leader Henry Campbell-Bannerman, sought to counter antisemitism within their movements (Hirshfield 1981: 102; Virdee 2017). Claire Hirshfield argues that by 1901, opposition to the war 'had largely lost its anti-Semitic edge' – but suggests that 'the anti-Semitic echoes refused to die entirely was probably due to [Hobson's] enduring influence', due to the 'impressive theoretical framework' of his analysis, reinforced by his personal observations on the ground in South Africa (1980: 628). Those who seek to defend Hobson from the charge of antisemitism argue that the antisemitic character of these 'personal observations' was the consequence of rushed, on-the-ground reportage, and not a true reflection of his theoretical stance (Allet 1981: 131). Indeed, by the time of *Imperialism*, explicit references to Jews and conspiratorial Jewish influence had been substantially pared down, and the underconsumption thesis given greater prominence. However, even here Hobson continued to highlight that the great financial houses were controlled 'chiefly by men of a single and peculiar race, who have behind them many centuries of financial experience, they are in a unique position to manipulate the policy of nations' (1902: 57).

For some, such as Hannah Arendt, Hobson's depiction of Jewish financial power in South Africa was based on an unfortunate but nevertheless empirically grounded observation of fact. Describing Hobson as a 'sober and reliable' historian, even after directly quoting his description of ravenous, befanged Jewish financiers, Arendt (1979: 24, 135) argues that 'Jewish international financiers' *were* 'especially suited for [the] essentially international business operations' entailed by the 'new imperialism'.[6] The few direct mentions of Jews in *Imperialism* compared with earlier works were because 'it had become obvious' by the time of *Imperialism* that Jewish 'influence and role [within imperialism] had been temporary and somewhat superficial' (135 n34). Hobson's apparent antisemitism was thus merely the consequence of the limitations of the empirical information available at the time. Once that information changed, so did his theory.

But, as Hirshfield (1980: 97) points out, in empirical terms, Hobson and others who focused on the Jewish influence in South Africa 'disregarded . . . the fact that many of the "Jewish" magnates maintained only the most marginal ties with their ancestral faith, that they pursued economic or class interests rather than communal ones; and that they were frequently at odds with each other'. The majority of Jews in South Africa opposed the war altogether (96). Moreover, Hobson's private letters from the time were even more forthright about Jews than his newspaper articles, talking of 'a strong strain of Jewish craft' in the region and describing Jews in Johannesburg as 'the veriest scum of Europe' (qtd in Holmes 1979: 138). Such an emotional response does not sit easily with claims of disinterested empirical observation. Indeed, it seems just as likely that for Hobson 'sentiment preced[ed] theory' (Koebner and Schmidt 1964: 250): already minded to blame the situation in South Africa on Jewish financiers before his arrival in the country, his 'empirical' observations were viewed through a prism shaded by anti-Jewish prejudice from the outset. And while the more structural theory of *Imperialism* removed most (though not all) of the direct references to Jews, the premises of that argument – the insistence that international, cosmopolitan finance was the driving force of imperialism, undermining the national interest by manipulation of public opinion, diverting resources from the social reforms that were so desperately needed at home – carried in its structure traces of the antisemitic 'sentiment' that had stimulated his initial writings on the subject. These traces, inherent in the structure of the general political-economic argument, provided a foothold for the remaining, relatively small number of explicitly antisemitic statements. More generally, they also allow, in different contexts, the Hobsonite, New Liberal theory of imperialism as such to be reconverted into more overtly antisemitic ideology.

While Hobson would never write so explicitly about Jews again, in 1918, just after the Balfour Declaration promising a 'Jewish homeland' in the British Mandate of Palestine, Hobson published a pseudonymous collection of satirical writings under the name 'Lucien' and entitled *1920: Dips into the Near Future*. Here he wrote of the prospective return of the 'Chosen People to the City of Their Choice' after which they would 'renounce . . . their sojourn in the House of Bondage so long and so unwillingly endured'. Hobson joked that the Jews would not, in fact, 'leave their bonds behind' but would rather

---

[6] Staudenmaier (2012) provides a comprehensive critique of Arendt's reliance on antisemitic readings of history and statistics.

lay them formally upon a temporary altar erected in the vestibule of the Temple, afterwards to be transferred to the vaults. One of the most interesting groups in the procession consists of representatives of the Transvaal Companies, who will with due solemn rites transfer the soul of the Rand, its share certificates, from Johannesburg to the New Jerusalem, thus completing the spiritual symbolism of the Golden City. ('Lucien', qtd in Allet 1987: 112)

The connection that Hobson makes here between international finance, the imperialism of the Transvaal and the establishment of a Jewish state – signified by the transfer of bonds and share certificates from the Rand to Jerusalem – prefigures in an intriguing way the contemporary Left's conceptualization of Israel as an 'imperialist' state, and the new modes of antisemitism that have emerged in the wake of Israel's existence, focused on Israel's supposed power over world affairs.

Conclusion: antisemitism as a marker of the nationalist stance against the wrong kind of capitalism

Hobson's antisemitism was emblematic of a broader tendency towards antisemitic critiques of capitalism across the liberal-left during this period. Where Hobson was exceptional was in his ability to integrate antisemitism within a far more theoretically robust explanation of capitalist crisis and imperialist expansion. While there was a tension between his underconsumptionist theory of imperialism and his conspiratorial focus on Jews – the former neither required nor necessitated the latter – this did not amount to a contradiction. It seems clear that Hobson had cultivated a personal streak of antisemitism, which waxed and waned but never entirely disappeared, based on racialized ascriptions of Jewish greed, self-interest and tribalism. His economic analyses, both domestic and geopolitical, were coloured with this animosity towards Jews from the outset, but they did not logically derive from them. Yet it is equally clear that those analyses – which regard capitalist appropriation of surplus value as a moral failing rather than the basis of the mode of production, and seek to divorce the nation-state from global processes of capital accumulation – were perfectly compatible with his antisemitic predilections.

Hobson's world view represented a departure from the liberal orthodoxy of the time, one justified given the huge disparities of wealth produced by the first century of industrial capitalism. Yet, for all its complexity and solid empirical basis, Hobson singularly failed to grasp that the 'distinction between the system of nation states and the capitalist world system is merely a distinction within a dynamic totality, that is, a totality whose different constituents are mutually constitutive and obey the same dynamic force that governs everything within the constellation' (Stoetzler 2019: 19). This misrecognition of the mutually constitutive relation of the nation and global capitalist relations, and his dichotomous opposition of material production and parasitical unproductive finance – which does not grasp how the two are inextricably entwined – is one that has been endlessly replicated within left-liberal political movements over the past century, no more than within parts of the British Labour

Party itself. And while such a perspective does not necessitate antisemitism – nor is it limited to the Left – it nevertheless dovetails neatly with classic antisemitic conspiracy theories of an exploitative international Jewish network pulling the strings of global affairs in order to disintegrate national communities. The 'truncated critique' embodied and popularized by Hobson's analysis of 'industrial society' not only left it open to antisemitic interpretations – an opportunity which he himself took – but also provides some insight into why a figure like Corbyn, whose opposition to capitalism is essentially liberal, remaining at the level of moral condemnation of its symptoms rather than a theoretically sustained critique of its essential dynamics, has been so susceptible to antisemitic positions, particularly in relation to questions of war, imperialism and Israel. Studying the relation between antisemitism and the foreshortened critiques of capitalism that can be discerned in Hobson's work, and from which the broader liberal-left was and is by no means inoculated, thus provides a clearer picture of the deep-rooted ideological underpinnings of antisemitism on the Left today.

References

Allet, J. (1981), *New Liberalism: The Political Economy of J. A. Hobson*, Toronto: University of Toronto Press.

Allet, J. (1987), 'New Liberalism, Old Prejudices: J. A. Hobson and the "Jewish Question"', *Jewish Social Studies*, 49 (2): 99–114.

Arendt, H. ([1948] 1979), *The Origins of Totalitarianism*, San Diego: Harvest.

Bell, D. (2009), 'Democracy and Empire: J. A. Hobson, Leonard Hobhouse and the Crisis of Liberalism', in I. Hall and L. Hill (eds), *British International Thinkers from Hobbes to Namier*, 181–206, New York: Palgrave Macmillan.

Beveridge, W. (1942), *Social Insurance and Allied Services*, vol. 942, London: HMSO.

Blair, T. (1996), *New Britain: My Vision of a Young Country*, London: Fourth Estate.

Cain, P. J. (2002), *Hobson and Imperialism: Radicalism, New Liberalism, and Finance 1887–1938*, Oxford: Oxford University Press.

Clarke, P. (1978), *Liberals and Social Democrats*, Cambridge: Cambridge University Press.

Collini, S. (1979), *Liberalism and Sociology: L. T. Hobhouse and Political Argument in England 1880-1914*, Cambridge: Cambridge University Press.

Crosland, A. ([1956] 2006), *The Future of Socialism*, London: Constable.

Cruddas, J. (2010), 'Our Labour', in R. Grayson and J. Rutherford (eds), *After the Crash*, 17–25, London: Lawrence & Wishart.

Emy, H. V. (1973), *Liberals, Radicals and Social Politics 1812–1894*, Cambridge: Cambridge University Press.

Feldman, D. (1994), *Englishmen and Jews*, Connecticut: Yale University Press.

Feldman, D. (2019), 'Jeremy Corbyn, "Imperialism", and Labour's Antisemitism Problem', *History Workshop*, 12 June, available at: www.historyworkshop.org.uk/imperialism-and-labours-antisemitism-problem/ (accessed 28 June 2023).

Fieldhouse, D. K. (1961), '"Imperialism": An Historiographical Revision', *Economic History Review*, 14 (2): 187–209.

Finkelstein, D. (2019), 'Corbyn's Praise for Deeply Antisemitic Book', *Times*, 30 April, available at: www.thetimes.co.uk/article/corbyn-s-praise-for-deeply-antisemitic-book-6jfcmh5fp (accessed 28 June 2023).

Freeden, M. (1973), 'J. A. Hobson as a New Liberal Theorist: Some Aspects of His Social Thought until 1914', *Journal of the History of Ideas*, 34 (3): 421–43.
Freeden, M. (1978), *The New Liberalism: An Ideology of Social Reform*, Oxford: Oxford University Press.
Green, T. H. (1986), *Lectures on the Principles of Political Obligation and Other Writings*, Oxford: Oxford University Press.
Hirshfield, C. (1980), 'The Anglo-Boer War and the Issue of Jewish Culpability', *Journal of Contemporary History*, 15 (4): 619–31.
Hirshfield, C. (1981), 'The British Left and the "Jewish Conspiracy": A Case Study of Modern Antisemitism', *Jewish Social Studies*, 43 (2): 95–112.
Hobhouse, L. T. (1994), *Liberalism and Other Writings*, Cambridge: Cambridge University Press.
Hobson, J. A. (1896a), *The Problem of the Unemployed*, London: Methuen.
Hobson, J. A. (1896b), *Problems of Poverty*, London: Methuen.
Hobson, J. A. (1900), *The War in South Africa*, London: Nisbit.
Hobson, J. A. (1902), *Imperialism: A Study*, London: George Allen & Unwin.
Hobson, J. A. (1906), *The Evolution of Modern Capitalism*, London: Walter Scott.
Hobson, J. A. (1909), *The Crisis of Liberalism*, London: P.S. King.
Hobson, J. A. ([1901] 1919), *The Social Problem*, London: Nisbit.
Hobson, J. A. (1930), *Wealth and Life*, London: Macmillan.
Hobson, J. A. ([1938] 2011), *Confessions of an Economic Heretic*, Oxford: Routledge.
Hobson, J. A. (2013a), 'The Subjective and the Objective View of Distribution', in R. E. Backhouse (ed.), *Writings on Distribution and Welfare*, 378–404, Oxford: Routledge.
Hobson, J. A. (2013b), 'Free Trade and Foreign Policy', in P. Cain (ed.), *Writings on Imperialism and Internationalism*, Oxford: Routledge.
Holmes, C. (1979), 'J. A. Hobson and the Jews', in C. Holmes (ed.), *Immigrants and Minorities in British Society*, 125–57, Winchester, MA: Allen & Unwin.
Holmes, C. ([1979] 2016), *Antisemitism in British Society 1876–1935*, Oxon: Routledge.
Julius, A. (2010), *Trials of the Diaspora*, Oxford: Oxford University Press.
Koebner, R., and H. D. Schmidt (1964), *Imperialism: The Story and Significance of a Political Word, 1840–1960*, Cambridge: Cambridge University Press.
Lenin, V. I. ([1917] 1988), *Imperialism, the Highest State of Capitalism*, London: Lawrence & Wishart.
Marx, K. (1974), 'Critique of the Gotha Programme', in D. Fernbach (ed.), *The First International and After*, 339–59, London: Penguin.
Morefield, J. (2005), *Covenants without Swords: Idealist Liberalism and the Spirit of Empire*, Princeton, NJ: Princeton University Press.
Porter, B. (1976), *Critics of Empire: British Radical Attitudes to Colonialism in Africa 1895–1914*, London: Macmillan.
Postone, M. (1993), *Time, Labor and Social Domination*, Cambridge: Cambridge University Press.
Ray, L. J. (1983), 'Eugenics, Mental Deficiency and Fabian Socialism between the Wars', *Oxford Review of Education*, 9 (3): 213–22.
Ruskin, J. (1985), *Unto This Last and Other Writings*, London: Penguin.
Sassoon, D. (2019), Letter to the *Guardian*, 2 May, available at: www.theguardian.com/news/2019/may/02/jeremy-corbyn-hobsons-imperialism-and-antisemitism (accessed 28 June 2023).
Say, J. B. ([1803] 2001), *A Treatise on Political Economy*, London: Routledge.

Schmitt, C. ([1950] 2003), *The Nomos of the Earth in the International Law of the Jus Publicum*, New York: Telos.

Semmel, B. (1960), *Imperialism and Social Reform: English Social-Imperial Thought 1895–1914*, Cambridge, MA: Harvard University Press.

Shaw, G. B. (1910), 'Lecture to the Eugenics Education Society', reported by *Daily Mail*, 4 March.

Staudenmaier, P. (2012), 'Hannah Arendt's Analysis of Antisemitism in the Origins of Totalitarianism: A Critical Appraisal', *Patterns of Prejudice*, 46 (2): 154–79.

Stoetzler, M. (2019), 'Capitalism, the Nation and Societal Corrosion: Notes on "Left-Wing Antisemitism"', *Journal of Social Justice*, 9: 1–45.

Virdee, S (2017), 'Socialist Antisemitism and Its Discontents in England, 1884–98', *Patterns of Prejudice*, 51: 356–73.

Weinstein, D. (2007), *Utilitarianism and the New Liberalism*, Cambridge: Cambridge University Press.

3

Antisemitism and the critique of society as economic object

Werner Bonefeld

The critical tradition associated with the work of Karl Marx, Max Horkheimer, Theodor W. Adorno and Moishe Postone conceives of the elements of antisemitism as essential to the existing social relations.[1] What is essential to society holds sway over its concept too. Critical Theory therefore formulates the critique of antisemitism as the critique of bourgeois society.[2] Instead of the promise of freedom (which would include the freedom from antisemitism), as Alex Honneth (2010) sees it, bourgeois society contains within itself the elements of antisemitism.

The contemporary Critical Theory of antisemitism chiefly draws on two classical texts: Horkheimer and Adorno's 'Elements of Antisemitism' ([1947] 1979), which was part of their *Dialectic of Enlightenment*; and Postone's 'Anti-Semitism and National Socialism' (1986). 'Elements of Antisemitism' conceives of the 'rumor about the Jews' as a form of paranoid rage against domination that is directly useful for the perpetuation of domination itself (Adorno 1974: 141). It is hatred of difference, of that which is not the same and which is therefore secretly longed for but remains repressed for the sake of self-preservation within domination.[3] According to Eva-Maria Ziege, the

---

I am most grateful to Marcel Stoetzler for his fabulous editorship.

[1] For an insightful account, see Lars Fischer (2018).

[2] Contemporary right-wing conservatives reject the Critical Theory associated with Adorno, Horkheimer and others as a 'cultural Marxism', which is itself an antisemitic trope (Braune 2019). The remaining defenders of the state-socialist orthodoxy, by contrast, view the Critical Theory of antisemitism with suspicion because they believe it is merely meant to shield the state of Israel from criticism. Following Moishe Postone, though, 'for many of the left, anti-Semitism has been a very relevant topic –not only because of its past, but also because, as a deeply reactionary ideology that can appear to be anti-hegemonic, it poses particular challenges for progressive movements. That the discourse on anti-Semitism can be and has been instrumentalized does not mean that the topic itself should be declared outside the pale of progressive critical discourse' (email to Werner Bonefeld and others, 30 June 2008, in a controversy that arose over the refusal by the hosts of an influential Marxist email list to circulate information about a conference on antisemitism on the grounds that it was 'not a Marxist topic').

[3] On 'Elements of Antisemitism', see Marcel Stoetzler's (2018a) insightful account. Karin Stögner's (2014) account employs the propositions of Critical Theory without expounding its critical acumen. She conceives of antisemitism as comparable to sexism in that it amounts to a 'critique' of perceived weakness by a cold masculine society. There is much to be said for her approach to social 'coldness', but without further conceptualization of the social relations, its meaning remains opaque. See,

central hypothesis of their work in the early 1940s was that antisemitism can only be understood through society, but society can only be understood through antisemitism (2009: 8). Moishe Postone approached antisemitism as a fetishized anti-capitalism, one which imagines a conflict between concrete nature (things for use, use values) and unnatural abstractness (money and the invisible power of the market).[4] While 'Elements' developed a critical social theory of antisemitism focusing on domination, Postone's approach expounded critical insights of Marx's critique of commodity fetishism for a critique of modern antisemitism.[5]

The account assembled here does not argue for the one or the other Critical Theory approach to antisemitism. I hold that political economy is the formula of an inverted social world. Society in the inverted form of the economic object is bewitched. I argue that antisemitism is the 'rumor about the Jews' as the intangible puppet masters of the capitalist wealth that makes itself manifest in the form of money as more money. Antisemitism amounts to a personalized critique of a crisis-ridden dynamic of real economic abstractions, of cash, profit and rent, and their regulation by the invisible hand of the market.[6] Modern antisemitism identifies the ghostlike character of society as an economic object, the form of society that the capital fetish (Marx) makes appear as an economic objectivity, with the power of 'the Jews'. The argument makes use of the classic texts but refrains from excessive referencing.[7]

The chapter is in three sections. It starts with an account of Critical Theory as a critique of the ghostlike character of capitalist society. This character was already identified by Adam Smith ([1776] 1981), who posited that it is regulated by an 'invisible hand'. There then follows a section about the elements of antisemitism, which, I argue, are innate to a critique of capitalist society that is enthralled by the spell society has put

---

however, Christine Achinger's (2013) excellent account, which expounds sexism and antisemitism in and through the definite social relations that manifest themselves as such.

[4] In a later contribution, Moishe Postone (2006) applied the notion of fetishized anti-capitalism to contemporary forms of anti-imperialism, which exonerate even the most reactionary movements, including, for example, Hamas and Hezbollah (see Butler 2010). In the UK, Butler's view defines the approach to internationalism by the Corbyn wing of the Labour Party (see Bolton and Pitts [2018]; and Chapter 11 in this volume). On this topic, see also Bonefeld (2014b) and Stoetzler (2018b).

[5] Postone's magnum opus, *Time, Labor and Social Domination* (1993), does not consider antisemitism, which is odd given that he considers antisemitism to be a fetishized anti-capitalism. Like the *Neue Marx Lektüre* that developed in West Germany post 1968, his book is an attempt at reinterpreting Marx's critique of political economy as a critical social theory. However, as I have argued elsewhere (Bonefeld 2004), his reinterpretation expunges the political in political economy, which leads his account towards a system theory of social action. The one contributor to the *Neue Marx Lektüre* who examines antisemitism in the context of *Capital* is Michael Heinrich (2012). He presents Marx's critique as a critique of capitalist social relations and, in this context, expounds the critical meaning of Marx's point about the capitalist individuals as personifications of economic categories. Antisemitism has to do with the personalization of capitalist social reality. For an appreciation of Postone's Critical Theory, see Elena Louisa Lange (2018) and Chris O'Kane (2018). On the *Neue Marx Lektüre*, see Bonefeld (2014a).

[6] 'Cash, profit and rent' stands as a reference to Marx's 'The Trinity Formula' (1966: chapter 48), in which he develops his theory of class.

[7] Readers familiar with these texts will spot the references and paraphrases. Those who are not might hopefully find themselves enticed to study them. Since I first wrote on this matter (Bonefeld 1997), my own work builds on the intersection between the Critical Theory of antisemitism and the Critical Theory of capitalism, developing Critical Theory as a critique of economic objectivity.

on it. The final section explores the meaning of the inscription at the gate of Auschwitz, 'Arbeit macht frei', as a condensed invocation and manifestation of the elements of antisemitism.

On the critique of political economy as a critical social theory

For a Critical Theory of society, it is not the independence of the economic categories of cash, profit and rent, money and profit that requires explanation. Rather, their comprehension rests on the understanding of social relations that assume the form of reified economic things. A Critical Theory of society aims to think against the spell of society's dazzling economic forms. It wants to get behind their forms of appearance as the fateful forces of economic nature. It therefore does not think *about* (reified) economic things. Rather, it thinks *in and through* them: at least this is its critical intention (Adorno 1990: 23, 149). Thinking by means of definitions or identifications is quite able to say what some-thing comes under, what it illustrates, exemplifies or represents. It does not, however, say what some-thing is. Thought is required to grasp reality, which in its immediacy does not tell us what it is. What, for example, really is money and what holds sway in its concept? 'Concepts', Adorno says, 'are moments of the reality that requires their formation' (11). Conceptualization thus does not mean 'thinking' *about* things. Rather, it means thinking *out of* things (33). If it were really *about* things, then conceptualization would be external to its subject matter.

Thought that does not go into its object does not recognize its object. Instead, it treats it as a theoretical hypothesis. Just as the critique of religion does not criticize God on the basis of God, a Critical Theory of capitalist political economy does not criticize real economic abstractions on the basis of real economic abstractions. Regarding the critique of religion, it thinks out of God to decipher the social relations that assume the form of God and vanish in the idea of God only to reappear as cowed believers in God, mere human derivatives of divine rule. Similarly, the critique of capitalist society is not a critique from the standpoint of economic nature. Like the critique of religion, it too deciphers the definite social relations that manifest themselves in mysterious, seemingly extra-mundane economic forces that prevail in and through the social individuals as personifications of a ghostlike economic objectivity. For a critical social theory, the fetishism of commodities entails the movement of some abstract, by themselves quite incomprehensible, economic forces that assert themselves over society as if by their own volition. Yet, however objective in its nature, economic nature is in its entirety a socially constituted nature. The question of the social nature of a fateful movement of coins, which has the capacity to force a whole class of people into abject poverty without a moment's notice, is therefore one about the specific character of the capitalistically constituted social relations that assert themselves in the form of a movement of coins beyond human control. The money form disappears as a social relationship, and instead asserts an abstract economic logic, which, for a Critical Theory of society, manifests the vanished social subject in her own social world as a mere personification of economic categories. The capitalist social subject is a coined subject, which on the pain of ruin, bloodshed and disaster, entails the promise of freedom as the freedom of money to beget more money.[8] In this freedom, the social individual is 'governed by the products of his own hand', and it is therefore his own social product that acts 'with the force of an elemental natural process' (Marx 1990: 772). Money does nothing unless it is furnished with a consciousness and a will. In Marx's argument, it is the acting individuals that bestow the economic forces with such an independent will and consciousness, one that 'takes care of both the beggar and the king' (Adorno 1990: 251). In this community of equals before money,

> each pays heed to himself only, and no one worries about the rest. And precisely for that reason, either in accordance with the pre-established harmony of things, or under the auspices of an omniscient providence, they all work together to their mutual advantage, for the common weal and in the common interest. (Marx 1990: 280)

Marx's ironic take on the magic of the invisible hand as the regulative principle of bourgeois freedom as economic compulsion is founded on the understanding that the social practice of the individuals manifests itself not only behind their backs but that it also prevails only in and through them.

Marx captures well the inversion of human practice as an action of things when he writes in the section on the money fetish that 'a social relation, a definite relation between individuals ... appears as a metal, a stone, as a purely physical external thing which can be found, as such, in nature, and which is indistinguishable in form from its natural existence' (1973: 239). Social objectivity does not lead a life of its own. It is not a force of nature. Rather, it is a socially constituted objectivity. Social relations vanish from sight, though, when they take the form of appearance of a piece of metal or a stone, and this appearance is as real as the circumstance that the economic object imposes itself on the acting subjects as if regulated by an invisible hand. There is only one world, and that is the world of appearances. What appears in society as a 'coin' in its fateful movement is in fact the manifestation of a definite social relationship between individuals that takes the form of a relationship between coins. Marx's point that 'the monstrous objective power which social labour itself created opposite itself as one of its moments' is key to the critique of political economy as a critical social theory (831). He argues that the monstrous economic power is not only a product of

---

[8] According to Marx's critique of political economy, capitalist wealth appears in the form of an equivalent exchange relationship in which 'money ... is worth more money'. This manifestation of a 'value which is greater than itself' is core to Marx's conception of capital as a social subject that has 'acquired the occult ability to add value to itself'. He asks where it gets this quality from and argues that 'money which begets money' entails the existence of a particular commodity, that is, labour power, whose consumption creates this surplus in value (Marx 1990: 257, 255, 256). The comprehension, then, of money as the form of value, does not lie within itself. Rather, the mysterious appearance (*Schein*) of a value equivalence between unequal values (M ... M') lies in the concept of surplus value, which presupposes the class relationship between buyers and sellers of labour power (on this, see Adorno 2022: 246 and 249). The equivalent exchange between the traders of labour power is fundamentally one between the buyers of labour power and the producers of surplus value.

social labour but also beyond the control of the social individuals who appear as mere personifications of their own social world. He thus characterizes the commodity as a sensuous supersensible thing. The fetishism of commodities does not *disguise* the 'real' social relations of capitalism. Rather, the fetishism of commodities *expresses* the 'real' social relations in the form of a movement of economic quantities. That is to say, the economic world contains the social individual within itself as the sensuous personification of her own reified social world.

Marx's work focuses on forms, 'at first on forms of consciousness (i.e., religion, philosophy, morality, law), then later on the forms ... of political economy. For Marx, the focus on forms was identical with the critique of the inverted forms of social existence, an existence constituted by the life-practice of human beings' (Reichelt 2000: 105). That is, every social 'form', even the simplest form like, for example, the commodity, 'is already an inversion and causes the social relations to appear as relations between things', and this appearance is real (Marx 1972: 508). The things objectify themselves in the social individuals as 'the bearers of particular class-relations and interests' (Marx 1990: 92). In this inverted world the individuals subsist as coined factors of production, 'mere exploited human material' and yet entirely dependent on the profitability of their living labour in competition with all other exploited human material on a global scale (740). 'Men owe their life to what is being done to them' (Adorno 1989: 275), although they 'are little better than cogs' to the capitalist form of social wealth. They depend on the global competitiveness of their exploitation to 'dodge the freedom to starve' (Adorno 2006: 201). Unprofitable employers of labour power go under, shedding labour, thus weakening the strength of the link to the means of subsistence for the redundant surplus value producers. Profit is primary; the satisfaction of human needs a 'mere sideshow' (51). Capitalist wealth appears in the form of money as more money, and the necessity of more money objectifies itself in the persons as mere 'agents of value' who depend for their life on the manner in which the logic of economic things unfolds.[9] What a monstrosity! An economic thing, this coin, which is thrown into circulation so that it yields more money, that in its nature really is nothing more than a piece of metal, manifests itself as a seemingly independent economic force, which 'the life of all men hangs by' (Adorno 1990: 320). For the acting subjects, society thus appears as an uncontrollable economic subject to which they are bound by seemingly invisible threads. Indeed, the individuals carry their relationship with society, and, therewith, their access to the means of subsistence, in their pockets (Marx 1973: 156-7).

Although coins tend to inflate or become depressed, they are not subjects. Yet, they are the subject of society as essentially a process of money making, imposing themselves on, and also in and through, the acting individuals to the point of madness and disaster, from the socially necessary consciousness of cash, profit and rent, to abject misery and bloodshed. Man is turned 'into money, or money is incorporated

---

[9] Marx posits the general formula of capital as 'value in process, money in process' and expounds 'value in process' as the process of 'valorization', that is, the *Verwertung* of social labour (1990: 256). Capitalist wealth is entirely abstract or, as Riccardo Bellofiore (2009: 185) put it, value is 'strictly speaking a ghost' – of a social labour time 'made abstract' (Bonefeld 2010: 262).

in him. *Human individuality*, human *morality* itself, has become both an object of commerce and the material in which money exists. Instead of money, or paper, it is my own personal existence, my flesh and blood, my social virtues and importance, which constituted the material, corporeal form of the *spirit of money*' (Marx 1975: 215; emphases in the original).[10] The mythological idea of fate becomes no less mythical when it is demythologized 'into a secular "logic of things"' that akin to an abstract system-logic structures the behaviours of the actual individuals by means of competing price signals and threatens their livelihood through loss of access to the means of subsistence because the expenditure of their living labour turned out to have been unprofitable, bankrupting their employer and making them redundant (Adorno 1990: 319). That is, the logic of things 'prevails *over* mankind as something that prevails *in* them' as traders in labour power, the one buying to make a profit, the other selling to gain wage-based access to the means of subsistence (Adorno 2006: 26; emphases in the original). In this society the products of labour that cannot be converted into money are valueless regardless of the needs that they could satisfy. What has no value in exchange has no utility and is therefore burnt or left to rot. That is, however much the individual might try to raise herself above the law of value – and raise she must for the sake of maintaining the civil character of capitalist labour economy preventing cut-throat competition and thus 'bloodshed' – she remains a coined subject of cash, rent and profit. The strength of her connection to the means of life depends on the movement of the abstract economic things over which she has no control, and which impose themselves with at times devastating force, cutting society off from the means of subsistence in the blink of an eye. For the producers of surplus value, the inability to sell her redundant labour power spells disaster to the point of destitution and death. Keynes ([1936] 2007) characterized this inability to trade as involuntary unemployment. Nobody can price themselves into work even for an apple and a pie. What is the price of a kidney? What is the value of life?

On the elements of antisemitism

I have argued that in capitalism the individuals are governed by the fateful movement of economic abstractions. The point of critique can therefore not be to 'make the individual responsible for relations whose creature he socially remains' (Marx 1990: 92).[11] It is therefore not sufficient to criticize capitalists for their seemingly excessive addiction to profit, nor is it sufficient to criticize bankers for pursuing money for the sake of more money. On the pain of ruin, these behaviours manifest the 'objective necessity' of capitalistically constituted social relations.

In this context, the question 'what is criticized' becomes an important one. How does one oppose the fateful movement of coins? Who really is responsible? Clearly,

---

[10] See Bonefeld (2020) for an account of money as a real abstraction of capitalist wealth and as a corporeal social power.
[11] Michael Heinrich (2012: chapter 10.2) similarly expounds antisemitism as personalization of the capital fetish.

the critique of the banker, or any other socio-economic operative in a system that asserts itself as an independent force over and through the social individuals, misses the object of critique. As a Critical Theory, the critique of political economy is not a critique of the personifications of the economic categories. Rather, it is a critique of the capitalistically organized social relations of reproduction that assume the form of a movement of economic things and in turn objectify themselves in the individual person as the human agent of her own forsaken world.

Nevertheless, while every individual is 'ruled by economic abstractions', the owners of great wealth experience this rule as a source of great enrichment and power. In this context Horkheimer and Adorno have argued that the 'rulers' are safe for as long as the 'ruled' struggle under the spell of the inverted world, in which, say, the cause of financial crisis, economic downturn, conditions of austerity and abject poverty, and competitive pressures are attributed to the greedy behaviour of some known peddlers of misery (1979: 179). A spell-bound critique of capitalism demands more of this and less of that. It attributes the fateful movement of the economic forces to the individual will of the greedy money-maker, apportions blame and proclaims to know 'how to set things right'. It is founded on the rumour that the capitalist economy has been corrupted by some greedy self-seekers, and that capitalism can therefore be made to work for the benefit of the national friends once the ghostlike power of the peddlers of misery has been curbed for good. This critique of capitalism does not reject capitalism. It demands a better capitalism, one that manifests the promise of the wealth of nations in opposition to the freedom of world market profits. This critique of capitalism is entirely false to the point of murder. Not only does it leave capitalist society entirely untouched by thought but it also attributes capitalist conditions to the conscious activity of some supposedly guilty party and demands action to sort things out. This personalization of the movement of economic categories entails a number of differentiations, most importantly between the productive or indeed creative capitalist as a 'producer' of 'real' wealth employing hard-working and creative people, and the financial or indeed parasitic capitalist who makes his fortune by speculating in money to the detriment of the established system of national wealth. Here the distinction between material (national) wealth and the financial wealth of money appears in the forms of distinct personalities – pitting the creative industrialist against the parasitic banker-cum-speculator. There emerges, then, the idea of a capitalism that is corrupted by the financial interests, for the benefit of the few and to the detriment of the many. Finance stands accused of turning capitalism into a profit-making system that at the expense of national industry, national wealth, national progress, national fortune and harmony of interests seeks money for the sake of more money.

In this view the capital fetish, which manifests itself in the form of money as the 'most senseless, incomprehensible form' of wealth, is not a fetish at all (Marx 1987: 487). Rather, it presents the wealth of parasites, of some intangible external enemy within, and wealth in money accumulates as the consequence of the allegedly parasitic activity of the bankers, the financiers and the speculators. In a society that asserts itself behind the backs of the acting subjects, the elements of antisemitism project the acting bearers (*Träger*) of the economic categories of money and finance as the hostile cosmopolitan subjects that, having no roots in the industry of the nation, grow rich by speculating on the wealth created by a hard-working national people. That is, a definite form of social relations manifests itself in the form of a movement of coins and then, under the spell of this coined movement, rebels against the personifications of a world governed by coins. This rebellion is entirely conformist and regressive. Instead of rejecting the capitalist social relations, which contain the 'pauper' in its conception of wealth (Marx 1973: 604), it seeks the promise of freedom from the speculators' yoke and a better market position for itself at the expense of the identified wrongdoer, the so-called merchants of greed. For the sake of the nation, something needs to be done. Something can be done! The personalized critique of the capitalist social relations is open to abuse from the outset. It thinks akin to a register of blame and, once radicalized to the point of maddening fury, condemns the identified party as a bloodsucker who drains the living life out of the national community of a hard-working people. It demands renewal of the nation, to make the nation strong again, in opposition to the world market society of capital, which is condemned as a network of money and power that conspires against the supposed nature of a national people who appear thus as hapless victims of the cosmopolitan peddlers of greed and their military backers.[12]

The identification of the 'guilty parties' personalizes the relations of economic objectivity. It points the finger accusingly at the identified foe of the national community. Under the spell of identification, it denounces the alleged wrongdoer and once radicalized into blind resentment, becomes demagogic in its demand for retribution. Who hides behind the invisible hand of the market, what is his name, where does she live, how do they look, walk, pray? How can the invisible wrongdoer of the nation be made visible? According to Adorno and Horkheimer in *Dialectic of Enlightenment*, the image of the Jew is readymade for this personalization. Modern antisemitism feeds on the Christian antisemitism that indicts the 'Jew' as the assassin of Jesus, they have blood on their hands, and as a trafficker in money, and it thus accuses the Jew to pursue unholy unproductive activities. The image of the Jew is that of a parasite – money and finance, speculators and bankers. 'No matter what the Jews as such may be like, their image, as that of the defeated people, has the features to which totalitarian domination must be completely hostile: happiness without power, wages without work, a home without frontiers, religion without myth. These characteristics are hated by the rulers because the ruled secretly long to possess them' (Horkheimer and Adorno 1979: 199, 185). The projected Jew thus appears as a figure of undeserved liberation from sweat and toil, that is, as one that does not submit to hard work, factory organization, struggle to make ends meet and is hated as such. Antisemitism turns the 'longing' for a freedom from want and for a life beyond the mere existence as human material of 'personified labour time' (Marx 1990: 352–3)[13] into a devastating denunciation: it rejects the Jew as the one who lives in comfort by exploiting the many

---

[12] The idea that so-called neoliberal capitalism resulted from a Washington-based agreement between money and power, the so-called Washington consensus, purports the idea, at least by implication, of a conspiratorial construction of a finance-driven world economy that, buttressed by the political and military might of the United States, exploits the nations of the world for financial gain (e.g. see Petras 2006).

[13] As Marx observed, if 'time is everything, [then] man is nothing; he is, at the most, time's carcass' (1976: 127).

for monetary gain. The antisemite says: our misery is the foundation of Jewish wealth. Horkheimer and Adorno thus argue that the 'rulers' are safe for as long as the 'ruled' struggle under the spell of the inverted world, in which, say, the cause of financial crisis, economic downturn and conditions of austerity, desperate struggle to make ends meet, are attributed to the greedy behaviour of some identifiable Others (1979: 179). For the apologists of capitalist society, the reference to the invisible hand operates like an explanatory subterfuge. It explains everything with reference to the Invisible. For the antisemite, however, behind the Invisible stands 'the Jew', so that the invisible power of the market is explained, too.

The category 'Jew' does not refer to a concrete person. It refers to an abstraction. For the antisemite the 'Jew' is the intangible and all-powerful puppet master of national misery. It is not capitalism as such that is rejected. What is rejected is so-called Jewish capitalism, that is, financial capitalism. According to contemporary economic thinking, this capitalism is said to extract 'financial profit directly out of the personal income of workers and others', which 'may be called financial expropriation' (Lapavitsas 2012: 16). This argument about financial capitalism denies that capitalism is in fact a monetary system.[14] The point here is not that the critique of financial capitalism as a system of greed is in itself antisemitic.[15] However, its incomprehension of money as the form of value opens the Pandora's box in which the elements of antisemitism lie in wait. Hardened by the cold stare of the elements of antisemitism, it posits the financialization of capitalism as a suckers' paradise, one in which the promise of opulence for the many brought about by a well-functioning national labour economy is crushed by a few cosmopolitan peddlers of misery. What makes money Jewish, what is Jewish capitalism and what is the concrete nature of a (capitalist) labour economy? For the antisemite, the radicalized subject of conformist rebellion, financial capitalism amounts to a Jewish conspiracy. He demands jobs and conditions for a people of an imagined national nature, defined by the camaraderie of soil and blood, and seeks the imaginary power and the money wealth of the projected foe for himself. Antisemitism articulates a senseless and barbaric discontent with conditions. Its rebellion for concrete nature eliminates even the glimpse of a life beyond 'domination'. Because its anti-capitalism leaves capitalism entirely untouched, it is totalitarian in character as 'it seeks to make the rebellion of suppressed nature against domination directly useful to domination' to the point of utter destruction (Horkheimer and Adorno 1979: 195). Auschwitz is this destruction. For Adorno, it confirmed the bourgeois relations of pure identity as death. It identified Man as a metaphysical distraction to the business at hand. What counts is what can be numbered and subsists as such in a numbered

---

[14] The insight that capitalism is a monetary system is of crucial significance to the *Neue Marx Lektüre*; see Backhaus (1975); Arthur (2005); Lotz (2014); and Heinrich (2017).

[15] It is however the case that the contemporary populism proclaims against financial globalization ostensibly in order either to make the nation great again or to make the economy work for the many. Whilst the nationalism of the right articulates a nativist prejudice against globalization, the 'progressive nationalism' of the Left endorses an inward-looking, national-Keynesian response to financial globalization ostensibly in support of the national labour economy. On the nationalism of the left, see Radice (2014) and Bonefeld (2008). On the differences between them and on the 'national' logic that holds sway in the overlap, see Abromeit (2018).

manner – mere material. Every number is a resource, and if it is not, it is not worth anything at all. What cannot be used (anymore) is gassed and burnt. There is no time to waste.

Arbeit macht frei

It is important to distinguish between the *elements* of antisemitism, which are often unacknowledged and refuse to answer to that name, and fully fledged antisemitism, which is openly recognizable and goes by that name. Fundamentally, antisemitism 'is the rumor about the Jews' (Adorno 1974: 141). The rumoured Jew has no concrete existence. The Jew exists as an abstract and appears as an invisible, entirely intangible and cunning foe who is difficult to pin down. The elements of antisemitism reject the hated forms of capitalism and attribute them to the hidden nature of the intangible Jew, who like the Invisible Hand is everywhere and meddles in everything. The elements of antisemitism are innate to the conspiracy theory of capitalist development. According to the rumour, the cunning Jew stands behind phenomena, and who stands behind the phenomena is the hidden and invisible puppet-master of the world. Antisemitism is first of all an attempt at unmasking and making visible 'the Jew', be it by desecrating the soil of her final resting place or by attaching a star to her clothes and place of business. It is an attempt at making visible the grinning speculator behind the human facade. It does not matter who the concrete individual is. What matters is visibility, and what is made visible is marked out for ridicule, arson and destruction. What has fallen from its pedestal can be kicked with joyless pleasure and cheerful persistence. The elements of antisemitism, by contrast, do not necessarily entail the pogrom as its automatic destiny. They prepare the ground, point the finger, spread the rumour and establish the legitimation for this perverted rebellion against capitalism. Ulrike Meinhof, the late co-founder of the German Red Army Faction, gave a frighteningly poignant example of the rationalization of antisemitism as a hatred of capitalism when she wrote that

> Auschwitz meant that six million Jews were killed, and thrown on the waste-heap of Europe, for what they were: money Jews. Finance capital and the banks, the hard core of the system of imperialism and capitalism, had turned the hatred of men against money and exploitation, and against the Jews . . . Anti-Semitism is really a hatred of capitalism. (Meinhof, qtd in Rose 2014: 304)

Jews are murdered supposedly 'for what they are'; supposedly antisemitism 'really' is anti-capitalism: Meinhof slides here, possibly without being aware of it, from describing to articulating and voicing one of the most potent elements of antisemitism. When antisemites attack capitalism, what counts as success?[16]

The previous section argued that antisemites divide the social world between the hated abstract forms of capitalism, especially finance and money capital, and the

---

[16] On the question of success, see the contributions to Stoetzler (2014).

social world's concrete natural substance. The concrete is conceived as immediate, direct, matter for use, as well as rooted in industry and productive activity. Money, on the other hand, is not only conceived of as the root of all evil but also as rootless. It is judged to exist not only independently from industrial capital but also over and against it: the dynamic movements of money for the sake of more money erode the natural substance of the nation, its soil and its blood, its industry and productive enterprise. In this way, money and financial capital are identified with capitalism while industry and productive labour are perceived as constituting the concrete and creative being of a national people. Thus, industry and enterprise are 'made' capitalist by (Jewish) money: money penetrates all expressions of industry and thus perverts and disintegrates the community of the people in the name of finance capital's destructive quest for self-expansion. The force and power of money is seen to undermine the individual in terms of entrepreneurship, the creative in terms of national industry, the rooted in terms of the imagined traditions of blood and soil, the community in terms of a paternalist direction of use-value production. These elements of their ideology enable the antisemites not only to embrace and promote a productive, national form of capitalism but also to declare that labour leads to freedom.

The approval of the *Volksgenosse*, the comradely member of the national-racial community, as the personification of concrete nature, blood, soil and industry goes hand in hand with the denunciation of 'the Jew' as the personalized power of economic abstractions. In this manner, the ideology of blood and soil, on the one hand, and that of machinery and unfettered industrial expansion, on the other, are projected as images of a healthy nation that stands ready to purge itself from the perceived enemies of the national labour economy, that is, the abstract, universal, rootless, mobile, intangible, international 'vampire' of 'Jewish capitalism'. Extermination is itself an effort exerted in terms of concrete nature, directed at concrete human bodies and consisting of a material process, and thus industrialized. All *Volksgenossen* have committed the same deed and have thus become truly equal to each other: their efficiently discharged occupation only confirmed what they already knew – they had lost their individuality and were set loose as a hard-working subject of extermination. Antisemitism is the national fury that is set loose in the shape of a maddened subject seeking liberation from an imaginary foe whom it has identified and nailed down with name and address. Its furious affirmation of its own maddening reality is 'the substitute for the dream that humanity could organize its world humanely, a dream that a man-made world is stubbornly rejecting' (Adorno 1986: 124). Indeed, Auschwitz confirmed the 'stubbornness' of the principle of 'abstraction' not only through extermination for extermination's sake but also, and because of it, through 'abstractification'. The abstract concept 'Jew' was made into a cipher and thereby *made* abstract: whatever could be used was consumed and taken away – teeth, hair, skin, labour-power; whatever remained was made abstract, invisible, smoke disappearing into the air.

Everything is thus changed into pure nature. The economic abstraction was not only personalized but also 'abstractified'. At the gates of Auschwitz, the *Volksgenossen* made clear that money does not liberate anybody from concrete nature; in fact, they put up a sign there that pronounced with deadly intent that the labour of Auschwitz is to liberate the concrete from the abstract to the vanishing point of death. Not money but 'labor makes you free' – *Arbeit macht frei* – until the labouring ceases because the labourer is dead. Labour liberates the concrete from the abstract. Normality is death. Industry is the bond of soil and blood. Extermination is efficiently discharged. It manifests 'the stubbornness of the life to which one has to conform, and to resign oneself' (Horkheimer and Adorno 1979: 171).

Upon arrival at the factory of death, everybody was assessed for use. Those deemed unable to work were discarded without second thought. Those deemed able to work were worked until death liberated them from life. Auschwitz was a factory 'to destroy the personification of the abstract. Its organization was that of a fiendish industrial process, the aim of which was to "liberate" the concrete from the abstract. The first step was to dehumanize, that is, to strip away the "mask" of humanity, of qualitative specificity, and reveal the Jews for what "they really are" – shadows, ciphers, numbered abstraction', mere disposable human material. Then followed the process to 'eradicate that abstractness, to transform it into smoke, trying in the process to wrest away the last remnants of the concrete material "use-values": clothes, gold, hair, soap' (Postone 1986: 313–14). Adorno and Horkheimer's point that 'anti-Semitic behavior is generated in situations where blinded men robbed of their subjectivity are set loose as subjects' describes a pogrom: it does not capture the labour of Auschwitz (Horkheimer and Adorno 1979: 171). Nobody there was set loose. Everybody worked in a disciplined manner until the end with relentless dedication to achieve the task at hand. *Arbeit macht frei* addresses the rumour about the easy living Jews with industrialized intent. It says, Jews are put to work here until they are no more, and that is the *Volksgenossens'* labour of liberation.

Conclusion

In his critique of Carey's economic-nationalist ideas, Marx argued forcefully that 'these world-market disharmonies are merely the ultimate adequate expressions of the disharmonies which have become fixed as abstract relations within the economic categories, or which have a local existence on the smallest scale' (1973: 887).[17] Global 'disharmony' exists in and through the 'domestic relations' and vice versa. Yet it appears as if national state and economy are accountable to, and at the mercy of, a nebulous force personified as the global economy. 'National wealth', national industry, and national employment and wages are seen to be at the mercy of intangible outside forces that impose themselves upon a hard-working national people with devastating effect. Here on this side of the line, then, is the real community of a people, and over there, then, is the rootless, cosmopolitan speculator. The perception of the *nation* as a community of a people who are kept in submission to the exigencies of a (financialized)

---

[17] Henry Charles Carey (1793–1879) was the chief economic advisor to President Abraham Lincoln. He argued for an 'America First' economic strategy in line with Maddison's and later List's nationalist economic ideas, arguing that economic development ('infant industry') needs to be protected from world market pressures through a system of tariffs until it is able to conquer the world of wealth by its own efforts.

global economy is entirely regressive. It lends itself to the ideology of the nation as a subject of liberation, which is as irrational as the belief in a national nature, a national homogeneity of purposes and a national destiny, from the national industry via the national interest and the national history to the national being. The idea of the nation as the foundation of being and becoming turns the concept of 'cosmopolitanism' into a term of abuse. In its stead, it puts its faith in the imagined community of the nation as some naturally rooted and active thing, which it idolizes as the 'spirit of the people'. If indeed it is permissible at all to speak about the national spirit of the people, it is a national spirit not by nature but by history. By reducing history to nature or by reading nature into history, the struggle for national liberation from the strictures of the world market becomes delusional: peoples are forced to act as if they really are natural forces that have a national history.[18]

There is, says Adorno, a need for a 'practice that fights barbarism' (1962: 30). However, barbarism cannot be fought in a direct and immediate manner. What really does it mean to struggle against money, resist the movement of coins, combat the movement of interest rates, fight price movements and resist the law of (economic) value in a mode of social reproduction which is founded on a class of dispossessed surplus value producers? A 'practice that fights barbarism' is about the social relations that manifest themselves in the logic of seemingly self-moving economic forces. Clearly, it is impossible to hold coins responsible for their movement. The personalized critique of the movement of coins contains the elements of antisemitism. Personalization entails attribution. It attributes the fateful movements of the economic forces to the identifiable image of the national foe and demands retribution. The elements of antisemitism attribute blame and thus personalize the critique of the false society to the point of blind fury. The rumour about the Jews provides an outlet for anger and hatred, and a target which can be attacked at will.

The rumour about the Jews comprehends nothing. It is therefore all-pervasive and all-embracing. The Jew is said to stand behind the fateful economic phenomena and is thus condemned as a conspiring parasite. This condemnation is totalitarian in character in that it identifies the fateful dynamic of the economic forces with the character of the Jews, and what is identified as Jewish in character is secretly longed for. The antisemite speculates in death and banks the extracted gold teeth. Innate to (the elements of) antisemitism is the desire to live the beautiful life of the condemned Jew.

References

Abromeit, J. (2018), 'Frankfurt School Critical Theory and the Persistence of Authoritarian Populism in the United States', in J. Morelock (ed.), *Critical Theory and Authoritarian Populism*, 3–27, London: University of Westminster Press.
Achinger, C. (2013), 'Allegories of Destruction: "Women" and "the Jew" in Otto Weiniger's *Sex and Character*', *Germanic Review*, 88: 2.
Adorno, T. (1962), *Einleitung zur Musiksoziologie*, Frankfurt: Suhrkamp.

---

[18] This part draws on Adorno (2006: 100–2).

Adorno, T. (1974), *Minima Moralia*, London: Verso.
Adorno, T. (1986), 'What Does Coming to Terms with the Past Mean?', in G. Hartman (ed.), *Bitburg in Moral and Political Perspective*, 114–29, Bloomington: Indiana University Press.
Adorno, T. (1989), 'Society', in S. E. Bronner and D. Kellner (eds), *Critical Theory and Society*, 267–75, London: Routledge.
Adorno, T. (1990), *Negative Dialectics*, London: Routledge.
Adorno, T. (2006), *Lectures on History and Freedom*, Cambridge: Polity.
Adorno, T. (2022), 'Marx and the Basic Concepts of Sociological Theory', from a seminar transcript in the summer semester of 1962, in W. Bonefeld and C. O'Kane (eds), *Adorno and Marx*, 241–50, London: Bloomsbury.
Arthur, C. (2005), 'Value and Money', in F. Moseley (eds), *Marx's Theory of Money*, 111–23, London: Palgrave.
Backhaus, H.-G. (1975), 'Materialien zur Rekonstruktion der Marxschen Werttheorie 2', in *Gesellschaft. Beiträge zur Marxschen Theorie*, 3, 122–59, Frankfurt: Suhrkamp.
Bellofiore, R. (2009), 'A Ghost Turning into a Vampire', in R. Bellofiore and R. Fineschi (eds), *Re-reading Marx: New Perspectives after the Critical Edition*, 178–94, London: Palgrave.
Bolton, M., and H. Pitts (2018), *Corbynism*, London: Emerald.
Bonefeld, W. (1997), 'Notes on Anti-Semitism', *Common Sense*, 21, available at: www.academia.edu/5556368/Notes_on_Antisemitism (accessed 28 May 2023).
Bonefeld, W. (2004), 'On Postone's Courageous but Unsuccessful Attempt to Banish the Class Antagonism from the Critique of Political Economy', *Historical Materialism*, 12 (3): 103–24.
Bonefeld, W. (2008), 'Global Capital, National State, and the International', *Critique*, 36 (1): 63–72.
Bonefeld, W. (2010), 'Abstract Labour: Against Its Nature and on Its Time', *Capital & Class*, 34 (2): 257–76.
Bonefeld, W. (2014a), *Critical Theory and the Critique of Political Economy*, London: Bloomsbury.
Bonefeld, W. (2014b), 'Antisemitism and the Power of Abstraction: From Political Economy to Critical Theory', in M. Stoetzler (ed.), *Antisemitism and the Constitution of Sociology*, 314–32, Nebraska: University of Nebraska Press.
Bonefeld, W. (2020), 'Capital Par Excellence: On Money as an Obscure Thing', *Estudios de Filosofía*, 62, available at: www.scielo.org.co/scielo.php?pid=S0121-36282020000200033&script=sci_arttext&tlng=en (accessed 28 April 2023).
Braune, J. (2019), 'Who's Afraid of the Frankfurt School? "Cultural Marxism" as an Antisemitic Conspiracy Theory', *Journal of Social Justice*, 9: 1–25, available at: https://transformativestudies.org/wp-content/uploads/Joan-Braune.pdf (accessed 28 June 2023).
Butler, J. (2010), 'AVIVA-Interview with Judith Butler', *Online Magazine für Frauen*, 9 July, available at: https://aviva-berlin.de/aviva/Found.php?id=1427323 (accessed 11 April 2022).
Fischer, L. (2018), 'Antisemitism and the Critique of Capitalism', in B. Best, W. Bonefeld and C. O'Kane (eds), *The Sage Handbook of Frankfurt School Critical Theory*, vol. II, 916–31, London: Sage.
Heinrich, M. (2012), *An Introduction to the Three Volumes of Karl Marx's Capital*, New York: Monthly Review Press.
Heinrich, M. (2017), *Die Wissenschaft vom Wert*, Münster: Westfälisches Dampfboot.

Honneth, A. (2010), *The Pathologies of Individual Freedom*, Princeton, NJ: Princeton University Press.
Horkheimer, M., and T. Adorno ([1947] 1979), *Dialectic of Enlightenment*, London: Verso.
Keynes, J. M. ([1936] 2007), *The General Theory of Employment, Interest, and Money*, London: Palgrave.
Lange, E. L. (2018), 'Moishe Postone: Marx's Critique of Political Economy as Immanent Social Critique', in B. Best, W. Bonefeld and C. O'Kane (eds), *The Sage Handbook of Frankfurt School Critical Theory*, vol. I, 514–32, London: Sage.
Lapavitsas, C. (2012), 'Financialised Capitalism: Crisis and Financial Expropriation', in C. Lapavitsas, *Financialisation in Crisis*, 15–50, Leiden: Brill.
Lotz, C. (2014), *The Capitalist Schema*, Lanham, MD: Lexington.
Marx, K. (1966), *Capital*, vol. 3, Moscow: Progress.
Marx, K. (1972), *Theories of Surplus Value*, vol. III, London: Lawrence & Wishart.
Marx, K. (1973), *Grundrisse*, London: Penguin.
Marx, K. (1975), *Comments on James Mills. MECW*, vol. 3. London: Lawrence & Wishart.
Marx, K. (1976), *The Poverty of Philosophy, Collected Works* 6, London: Lawrence & Wishart.
Marx, K. (1987), *From the Preparatory Materials, Collected Works* 29, London: Lawrence & Wishart.
Marx, K. (1990), *Capital*, vol. I, London: Penguin.
O'Kane, C. (2018), 'Moishe Postone's New Reading of Marx', *Consecutio Rerum* (3), available at: www.consecutio.org/2018/11/okane_moishe-postones-new-reading-of-marx-the-critique-of-political-economy-as-a-critical-theory-of-the-historically-specific-social-form-of-labor/ (accessed 11 April 2022).
Petras, J. (2006), *The Power of Israel in the United States*, Atlanta, GA: Clarity.
Postone, M. (1986), 'Anti-Semitism and National Socialism', in A. Rabinbach and J. Zipes (eds), *Germans and Jews since the Holocaust*, 302–14, New York: Holmes & Meier.
Postone, M. (1993), *Time, Labor and Social Domination*, Cambridge: Cambridge University Press.
Postone, M. (2006), 'History and Helplessness: Mass Mobilization and Contemporary Forms of Anticapitalism', *Public Culture*, 18 (1): 93–110.
Radice, H. (2014), *Global Capitalism*, London: Routledge.
Reichelt, H. (2000), 'Jürgen Habermas' Reconstruction of Historical Materialism', in W. Bonefeld and K. Psychopedis (eds), *The Politics of Change*, 105–46, London: Palgrave.
Rose, P. L. (2014), *German Question/Jewish Question*, Cambridge, MA: Princeton University Press.
Smith, A. ([1776] 1981), *The Wealth of Nations*, Oxford: Oxford University Press.
Stoetzler, M. (ed.) (2014), *Antisemitism and the Constitution of Sociology*, Lincoln: University of Nebraska Press.
Stoetzler, M. (2018a), 'Dialectic of Enlightenment. Philosophical Fragments', in B. Best, W. Bonefeld and C. O'Kane (eds), *The Sage Handbook of Frankfurt School Critical Theory*, vol. I, 142–60, London: Sage.
Stoetzler, M. (2018b), 'Critical Theory and the critique of Anti-Imperialism', in B. Best, W. Bonefeld and C. O'Kane (eds), *The Sage Handbook of Frankfurt School Critical Theory*, vol. III, 1467–87, London: Sage.
Stögner, K. (2014), *Antisemitismus und Sexismus. Historisch-gesellschaftliche Konstellationen*, Baden-Baden: Nomos.
Ziege, E. M. (2009), *Antisemitismus und Gesellschaftstheorie*, Frankfurt: Suhrkamp.

4

Jews and other 'others': Identity and constellation in intersectional and Critical Theory

Christine Achinger

The rise of right-wing, populist and authoritarian politics all over the world gives a renewed urgency to seeking connections between struggles against racism, nationalism, antisemitism, misogyny, homo- and transphobia and other forms of hatred and exclusion.[1] At the same time, forging alliances between these causes seems to have become ever more difficult. The reasons for this are multiple and complex. Among them are what have been obstacles to solidarity for a long time: chiefly, perhaps, despite a growing general awareness of its disastrous trajectory, the capitalist status quo has a way of appearing without alternative and of undermining the subjective preconditions of effective critique of the social whole (cf. Fisher 2009). Relatedly, there is a refusal on the part of many in society to recognize discrimination and inequality and the need to remedy it, including a simple lack of empathy and urgency on the part of those who, as yet, still live comfortable lives. But some obstacles have also emerged from within radical politics. They include the rise of exclusionary forms of identity politics of various political stripes,[2] a notion that access to social recognition of past and present suffering is a zero-sum game, putting discriminated groups in a relationship of competition,[3] and the abandonment of a concept of society that would be able to theoretically grasp different forms of hierarchy, exclusion and discrimination and their origins and interconnections as socially rooted, instead of reducing them to the oppression of one group by another. The frequent reduction of forms of racialization to questions of skin colour makes it difficult to recognize antisemitism and forms of

---

[1] This contribution expands on Achinger 2022.
[2] Meyer (2002) and Haider (2018); instructive on the moralization of left-wing discourse also Fisher (2013). This is obviously not to say, though, that political practice that takes its starting point from specific experiences of discrimination and exclusion therefore has to be incapable of forming alliances; see on this, for example, the discussion of 'transversal politics' in Yuval-Davis (1997: 116–33).
[3] There is, of course, a sense in which teaching hours, museum space and funding for monuments or educational programmes are indeed limited resources, but such conflicts usually emerge not at the point where these limitations really turn into practical obstacles but at a much earlier stage of competing interpretations.

cultural and other racisms that do not follow this pattern,[4] restricts our understanding of the origins of racialization[5] and can facilitate the naturalization of racism itself. Furthermore, dualistic and reductive variants of anti-imperialism and increasingly polarized and simplistic perceptions of conflicts in many parts of the world, including, but by no means restricted to, the multiple conflicts in the Middle East and their complex history, also structure debates on antiracism and the struggle against antisemitism.[6] All of these factors promote what Paul Gilroy has called 'camp thinking', characterized by Manichean, moralizing and personalizing patterns of thought, the logic of 'the enemy of my enemy is my friend', a homogenizing and essentializing perception of groups and group interests, and the refusal to acknowledge historical and social complexity and contradictions (Gilroy 1999: 189).

This seems to make it all the more urgent, theoretically as well as politically, to investigate the connected origins of these various forms of projection and discrimination without denying their specificities, and to develop theoretical approaches able to describe their entanglement. On the one hand, approaches in the tradition of Critical Theory seem promising here. By 'Critical Theory', I mean the tradition from Marx to today that understands modernity as based on a conception of capitalist society, its changes and contradictions. This kind of analysis is not restricted to class relations: it understands capitalism as characterized by specific forms of social mediation, and aims at a comprehensive, historically specific theory of modernity that seeks to understand how social imperatives and dynamics assert themselves behind the backs of the people whose collective practice produces them in the first place. Critical Theory seeks to understand how this society generates new forms of subjectivity and intersubjectivity, and profoundly reshapes our relationships to the social and natural worlds. In this way, it opens up a perspective not only on the immanent *logic* and instrumental *rationality* of a capitalist society that increasingly subsumes all dimensions of individual and social life, but also on the systematic *irrationality* and the hate-filled projections of the 'other' that this society produces.

The first generation of thinkers of the 'Frankfurt School' have developed seminal analyses of modern antisemitism as integral to an understanding of capitalist society (Fischer 2018, Rensmann 2017). Other processes of essentialization, racialization[7]

---

[4] This is in part due to the dominance of British and US-American discourses in debates on racism and racialization and the specific histories of violence they respond to, but leads to erasures even in those historical contexts, as – among many other examples – the colonial and migration history of the Irish illustrates (cf. Virdee 2014: 3–4).

[5] Illuminating on capitalism and racialization is Guillaumin ([1977] 1988, 1995), whose work is also a key reference for Étienne Balibar's (1991a, 1991c) reflections on these issues.

[6] On anti-imperialism, see Postone (2006) and Stoetzler (2018).

[7] There is a long-standing debate on whether antisemitism should be seen as a form of group hatred *sui generis* or one very specific form of racialization. This debate derives some of its charge from the fact that in some political contexts, antisemitism is subsumed to a simplistic notion of racism as oppression, exploitation or political and economic exclusion. Seen through this lens, antisemitism – which works in very different ways – becomes hard to recognize, and can be downplayed or rendered invisible. (On the complex relationship of both see also Fischer 2016). On the other hand, attempts to describe antisemitism as completely disjunct and categorically different from all forms of racism can also tend to ignore the historical complexities of either by reducing them to diametrically opposed ideal types. These political issues make it harder to approach the question of appropriate conceptualization, which largely hinges, it seems to me, on the concepts of 'racism' and 'racialization' employed. The issue requires more extensive discussion, but in view of the wide

and constructions of gender, though, clearly play a more marginal role in their theoretical efforts, in spite of illuminating reflections whose potential ought to be further developed.[8] On the other hand, conceptions of intersectionality seem obvious candidates to turn to when trying to understand the connections between different constructions of 'otherness'.[9] The primary focus of most intersectional approaches is not so much the connections between ideologies, between different kinds of othering and discrimination where they emerge, in a specific society at a specific historical moment, but rather their connections at their point of impact, as it were, in their consequences for individuals who are subject to several such forms of inequality and oppression. There are nevertheless, within this theoretical field, extensive debates on the question of how to describe the interrelation between different forms of oppression and their origins (Stoetzler 2016). And while the potential of Critical Theory to illuminate processes of racialization and discrimination based on gender or sexuality is still underdeveloped, conversely, many variants of intersectional politics do not even include anti-Jewish hostility in their universe of intersectional discrimination (Stögner 2019), or even

---

range of cultural racisms and racisms not based on skin colour, many of which do not conform to the dominant paradigm of biologizing colonial racism against people imagined as inferior, a broad conception of racism and racialization as an essentializing construction of groups characterized by certain ascriptions (as e.g. in Balibar 1991a and 1991b) seems most productive to me. Such a conception would encompass antisemitism as one very specific kind of group hatred, but would by no means lessen the importance of understanding the specificities of modern antisemitism as, crucially, a fantasy of immense, but invisible power and conspiracy that associates Jews with the dark sides of capitalist modernity and sees them as threats to an imagined community. This makes antisemitism appear as a defence against the powerful and is also responsible for the fact that simplistic forms of left-wing politics seem more open to antisemitism than to (other forms of) racism.

[8] Adorno and Horkheimer's critique of instrumental rationality in *Dialectic of Enlightenment* was important for some strands of feminist theory, and the work contains insightful remarks on notions of femininity and the origins of misogyny, and connects these impulses also to antisemitic sentiments: The hatred of women, as of Jews, is the hatred of nature, perceived as threatening, with which they are both associated ([1947] 1969, 119–20; see also my discussion of Weininger below). Adorno's *Minima Moralia* ([1955] 1987: 119–21) also contains some astute observations about the notion of the 'feminine character'. These reflections remain unsystematic and disconnected, however (more generally on Adorno, the Frankfurt School and feminist theory, see Ziege [2004, 2007], Heberle [2006], Hewitt [1992] and O'Neill [1999]). Regarding analyses of racism and racialization: in *The Authoritarian Personality* (Adorno et al. 1950), both antisemitism and racism/ethnocentrism are among the attitudes measured and linked to this personality type, and authoritarian aggression, as described in this study, continues to be one powerful explanation for racist and anti-migrant attitudes (cf. Rensmann 2017: 65–143; see e.g. Marz [2017] on the degree to which these concepts can still be useful to describe contemporary racism and antisemitism). The explanatory potential of the concept of projection employed so productively in Adorno's and Horkheimer's reflections on antisemitism, though, seems underdeveloped in particular when it comes to their engagement with other forms of racialization (though some other authors more recently productively referred to their thinking to approach related issues; see e.g. Gilroy [1993 and 2000]; Fischer [2016]), and in spite of the fact that Adorno and Horkheimer insist on the social origins of all these forms of hatred and exclusion, their interrelations remain underexplored in their work.

[9] The term is frequently credited to Crenshaw (1989), but debates on questions of intersectionality, in particular within Black Feminism, date back further (e.g. Combahee River Collective [1977] 1983; see also hooks 1981 and Hill Collins 1990), and from a contemporary perspective, e.g. the criticisms by socialist and working class women of the mostly middle-class women's movement of the late 19th century can be said to explicitly address intersectional issues.

contribute to such hostility.[10] It therefore seems politically and theoretically all the more important to explore the possibilities of a productive dialogue between Critical Theory and those theories of intersectionality that do not reproduce these patterns, a dialogue aimed at challenging these various blind spots and their underlying causes, and to gauge what each of these approaches can contribute to an understanding of the connections and contradictions between ideas of race, gender and Jewishness. As a first step towards such an investigation, this chapter is going to explore some implications of Adorno's concept of the constellation for such a critical dialogue.

In order to give some historical grounding to my reflections, though, I would first like to introduce three examples for varying conceptualizations of alterity and their interrelation from different moments in Germany's and Austria's 'long nineteenth century'. They illustrate how different discourses of alterity respond to new and changing problems connected to the rise of capitalist modernity, and hence are linked to each other even where they do not directly intersect. They also highlight how these developments fundamentally reconfigure pre-capitalist forms of difference, so that both their continued existence and their transformations have to be understood as aspects of this new society.

The state as the sphere of abstract equality: Jewish and female emancipation in the eighteenth century

My first example consists of two interconnected late-eighteenth-century Enlightenment texts: firstly, Christian Wilhelm Dohm's influential call for Jewish emancipation, *Über die bürgerliche Verbesserung der Juden* (*On the Civic Improvement of the Jews*), published in 1781, followed in 1783 by a second part under the same title documenting the ensuing debate; and secondly, an early feminist satirical diatribe by Theodor Gottlieb von Hippel, *Über die bürgerliche Verbesserung der Weiber* (*On the Civic Improvement of Women*) from 1792, borrowing the title of Dohm's widely discussed intervention.[11] Both texts can be seen as paradigmatic illustrations of the connection between philosophical, political and social change during the rise of bourgeois society, and they already give an inkling of what could be described, with Horkheimer and Adorno, as a kind of 'dialectic of Enlightenment'. Both demand to take seriously the programmatic emphasis on equality that accompanied the revolutions of the late eighteenth century, and to extend this political equality beyond its initial restriction to – depending on the national context and historical moment – white, gentile and/or protestant men of property. In both cases, though, the ensuing debates already point

---

[10] This has also become apparent in some particularly high-profile political conflicts, such as the debates within the anti-Trump 'Women's March' movement in 2017/18, or the events at the Chicago Dyke March in June 2017, where some participants were ejected from the march for carrying a rainbow flag with a Star of David, and the debates surrounding both events (cf. Stögner 2019: 386–90). On the exclusion of antisemitism from anti-racist and other forms of left-wing activism, see also Stögner (2017: 28); Taylor (2017); Arnold (2015); Arnold and Taylor (2019).

[11] In spite of the historic significance of Dohm's text and the ensuing debate, there is still no complete English translation. All translations from the German original are therefore my own.

towards the emergence of new notions of essential – national or biological – difference along the lines of Jewishness, race and gender that should come to justify novel forms of exclusion.

In spite of all differences of genre – Dohm's is an earnest sociopolitical argument for reform in the best interest of both the Jews and the common weal, Hippel's a biting satirical attack – both argue for legal equality in similar ways, on the one hand by invoking a universalist idea of human rights, and on the other with pragmatic reference to the *raison d'état*. According to Dohm, by maintaining a feudal system of group-specific rights and privileges and the exclusion of Jews from full participation in society and productive activity, the state deprives itself of an important resource (1781: 1–12, 28). Furthermore, this exclusion creates an impoverished segment of the population, reduced to peddling, pawnbroking and begging for survival, a situation that undermines moral principles and is detrimental to the common good (31–5). Moreover, the legal discrimination of Jews, according to Dohm, constitutes an obstacle for social, legal and economic modernization (25–6, 114). He counters the argument that the unequal treatment of Jews is only a response to their moral corruption by pointing out that this constituted 'the fallacy . . . of invoking the ill produced by the heretofore faulty politics to justify those same politics' (33–4).

Instead, according to Dohm, religious – and hence also Jewish – difference should become but one among many in emerging bourgeois society: 'Thus nobility, bourgeois and peasant; town-dweller and countryman; warrior and unarmed man; scholar and layman; artist and amateur [*Ungeweihter*] separate. In this way one guild, one trade, one occupation within the state separates its adherents from all others, and thus Christian, and Jew, and Moslem segregate from each other' (25–6; my translation). It is therefore

> the great and noble task of the government . . . to tone down the excluding contradictions of all these different associations in such a way that they are not detrimental to the great community that encompasses them all; that each of these divisions only incites competition and activity without producing aversion and distance, and that they all dissolve into the great harmony of the state. (26)

In this way, Dohm clearly situates his political suggestions in the radical social transformation from feudal to bourgeois society, in the process of separation of civil society, as the sphere of concrete difference and beneficial competition of the *bourgeois*, and the state as the sphere of abstract equality of the *citoyen*, turning the individual who belongs to both into a dual being.[12]

---

[12] This contradiction between particular identity and general human 'essence' is inherent in the way the subject is constituted within and by bourgeois society. 'The qualitative and particular differences which concretely make individuals who they are appear inessential to them, while the generic equality which appears to characterize their subjectivity is abstract, formal and illusory. The 'ideal community' of the state is grounded in this denial of difference (whilst concretely regulating the relations which constitute it)', as Derek Sayer (1991: 87) sums up Marx's analysis of this process. Sayer thus already points out the fact that these 'qualitative and particular differences' – whether those of the individual or pertaining to, and defining, groups – are themselves, at least in part, constituted by the same society that upholds the illusion of their absence in the political

For Dohm, religious – and hence also Jewish – difference should become merely one among many forms of 'private' difference in emerging civil society, alongside status, wealth or occupation. Even differences between the estates, which formerly determined the legal position of the individual, are depoliticized and transformed into mere elements of a pluralist society. The state, as the sphere of abstract synthesis, takes on the role of taming all those antagonisms and of transforming them into nothing but beneficial economic competition and the enlightening contest of opinions. 'It has achieved its great aim when the nobleman, the peasant, the scholar, the craftsman, the Christian and the Jew is, above all this, a citizen' (26).

With this model, Dohm is far ahead of the societal reality of the Prussia of his days, but he indicates where he expected the journey to go. The measures he suggests amount to the near-complete legal equality of Jews – only public office was to be opened to Jews just in exceptional cases until the process of assimilation had further progressed (118) – accompanied by measures to incite parts of Prussian Jewry to take up a craft or move into agriculture and to reduce their concentration in trade, flanked by educational measures directed at both Jews and Christians to reduce mutual prejudice, and the granting of independence in religious affairs to Jews.

None of the German states, though, subsequently enacted Dohm's suggestions, and the debate documented in the second volume of his work already indicates that the arguments of the opponents of Jewish emancipation were already beginning to undergo a modernization of sorts that pointed ahead to the rise of modern antisemitism. Firstly, rather than following Dohm's suggestion of immediate and near-complete emancipation as a matter of principle and a path to assimilation, in the German countries, evidence of assimilation was in fact made a *precondition* for a slow and gradual granting of equal rights, with momentous consequences. Not only did it place Jews under permanent observation and suspicion, measured against a mutable standard they could never meet, but it also introduced a more fundamental distinction. Feudal society had been based on different rights and privileges for a whole range of different groups. In this new political universe, however, where abstract legal equality as *citoyen*, as citizen, is supposedly rooted in the equality as *homme*, as human being, to deny equality as man and citizen specifically to just this one group because of their concrete inequality as *bourgeois*, as participants in civil society, transforms Jewish difference from one difference among many into a categorical issue. It de facto excludes Jews from full, legally enshrined humanity and undermines Dohm's insistence that 'the Jew is even more a man than he is a Jew!' (26).

Secondly, in response to Dohm's enlightened attack on the relevance of religion in the political and legal sphere, we can see a secularization of the frame of reference on the part of the opponents as well, who now move the debate onto the field of cultural, national and eventually ethnic difference. The prominent theologian and orientalist Johann David Michaelis, for example, transforms the relevant opposition from that of Jews versus Christians to Jews versus Germans, thus pre-empting

---

sphere. They do not, therefore, constitute some sort of 'authentic' identity that could serve, in an unproblematic manner, as an emancipatory counterpoint to abstract and illusory universalism.

the later exclusion of Jews from the German nation.[13] This kind of rationalization and ultimately naturalization of difference, once older religious or traditionalist justifications for inequality lose their power, connects Enlightenment debates on Jewishness with contemporary discussions on race or gender (e.g. see Honegger 1996; Hentges 1999).

Hippel's witty attack on the misogynist status quo on the one hand rejects the invocation of 'nature' as biological difference with a range of different arguments, and on the other hand affirms 'nature' in a different sense, referring to 'natural rights' and the appeal to equality as the natural order of society. Like others at the time, Hippel's text raises the question if this equivocation in the concept of 'nature' inadvertently might have left an opening to an argument that in different ways would also complicate debates on Jewish emancipation: the notion that ontological, empirically observable equality of some kind would have to be the basis and precondition of legal equality, a kind of equality that in fact is only constituted by society. In the words of Hannah Arendt: 'We are not born equal; we become equal as members of a group on the strength of our decision to guarantee ourselves mutually equal rights' ([1951] 1979: 301). Both in the case of the emancipation of Jews and that of women, debates soon shifted from a dispute about dogma and tradition towards the assertion of ontological, empirically demonstrable difference that was to serve as a novel, pseudo-rational legitimization of inequality (cf. also Honegger 1996).

In spite of those parallels, though, one can also observe a telling divergence in the relationship of emancipation and modernization in both writers. When Hippel sounds the attack against 'those chivalrous *Bastilles*, those domestic prisons and bourgeois dungeons that the fair sex finds itself in' ([1792] 1977: 17–18), he pinpoints the emerging separation of domestic and public sphere that should become a basis for the growing polarity of gender roles and images – the association of masculinity with rationality, autonomy, competition and struggle, and of femininity with emotion, family bonds and care – as a key issue. The social constitution of a supposedly extra-social sphere, the historically produced notion of a place outside history are core features of the construction of gender in bourgeois society (cf. Hausen 1992; Frevert 1988: 16).

The very same process – the rise of modern, bourgeois society with a homogenous political and social sphere – that, according to Dohm, turned any special status for Jews into an anachronism, thus also reinforced the separation of the public and domestic spheres that should become the foundation of increasingly polarized notions of gender difference. As noted before, the debate about Jewish difference was also soon caught in the maelstrom of nationalization and naturalization that had already been inherent in the Enlightenment opening. Seeing both texts and the surrounding debates as part of the same picture thus illustrates how the rise of bourgeois society simultaneously produced a dynamic in the direction of increased equality *and* new, essentializing notions of difference that underpinned *new* kinds of exclusion, and

---

[13] Cf. Dohm's reprint of Michaelis's review of his book in its second volume (1783). Moses Mendelssohn promptly identifies this shift in the terms of the debate, in a comment published in the same volume, as a strategy of permanent exclusion from the community (1783: 75–6).

how the same processes of social change can have divergent effects on different groups. Both texts also illustrate, however, that neither the postmodern dismissal of the Enlightenment as totalitarian and responsible for racist, sexist and antisemitic exclusions nor the liberal notion that the problem with the eighteenth-century Enlightenment was only the incomplete realization of its ideals can do justice to the entanglement of historicization and naturalization, emancipation and exclusion.

The nation as concrete community in Gustav Freytag's *Debit and Credit*

My second example, Gustav Freytag's 1855 novel *Debit and Credit* (*Soll und Haben*), is virtually forgotten today but was the most widely read German novel of the second half of the nineteenth century. In it, constructions of Jewishness, racializing colonial discourses, notions of status and estate and intersectionally diverse images of gender interact to paint the picture of a specifically German path to capitalist modernity, free of antagonism and alienation. While for Dohm, the guarantor of social cohesion after the gradual demise of the static feudal order was still the state as the sphere of abstract synthesis, for Freytag it is the nation as concrete community.

As a novel of education, the text narrates the development of young Anton Wohlfart from a romantic youth to a steadfast young merchant. Anton is almost lured off the path to a solid middle-class existence by his infatuation with the young noblewoman Lenore von Rothsattel, and has to struggle with Polish insurgents against Prussian rule and an assortment of Jewish crooks, led by the novel's anti-hero Veitel Itzig and the Jewish trader Ehrenthal. Anton's return into the fold of the middle classes is eventually sealed by his engagement to Sabine, the younger sister of his employer, the upstanding merchant Schröter, and his entry as a partner in Schröter's trading company.

The novel is thus structured through a number of oppositions and conflicts: between nobility and middle class, German merchants and Jewish traders, German settlers and Polish rebels, and conflicting models of aristocratic and bourgeois masculinity and femininity. All these oppositions also articulate core problems associated with the rise of capitalist modernity in the nineteenth century and translate them from inherent social tensions and contradictions into external conflicts between groups. At their centre is a notion of 'German labour' as concrete mediation and productive, morally directed and community-building activity (Freytag [1855] 1923: vol. 2, 302). This kind of labour is the preserve of the German middle class in the text. The nobility and the Poles appear incapable of methodical and dedicated work, and while the Jews are restlessly busy, their activity is only motivated by egoistic profit interest (see also Achinger 2018).

More specifically, those parts of the novel set in Poland develop a colonial discourse of the East: The Poles are stuck on the feudal rung of the historical ladder, in an unproductive and disorganized pre-modernity, and in their own best interest have to be dragged – by force if necessary – into a productive, ordered, 'German' modernity. As the narrative develops, this justification shifts, the ability to perform 'German labour' and the associated economic and military strength increasingly turn into a testament of quasi-racial superiority, and domination is legitimized solely through this hierarchy (for more detail on these racial discourses, see Achinger 2007: 131–65).

This contrast between beneficial German modernity and unproductive Polish pre-modernity is supplemented by a split in the image of modernity itself, opposing a 'good' German to a 'bad' Jewish kind of modernity. The former represents progress, productivity and community, while the latter comes to stand for all those aspects of modernity that seem to threaten this national community, for materialism, antagonism and fragmentation, and in general the domination of abstract over concrete dimensions of social and economic life.[14] These oppositions become apparent in the contrast between the 'Jewish' and 'German' faces of the city as well as in the economic realm, though not in the familiar antisemitic opposition between 'German' production and 'Jewish' circulation, but running through both spheres: as a contradiction between good versus bad, credit-based industrial production, and beneficial versus destructive forms of trade. German agricultural industry seems to grow out of the soil, its pipes mimicking the stems of plants, it reconciles old and new modes of production and itself appears alive and natural (Freytag [1855] 1923: vol. 1, 447). Industrialization financed through credit, as instigated by the Jewish crooks, however, takes a different course. It is subject to the imperative of profit maximization, which constitutes a form of abstract domination and demands the violation of nature; crop failure and social decline will ensue. The destructive potential of this kind of modernization lies, therefore, not in industrial technology itself but in the growth of the credit sector and the lust for profit.

The most striking illustration of this contrast between 'Jewish' and 'German' modernity, however, lies in both groups' relationship to the commodity itself. Itzig's activity is exclusively directed towards exchange value; the concrete, material qualities of the goods he trades only matter to him to the extent that they influence the price. For him, objects only count as carriers of value. Even the concrete character of his own feverish activity is insubstantial to him, it is reduced to a series of transactions directed towards ever more of the same, of increased profit, and can never come to rest in any final satisfaction.

In the world of the German merchants, on the other hand, use value is all that matters. Over many pages, readers can perceive, as it were, the shapes, colours and smells of the colonial goods in the vaults and attics of the merchant's house in all their sensual richness through Anton's eyes and nose; their character as carriers of value is hardly ever mentioned. The magic and mystery of the world of commodities result from the fact that the global context of production is made visible in the objects: 'These bast-fibre mats had been woven by a Hindu woman, that chest had been painted with red and black hieroglyphs by a diligent Chinese, the wickerwork over there had been tied

---

[14] Postone (1993) analyses the social origins of the apparent separation of abstract and concrete dimensions of capitalist society, where only the former appear as historically and socially specific, the latter as transhistorical and natural. Already in 'Anti-Semitism and National Socialism: Notes on the German Reaction to "Holocaust"' (1980), he describes the association of forms of abstract domination in capitalism with 'the Jews' in modern antisemitism. The perception of Jews as personified counter-principle of the national community inherent in this association, already described by Postone, is studied more extensively in Holz (2001) and – with specific reference to antisemitism on the Left – Haury (2002).

over the bale by a negro [*Neger*] from Kongo in the services of the Virginian planter' (Freytag [1855] 1923: vol. 1, 70). Here, commodities appear as products of concrete human labour, performed by various individuals in all their diversity. For Anton, they turn into the 'source of a peculiar kind of poetry' (70), at the same time tokens of exotic enchantment and materialization of a totality produced through concrete labour and spanning the globe. Not just the colonial context and the dimension of direct coercion and violence are actively denied in this description – as when slave labour is rendered invisible as 'service' for the planter – but the context of a capitalist world market has likewise disappeared. Commodities are being described as if they had been produced with their use in mind, not their sale, let alone profit. This description narratively replaces mediation through the market, motivated by self-interest, with the suggestion of a consciously social form of production. Accordingly, Anton sees himself as participant in a conscious global mediation between producers and consumers that is governed by moral imperatives. Atomization and alienation are remedied, the fact that – in Marx's slightly later diagnosis – social relations in capitalism appear 'not as directly societal relations between individuals in their labours but as what they really are, material relations between persons and societal relations between things (*sachliche Verhältnisse der Personen und gesellschaftliche Verhältnisse der Sachen*)' (Marx [1867] 1972: 87; Marx 1976: 166 [translation amended])' is narratively reversed. In this way even colonial trade turns into a moral enterprise, and the powerlessness of the individual in the face of social and economic forces is transformed into free decision-making and agency.

At the same time, in the Jewish characters, alienation, self-interest and the destructive consequences of abstract social mediation are presented as merely the contingent and avoidable result of a malicious Jewish attitude. In spite of their contrary character, then, the anti-Slavic colonial racism and the antisemitism of the novel combine to stabilize the idea of a German path to an unalienated, beneficial modernity.

The intersectionally diverse gender discourses of the novel are intertwined with this narrative of modernity in multiple ways.[15] In the decline of the Rothsattel family and in Anton's turning away from his youthful fascination with the splendour of their world, the replacement of an ideal of warlike, passionate, splendid and status-conscious aristocratic masculinity by the self-disciplined, rational, self-controlled bourgeois man, committed to achievement and the common good, is enacted. However, in Anton's relationship to Lenore, this education of the bourgeois man becomes visible as a schooling in renunciation and a prohibition on female passion.

Lenore is a child of nature; she pushes into the open, transcending physical, national, class and gender boundaries. While young Anton is fascinated by Lenore's vitality, once matured into a bourgeois man, the hero increasingly rejects her violations of bourgeois norms of femininity. At a ball on a Polish nobleman's estate, for example, the bourgeois Anton acts as guardian of national values and borders against the cosmopolitan nobility (Freytag [1855] 1923: vol. 2, 155). Their blurring is in particular blamed on Lenore, whose passion in dance breaks with explicitly nationally defined gender norms. Worse still, her flirtation with Polish officers directly

---

[15] On the complex gender discourses of the novel, see also Achinger (2007: 245–89).

violates her female role as biological reproducer of national boundaries. Here, female honour turns into a symbol of national honour.[16] The figure of Lenore throws the entanglement of all these demarcations along the lines of class, gender and national identity into stark relief.

When Anton begins to turn his back on Lenore, however, this is not due to an actual loss of attraction but due to a moral taboo. Contrary to all programmatic statements by the hero and the narrator, again and again the text reveals deep ambivalence surrounding the taboo against female passion, which also presupposes the suppression of male desire. Each time Anton becomes aware of Lenore's vital attractiveness, this insight is neutralized immediately – as if startled by this recognition – in the assertion of her lack of femininity (e.g. Freytag [1855] 1923: vol. 2, 231). It becomes clear, however, that Anton's secret desires continue to exist – what has changed is merely that he is now ready to renounce and deny them, to censor whatever does not correspond to bourgeois norms.

While Lenore represents the 'other' outside of bourgeois society, temptation through nature, Sabine with her 'attitude of a homemaker' (*hausmütterliche Haltung*) (vol. 1, 294) embodies the 'other' within bourgeois society that compensates its coldness and sobriety. Against the young nobleman Fink's admiration of American unsentimentality, Sabine fights to endow the disenchanted world again with colour and meaning by means of the imagination (vol. 1, 300–1). This defence of the 'German' variant of modernization against the American, and implicitly the Jewish, one can be read as an exposition of the poetic programme of 'sublimation' (*Verklärung*), of the compensation of alienation through narrative production of meaning, to which *Soll und Haben* is committed.

Freytag's novel renders visible how different constructions of race, nation, gender and Jewishness are interconnected as parts of an ideological picture of the German path to modernity. This picture is shaped by changing socio-historical experience: Where in Dohm and Hippel it is still the state as the sphere of abstract equality that is supposed to guarantee social synthesis, in Freytag it is the nation as ethnic/cultural, concrete community and haven from the devastations of capitalist modernity that takes over this role.

Identity as quasi-biological substance: Otto Weininger's *Sex and Character*

My third example is Otto Weininger's equally influential and infamous 1903 book *Sex and Character* (Geschlecht und Charakter), which seeks to deduct the crisis of modernity from the conflict of male and female principles and the opposition of Aryan and Jew. While in the first, much shorter part of the book, described by Weininger as 'biological and psychological', he writes as a follower of empirical psychology, the second and main 'psychological and philosophical' part is written from an explicitly

[16] On the different dimensions of women's role in reproducing national and ethnic boundaries see Yuval-Davis (1997: 45–6), Anthias and Yuval-Davis (1989: 9–10) and McClintock (1997: 90).

anti-positivist perspective, tackling the 'most elevated and ultimate questions' (Weininger [1903] 1908: 5) and proudly venturing into metaphysics. From one part of the book to the other, Weininger transforms himself from a modernist sceptic of the idea of a coherent self, detached from the realm of biology and physiology, to its staunch defender. Correspondingly, his initial theory of universal bisexuality, where masculinity and femininity are still imagined akin to two substances that can be found in every cell of the body, is quickly replaced by a polar discourse of sex and gender. Weininger's 'ideal man' and Aryan is a kind of hypertrophy of the notion of the Enlightenment subject as rational, autonomous, self-transparent, characterized by self-control and impermeable subject boundaries, and elevated above time and decay. The 'ideal woman' and 'the Jew', on the other hand, are both 'blurrers of boundaries' (424) and mortal threats to the ideal man, even though in different ways.

Substantial amounts of research have focused on the commonalities between Weininger's 'ideal woman' and 'the Jew'. Weininger's insistence on the categorical *differences* between 'woman' and 'Jew', however, have rarely if ever been studied. This concerns, for example, the diverse reasons for their apparent commonality in adaptability and their lack of stable personality: While the 'woman' is 'matter' that '*passively* takes on any form', the Jew is active and aggressive; he 'actively adapts to any environment and any race, just as the parasite who becomes a different one in every host'. Moreover, 'the woman is *not at all*, the Jew is *eminently* gifted for *conceptual thinking*' (436–7; here and in the following, all italics and bold face in the original). The intellectual activity of the Jew, however, is not creative like that of the Aryan; he is a critic and sceptic, '*the* **unbelieving** human', who 'does not put down roots', which is also manifest in 'his preference for mobile capital' (437–8; the word 'unbelieving' is bold in the original), his talents for corrosive journalism, instrumental rationality in the sciences and his close connections to capitalism as well as communism. In short: '*The spirit of modernity* is *Jewish*, whichever way you look at it' (440). In this way, Weininger's characterization of 'the Jew' radicalizes modern antisemitism, whose early forms can already be found in Freytag, as well as the former's still ambivalent association of woman and nature, now based on a disenchanted notion of nature as mere material.

As I have argued elsewhere, reading Weininger with Horkheimer and Adorno's *Dialectic of Enlightenment* ([1947] 1969) can illuminate this double opposition against 'the ideal woman' and 'the Jew' (Achinger 2013). These two different counter-poles against the Aryan male can be read as personifications of two fundamental contradictions in the constitution of the modern subject itself. In this perspective, the 'ideal woman' appears as an embodiment of the threat to the supposedly rational, autonomous, clearly bounded bourgeois subject, connoted as male, from its own embodied existence, from what Horkheimer and Adorno describe as 'nature within the subject' ([1947] 1969: 47). This embodied existence makes it impossible to ever really rise above physical and emotional needs, sexual impulses, age, sickness and decay. 'The effort to hold itself together attends the ego at all its stages, and the temptation to be rid of the ego has always gone hand-in-hand with the blind determination to preserve it' (40; Horkheimer and Adorno 2002: 26). The constant fear of relapsing into nature is projected outward in the hatred of women as temptresses. In the words of

Horkheimer and Adorno: 'Woman as an allegedly natural being is a product of history, which denatures her . . . To eradicate utterly the hated but overwhelming temptation to lapse back into nature – that is the cruelty which stems from failed civilization; it is barbarism, the other side of culture' (119; Horkheimer and Adorno 2002: 87–8).

'The Jew', by contrast, seems associated with the threat originating from modern society itself. It produces the allegedly autonomous individual as an ideal, while constantly revoking that autonomy and uniqueness through a network of dependencies, through a social dynamism beyond individual and collective control, and the levelling of individuality in mass society.

Modern bourgeois individuals can never truly overcome their embodied existence or their dependency on a society that threatens to abolish them. Therefore, these threatening aspects continually have to be exorcized through outward projection on 'the woman' or 'the Jew' in Weininger's text. Thus personified, they can be fought, controlled or overcome. To see those two figures and their commonalities as well as differences as part of one and the same picture facilitates a more differentiated understanding of the dual crisis of modernity and masculinity at the turn to the twentieth century.

Identity and constellation

These three examples might give an impression of how, in a particular textual universe and a specific historical moment, discourses of alterity respond to changing configurations in the development of capitalist modernity. Such discourses are therefore connected and mutually illuminate each other – and the society that gives rise to them – even where they do not directly intersect, as in the image of the 'effeminate Jew' or racialized femininity.[17] Even though these examples are textual representations, they are deeply interwoven with the real social production of inequality. These discourses of gender, race and Jewishness emerge in part as rationalizations of existing or justifications of newly produced inequalities and forms of domination. In other cases they are personifying projections of longings, taboos or fears resulting from the threatening, alienating and opaque aspects of capitalist modernity or the precarious and contradictory constitution of the modern subject in it. The comprehensive understanding of capitalist modernity suggested by Critical Theory therefore allows to analyse the changing and contradictory images of various 'others' as embedded in structured forms of social practice, rather than as mere cultural artefacts.

These images shape social practice in turn, and the concrete experiences of those who are subsumed under them. Identities are formed in the tensions between inclusive or exclusive practices and ascriptions, and the individual and collective resistance against them. Individual and collective identities are therefore, to riff on de Beauvoir, not simply a question of who we are but who we have become, that is, who we have

---

[17] On the social co-constitution of images of femininity and Jewishness, see also Stögner (2014) and AG Gender-Killer (2005).

been turned into. This raises two closely interrelated and equally challenging issues, that of the materiality of identity and that of the standpoint of critique.

Firstly, when de Beauvoir insists that women are not born but made, she does not thereby declare women or femininity to be mere figments of the imagination. The way we have been socially 'made' cannot easily be undone, and this making does not just concern such seemingly changeable features as clothing, gender roles or social position, but the very ways bodies are imagined and experienced and the – often violent – histories inscribed in them. These social constructions do not just shape the valuation of certain identities but create the very boundaries that define who belongs and does not belong to a certain group, even if that group is perceived as 'natural'.[18] The twin facts that identities are both socially and culturally created and yet have material force need to be reflected in all analyses. This raises the question how a non-essentialist politics can be developed that still does not deny, in the name of some abstract universalism, the reality and material power of socially created identities, and does not end up taking away voice and visibility from those who have been denied either for centuries[19] – but that also does not conflate subjective experience and belonging with political positioning, in a move where ultimately each group is perceived as only having legitimate interest in its own liberation (Ibrahim et al. 2012).

Secondly, because the subjects of emancipatory politics are at the same time parts and products of the very status quo that they oppose, any social critique necessarily has to have a self-reflective moment. This is where Critical Theory converges with those versions of intersectional theory that problematize essentializing notions of identity in similar ways and seek to form alliances, rather than turning intersectionality into the identity-political fundament of ever more narrowly circumscribed group identities, defined by an agonistic or competitive relationship to other such identities.[20] This view of identities as produced does not, of course, foreclose a political practice based on shared experiences of oppression and exclusion, whether this is described with Spivak's notion of 'strategic essentialism' (1993: 60–1) – since disavowed by her because of its widespread use to justify nationalist essentialism (2008: 260) – with Yuval-Davis's (1997: 116–33; 2011: 197–9) concept of 'transversal politics' or simply as solidarity. But it does open up such politics for the formation of coalitions and helps guard against naturalization and group homogenization, against the erection of rigid outward boundaries.

In Critical Theory, we can already find attempts to engage with these dialectical tensions. Much of Adorno's philosophy is an extended reflection on the fact that we have been constituted as subjects by the very society we try to criticize and hope to change, and he does so conscious of his own positionality as one who, in this society, has been empowered to speak: 'Criticizing privilege becomes a privilege – the world's

---

[18] For example, the issue is not just that Blackness, in the context of colonialism and slavery, has been devalued in most of Western culture for the past centuries, but the very notion of 'Blackness' and who is seen as 'Black' is a consequence of social relations (Guillaumin ([1977] 1988; Miles 1993: 2–9; Goldberg 1993: 148–55).

[19] bell hooks (1991) traces the manifestations of this tension in the classroom. Illuminating in this context are also Anthias and Yuval-Davis (1989: 4).

[20] See also Yuval-Davis (2006: 195; 2010: 268).

course is as dialectical as that' ([1966] 1973: 41) ('Kritik am Privileg wird zum Privileg: so dialektisch ist der Weltlauf'; Adorno [1966] 1988: 49). And his reflections on the 'primacy of the object' could, among many other things, be seen as attempts to come to grips with the simultaneous materiality and social genesis of subjects and subjectivities. In true materialistic fashion, for Adorno, the body itself and the way it is lived and experienced is deeply shaped by society and culture, as is the very notion of a realm of 'nature' that is opposed to history, while at the same time there is no intellectual impulse that is not rooted in our physical being.

Adorno describes the experience of the contradiction between the particular and the general concept, between the individuals and the ascriptions of identity under which they are subsumed, as experience of 'non-identity'. His characterization of the process by which this experience necessitates not the rejection of conceptual thinking per se but, on the contrary, the invocation of further concepts, further differentiations, which are gathered around the object without ever fully grasping it, is reminiscent of the inherent logic of some intersectional analyses.

When Kimberlé Crenshaw (1989) points out that the situation of Black women is not reflected in a legal system that operates with generalizing conceptions of 'woman' based on the experience of white women, and assumptions about the discrimination of 'Black' people that are based on the reality of Black men, and that neither of them nor their combination is able to do justice to the intersectional discrimination experienced by Black women, it seems an obvious conclusion that the victims of that discrimination would organize *as Black women* to confront this situation. However, it does not follow that this categorization in any way exhausts *who* they and their positionalities actually are. It is within the inherent logic of this analysis not to be content with these determinations but to advance to further specifications through class, sexuality and so on, in a process whose vanishing point is the individual. As all categories involved are shaped – or, depending on terminology, co-constituted – by all others (e.g. see Yuval-Davis 2006: 202), and even their sum total is unable to exhaust a particular person's unique situatedness and story, the actual individual will in this perspective always escape any definitive conceptual determination, though.

Structurally, this movement is similar to the one Adorno describes as the emergence of conceptual constellations that point towards the particular without ever being able to fully reach it: 'The determinable flaw in every concept makes it necessary to cite others; this gives rise to those constellations which alone inherited some of the hope that is in the name' ([1966] 1988: 62; [1966] 1973: 53, translation amended). In this perspective, constructions of collective identities, which are not just constituted discursively, but through social practice, would appear as a specific instance of Adorno's 'concepts'. This is entirely compatible with Adorno's description: 'That the concept is a concept, even when dealing with things in existence, does not change the fact that on its part it is entwined with a non-conceptual whole. It insulates itself from that whole through its reification, which in fact establishes it as a concept' ([1966] 1973: 12, translation amended).

This concept of a 'constellation' may not only be helpful to describe the intersectional position of the individual, however, but it might in other ways be useful to illuminate the interrelation between different constructions of alterity. Theories of intersectionality offer a broad spectrum of positions regarding the question of how to imagine the interrelations between different forms of discrimination. On the one hand, we find fairly simplistic conceptions of 'triple', 'quadruple' or other counts of multiple oppressions that understand different forms of discrimination as merely additive layers. Such approaches, however, have been criticized for decades as reductive within intersectional debates (e.g. Anthias and Yuval-Davis 1983), and the question of how to describe the interrelations between different dimensions of identity or different forms of hierarchy and oppression has produced a whole range of different models and metaphors. They have been described, for example, as 'interlocking' (Combahee River Collective [1977] 1983: 210), 'mutual constitution' (Davis 2008: 71), 'mutual shaping' (Walby, Armstrong and Strid 2012: 235), 'entanglement' (Anthias and Yuval-Davis 1983: 62-3), 'mutual enveloping' and so forth. Attempts to go beyond such debates on the most appropriate image to describe these interrelations and instead to ground such an analysis in a developed concept of social totality are, however, comparatively rare.[21] It seems to me that this is one among a number of areas where Critical Theory could make an important contribution. It also allows us to see constructions of 'otherness' as interconnected, as part of the same overall social totality even where they do *not* directly constitute each other, that is, even where we are not talking about overlapping ascriptions, as in the image of the 'effeminate Jew', the parallels between notions of femininity and certain colonial stereotypes and so on.

While etymologically, the term 'constellation' points towards the relative positioning of the stars and describes a connection that only emerges in the eye of the beholder, Adorno's constellation traces the immanent social connections of these different determinations: it is an unfolding of the history sedimented in each one. If we reversed the perspective and turned it towards the social origins of these identifications, the notion of a 'constellation' could also be applied to the interrelation of these different constructions of alterity. As outward projections of immanent social contradictions and tensions, as phantasmal responses to real problems or as rationalizations of socially produced inequality, they reflect back from the margins to the societal centre. They do so from different directions, however, and hence reveal a more complex, three-dimensional picture of the society that has produced them, and of its fissures and contradictions.[22] In this sense they, too, form constellations. Only their specific relationships to each other

---

[21] For an illuminating attempt to do so with reference to Adorno, see Stoetzler (2016: 463–8). Patricia Hill Collins includes a section on the Frankfurt School in her reflections in *Intersectionality as Critical Social Theory* (2019: 57–65), but the focus of her discussion remains largely restricted to Adorno and Horkheimer's critique of the culture industry in the *Dialectic of Enlightenment* and Horkheimer's discussion of 'Traditional and Critical Theory', and on the anti-positivist and self-reflexive dimensions of Horkheimer's and Adorno's thought. The Marxian dimension of Frankfurt School thinking, understanding capitalism as a system of abstract domination that is generative of new forms of subjectivity and intersubjectivity, largely remains out of sight.

[22] This would seem to be in tension with Nira Yuval-Davis's view that 'each social division has a different ontological basis, which is irreducible to other social divisions' (Yuval-Davis 2006: 195). While social divisions along the lines of gender, race, class and so on are indeed not simply reducible to one another, their ontological bases, in the perspective presented here, seem closely interconnected as dimensions of globalized capitalist modernity.

fully reveal what they point towards – in this case not the particular, the individual, which is subsumed under these designations, but the society that produces them.

In order to ground such intersectional analyses in critical social theory, however, the concept of capitalist modernity itself has to be expanded – in the manner begun by Critical Theory – in order to include other forms of inequality than just that of class, not as a side contradiction, but as socially constitutive (cf. Bohrer 2018). Modern capitalist society produces multiple kinds of oppositions, exclusions and hierarchies that contradict its programmatic universalist constitution, even if that equality is only that of market participants.

The apparent particularities of gender, race, Jewishness and so on thus become visible, at least in part, as dimensions of the social totality that produced them, not its counter-principles; as results of social relations, not qualities inherent in the subjects. Critical theory starts from damaged life, from the negation of such socially imposed identities and their limitations, as a politics of non-identity. Such a politics would not speak in the name of what we have become, but in the name of a life that still stands to be realized. Or, in the words of Adorno, 'the means by which negative dialectics permeates its hardened objects is possibility – the possibility of which their reality has cheated them, and which is nonetheless visible in each one' ([1966] 1988: 62; [1966] 1973: 52, translation amended). Critical Theory's critique of antisemitism is committed to holding open a perspective on those possibilities.

References

Achinger, C. (2007), *Gespaltene Moderne: Gustav Freytags Soll und Haben – Geschlecht, Nation und Judenbild*, Würzburg: Königshausen und Neumann.
Achinger, C. (2013), 'Allegories of Destruction: "Woman" and "the Jew" in Otto Weininger's *Sex and Character*', *Germanic Review: Literature, Culture, Theory*, 88 (2): 121–49.
Achinger, C. (2018), '"Deutsche Arbeit" und die Poetisierung der Moderne', in F. Axster and N. Lelle (eds), *"Deutsche Arbeit": Kritische Perspektiven auf ein ideologisches Selbstbild*, 251–82, Göttingen: Wallstein.
Achinger, C. (2022), 'Bilder von Geschlecht, Judentum und Nation als Konstellation. Intersektionalität und kritische Theorie', in K. Stögner and A. Colligs (eds), *Kritische Theorie und Feminismus*, 75–96, Frankfurt: Suhrkamp.
Adorno, T. W. ([1955] 1987), *Minima Moralia: Reflexionen aus dem beschädigten Leben*, Frankfurt: Suhrkamp.
Adorno, T. W. ([1966] 1973), *Negative Dialectics* (trans. E. B. Ashton), London: Routledge.
Adorno, T. W. ([1966] 1988), *Negative Dialektik*, Frankfurt: Suhrkamp.
Adorno, T. W., E. Frenkel-Brunswik, D. Levinson and N. Sanford (1950), *The Authoritarian Personality*, New York: Harper.
AG Gender-Killer (2005), *Antisemitismus und Geschlecht: Von 'effeminierten Juden', 'maskulinisierten Jüdinnen' und anderen Geschlechterbildern*, Münster: Unrast.
Anthias, F., and N. Yuval-Davis (1983), 'Contextualising Feminism – Gender, Ethnic and Class Divisions', *Feminist Review*, 15: 62–74.

Anthias, F., and N. Yuval-Davis (1989), 'Introduction', in F. Anthias and N. Yuval-Davis (eds), *Woman-Nation-State*, 1–15, Basingstoke: Macmillan.

Arendt, H. ([1951] 1979), *The Origins of Totalitarianism*, San Diego: Harvest.

Arnold, S. (2015), 'From Occupation to Occupy: Antisemitism and the Contemporary Left in the United States', in A. Rosenfeld (ed.), *Deciphering the New Antisemitism*, 375–404, Bloomington: University of Indiana Press.

Arnold, S., and B. Taylor (2019), 'Antisemitism and the Left: Confronting an Invisible Racism', *Journal of Social Justice*, 9: 1–33.

Balibar, É. (1991a), 'Is There a "Neo-Racism"?', in É. Balibar and I. Wallerstein (eds), *Race, Nation, Class: Ambiguous Identities*, 17–28, London: Verso.

Balibar, É. (1991b), 'Racism and Nationalism', in É. Balibar and I. Wallerstein (eds), *Race, Nation, Class: Ambiguous Identities*, 37–67, London: Verso.

Balibar, É. (1991c), 'Class Racism', in É. Balibar and I. Wallerstein (eds), *Race, Nation, Class: Ambiguous Identities*, 204–16, London: Verso.

Bohrer, A. (2018), 'Intersectionality and Marxism: A Critical Historiography', *Historical Materialism*, 26 (2): 46–74.

Combahee River Collective ([1977] 1983), 'A Black Feminist Statement', in C. Moraga and G. Anzaldúa (eds), *This Bridge Called My Back: Writings by Radical Women of Color*, 210–18, New York: Kitchen Table, Women of Color Press.

Crenshaw, K. (1989), 'Demarginalizing the Intersection of Race and Sex', *University of Chicago Legal Forum*, 1: 139–67.

Davis, K. (2008), 'Intersectionality as Buzzword', *Feminist Theory*, 9 (1): 67–85.

Dohm, C. W. (1781/83), *Über die bürgerliche Verbesserung der Juden*, 2 vols, Berlin: Nicolai.

Fischer, L. (2016), "A difference in the texture of prejudice": *Historisch-konzeptionelle Überlegungen zum Verhältnis von Antisemitismus, Rassismus und Gemeinschaft*, Graz: Grazer Universitätsverlag.

Fischer, L. (2018), 'Antisemitism and the Critique of Capitalism', in B. Best, W. Bonefeld and C. O'Kane (eds), *The SAGE Handbook of Frankfurt School Critical Theory*, vol. 2, 916–31, London: Sage.

Fisher, M. (2009), *Capitalist Realism: Is There No Alternative?*, Winchester: Zero.

Fisher, M. (2013), 'Exiting the Vampire Castle', *Open Democracy*, 24 November, available at: www.opendemocracy.net/en/opendemocracyuk/exiting-vampire-castle/ (accessed 18 March 2021).

Frevert, U. (1988) 'Einleitung', in U. Frevert (ed.), *Bürgerinnen und Bürger: Geschlechterverhältnisse im 19. Jahrhundert*, Göttingen: Vandenhoeck & Ruprecht.

Freytag, G. ([1855] 1923), *Soll und Haben*, 2 vols, Berlin: Knaur.

Gilroy, P. (1993), *The Black Atlantic: Modernity and Double Consciousness*, London: Verso.

Gilroy, P. (1999), 'Between Camps: Race and Culture in Postmodernity', *Economy and Society*, 28 (2): 183–97.

Gilroy, P. (2000), *Between Camps: Race, Identity and Nationalism at the End of the Colour Line*, London: Allen Lane.

Goldberg, D. T. (1993), *Racist Culture: Philosophy and the Politics of Meaning*, Cambridge, MA: Blackwell.

Guillaumin, C. ([1977] 1988), 'Race and Nature: The System of Marks', *Feminist Issues*, 8: 25–43.

Guillaumin, C. (1995), *Racism, Sexism, Power and Ideology*, London: Routledge.

Haider, A. (2018), *Mistaken Identity: Race and Class in the Age of Trump*, London: Verso.

Haury, T. (2002), *Antisemitismus von links: Kommunistische Ideologie, Nationalismus und Antizionismus in der frühen DDR*, Hamburg: Hamburger Edition.

Hausen, K. (1992), 'Öffentlichkeit und Privatheit: Gesellschaftspolitische Konstruktionen und die Geschichte der Geschlechterbeziehungen', in K. Hausen and H. Wunder (eds), *Frauengeschichte – Geschlechtergeschichte*, 81–8, Frankfurt: Campus.

Heberle, R. (ed.) (2006), *Feminist Interpretations of Theodor Adorno*, University Park: Pennsylvania State University Press.

Hentges, G. (1999), *Schattenseiten der Aufklärung: die Darstellung von Juden und 'Wilden' in philosophischen Schriften des 18. und 19. Jahrhunderts*, Schwalbach: Wochenschau-Verlag.

Hewitt, A. (1992), 'A Feminine Dialectic of Enlightenment? Horkheimer and Adorno Revisited', *New German Critique*, 56 (Spring–Summer): 143–70.

Hill Collins, P. (1990), *Black Feminist Thought: Knowledge, Consciousness, and the Politics of Empowerment*, Boston, MA: Unwin Hyman.

Hill Collins, P. (2019), *Intersectionality as Critical Social Theory*, Durham, NC: Duke University Press.

Hippel, T. G. von ([1792] 1977), *Über die bürgerliche Verbesserung der Weiber*, Frankfurt: Syndikat.

Holz, K. (2001), *Nationaler Antisemitismus: Wissenssoziologie einer Weltanschauung*, Hamburg: Hamburger Edition.

Honegger, C. (1996), *Die Ordnung der Geschlechter: Die Wissenschaften vom Menschen und das Weib*, Munich: dtv.

hooks, b. (1981), *Ain't I a Woman? Black Women and Feminism*, Boston, MA: South End.

hooks, b. (1991), 'Essentialism and Experience', *American Literary History*, 3 (1): 172–83.

Horkheimer, M., and T. W. Adorno ([1947] 1969), *Dialektik der Aufklärung*, Frankfurt: Suhrkamp.

Horkheimer, M., and T. W. Adorno (2002), *Dialectic of Enlightenment: Philosophical Fragments* (ed. G. S. Noerr, trans. E. Jephcott), Stanford, CA: Stanford University Press.

Ibrahim, A., J. Karakayalı, S. Karakayalı and V. S. Tsianos (2012), 'Decolorise it! Die Rezeption von Critical Whiteness hat eine Richtung eingeschlagen, die die antirassistischen Politiken sabotiert', *analyse & kritik – zeitung für linke Debatte und Praxis*, 575 (September), available at: www.akweb.de/bewegung/diskussion-um-critical-whiteness-und-antirassismus-decolorise-it/ (accessed 6 January 2023).

Marx, K. ([1867] 1972), *Das Kapital*, vol. 1 (*Marx-Engels-Werke*, vol. 23), Berlin: Dietz.

Marx, K. (1976), *Capital*, vol. 1 (trans. B. Fowkes), Harmondsworth: Penguin.

Marz, U. (2017), 'Annäherungen an eine kritische Theorie des Rassismus', *Peripherie*, 146/147: 250–70.

McClintock, A. (1997), '"No Longer in a Future Heaven: Gender, Race and Nationalism', in A. McClintock, A. Mufti and E. Shohat, *Dangerous Liaisons: Gender, Nation, and Postcolonial Perspectives*, Minneapolis: University of Minnesota Press, 89–112.

Mendelssohn, M. (1783), 'Anmerkungen über diese Beurtheilung von Hrn. Moses Mendelssohn', in C. W. Dohm (1783), *Über die bürgerliche Verbesserung der Juden*, vol. 2, 72–7, Berlin: Nicolai.

Meyer, T. (2002), *Identitätspolitik: Vom Missbrauch kultureller Unterschiede*, Frankfurt: Suhrkamp.

Michaelis, J. D. (1783), 'Hr. Ritter Michaelis Beurtheilung: Über die bürgerliche Verbesserung der Juden von Christian Wilhelm Dohm', in C. W. Dohm (1783), *Über die bürgerliche Verbesserung der Juden*, vol. 2, 31–71, Berlin: Nicolai.

Miles, R. (1993), *Racism after 'Race Relations'*, London: Routledge.

O'Neill, M. (ed.) (1999), *Adorno, Culture and Feminism*, London: SAGE.

Postone, M. (1980), 'Anti-Semitism and National Socialism: Notes on the German Reaction to "Holocaust"', *New German Critique*, 19 (Winter): 97–115.

Postone, M. (1993), *Time, Labor, and Social Domination: A Reinterpretation of Marx's Critical Theory*, Cambridge: Cambridge University Press.

Postone, M. (2006), 'History and Helplessness: Mass Mobilization and Contemporary Forms of Anticapitalism', *Public Culture*, 18 (1): 93–110.

Rensmann, L. (2017), *The Politics of Unreason: The Frankfurt School and the Origins of Modern Antisemitism*, New York: State University Press of New York.

Sayer, D. (1991), *Capitalism and Modernity: An Excursus on Marx and Weber*, London: Routledge.

Spivak, G. C. (1993), *Outside in the Teaching Machine*, London: Routledge.

Spivak, G. C. (2008), *Other Asias*, Malden, MA: Blackwell.

Stoetzler, M. (2016), 'From Interacting Systems to a System of Divisions: The Concept of Society and the "Mutual Constitution" of Intersecting Social Divisions', *European Journal of Social Theory*, 20 (4): 455–72.

Stoetzler, M. (2018), 'Critical Theory and the Critique of Anti-imperialism', in B. Best, W. Bonefeld and C. O'Kane (eds), *The Sage Handbook of Frankfurt School Critical Theory*, vol. 3, 1467–86.

Stögner, K. (2014), *Antisemitismus und Sexismus: Historisch-gesellschaftliche Konstellationen*, Baden-Baden: Nomos.

Stögner, K. (2017), '"Intersektionalität von Ideologien" – Antisemitismus, Sexismus und das Verhältnis von Gesellschaft und Natur', *Psychologie & Gesellschaftskritik*, 41 (2): 25–45.

Stögner, K. (2019), 'Wie inklusiv ist Intersektionalität? Neue soziale Bewegungen, Identitätspolitik und Antisemitismus', in S. Salzborn (ed.), *Antisemitismus seit 9/11*, 385–402, Baden-Baden: Nomos.

Taylor, B. (2017), 'Ruthless Critique or Selective Apologia? The Postcolonial Left in Theory and Practice', *Amerikastudien – American Studies*, 62 (4): 649–61.

Virdee, S. (2014), *Racism, Class and the Racialized Outsider*, Houndsmills: Palgrave Macmillan.

Walby, S., J. Armstrong and S. Strid (2012), 'Intersectionality: Multiple Inequalities in Social Theory', *Sociology*, 46 (2): 224–40.

Weininger, O. ([1903] 1908), *Geschlecht und Charakter: Eine prinzipielle Untersuchung*, Berlin: Kiepenheuer.

Yuval-Davis, N. (1997), *Gender & Nation*, London: SAGE.

Yuval-Davis, N. (2006), 'Intersectionality and Feminist Politics', *European Journal of Women's Studies*, 13 (3): 193–209.

Yuval-Davis, N. (2010), 'Theorizing Identity: Beyond the "Us" and "Them" Dichotomy', *Patterns of Prejudice*, 44 (3): 261–80.

Yuval-Davis, N. (2011), *The Politics of Belonging: Intersectional Contestations*, London: SAGE.

Ziege, E.-M. (2004), 'Die "Kritik des Weiblichen" bei T.W. Adorno und die Frühe Kritische Theorie', *Die Philosophin: Forum für Feministische Theorie und Philosophie*, 15 (30): 129–40.

Ziege, E.-M. (2007), 'Die Geschlechterthematik in der Zeitschrift für Sozialforschung/ Studies in Philosophy and Social Science (1932–1941)', in R. Faber and E.-M. Ziege (eds), *Das Feld der Frankfurter Kultur- und Sozialwissenschaften vor 1945*, 89–106, Würzburg: Königshausen & Neumann.

5

Antisemitism, anti-capitalism, community: (Con)fusing reft and light

Marcel Stoetzler

Theorizing antisemitism in the framework of Critical Theory requires relating it to the dialectic of capitalism and emancipation.[1] Capitalism, being a force that constructs as well as destroys, itself creates the conditions of, and the means for, overcoming capitalism, and this produces the space of ambiguity and confusion in which antisemitic forms of anti-capitalism emerge, some of which can appear to be 'left-wing'. It is a 'missive mastake' to assume that 'reft and light cannot be foncused' (Jandl [1966] 1976: 135).[2]

Strictly speaking, as the concept of 'the left' is customarily defined in terms of the ideas of *liberté, égalité* and *fraternité*, 'left-wing antisemitism' is a contradiction in terms: antisemitism clearly denies these ideas. More loosely speaking, though, not only is there 'antisemitism *on* the left' – that is, antisemitic attitudes and behaviours by people who otherwise are committed leftists – but there is even an 'antisemitism *of* the left', that is, a form of antisemitism that is *specific* to the overall perspective of 'leftism', following from how 'the left' interprets, develops and actualizes the classic trinomial of concepts that define it. My proposition is that this distinction could help in making critiques of 'left-wing antisemitism' more precise. In this chapter, I run through a number of arguments in an attempt thereby to clarify the concept.

In the present period, 'being on the left' is often equated with opposing capitalism. In nineteenth-century Europe, when capitalism was a new phenomenon and conservatives were still in two minds concerning the revolutionizing new mode of production, few people would have made this equation so easily. 'Being on the left' means being 'for emancipation' rather than merely 'against capitalism'. Anti-capitalism is not an axiom

---

[1] This chapter draws on several previous publications in which I groped my way towards an argument, the most wide-ranging of which is Stoetzler (2019a). The present chapter is, I would like to believe, conceptually clearer than this article from 2019, but the latter contains more detailed reflections on some particular antisemitism disputes, including some that initially got me started thinking on these matters. An earlier version of sections of the present chapter was published in Spanish and in Catalan (Stoetzler 2021, 2022).

[2] Jandl's famous poem 'Lichtung' where this formulation is from seems to be a sarcastic comment on Heidegger and 'left-wing' Heideggerians.

or an *a priori* but follows from the commitment to emancipation. The roots of some of the ideas of the left may be older than the capitalist mode of production, but the left as an actual movement or social force sprung from and grew with it and must be mindful of this link. The left is anti-capitalist to the extent that capitalism hinders emancipation but seeks to exploit the emancipatory possibilities generated by capitalism's corrosion of some of the oppressive and dehumanizing aspects of human civilization writ large.³

In *Dialectic of Enlightenment*, Horkheimer and Adorno ([1947] 2002) theorized the oppressiveness of this civilization in terms of the forward march of unreflective rationality, relentless productivism and obsessive, compulsive labour (Stoetzler 2019b), but there are other perspectives relevant to a dialectical critique of civilization, too: feminists, most prominently, have theorized the same civilization under the name of patriarchy. Political ecologists have developed arguments that in many ways echo those of *Dialectic of Enlightenment*. The capitalist mode of production has helpfully corroded some aspects of the sex-gender-sexuality matrix of domination as well as the traditionalist ur-racism of caste societies, to name two examples, but restabilized and reconstituted them *in capitalist form*. This is the inconclusive and confusing situation humanity now finds itself in.

Today, only few people oppose the capitalist mode of production as such (although very many oppose some particular version of it, such as 'neoliberalism'). Nevertheless, there are some on the right as well as on the left who claim the epithet of 'anti-capitalist', usually without making explicit what they mean by it.

This chapter reflects on the meanings of the concepts 'left-wing' and 'right-wing', relating them to what is commonly called 'the ideas of the French Revolution', and in this framework examines the distinctions between the three principal types of modern antisemitism: left-wing, right-wing and 'Conservative-Revolutionary'. The chapter then zooms in on two elements that played a part in recent scandals concerning leftists who accommodated, hosted and celebrated ultraconservative antisemites. I suggest that a poorly understood longing for, and myopia about, 'community' is a key driver in such constellations. One of my contentions is that 'anti-imperialism', in the sense of the mostly nationalist resistance to the global spread of the capitalist mode of production, constitutes one of the contexts in which contemporary antisemitism is a symptom of confusion between 'left' and 'right', while another, indirectly related source of confusion is the ethnicized concept of 'community' inherent in the state-centric, bureaucratic, communalist version of multiculturalism, that is, the modern state's reification and containment of culture.⁴

Central to the argument is the contention that Marx and Engels proposed, most prominently in the *Communist Manifesto*, a dialectical view of capitalism that is not straightforwardly anti-capitalist, and that this perspective can be put to work for theorizing antisemitism. Antisemitic 'anti-capitalists' who refer by 'Jewish capitalism'

---

³ I have developed this notion in a discussion of the concept of 'anti-imperialism' (Stoetzler 2018) to which the present chapter is complementary.

⁴ By 'containment' I mean making an infinite finite in the sense in which Christopher D. Wright (in this volume) uses these terms. I have discussed the concept of culture in this sense in Stoetzler (2020).

to corrosive and exploitative capitalism silently presuppose the possible existence of other, 'non-Jewish', benign types of capitalism imagined as productive, harmonious and peaceful. (This means, of course, that their 'anti-capitalism' is not one.) By contrast, being a left-wing anti-capitalist properly understood means *embracing* the corrosive effects capitalism has on enduring oppressive and exploitative societal-civilizational structures that long predate capitalism, such as patriarchy: these 'critical' or 'corrosive' ones are exactly the dimensions of capitalism which reactionaries tend to denounce as 'Jewish'.

The concepts of 'left' and 'right'

The concepts of 'left' and 'right', dating from the period of the French Revolution, are usually defined in terms of a commitment to the idea of either the (ontologically given as well as normatively desired) equality or the natural *in*equality of all human beings. Beyond that, though, the notion of 'the left' resonates with *liberté* and *fraternité* in addition to *égalité*. The more traditional definition references the entire trinomial phrase and therewith includes liberalism in the concept of 'the left' (in this sense, see, e.g., Solty 2015). A simplified definition, by contrast, was proposed by Norberto Bobbio (1996: chapters 6–8) who equates 'leftism' with egalitarianism only, to the effect that 'classical' liberalism is out, as for him liberty as such is not a 'left-wing' value, whereas 'social liberalism' is included.

In my view, the full trinomial definition is more in keeping with the actual usage of the concept also in the present; the fact that it is vaguer and contradictory, as it is far from obvious how *liberté, égalité, fraternité* relate to each other, is a reflection of the reality of its referent, and in this sense a strength rather than a weakness of the concept. Maybe we still talk so much in terms of 'left' and 'right' *because* of its polyvalence (a.k.a. vagueness).

Although the concept of 'the left' has, on the one hand, a core meaning in the reference to *liberté, égalité, fraternité*, it is, on the other hand, also very much a relational, floating concept whose meaning is only loosely circumscribed by these three concepts: there can be 'a left' within pretty much any group or subcategory of people, as well as within society as a whole. The 'Tory left', the 'Marxist left', the 'fascist left' can all be meaningful phrases. This polyvalence is made possible by the fact that different interpretations of *liberté, égalité, fraternité* and how they relate, or should relate, to each other must result in different politics, usually prioritizing one or two elements of the revolutionary trinomial. The leftness of 'the Tory left' is very different from the leftness of 'the Marxist left': if the latter is the anti-Bolshevik, anti-authoritarian left that critiques or rejects the organizational form of the centralized party along with the capitalist mode of production and the modern bureaucratic state, consistent with the full trinomial of *liberté, égalité, fraternité*, the former seems almost exactly the opposite, namely advocacy of a more interventionist state that is meant to stabilize class hierarchy by improving the material situation of the lower orders. In nineteenth-century Germany, 'left-liberal' denoted a free-market, small-state liberal, whereas a more socially conservative national-liberal supporter of the monarchical,

Bismarckian welfare state would have been perceived as more right-wing, similar to what in the UK is called a 'One-Nation Tory' (a phrase that seems to go back to Disraeli, the conservative modernizer). The 'fascist left' are those populist agitators who take literally the anti-capitalist pretensions of fascist ideology (the SA leader Ernst Röhm, the Strassers, today's 'third-positionist' fascists such as the Italian MSI, Casa Pound, etc.): they are fascists who (pretend to) fight for more class equality, as it were – the soldierly elite who (think they) fight the conservative/liberal/democratic establishment (Ross 2017).[5]

The notion of 'the Labour (Party) left' is particularly complicated. It makes little sense when leftness is defined in terms of all three of *liberté, égalité, fraternité*: many of those considered to be on 'the left' of the Labour Party are associated with (supposedly progressive, 'patriotic') nationalism and nation-state-centric politics of redistribution that might score high in terms of *égalité* and *fraternité* (assuming their policies work) but not so high (potentially very low) on *liberté*. Somewhat paradoxically, a stronger commitment to statism counts in this context usually as *more* 'left-wing', not less.[6] In the context of social-democratic political parties, the definition of leftness in terms of egalitarianism *alone*, as proposed by Bobbio, seems therefore more appropriate as it allows direct comparisons: politician A is 'more left-wing' than politician B because A is more strongly committed to state-mediated redistribution (scores high for *égalité* and *fraternité*). B might perhaps be more strongly and explicitly opposed to the politics of clerical ultraconservatives and other Conservative Revolutionaries (scores higher for *liberté*) but would not be perceived as 'left wing' in this context.

Bobbio, the Weberian sociologist who proposed the narrower definition, himself a supporter of centre-left social democracy, argues that the 'camps' of left and right consist 'on the one hand, of people who believe that human beings are more equal than unequal, and on the other, people who believe that we are more unequal than equal' (1996: 67), conventionally represented by the philosophers Rousseau and Nietzsche respectively: 'The same degeneration which created inequality for Rousseau created equality for Nietzsche' (68); 'the egalitarian condemns social inequality in the name of natural equality, and the anti-egalitarian condemns social equality in the name of natural inequality' (68–9). In practice, the two camps assess differently 'what is relevant to the justification or repudiation of discrimination': they produce arguments 'for and against the proposal that characteristics belonging to individuals within the group under consideration ... constitute grounds for equal treatment' (69). 'The egalitarian tends to play down the differences, the inegalitarian to overstate them' (70).[7]

---

[5] The plebeian Nazis found out the hard way that their Führer had other ideas when they met their death in June 1934. Lipset named Peronism as the paradigm of left-wing fascism (Lipset 1960: 133–4).

[6] There is a small anti-authoritarian tendency among 'the Labour left' (relatively vocal during the Corbyn years), but anti-authoritarianism – a socialist interpretation of *liberté, égalité, fraternité* that would include anti-nationalism and anti-statism – does not define how the phrase 'the Labour left' is commonly used.

[7] Importantly, Bobbio defines egalitarians rather strictly as 'those who, while not ignoring the fact that people are both equal and unequal, believe that what they have in common has greater value in the formation of a good community' (66–7): those who *deny* difference, or want to abolish it, are not egalitarians in the sense of Bobbio's definition. In his view, egalitarians simply say that certain

The British discourse on antisemitism in the Labour party, for example, can in this perspective be addressed as a case of 'antisemitism on the left' only when the less complex definition of 'the left' is applied: it is about politicians who are concerned with egalitarian social reform rather than the *encompassing* revolutionary idea of emancipation in terms of the full trinomial of *liberté, égalité, fraternité*[8]. They are intensely relaxed about capitalism, the state and nationalism, as long as they (are hoped to) serve the societal redistribution of wealth; this means that they (attempt to) pursue *égalité* by sacrificing *liberté* (denied by the nation-state and its border regimes as well as national culture's clampdown on transcendence by making culture static, i.e., state-ic) and *fraternité* (denied by capitalism's reliance on reproducing class antagonism and exploitation). It is therewith also perhaps not too surprising that they are, like Ferdinand Lassalle back in the post-1848 period, not entirely disinclined to having friendly ties to modernizing ultraconservatives whom they misperceive as populists like themselves (as when they refer to Hamas functionaries as 'friends').[9]

Applying this definitional reflection to the current antisemitism disputes may help clarify what we actually mean when we talk about 'left-wing antisemitism'. Antisemitism *of* the left – proper, genuinely left-wing antisemitism – could be defined first of all as an antisemitism that presumes that there is something in the essence or spirit of 'the Jews' that makes them impediments to the pursuit of the ideas of the French Revolution: the Jews are *by their nature* supporters of the status quo or even of reaction.[10] They are perceived to be against equality and liberty, let alone fraternity, an accusation that can be found frequently in pamphlets written by nineteenth-century petty-bourgeois antisemites of liberal, democratic or socialist backgrounds.[11]

(if not all) differences are irrelevant for the allocation of goods or rights. Therewith, Bobbio has (unintentionally) defined such a phenomenon as 'left-wing antisemitism' out of existence: since Bruno Bauer, *antisemitic* egalitarians and democrats wanted to dissolve and destroy the differences of certain others that seemed to them as obstacles to progress, against which Marx was the first to propose what Bobbio presupposes: deliberate *indifference to difference*, the assertion that difference does not matter and should not stand in the way of equality. In Bobbio's definition, though, the Bruno Bauers are not in fact egalitarians, and therewith not 'on the left'. (Hence, they are not our problem.) He solves the problem by way of tweaking the definition (i.e. through logocentrism) rather than dialectical historical analysis. In my view it is more helpful to accept that egalitarians *can be* antisemites, and that egalitarians who disregard *liberté* are not 'on the left', strictly speaking: the (revolutionary, authentic) left aims for equality/fraternity *on the basis of* liberty. (This is in fact the opposite of the conservative argument that egalitarianism is *inherently* 'totalitarian', i.e., *incompatible* with liberty.)

[8] Bolton and Pitts (2018) demonstrate the overlap between Corbynism and 'Blue Labour', which I would describe as a form of 'lower case', socially-minded conservatism. This conservative strand of the Corbyn coalition was difficult to be reconciled with its anti-authoritarian, genuinely left-wing elements.

[9] By populism I mean the perspective that replaces differentiated class analysis by an assertion of a conflict between 'the people' and some kind of elite, central to fascism but by no means exclusive to it. To the extent that ultraconservatives or reactionaries defend, or want to reinstate, some traditional form of elite (clerical, for example), they are not populists.

[10] This could be distinguished from 'antisemitism *on* the left' (see below), that is, the theoretically less interesting case of leftists saying antisemitic things that contradict their leftism; the litmus test is perhaps whether they can be talked out of it with the help of (their own) left-wing arguments.

[11] This is a central theme of Hannah Arendt's discussion of antisemitism in the first part of *The Origins of Totalitarianism* (especially the chapter on 'Leftist antisemitism' (1973: 42–50)).

A second dimension of the 'antisemitism of the left' consists of elements of antisemitism that follow from a mechanical, dogmatic and undialectical interpretation of the ideas of *liberté, égalité, fraternité* that turns them against difference. A left that misreads its own ideals thereby becomes their enemy. Adorno reacted to this form of antisemitism with his famous reference to 'the state of things (Zustand) where one can be different without fear' (1978: #66) as the longed-for state of things: a state of equality that allows for and encourages difference.

This points to a question that is central to Critical Theory: *how can we articulate a defence of difference within the framework of a belief in equality?* Within the Marxist canon, the first important treatment of this problem is Marx's own 'On the Jewish Question' (Fine 2014). Reflections on how capitalist modernity *creates* but also *undermines* equality and sameness, difference and identity, particularism and universalism in their dialectical interplay can be found in contemporary discussions of race, class, sex and gender and others: all emancipatory social movements of the last century or so have reflected, in different manners, on the modern dialectic of difference and equality.[12] Critical Theory links this dialectic to that of the commodity form, which produces the totalizing dynamic characteristic of modern society whose chief mechanism of mediation it is (Postone 1980, 1986, 2003): the capitalist mode of production produces a schizophrenic reality of total, mind-numbing ever-sameness based on antagonism, separation and a bad infinity of particularisms. Similarly, albeit coming from a different theoretical background, Etienne Balibar gave expression to this in his formulation that racism is 'encore un universalisme', 'yet another form of universalism': although racism professes to be a strong form of particularism and claims to defend difference, it is also a universalism, one of the signatures of the global order (Balibar 1989a, 1989b). As much as the concept of the 'universally human' cannot be defined except in terms of criteria which throw up boundary problems that destabilize the concept, as much racism is a universal social form in modern society (i.e. the world system). Racism produces communities by creating, together with sexism, 'types of ideal Humanity', that is, particular universalisms. Although it does so differently in every specific 'racial' context, it does so universally. Racism cannot therefore be fought by simply invoking universalism as such: the constitution of *a new kind of universalism* is required (Postone 1993: 396).

Leftism that turns against difference, or even makes one fearful of being different, is (historically, but perhaps also logically) first of all nationalist, before it is racist or antisemitic. Nationalism is difficult to chart in terms of 'left' and 'right', but it is linked historically to the French Revolution and has been an aspect of most liberal, democratic and socialist movements throughout the last two hundred years. Factions of the left have often assumed that building the nation will deliver legal equality, welfare and dignity for all its members, underestimating in the process the problems involved in saying who these members are or should be: any nationalism, however left-wing it may be, must at least *sotto voce* define who belongs and who does not belong to the

---

[12] Wallerstein (e.g. 1990) and Postone (1993: 396) can be seen as converging on this, although coming from reassuringly different directions. On Postone's argument in relation to social movements, see Stoetzler (2004).

nation and therefore deserves its solidarity, and consequently relies on some set of mechanisms of exclusion: you cannot have a nation without borders and boundaries.

Historically speaking, nationalism first of all has been a project of the liberal, democratic and socialist movements of the nineteenth century in their interplay with the becoming hegemonic of the capitalist mode of production. However, since the nation form has become the established, predominant political form of capitalist society in the world system, a process that was more or less completed in the post-Second World War era of decolonization, it is, in fact, a *conservative* political form: seen in this perspective, accordingly, the antisemitism of a nationalist is *today* a form of conservative, right-wing antisemitism in spite of nationalism's liberal, left-wing nineteenth-century roots. This includes the kind of nationalist antisemitism that can be found in some anti-imperialist or postcolonial nationalisms. Nationalism has not, though, entirely changed its character in these different contexts: it seems rather that 'left' and 'right', progressive and conservative, fail to function as classificatory categories in the case of a political form, the nation, that is fundamentally ambiguous: the nation form stands, and always stood, for a conservative kind of progressiveness, circumscribed emancipation, equality by way of difference, unity through separation.[13] 'Left' and 'right' are useful in this context only as dynamic, historical-dialectical, not logical-classificatory categories.

'Conservative-Defensive Antisemitism' versus 'Liberal, Democratic and Socialist Antisemitism'

In terms of its social content, the messy phenomenon of antisemitism can be broken down into three principal types. The first type is the 'Conservative-Defensive Antisemitism' (CDAS). It aims to defend an established order of domination and exploitation from rising newcomers who want to join and potentially transform it. This is, in the first instance, the kind of anti-Jewish snobbery that is practised in upper-class circles as a conventional means of bonding and boundary maintenance. It has none of the characteristics of being a quack medicine meant to soothe grievances about capitalist modernity: those who do not suffer the grievances do not need the medicine. Especially before the consolidation of the capitalist mode of production as the core element of the ruling order, it would have contained elements of conservative, anti modernization anti-capitalism, whereas thereafter such elements would have been downgraded to merely rhetorical flourishes or 'traditionalist' coquettishness. The ruling classes learned to take capitalism as much for a natural phenomenon as they have always thought patriarchy, aristocracy, Christianity and 'the straight mind' were and do not suffer from any paranoia about globalization or the 'Judaization' of society

---

[13] By nationalism I mean the idea, or demand, that the territorial unit of the state ought to be congruent with a cultural unit, often nominally defined in terms of language but loaded with much more than that, especially ideas about sex and gender (Yuval Davis 1997). It is 'progressive' (i.e. functional to capitalist progress) inasmuch as its creation of borders brings people together, into communication; helps build all kinds of disciplinary institutions; and therewith is 'educational'.

threatening their 'cultural identity': they know too much about the actual workings of society to fall for any such nonsense. As their anxiety levels are usually much lower, the antisemitism of the established elites generally also lacks the systematic viciousness of modern genocidal antisemitism.

The second type is the 'Liberal, Democratic and Socialist Antisemitism' (LDSAS), dating from the nineteenth century, or else the antisemitism of 'the left' broadly conceived.[14] More often than not, those on the broad left believe that they have worked out which measures are necessary to institute a reconciled, reasonable and humane society, but are also aware that existing society is, and largely remains, anything but reasonable and humane.[15] Belief in plans and programmes can become problematic when the believers find themselves in positions of power: the more they have put into practice their respective programmes, without, though, achieving the desired results, the more they need a culprit to explain the failure.[16] Antisemitism is in this context an attempt to explain the failure of post-1789 modernity – liberalism, capitalism, republicanism, democracy, socialism – to usher in a New Jerusalem. Blaming it on the Old Jerusalem is an obvious and convenient solution.

Again, depending on historical context, LDSAS comes in variations: left-wing antisemites denounce 'the Jews' either as allies of the old regime, a 'financial aristocracy' that props up a modern form of feudalism, or, once this becomes too obviously implausible, as representatives of *the wrong kind of* capitalist modernity: usurious, rapacious, anti-national, cosmopolitan, rootless, commercial, immoral, financial, Zionist, East Coast and so on. Although a nineteenth-century phenomenon, LDSAS inherits premodern anti-commercial ideologies that depicted 'usury', the 'sterile' begetting of money off money, as immoral and found acceptable only wealth that was earned the sweaty way from working in the fields and workshops.[17] This 'producerist' kind of ideology that is central to the ideology of the bourgeois revolution, its manifesto being Sieyes' hugely influential 1789 pamphlet *What Is the Third Estate?*, is prone to

---

[14] The phrase 'left-wing antisemitism' may refer to 'antisemitism *on* the left', often rooted in the wider social milieu or national context of a left-wing individual, or 'antisemitism *of* the left', that is, antisemitism that is 'left-wing' *in itself* (see above). In practice, a left-wing racist or antisemite may be both, a racist *in spite of* being a leftist, and *because of* being a racist-antisemitic *kind of* leftist. In other words: on the one hand, a particular individual who is predominantly a leftist may, at the same time, also be a bit of a conservative or a reactionary, whereas, on the other hand, his or her leftism may be of the unreflective, mechanical kind that *in itself* has a racist dimension.

[15] Conservatives, by contrast, tend to be more relaxed about living in an imperfect, unequal and unjust society as they believe this to be 'natural', and are correspondingly more inclined to muddle through than work out a grand plan. In this specific sense, the 'postmodern' critique of 'grand narratives' was conservative (although it was simultaneously anti-metaphysical, like Comte, *and* hostile to the modernism of the Comtean project of bureaucratic-positivist-capitalist plan rationality).

[16] As long as 'the left' neglect to abolish the capitalist mode of production, the state and patriarchy, failure is inevitable, and the search for culprits and traitors is a feature rather than a bug. Conservatives, again, have it much easier: they don't see a big problem, hence do not devise a big plan and *ipso facto* cannot fail.

[17] Such agrarian ideology was classically expressed by Aristotle and Thomas Aquinas, but can be found earlier, for example, in the Torah. On the role of the notion of 'making (people) productive' for antisemitism, see Bermann (1973).

turn antisemitic if and when circumstances and cultural traditions make it plausible, that is, when there is a cultural tradition that depicts Jews as money-grabbing non-producers.[18] (Depending on historical context, other population groups may be stereotyped this way and cast accordingly.[19])

These two types of antisemitism are opposed to each other in their commitment to the concepts of equality and inequality, respectively: the right-wing type hates the Jews as equalizers and levellers, newcomers who destroy natural differences and hierarchies (caste or estate systems, patriarchy, etc.); the left-wing type sees them standing in the way of a more equal, emancipated, fair and just society. Rather than melting into the modern 'society of equals' (a notion that in the nineteenth century was shared by liberal, democratic and socialist traditions that differed mostly in their ideas about how to get there), 'the Jews', it was thought, stubbornly remained allies of the old regime of the aristocracy. In the twentieth century, leftist antisemites would see 'the Jews' allied to whichever social forces appeared to them as the reactionary aristocracy's inheritors: imperialism, the United States, the cosmo-metropolitan elites or others. The internationalism (or, more precisely, pre-nationalism) of the European old-regime aristocracy (the principal enemy of the left in 1789 and through much of the nineteenth century) reverberates in the globalism of capitalism-as-imperialism[20]; as long as liberals, democrats and socialists hope to achieve the goal of human emancipation through a nationalist kind of (liberal or socialist) democracy 'in one country' (just as Sieyes had seen the revolution of 1789 embodied in 'la nation'), they are liable to perceive the nation-transcending aspects of capitalism (imperialism and empire) as the main obstacles to their efforts: cue LDSAS, or whatever other racist scapegoatism is historically available.

---

[18] Socialist movements, ideologies and regimes, in contradistinction to liberal ones, aim to govern in the name of society against a perceived preponderance of individualism. They are not typically opposed to capitalism, though, even when, in the name of 'state socialism', they eliminate the predominance of private ownership, as all or most other descriptors of the capitalist mode of production (including wage labour, societal mediation by money, commodity exchange, creation of societal wealth mostly in the form of value) remain unchallenged. Liberalism, democracy and socialism are historically closely related phenomena, often forming coalitions against common enemies such as feudalism, in spite of their differences. The shared capitalist nature of all liberal, democratic or socialist projects is central to their inevitable failure to realize their goals, and therewith also their need to blame their failure on a supposedly external factor, such as 'the Jews'. Furthermore, a fetishism of labour and productivity is common to most strands of 'the left' across the spectrum. I discuss Sieyes' pamphlet *What Is the Third Estate* and how its racialized producerism anticipated left-wing antisemitism in Stoetzler (2007).

[19] For a discussion of 'producerist populism', see Abromeit (2017) and Loeffler (2017).

[20] It helps here to keep in mind that the current social order is not simply the result of one ruling class being overthrown and replaced by another. Rather, it takes the form of a system which has developed a most sophisticated form of class exploitation into its central operating mechanism but has also subsumed classes themselves (as they existed before capitalism) entirely under its dynamic totality, reprogramming rather than going to the trouble of overthrowing or dissolving them. The aristocracy still exists in many countries, but it operates now according to the logic of the new regime. The antisemitic slogan of the Jews as the new 'financial aristocracy', implying that the revolution was a con, both reflects and obscures the fact that the new society is the old one, just working in a different key.

Beyond left and right: 'Conservative-Revolutionary Antisemitism'

CDAS and LDSAS, the two principal nineteenth-century forms of antisemitism, produced discrimination, exclusion and pogroms, depending on context. This distinguishes them from the third, most modern type that is much more consistently and dynamically violent and tends towards genocide: the antisemitism that is associated with Conservative-Revolutionary ideology, which comes in a range of varieties from fascist-plebeian to aristocratic-clerical.[21] In 'Conservative-Revolutionary Antisemitism' (CRAS), ordinary resentment, envy and sadism have been translated into the quasi-metaphysical expectation that salvation of the world will come from the destruction of the Jews. Although ultraconservative (it wants to restore 'natural hierarchy'), it is also meta-political, aiming to transcend the categories of 'left' and 'right'.[22] Its anti-bourgeois, anti-liberal and seemingly anti-capitalist aspects have always confused and attracted some of those on both 'the right' and 'the left' broadly conceived.[23]

The antisemitism of the first two types has been described as a 'cultural code'.[24] A code by definition *stands for* something else: the snobbish-conservative and liberal-democratic-socialist antisemitisms point to a larger agenda that has nothing intrinsically to do with Jews. Hating Jews is a sign of distinction, a badge of honour

---

[21] On the concept of 'Conservative Revolution', see the source materials in Kaes, Jay and Dimendberg (1994). Although Breuer rejects the concept, he (1990) gives a very good survey of what it means, including how nebulous it inevitably is: analytical precision is not a natural characteristic even of the brightest minds of the far right. See also Herf (1984); a different twist on Herf's 'reactionary modernism' argument, closer to Critical Theory, is by Rohkrämer (1999). See also Pfahl-Traughber (1998), Bar-On (2011), Schlembach (2013) and Cooper (2008).

[22] To my knowledge, the first author to point to the importance of fascist pseudo-anti-capitalism was Daniel Guérin, who discussed this already in 1936 in his book *Fascism and big business* ([1936, 1965] 1973). Guérin's book is much more perceptive and multifaceted than its title suggests: in the chapter 'Fascist Demagogy: "Anti-capitalist" Capitalism' (1973: 105–37), he shows through a wide range of quoted sources how different sections of the fascist movement in Italy and National Socialism in Germany were differently serious about offering an anti-capitalism that was not one. The chapter contains a passage on antisemitism (108–11), some of which must have been added in one of the later editions as he refers there to 'the most abominable genocide of all time' (111; the 1973 English edition mentions that revisions were made in the 1965 edition but does not indicate what they were). Guérin was a libertarian socialist (although at the time close to the Fourth International) and a key figure of the French gay liberation movement (Berry 2014; Stangler 2017). Guérin travelled Germany from summer 1932 to summer 1933 by bicycle and published quasi-ethnographic reports in French journals (Saintin 2013). It is interesting, and depressing, to note that one of these reports seems to have contained an expression of (class-related, i.e., anti-bourgeois) anti-Jewish resentment that shows 'the social limitations' of 'Guérin's compassion' (24). Saintin points out that Guérin 'évolue dans une sphère intellectuelle et militante imprégnée d'antisémitisme économique' (24).

[23] Rebecca Pierce (2019) makes a similar argument on the occasion of an antisemitic shooting in Jersey City in the United States in 2019: 'Though movements like BHI [Black Hebrew Israelites] and NOI [Nation of Islam] are often labelled as [left-wing] … they are actually culturally conservative and invested in patriarchal family values, homophobia, free market capitalism, and opposition to abortion and miscegenation.'

[24] Shulamit Volkov has explained the background and genesis of this phrase, which she famously coined, in a more recent contribution (Volkov 2006). She describes her experience of 'campus antisemitism' in the 1960s as an ideology that treated 'the Jew' as a sort of free-floating signifier for a variety of other things and ideas, rather than constituting an actual genocidal threat.

or a signifier signalling a commitment to this or that social and political agenda. By contrast, the more modern, twentieth-century, revolutionary, ontological, utopian, eliminatory, cosmological, apocalyptic, eschatological antisemitism is cut from a different cloth: it does not 'stand for' anything else. It is what it is: genuine, raw, visceral hatred that has its own rationality, energy and logic. This third type of antisemitism, the far-right, Conservative-Revolutionary type, which is a key ingredient of fascist antisemitism, is more than just a more extreme version of the 'antisemitism as cultural code'. It is a phenomenon of its own kind.[25]

Genocidal and eliminatory antisemitism, the full-blown Nazi variety, is part of the modern, Conservative-Revolutionary reaction to modernity. Failure to distinguish it from the more ordinary forms – evil, damaging and repulsive as they are – amounts to relativizing or downplaying, if not denial, of the Holocaust.[26] Although it is tempting to do so, one must not transfer the opprobrium that belongs to the Holocaust to descriptions of the casual stupidities of everyday forms of antisemitism.[27] Vulgar, garden-variety antisemites do sometimes turn into fascist ones, but it is at least equally problematic that the widely shared, socially accepted, non-fascist forms of antisemitism protect fascist antisemites from detection. The widespread habit of equating CDAS/LDSAS with CRAS gave Hitler cover: for far too long, too few people took Hitlerite antisemitism for more than the kind that was familiar to everybody as a 'cultural code'. It was therefore not taken literally. Likewise, today, heavily armed apocalyptic antisemites will find it the easier to hide the more the internet teems with casual, complacent and unthinking cultural-resentment antisemites left, right and centre. The latter need to be challenged and confronted not so much because they are all future Hitlers but because the future Hitlers can hide in the smoke and confusion they create.

Radical antisemitism – the kind that is more than a 'cultural code' – is meta-political.[28] Its principal strength and attraction lie in its being beyond ordinary politics: it connects to and invites the opposite side. The ambiguous meaning of the word 'Socialism' in its name was crucial to the success of National Socialism, as it allowed the party to reach out across class divides. At the same time, the word 'National' reduced the ambiguity of the 'Socialism' to a safe minimum: Hitler was perfectly clear that his was a *community*-based socialism 'the German way', that is, without the corrosive Jewish-Marxist talk about class struggle. Importantly, this was not 'code' – it was what it was, singularly brutal and eliminatory. This puts it into a category all its own. Nevertheless, it also belongs into the much wider category of nationalist socialisms that affirm the capitalist mode of production but claim

---

[25] On the other hand, though, the fact that some individuals do cross over from the latter to the former may suggest that the meta-political virus is already built into the 'antisemitism as cultural code'. There is perhaps a hidden code within the code.

[26] The German term *Verharmlosung* is pertinent here: 'making it appear to be rather harmless'.

[27] The genocide of the Holocaust is not simply the fully developed form of an antisemitic Twitter meme in the way the oak tree is of the acorn.

[28] 'Meta-political' denotes a move away from, or beyond, party politics and the framework of nation-states towards the level of culture, 'race' or civilization (Payne 1995). The term seems to have been coined by Ernst Nolte in *Three Faces of Fascism* (1966).

to be 'anti-capitalist' in their rejection of some aspects of capitalist circulation and reproduction – greedy immoral bankers who behave like locust swarms and so on – and seek a solution to 'the social question' at the level of the nation-state. The more eccentric side of Nazi ideology, its cosmic-racial-civilizational meta-politics, seemingly contradicts its more prosaic register of extreme 'palingenetic' (i.e. rebirth-) nationalism, but the latter was both the basis of the former and the default fall-back option when the cosmic ambitions hit the buffers.

The Nazis' National Socialism is simultaneously unique and representative of a genre. There are many forms of nationalist socialism, and they are as current and popular as ever. They are by nature receptive to antisemitism if and when the cultural-historical context makes 'the Jews' plausible victims whose destruction can be presented as being in the service of national regeneration or liberation.[29]

Conservative versus corrosive capitalism

Although antisemitism is not mentioned in it, I would like to argue that the most important text for understanding modern antisemitism is Marx and Engels' *Communist Manifesto*. Its first section sets out with relish why the ruling classes of Europe had to fear capitalist modernity that increasingly, whether they liked it or not, was becoming the material basis of modern domination and exploitation, and which they could only adopt, or be swept away by. The bourgeoisie, by which they actually meant the capitalists as Engels later clarified in a footnote, destroyed all ideas of 'natural' superiority or hierarchy, all sentimental illusions and prejudices, including religion, family, patrimonialism, parochialism and nationality: rational, egotistic, centralizing, state-building but cosmopolitan capitalism seems to signal here the end of ideology as new illusions are outdated before they can even 'ossify'. Communism appears as a 'spectre', a conspiracy of shady, isolated radical individuals, only to those who fail to see it as the product of the dialectical dynamics of bourgeois society. Behind the alleged uncanniness of communism stood the Jekyll- and Hyde-character of capitalism itself that not only has destroyed the old regime but also has produced, in the proletariat whose humanity it negates, its own imminent negation.[30]

---

[29] The historical-cultural context that makes modern antisemitism plausible (and likely to occur in the type of situation described) is roughly what Nirenberg (2013) described in *Anti-Judaism*: the entire 'Western' (i.e. Christian-Islamic) civilization whose intellectuals construct Judaism as a negative foil for reflecting on itself.

[30] This argument, very condensed in the *Manifesto*, is first developed in the *German Ideology*. Lenin echoed this train of thought on the concluding pages of *The Development of Capitalism in Russia* (in the section titled 'The "Mission" of Capitalism') where he asserted that 'recognition of the progressiveness of [the historical role of capitalism in the development of Russia] is quite compatible ... with the full recognition of the negative and dark sides of capitalism' (1956: 654). He attacks the Narodniki for claiming 'that an admission of the historically progressive nature of capitalism means an apology for capitalism', thereby making invisible its contradictions. Lenin briefly mentions the 'increase in the productive forces of social labor' and then goes into much more detail on 'the socialisation of that labor', which he defines quite broadly. Apart from all the usual suspects (expansion of production, centralization, mobility, urbanization), he also mentions that 'capitalism eliminates the forms of personal dependence that constituted an inalienable component of preceding systems of economy', naming 'patriarchalism' in particular, that 'capitalist

The remainder of the *Manifesto* elaborates on the notion that communism is *not* that spectre-like conspiracy but the light-as-day consequence of the bourgeois order, and lays out what the communists should *avoid* being: nationalist, sectarian, secretive, positivist, authoritarian. The communists only need to abolish institutions that are *in their bourgeois form* chimerical already, such as property, nationality and family: the latter are the spectres; they hardly exist. No mystery here, no secret blueprint, no conspiracy. (The rejection of conspiratorial politics was one of the hallmarks of Marx's politics throughout his life.)

Understanding the dialectic of capitalist civilization itself, and the dialectical dependency of the communist movement on capitalist modernity, requires dialectical thinking, which probably springs from an individual's strongly felt experience of non-identity. In a world that sees identities everywhere, admitting non-identity is hard to do. Those condemned to possess a straight mind, identical to themselves, smug, happy, undisturbed, well-balanced, integrated subjects, are likely to find ways of thinking about the contradictory realities of our civilization that will de-dialecticize and obscure them. To recognize the self-destructive dynamics of the capitalist mode of production as the engine on which rests our hope of overcoming capitalism is perhaps the hardest thing to think. It is easier to think either of ourselves as 'the other' of capitalism that will confront and defeat it (say David 'Lifeworld' fighting Goliath 'System'), or else to confront bad (bureaucratic, 'iron cage', alienating, greedy) from the standpoint of good (heroic, ethical, fair-trade, productive, creative) capitalism. Robbed of its dialectical dynamics, thinking becomes dichotomous. The third section of the *Manifesto* consists of a roll-call of contemporary socialisms all of which are censured for lacking a dialectical understanding of capitalism and its overcoming; a closer inspection would show that quite a few of those at the receiving end of Marx and Engels' polemic also showed elements of antisemitism, the 'socialism of fools'.[31]

In a world that has the nation-state for one of its principal political structures, benign, productive, harmonious, all-round enriching capitalism is most easily imagined as a nationalist form of state capitalism (what presumably most people think of as 'socialism'). Anything national, though, can easily tip over into its racial complement (Balibar 1991). Depending on context, capitalism with, say, German characteristics can morph into 'Aryan' capitalism and back, and needs to define itself against the foil of French, English, Yankee or Jewish capitalisms, as the case may be. The dichotomy between, say, a German and a Jewish 'kind' of capitalism, the former concrete and wealth-creating ('schaffend'), the latter abstract, exploitative

---

society increases the population's need for association' and effects a 'change in the mentality of the population' (357–9).

[31] The *Manifesto* (first published in early 1848) does not engage with antisemitism, which probably did not seem like an important enough dividing line at the time. Marx had famously called out and challenged Bruno Bauer's opposition to Jewish emancipation four years earlier in his review essay of 1844, 'On the Jewish Question' (Marx 1961). Engels later ([1877] 1975) devoted one of his most influential books to a comprehensive critique of the socialist philosopher Eugen Dühring, whose antisemitism Engels mentions in passing. Like Bruno Bauer in the 1860s, Dühring became in the 1880s one of the most radical antisemites of the time. Although Marx and Engels did not develop an actual critique or theory of antisemitism, it is arguably no coincidence that some of those against whom they directed their fiercest polemics were, or became, key figures of political antisemitism.

and value-appropriating ('raffend'), is one of the elements of continuity that linked the antisemitism of nineteenth-century German liberals such as Gustav Freytag or Heinrich von Treitschke,[32] and that of socialists who dreamed of harmonious, national-capitalist development such as Eugen Dühring, to Hitler's.

Without a concept of capitalism that differs from that which underpins antisemitic 'anti-capitalism', it is impossible to argue that the latter is either not an anti-capitalism at all or not one that might lead to emancipation.[33] Marx spent the two decades after 1848 to develop such a concept; the helplessness of most liberals and socialists in dealing with antisemitism in their own ranks (LDSAS) stems not least from their lack of a theoretically grounded critical concept of capitalism with which to debunk the antisemites' pseudo-anti-capitalism.

State, nation, world system

Nationalism, in any of its many varieties from social-democratic republican 'patriotism' to fascist National Socialism, is, in the realms of politics and culture, the signature of the attempt to create non-corrosive capitalism, capitalism minus its in-built contradictions and tensions that contain the potential of its self-transcendence: capitalism of a calm complexion, anodyne, undisturbed by struggle, discreetly self-perpetuating, non-partisan, anti- or meta-political. As the medicine does not, in fact, work like that, the dosage tends to be steadily increased, and the analgesic becomes a universal fire-starter: when nationalism, on the one hand, is meant merely to stabilize civilization by showing women, gays, the dangerous classes, foreigners and others their places, on the other hand, it becomes in fascism and imperialism a threat to civilization's very existence.

The modern state is constituted, and reconstituted continuously, by capitalist world society itself, whose political form the state system is: the modern state system and the capitalist world system are different dimensions of the same historical constellation (von Braunmühl 1978; Bonefeld 1992; Song 2011). The distinction between the system of nation-states and the capitalist world system is merely a distinction within a dynamic totality, that is, a totality whose different elements are mutually constitutive and obey the same dynamic force that governs everything within the constellation. For this reason, it is misleading, and politically a dead-end, to assume that the national state can be an instrument for 'fighting back' against the world system: it is an aspect of that system itself. One must avoid fetishizing the distinction between the individual state and the global system. This is difficult because anyone who can perceive the obvious ugliness of global capitalism is susceptible to being mobilized, often in good faith, to defend the national state from the global-capitalist onslaught as the nation-state speaks to its particular constituents *as its nationals*. This is a reality, but one that must not be taken at face value: accepting being addressed in this form means potentially also accepting the drift towards fascism, or at least will undermine any effective resistance.

---

[32] On this, see Achinger and Stoetzler (2013).
[33] On the relationship between anti-capitalism and emancipation, see Stoetzler (2012).

The strategy of turning the capitalist nation-state into a rampart against capitalism, of making national community overcome capitalist society, is fundamentally and logically impossible, but its futility can be masked by making the effort ever more virile and martial. The strong believer in the nation's ability to defend state and society from the ugly sides of capitalist modernity will be tempted to blame the inevitable failure of the project on the feebleness of milquetoast liberal-civic nationalism whose politics are not undergirded by cultural-ethnic-religious-racial claims of identity: failure will make the liberal-nationalist or social-democrat either retreat or give in to more robust and muscular, ultimately violent and paranoid nationalism – *et voilà*, fascism is only a step away.[34] 'We are all in this together' becomes *Volksgemeinschaft* when empty coffers demand clarification as to who belongs to the 'we' and who does not.

Unfortunately, the muscular nationalists, in their delusion, have a point: civic nationalism is ill-prepared on its own terms to survive the fascist onslaught. In the current situation, many of the world's largest countries are governed by authoritarian nationalists, while liberals and democrats generally fail to propose exciting new policies on the back of which they could defend the existing order from the proto-fascist surge. Furthermore, where they are still in control of the state, they try to *demobilize* those who look and fight for a non-fascist alternative. They tend to find this quite an easy task: as critical theorists suggested already in the early 1930s, the authoritarian and nationalist Communist Party of the Weimar period was designed to fail as it had produced and reinforced an authoritarian personality structure in its members that prevented many from resisting fascism (Murphy 2018; Durkin 2018). The same is true, more or less, of any modern political party. In the Critical Theory perspective, the touchstone of whether any social or political movement or project today is worth supporting must be whether it contributes to strengthening autonomous and anti-authoritarian individuals, that is, the types of people who are able to associate and cooperate without the imposition of heteronomous authority. Nothing less will do.

Nationalism is the central ideology of the capitalist world system not least because it functions well as the political form of diverse societal contents: national conflicts are also conflicts about differing conceptions of capitalist modernity and modern statehood. Nationalism is so powerful because it manages to present itself as the 'natural' form of such conflicts: it naturalizes any social conflict by making it appear national. Observers of a national conflict, like the Israel/Palestine conflict, will inevitably and automatically translate back what they observe into the language of conflicting social ideals and types of state and society, turning the postcolonial space in question into a mental space, a stage on which ideas collide and fight. In the process, outside observers may, for example, project latent antisemitic ideology onto the conflict in Israel/Palestine that would not impact their analysis of any other similar conflict.

---

[34] Postone suggests that the fascist cult of violence, in fact, mirrors a central aspect of the dynamics of the capitalist mode of production: 'An irony involved in this "radical" stance, in the idea of violence as creative, cleansing, and revolutionary, is that it expresses and affirms a central characteristic of capitalism: its ceaseless revolutionizing of the world through waves of destruction that allow for creation, for further expansion. (Like the liberal notion of the rational actor, the existentialist and anarchist notions of the self-constitution of personhood through violence entail a projection onto the individual of that which characterizes corporate entities in capitalism.)' (2006: 106).

Those in 'the West' brought up in a Christian-ish environment must, for example, take into account the real possibility that their judgement may be influenced by a kind of unacknowledged 'morality play': the 'Jewish state' may well trigger subconsciously held imaginings of heartless 'Jewish modernity' and greedy 'Jewish capitalism' that must conflict with the warm-as-blood, community-minded, non-greedy, hard-working capitalism of genuine, 'organic' nations. The parable of 'Jesus driving the money-changers and merchants out of the Temple', a week before he famously died, operates in the deep tissue of our civilization, and we better keep an eye on how it plays games on our minds.

Antisemitism is selective and also rather flexible as to *which aspects* of the complex, contradictory phenomenon that is capitalist modernity it finds undesirable: greedy bankers, egoistic trade unionists, unruly women, anything cosmopolitan, sexual reform, the emancipation of gays, imperialism – all can be coded 'Jewish'. All of these are, in fact, historically connected – directly or indirectly, albeit not necessarily causally – to the expansion of capitalist modernity in its liberal vein; they can therefore, in the mind of the antisemite, appear as so many different effects of the same Jewish machinations. The structure of antisemitic ideology does not require logical consistency. In the *Protocols of the Elders of Zion*, the Jews are supposed to promote liberal capitalism as well as social democracy only in the service of a global über-Bonapartist dictatorship; the former are merely strategic gambits. The antisemitic authors of the *Protocols* did not assume anyone, not even the Jews, would promote liberalism and/or socialism in good faith. The absurdity of antisemitic reasoning defends itself with the notion that nothing will be too absurd for 'the Jews' to do to advance their project of universal domination.

The shared ground that makes the meta-politics of antisemitism possible is characterized by the emphasis on community over class struggle, totality over fragmentation, defending identities over changing the world. In reality, though, there is no community in capitalist society except the 'societal community' (Parsons 1966) of the capitalist nation-state which is a unity based on division, fragmentation and antagonism ('division of labour', to use the sociological euphemism). Antisemitism with its boundary-transcending and taboo-breaking mystique is the signature of those who aim to transcend partiality, fragmentation, particularity and division by exorcising the fragmenters. They hope thereby to make true capitalist society's false claim to being a community.

The notion that there are good and bad capitalisms is mirrored by the notion that there are good and bad nationalisms. The fetishizing, dichotomizing mind of the inhabitant of a world shaped by the fetishism of commodities splits up the reality of nationalism as it actually is (featuring some nice things like a national health service or the national opera and a lot of bad things, including any nation-state's realpolitik that must serve its own national interest) into two ideal-types: on the one hand, the imaginary pure essence of the true heroic patriotism of communities that are imagined to lack divisions of class, politics, gender and so on against, on the other hand, oppressive, imperialist nationalism, which antisemites see epitomized in the evil scheming of the Jewish (anti-)nation and, in the present period, the imperialistic 'entity' of Israel. As the concept of the nation-state receives its meaning from its being an element of the global nation-state system, such a dichotomy is as nonsensical as that between benign, productive, homey capitalism and capitalism-as-imperialism: imperialism is nothing other than the expansion of capitalism, though, a system to which expansion is essential.

No apparently national conflict is just that. Local geopolitics, the interested rivalries of nation-state elites and their apparatuses, including those of states not yet in existence, matter but must not be overestimated: no elite succeeds in mobilizing a population for a particular political programme simply because they are the elite – to the contrary, they are (and remain) the elite only because they hit on a strategy that works in the context, and there are always societal reasons for why it does or does not do. The crucial question is therefore why any particular political position or movement, such as any particular form of nationalism, *resonates* among large numbers of people; this means asking about the societal content of any political phenomenon. Why do large groups of people, or even majorities, follow this rather than that faction of the elite? What makes them shift from one to the other, and why does, for example, Jew hatred at one point acquire an importance it did not have at a previous point? With reference to the Middle East, Postone points to the fundamental reality of socioeconomic changes in the capitalist world system, arguing

> that the spread of anti-Semitism and, relatedly, anti-Semitic forms of Islamicism [*sic*] (such as the Egyptian Muslim Brotherhood and its Palestinian offshoot, Hamas) ... may be sparked and exacerbated by Israel and Israeli policies, but its resonance is rooted in the relative decline of the Arab world against the background of the massive structural transformations associated with the transition from Fordism to neoliberal global capitalism. The result is a populist antihegemonic movement that is profoundly reactionary and dangerous. (2006: 101–2)[35]

---

[35] Islamism and other forms of modern 'fundamentalism' developed in tandem with and took inspiration from the European, anti-Enlightenment, post–First World War Conservative Revolution, a transfer that can be observed in the work of the Muslim Brotherhood's influential theorist Sayyid Qutb. 'Salafism is a political formation of the Far Right, one that is singularly focused on the sacralization of virtuous womanhood' (Cooper 2013: 30). Qutb understands capitalism as the expression of excessive, unregulated desire (Cooper 2008); his is a form of anti-capitalism that is centrally concerned with women's labour, understood as generalized prostitution and corrosive of societal order. Cooper argues that Qutb translates the concerns of the Conservative Revolution from the Christian idiom into an Islamic one. The Islamist vision is therefore, as Cooper states, 'in perfect alignment with the political transformations of the British and US neoliberal state over the last decades, which has progressively sought to outsource social service provision to the faith-based initiative' (2008: 28). The connection between the German/French/Italian tradition of Conservative Revolution and Islamism has been made by a variety of authors, including Al-Azmeh (1991, 2009), Bassi (2010), Bhatt (2006, 2014), Cooper (2008, 2013) and Halliday (2007). On the concept of 'fundamentalism', see Cowden and Sahgal (2017), Zubaida (2011), McDonald (2014) and Women Living under Muslim Law (2005). Qutb's text 'Our Struggle with the Jews', a key source of Islamist antisemitism first published in or around 1951 but disseminated widely only in the 1970s, is contained in Nettler (1987). Other source texts are included in Euben and Zaman (2009). Al-Azm (1993: 79) argues that the concept of 'fundamentalism', which stems from the context of Christianity, is valid also in the context of Islam because all forms of 'fundamentalism' are responses to the same global societal transformations irrespective of which particular cultural or national contexts they are articulated in; furthermore, in the cases of Judaism, Christianity and Islam, these contexts themselves are, in fact, much less different from one another than their 'fundamentalist' proponents may claim. The claim that there are 'civilizations' so fundamentally

He suggests that the decline of the Fordist accumulation model, much more than the Israeli army, destroyed the viability of more traditional, relatively secular Arab state-centric nationalisms; the latter's decline opened the space for Islamism's turning from a concern of elite factions to populist mass movements. Asking what (short term) *triggered* them is different from asking what (longer term) *caused* them, and what they *are*. A similar point is made by Melinda Cooper, who writes that

> a comparative historical view reveals a remarkable synchronicity to the worldwide resurgence of religion, even across the most intransigent geopolitical and doctrinal divides. In contexts as diverse and inimical as the United States, Egypt, and Iran, the return of political religion during the 1970s can be correlated with dramatic shifts in the gender, class, and ethnic composition of work, as the Fordist-developmental consensus around (masculine) formal, industrial labor succumbed to the flexible restructurings of post-Fordism. (2013: 35)

Imperialism, anti-imperialism and foolish associations

The tendency among anti-imperialists to make 'imperialism' the most significant category of analysis of the contemporary world implies the claim that capitalism has fundamentally changed since the days of *Das Kapital*. When imperialism – a word with a range of meanings in different contexts – still mostly meant the use of military power by states positioned at the core of the world system, it counted (correctly) as one important aspect of the capitalist world system among others. When in the period around 1900 the concept was substantially developed by the contributions of socialist economists and British 'New Liberals',[36] whom Lenin famously built upon in his canonical text on the matter, the augmented concept of 'imperialism' came to *replace* that of the capitalist mode of production among many of the subsequent advocates of anti-imperialism.[37]

> different that they are bound to 'clash' is itself fundamentalist. Al-Azmeh (2009) discusses a wide range of points of contact between Islamism and modern European anti-Enlightenment and Romantic thought, partly in terms of direct influences, partly in terms of shared origins in early modern and Enlightenment thought and its contradictions. Central ideas are the uniqueness of Islamic government that is neither categorizable with any of the established concepts such as liberalism or socialism, nor applicable to other civilizations; at the same time, it aims to bring about a society in a state of nature, or of 'natural reason', at which history will end and of which the pristine community of early Islam was a utopian premonition. Al-Azmeh points to the influence of a French proto-fascist, Alexis Carrel, whose writings on the 'degeneracy' of modern society and the need for an elite for the salvation of civilization 'entranced Islamist authors like Qutb and Shariati' (2009: 30). The philosophical naturalism that undergirds political Islam ironically results in extreme voluntarism, a nihilistic lack of concern for the specific historical conditions of political action, and the embrace of clandestine, avant-garde and putschist practices that are thoroughly modern, nineteenth-century inventions (31).

[36] In particular John A. Hobson, the textbook case of a liberal antisemite (Feldman 2019). See on this the chapter by Bolton in this volume.

[37] The notion that the period of liberal, competitive capitalism has ended and given way to monopoly or state capitalism of some form underlies also some of the arguments in *Dialectic of Enlightenment*, including the 'culture industry' thesis, as it is rooted in some of the same Marxist debates in the period around the First World War. The efforts, in particular, by Adorno in the period after the

The Leninist claim that imperialism represents the 'highest stage' of capitalism[38] implicitly suggests that the defining features of capitalism are not any longer the classic ones like generalized commodity production, wage labour and the appropriation of the surplus product in the form of surplus value. Any socialist will, of course, want to fight capitalism where it is at its 'highest stage', and if one believed this to be 'imperialism', then it followed logically that anti-imperialism would have to carry more weight than labour struggles, women's emancipation and other aspects that presumably related to capitalism's past 'stages'.

The charge of 'imperialism' can mean entirely different things, though. Some, following Marx's position, have accused European imperialism of *preventing* the global spread of the capitalist mode of production from destroying conservative social and cultural structures that stand in the way of human emancipation, notably clerical and other non-rational forms of the cultural legitimation of domination. This was a critique of the fact that metropolitan capitalism is quite happy to maintain and utilize 'traditional' social forms of oppression and domination, especially in the periphery. In the 1970s, this still would have been the predominant liberal and Marxist position: cynical European capitalists try to prevent capitalist development elsewhere, thereby preventing the globalization of the conditions for overcoming capitalism itself. Others, by contrast, accuse imperialism of actually doing what Marx, in fact, had *hoped* it would do: globalizing a secular modernity that would help destroy the cultural and political muck of ages as well as modernity's own principal engine, capitalism. This (essentially conservative) position is taken by many on 'the left' now: imperialism is fought because it destroys cultural identities and imposes universally identical monoculture. Whereas Frankfurt School Critical Theory reformulated the Marxian notion of the dialectical dynamic of capitalist modernity by updating and detailing the account of its more modern horrors while maintaining the basic position that there is no alternative to trusting the potentially redemptive powers of the dialectic of civilization (of 'enlightenment', as they called it), those who reject the Marxian dialectic give up on the notion of modernity as more humane and liberating: they embrace what, in fact, is the *conservative* critique of capitalist modernity that Marx spent a lifetime fighting against. If the expansion of capitalist modernity is a dialectical, contradictory force that creates labour as well as capital, racist particularism as well as anti-racist universalism (Wallerstein 1990), expressly rigidified gender norms as well as the destabilization of gender norms, then anti-imperialism, even more than anti-capitalism, is a category whose usefulness as a category of analysis very much depends on its being made specific (Stoetzler 2016, 2018): support of anti-imperialism must be made contingent on what the specific social content of any particular anti-imperialist

---

Second World War to bring back the careful study of the Marxian critique of political economy (which lay the groundwork for the 'new readings of Marx' and 'Open Marxism' as they emerged in the 1970s) can perhaps be seen as his attempt to paddle back against an undialectical understanding of this notion, against which he had expressed reservations already in the 1930s when the debate was raging among the Frankfurt School scholars.

[38] Usage of the bourgeois rhetoric of 'stages' is a hint that this does not represent the highest stage of Marxist theorizing.

struggle is. Before signing up, I must ask, who conducts the struggle and in the name of which societal goals – that is, what it actually means?

Cultural reactionaries and palingenetic ('rebirth') nationalists in various parts of the world utilize anti-imperialism as an umbrella under the cover of which they fight back against modernity's own – still largely undelivered – promise of emancipation, adopting to this end some of the most reactionary aspects of Western modernity itself, such as elements of the philosophy of 'revolutionary conservatism'. They are the heirs of the 'true', conservative, bourgeois and aristocratic socialists who were ridiculed in the *Communist Manifesto* whose authors would be horrified to see that some on the contemporary left welcome, or turn a blind eye to, authoritarian and patriarchal anti-liberalism driven by religious ethics, obvious flaws such as antisemitism, homophobia and sexism notwithstanding. This happens, in different ways, at various levels, the geopolitical, the national and the municipal: foolish associations with ultraconservative forces happen globally in the fight against imperialism, as well as domestically in the context of state-managed forms of multiculturalism.

Humans were not made for solitary life, but domination by capital and state keeps defeating and frustrating our longing for community, whether we acknowledge it or not. At least subconsciously, we have an inkling of the falseness even of the communities we advocate or partake in. We all look for something but we don't know what it is; we kind of know a lie even when we tell it ourselves. Admittedly, some are lucky enough to experience brief moments of effervescence – a protest, a walkout, an action – or the more subdued fires of a political, social or cultural project organized and maintained over time in solidarity, but most of the time the egalitarian community of struggle, the utopian lifeworld where we live the future already in the here and now, is imaginary. A society that makes the community of equals seem an unattainable utopia and covers society in the 'suffocating ash of everyday life' (Weber [1912] 2003: 94) makes people get their kicks elsewhere, mostly in the harmless offerings of the culture industry, but sometimes by turning unhealthy phantasies into murderous real-life catastrophes: an example would be those East London teenage girls who literally travelled through the end of the night into the false immediacy of the internationalist caliphate in Syria, swapping for promising but perhaps somewhat boring lives in London the hell of theological-political deceitful utopia. Other metropolitans, very sensibly lacking the guts for this level of self-destruction, project their unfulfilled communitarian longing onto the same or similar faraway places merely in the imaginary mode. Being too liberal and well-adjusted personally to fall for the charms of 'prophets of deceit' (Lowenthal and Guterman 1949), they partake in the deceits suffered by others elsewhere without the inconvenience of actually needing to travel there, and cheer even the most reactionary of 'my enemy's enemies' remotely from the comfort of their office chairs.[39]

---

[39] From a pragmatic-analytical perspective, Keith Kahn-Harris (2019) makes a similar argument: he points out that the New Left has always had a tendency to project onto anti-colonial struggles a redemptory quality they could never live up to, having previously misconstrued the struggles of the proletariat in the industrialized countries similarly: 'Too often, the heroic liberation fighter became a repository for Western fantasies and desires' (100, referencing Sartre's embrace of Maoism). He recommends 'decoupling victimhood from redemption' (103), something people who grew up in

A peculiar kind of Eurocentrism prevents some leftists from recognizing antisemitism and other proto-fascist elements of the ideology of the 'Conservative Revolution', developed in Europe in the 1920s, when it emerges in the updated form given to it by non-Europeans, who use it to express their own resentment of liberal modernity. In this context, antisemitism comes into play, as if through the back door, as part of a strategy that defends 'this' particular, concrete culture from being robbed of its identity and stability. Culture is today increasingly often articulated in religious terms and contrasted with the imperialism of generic, overwhelming, 'Western', modern, liberal, capitalist and relatively secular civilization. Antisemites denote the latter as 'Jewish'. In this context, resistance to antisemitism depends on refuting the grand narrative of (particular) 'culture' versus (universal, imperial) 'civilization' as well as the coding of the corrosiveness of capitalist modernity as somehow specifically 'Jewish' (Stoetzler 2020). Overcoming Eurocentrism must include acknowledging that people from East, West, North, South all over the world have been, and are, equally able to study and adopt ultra-right-wing attacks *on* 'the West' that were first produced *in* 'the West'. Anyone, whatever their background, who expresses the need to defend 'their culture' from unruly women, greed, the rule of money, homosexuals and so on may choose to blame the liberal-capitalist modernity that brought about all these 'corruptions' on 'the Jews'.[40] It is Eurocentric and patronizing, bordering on racist, not to take them at their word and not to oppose them.

Fantasies about valiant communities-in-resistance can also be projected onto an equally complex reality that is found in parts of the metropole itself. The imperialist logic of divide and rule that nineteenth-century liberals developed in the colonies is also applied in the metropole in the form of management by empowerment and co-opting of 'the communities'. State-centric liberal multiculturalism, a governmental technique for conditioning and containing the societal multiculture that is the normal reality of modern urban everyday life, tends to utilize and consolidate the power of established 'community leaders'. If ultraconservatives succeed in establishing themselves as 'community leaders', bureaucratic multiculturalism empowers them further also to fight 'westoxification' and uppity women within the communities they lead.[41] When the Greater London Council under Ken Livingstone pioneered state-managed communitarianism in the early 1980s, it aimed to 'empower communities' in the struggle against white British racism but inadvertently also weakened the left's resistance

a Christian environment should find rather difficult to do, though. 'Desperately, selected Islamist movements are treated as if they are anti-imperialists with unfortunate rhetoric', while the Israel–Palestine conflict has become 'a metaphor for the world' (101). The latter can perhaps be seen as an ironic reflection of the way a liberal-democratic public has turned the Holocaust into a global metaphor, a universal signifier for evil as such, rather than a very specific historical event that demands very specific historical interpretation.

[40] Buruma and Margalit (2005) emphasize anti-urbanism as a key ingredient of their very broad conceptualization of a phenomenon similar to what I refer to here as 'Conservative Revolution'. Their brief comments on, for example, Japanese 'occidentalism' are very useful as they take away the focus from Islam: this is a pretty universal phenomenon.

[41] 'Westoxification' or 'occidentosis' is a term denoting cultural imperialism (Western culture being 'toxic') in Khomeinist ideology. The term was first coined by a secular follower of Khomeini, Jalal Al-e Ahmad (Abramson 2017).

to ultraconservatism in places where it did not recognize it.[42] Liberal politicians end up helping to empower the 'community leaders' of embattled and racialized minorities in the metropole when they see them only as victims of discrimination and fail to ask about the class, age and gender structures of the 'communities' and how 'community leadership' is established. Those of us who are painfully aware of our lack of, and hunger for, community are too easily awed by its actually existing semblances.[43]

Due to its dissemination in the hand luggage of Western civilization, modern political antisemitism, initially a European problem, is now a global one. The unpredictable feedback loops of globalization allow some religious instructors to reimport to Europe (sometimes in the name of 'authenticity', another nineteenth-century European invention) anti-traditional political theologies purged of the 'impurities' and 'corruptions' that mark actual traditions.[44] These purified, anti-traditional theologies are leavened with some of the least attractive ideas about modernity that Europeans developed in the late nineteenth and early twentieth centuries, including (modern) antisemitism, anti-feminism and other related ideologies. Its adoption by some non-Europeans is a sign of the latter's successful integration into a world system dominated by Europeans and their descendants and explained by Western ideas: imperialism and all the master's tools shape also the fight against imperialism, for better or for worse. Current immigrants to Europe are as well able as anyone else, though, to figure out which of the many contradictory things and ideas that the dialectic of enlightenment and modern capitalism have produced – from brain surgery to the atom bomb, from multicultural society to the Holocaust – are emancipatory and useful and which are not, unless European society denies them the breathing space to do so. If liberal society can defeat its own illiberalism, then enlightenment can still 'master itself' and 'assume its own power' (Horkheimer and Adorno 2002: 172) and figure out how to get to 'the better state of things ... where one can be different without fear' (Adorno 1978: #66).

---

[42] The paradox of multicultural liberalism inadvertently empowering ultraconservatives was discussed at the time primarily with reference to Hindu fundamentalism (Sahgal and Yuval-Davis 1990, 1992). Floya Anthias and Nira Yuval-Davis analysed the ambiguities of 'community' and bureaucratic multiculturalism in their *Racialised Boundaries* (1992). See also Anon. (2009).

[43] As it befits a totality, micro and macro levels are here in striking harmony: the ultraconservatives who are unintentionally empowered as 'community leaders' to gain oversight over a women's refuge in London may sing from the same hymn sheet as their fellow reactionaries who, at the level of world politics, take charge of the struggle against 'the West'. Ken Livingston's hosting of Yusuf Al-Qaradawi, the 'spiritual leader' of the Muslim Brotherhood, at London's City Hall in 2004 symbolized both tendencies in a single act. Both communitarianism, initially invented as a strategy of imperial rule (Mantena 2010), and modern anti-imperialist ideology – antisemitic undertones included (as in J. A. Hobson) – can be found in late nineteenth-century liberalism.

[44] It is important to keep in mind that 'fundamentalism' is the opposite of 'traditionalism'. The argument made by some in 'the West' that Islam as such is *intrinsically* Judeophobic, or even antisemitic, is in agreement with a fundamentalist reading of the 'sacred texts'. Those who want to make the argument that Islam *as such* is Judeophobic would need to demonstrate that the Judeophobic passages in the 'sacred texts' are constitutive of their overall thrust. Theology constructs a larger meaning out of a 'sacred' text that in itself is inevitably contradictory and polyvalent, by asking what is the relative importance of different parts of the text. For a historical critique of the concept of 'Islamic antisemitism', see Schroeter (2018).

Accentuate the negative!

Eric Hobsbawm remarked already in 1980 that a thirty-five-year period of 'striking though not universal recession of anti-semitism', some aspects of which he wrote were nothing less than 'amazing', was about to end (1987: 374).[45] For Hobsbawm, the phenomenon that needed explanation in 1980 was the thirty-five-year relative *absence* of antisemitism, not its resurgence. More naïve observers may have assumed the relative quiet was the signature of the progress of civilization. In fact, merely incidental factors had temporarily hidden antisemitism, the ugly flipside of a civilization that has after, and in spite of, Auschwitz not changed any of its fundamental structures. What happened was exactly what for Adorno and others counted as the worst-case scenario: civilization resumed its day-to-day operations where, in 1933, according to liberal-democratic opinion, it had suddenly been interrupted. After the interlude of National Socialism, business as usual was resumed. Therefore (once more Hobsbawm writing in 1980): 'There is no reason to believe that the roots of xenophobia, racism in general, or anti-semitism in particular, have permanently atrophied anywhere' (1987: 377). Some commentators suggest that antisemitism is now more common than in previous periods. Such a claim is difficult to assess: it seems problematic to make any judgement as to whether antisemitic *attitudes*, as opposed to the *manifestations* of such attitudes, have increased or decreased over a longer timescale.[46] It seems fair to say, though, that the polarization of publicized *opinion* on such matters *has* increased; this is at least potentially a good thing. My own impression is that the space to discuss and challenge antisemitism on the left has increased over the last decades, and thanks to the resurgence of genuine discussions of the Marxian critique of political economy (labelled as 'Value Critique', 'Open Marxism' or 'New Readings of Marx') since the collapse of Bolshevism and Social Democracy, there are now far *more* individuals willing and able to do so.[47]

---

[45] The cause was, according to Hobsbawm, that three of the four obvious reasons behind the recession of antisemitism were losing force: 'the recoil effect of the holocaust' that had stigmatized expression of 'dislike and distrust of, or a contempt for, Jews' (note: its *expression*, not the dislike itself) as it had been common amongst, for example, 'English upper middle class people even of relatively liberal views' (375); second, the admiration of the military feats of Israel which showed that the Jews were not just a people of contemptible eggheads; third, general prosperity had 'blunted a good deal of the social and economic resentments which gave anti-semitism its cutting edge'. Another quarter-century on, these three factors of the 'amazing' post-Holocaust tendency of antisemitism to recede have continued to evaporate. A fourth factor named by Hobsbawm – namely that other immigrant minorities 'became the main targets for racism' so that 'the firing line moved away' from the Jews, a factor he saw as more persistent than the other three – is weakened but still in evidence presently.

[46] Unfiltered access for just about anyone to electronic media that record, distribute and preserve in searchable form any opinion anyone may have on anything has only existed for a decade or so: it seems plausible to assume that the media environment has multiplied the number of *manifestations* of antisemitic attitudes irrespective of whether these attitudes themselves have become more or less common. Methodological naivety also makes it appear that conservatives are less antisemitic than youthful progressives because the latter are wont to volunteer terabytes of evidence, whereas the former do not typically share their innermost feelings and convictions with the digital commons.

[47] It is historically remarkable and very encouraging that sustained critiques of antisemitism are among the best-known texts within the canon of renewed, serious engagement with Marx, including those by Postone, who first published on the subject of antisemitism in 1979 (Postone 1980, 1985a, 1985b,

Late nineteenth-century antisemites dismissed the Marxist labour movement as a 'Jewish-capitalistic' movement, a false flag operation by the Golden International, because they may have sensed (correctly) that Marx's perspective was not straightforwardly anti-capitalist but, in an ironic sense, *in-through-and-beyond-capitalist*.[48] The Marxian conception of transcending the capitalist mode of production depends on the latter's own dynamics and relies therefore on capitalism's most up-to-date version. A labour movement with an emancipatory rather than restorative perspective would not try to tame or dilute capitalism by subjecting it to the benign authority of the state: nothing could be more depressing than being stuck in a stable, well-tempered, steady-state kind of capitalism that looks like it will grind on forever.[49] In the name of the dialectical view of capitalism expressed in the *Communist Manifesto*, Marx and Engels rejected any suggestion the labour movement should ally itself with anti-liberal conservatives and the Christian ethics of the monarchic state. (Their antisemitic opponents might well have taken this as confirmation of their belief that the 'Red' and the 'Golden International', led presumably by Marx and the Rothschilds, respectively, were essentially the same thing.)

The left must stick by the Enlightenment's still largely undelivered promise of human emancipation. 'Left-wing antisemitism' strictly speaking – LDSAS – tars 'the Jews' with the brush of being enemies of *liberté, égalité, fraternité*, that is, enemies of the left and therefore undeserving of its support. It differs from the phenomenon that people who are otherwise 'on the left' can have some very conservative attitudes and opinions, including elements of *right-wing* antisemitism such as the myth that capitalist modernity is a Jewish conspiracy. At this point, the distinctions become blurred, though: ultraconservatives oppose capitalist modernity because it *furthers* liberty and equality, but destroys traditional hierarchies, while leftists oppose it because it creates inequality, unfreedom, oppression and division, that is, it *stands in the way of* liberty, equality, fraternity: both claims are true as much as untrue, which is where the confusion and the foolish associations come from.

Some ideas that in contemporary discourses count as left-wing commonplaces, such as the idea that it is the role of the state to alleviate social inequality, are, strictly speaking, more rooted in conservative thinking: they stem from modernizing, nationalist, 'enlightened' conservatism that aims to manage and alleviate, as opposed to overcome, inequality. This may help explain why some on the left are sympathetic to conservative, and equivocal towards even ultraconservative positions. Left/right

---

1986, [1979] 1992, 2003, 2006), and by Bonefeld, who first stated his perspective in 1997 (Bonefeld 1997, 2005, 2014, 2019 and in this volume).

[48] 'Ironic' not in the sense of 'jocular' but in the sense of 'historical irony', that is, a dialectical process in which a historical force produces the opposite of what it seems, or perhaps an actor intends, to be producing.

[49] Marxist theorists like Pollock, Horkheimer and others discussed in the 1940s whether capitalism can morph into a state-centric form that suppresses its recurring crises and becomes practically invincible, be it the Stalinist, fascist or liberal (Rooseveltian) way. Although analytically of great significance, in a *normative* perspective, this question is much less important: possible or not, one should not *want* it. Critical Theory looks to end, rather than stabilize, capitalism. Capitalism is not, and should not be made, sustainable.

confusion can lead on, furthermore, to the Conservative-Revolutionary mindset that claims to have transcended the ordinary distinction between 'left' and 'right'.

Key to these questions is the concept of the peculiar dialectic between modern, capitalist civilization and the hope for emancipation that is central to Marxian theory. By far most instances of what is commonly perceived to be 'antisemitic anti-capitalism' are not anti-capitalism at all, but rather the antisemitic version of the conservative-reformist search for a way of politically *framing* capitalism that does not threaten pre-existing societal hierarchies of power, including those of race, caste, creed, sex and sexuality. Most antisemites, including supposedly 'left-wing' ones, want capitalism minus its 'anomic' or, as Comte might have put it, 'critical' dimensions, that is, capitalism minus its negative, corrosive, anti-identitarian effects. Critical Theory, by contrast, suggests the latter are the real basis of our hope to *transcend* the misery of our civilization.

References

Abramson, S. (2017), 'The Iranian Intellectual Who Inspired the Islamic Revolution and Admired Israel', 26 June, available at: www.tabletmag.com/sections/arts-letters/articles/iranian-intellectual-admired-israel (accessed 7 November 2022).

Abromeit, J. (2017), 'Transformations of Producerist Populism in Western Europe', in J. Abromeit, B. M. Chesterton, G. Marotta and Y. Norman (eds), *Transformations of Populism in Europe and the Americas, History and Recent Tendencies*, 231–64, London: Bloomsbury.

Achinger, C., and M. Stoetzler (2013), 'German Modernity, Barbarous Slavs and Profit-Seeking Jews: The Cultural Racism of Nationalist Liberals', *Nations and Nationalism*, 19 (4): 739–60.

Adorno, T. W. (1978), *Minima Moralia, Reflections from Damaged Life*, London: Verso.

Al-Azm, S. J. (1993), *Unbehagen in der Moderne. Aufklärung im Islam*, Frankfurt/M: Fischer.

Al-Azmeh, A. (1991), 'Islamist Revivalism and Western Ideologies', *History Workshop Journal*, 31 (2): 44–53.

Al-Azmeh, A. (2009), *Islams and Modernities*, 3rd edn, London: Verso.

Anon. (2009), 'Croissants and Roses. New Labour, Communalism, and the Rise of Muslim Britain', *aufheben*, 17: 1–32.

Anthias, F., and N. Yuval-Davis (1992), *Racialised Boundaries*, London: Routledge.

Arendt, H. (1973), *The Origins of Totalitarianism*, San Diego, CA: Harcourt Brace.

Balibar, E. (1989a), 'Le racisme: encore un universalisme', *Mots*, 18: 7–20.

Balibar, E. (1989b), 'Racism as Universalism', *New Political Science*, 8 (1/2): 9–22.

Balibar, E. (1991), 'Racism and Nationalism', in E. Balibar and I. Wallerstein (eds), *Race, Nation, Class: Ambiguous Identities*, 37–67, London: Verso.

Bar-On, T. (2011), 'Transnationalism and the French Nouvelle Droite', *Patterns of Prejudice*, 45 (3): 199–223.

Bassi, C. (2010), '"The Anti-Imperialism of Fools": A Cautionary Story on the Revolutionary Socialist Vanguard of England's Post-9/11 Anti-war Movement', *ACME: An International E-Journal for Critical Geographies*, 9 (2): 113–37.

Bermann, T. (1973), *Produktivierungsmythen und Antisemitismus. Eine soziologische Studie*, Wien: Europaverlag.
Berry, D. (2014), 'Metamorphosis: The Making of Daniel Guérin, 1904–1930', *Modern & Contemporary France*, 22 (3): 321–42.
Bhatt, C. (2006), 'The Fetish of the Margins: Religious Absolutism, Anti-racism and Postcolonial Silence', *New Formations*, 59: 98–115.
Bhatt, C. (2014), 'The Virtues of Violence: The Salafi-Jihadi Political Universe', *Theory, Culture & Society*, 31 (1): 25–48.
Bobbio, N. (1996), *Left and Right. The Significance of a Political Distinction*, Cambridge, MA: Polity Press.
Bolton, M., and F. H. Pitts (2018), *Corbynism: A Critical Approach*, Bingley: Emerald.
Bonefeld, W. (1992), 'Social Constitution and the Form of the Capitalist State', in W. Bonefeld, R. Gunn and K. Psychopedis (eds), *Open Marxism. Vol. 1: Dialectics and History*, 93–132, London: Pluto.
Bonefeld, W. (1997), 'Notes on Anti-Semitism', *Common Sense*, 21: 60–76.
Bonefeld, W. (2005), 'Nationalism and Anti-Semitism in Anti-globalization Perspective', in W. Bonefeld and K. Psychopedis (eds), *Human Dignity: Social Autonomy and the Critique of Capitalism*, 147–71, Aldershot: Ashgate.
Bonefeld, W. (2014), 'Antisemitism and the Power of Abstraction: From Political Economy to Critical Theory', in M. Stoetzler (ed.), *Antisemitism and the Constitution of Sociology*, 314–32, Lincoln: University of Nebraska Press.
Bonefeld, W. (2019), 'Critical Theory and the Critique of Antisemitism: On Society as Economic Object', *Journal of Social Justice*, 9: 1–20, http://transformativestudies.org/wp-content/uploads/Werner-Bonefield.pdf (accessed 28 June 2023).
Breuer, S. (1990), 'Die "Konservative Revolution" – Kritik eines Mythos', *Politische Vierteljahresschrift*, 31 (4): 585–607.
Buruma, I., and A. Margalit (2005), *Occidentalism: The West in the Eyes of Its Enemies*, New York: Penguin.
Cooper, M. (2008), 'Orientalism in the Mirror: The Sexual Politics of Anti-modernism', *Theory, Culture & Society*, 25 (6): 25–49.
Cooper, M. (2012), 'Workfare, Familyfare, Godfare: Transforming Contingency into Necessity', *South Atlantic Quarterly*, 111 (4): 643–61.
Cooper, M. (2013), 'Why I Am Not a Postsecularist', *Boundary 2*, 40 (1): 21–39.
Cowden, S., and G. Sahgal (2017), 'Why Fundamentalism?' *Feminist Dissent*, 2: 7–38.
Durkin, K. (2018), 'Erich Fromm: Psychoanalysis and the Fear of Freedom', in B. Best, W. Bonefeld and C. O'Kane (eds), *The Sage Handbook of Frankfurt School Critical Theory*, vol. 1, 55–71, London: Sage.
Engels, F. ([1877] 1975), 'Herrn Eugen Dühring's Umwälzung der Wissenschaft', in *Marx Engels Werke, Vol. 20*, 1–303, Berlin: Dietz Verlag.
Euben, R. L., and M. Q. Zaman (eds) (2009), *Princeton Readings in Islamist Thought: Texts and Contexts from al-Banna to Bin Laden*, Princeton, NJ: Princeton University Press.
Feldman, D. (2019), 'Jeremy Corbyn, "Imperialism", and Labour's Antisemitism Problem', *Histories of the Present*, 12 June, available at: www.historyworkshop.org.uk/imperialism-and-labours-antisemitism-problem (accessed 4 January 2020).
Fine, R. (2014), 'Rereading Marx on the "Jewish Question": Marx as a Critic of Antisemitism?' in M. Stoetzler (ed.), *Antisemitism and the Constitution of Sociology*, 137–59, Lincoln: University of Nebraska Press.
Guérin, D. ([1936, 1965] 1973), *Fascism and Big Business*, New York: Pathfinder.
Halliday, F. (2007), 'The Jihadism of Fools', *Dissent*, 54 (1): 53–6.

Herf, J. (1984), *Reactionary Modernism: Technology, Culture and Politics in Weimar and the Third Reich*, New York: Cambridge University Press.

Hobsbawm, E. ([1980] 1987), 'Are We Entering a New Era of Anti-Semitism?' in H. Fein (ed.), *The Persisting Question: Sociological Perspectives and Social Contexts of Modern Antisemitism*, 374–9, Berlin: Walter de Gruyter.

Horkheimer, M., and T. W. Adorno (2002), *Dialectic of Enlightenment, Philosophical Fragments* (ed. G. S. Noerr, trans. E. Jephcott), Stanford, CA: Stanford University Press.

Jandl, E. ([1966] 1976), *Laut und Luise*, Stuttgart: Reclam.

Jones, S. H. (2019), 'Book Review: *British Muslims: New Directions in Islamic Thought, Creativity and Activism*', *London School of Economics*, https://blogs.lse.ac.uk/politicsandpolicy/new-directions-in-islamic-thought-creativity-and-activism/ (accessed 7 November 2022).

Kaes, A., M. Jay and E. Dimendberg (eds) (1994), *The Weimar Republic Sourcebook*, Berkeley: University of California Press.

Kahn-Harris, K. (2019), *Strange Hate: Antisemitism, Racism and the Limits of Diversity*, London: Repeater Books.

Lenin, V. I. (1956), *The Development of Capitalism in Russia: The Process of the Formation of a Home Market for Large-Scale Industry*, Moscow: Foreign Languages Publishing House.

Lipset, M. S. (1960), *Political Man: The Social Bases of Politics*, New York: Doubleday.

Loeffler, M. (2017), 'Populists and Parasites: On Producerist Reason', in J. Abromeit, B. M. Chesterton, G. Marotta and Y. Norman (eds), *Transformations of Populism in Europe and the Americas, History and Recent Tendencies*, 265–92, London: Bloomsbury.

Lowenthal, L., and N. Guterman (1949), *Prophets of Deceit*, New York: Harper, available at: www.ajcarchives.org/main.php?GroupingId=6530 (accessed 28 June 2023).

Mantena, K. (2010), *Alibis of Empire: Henry Maine and the Ends of Liberal Imperialism*, Princeton, NJ: Princeton University Press.

Marx, K. (1961), 'Zur Judenfrage', in *Marx Engels Werke, Vol. 1*, 347–77, Berlin: Dietz Verlag.

Marx, K., and F. Engels (1974), 'Das Manifest der kommunistischen Partei', in *Marx Engels Werke, Vol. 4*, 459–93, Berlin: Dietz Verlag.

McDonald, K. (2014), 'Islamic State's "Medieval" Ideology Owes a Lot to Revolutionary France', *The Conversation*, 8 September, available at: https://theconversation.com/islamic-states-medieval-ideology-owes-a-lot-to-revolutionary-france-31206 (accessed 7 November 2022).

Murphy, J. (2018), 'On *The Authoritarian Personality*', in B. Best, W. Bonefeld and C. O'Kane (eds), *The Sage Handbook of Frankfurt School Critical Theory*, vol. 2, 899–915, London: Sage.

Nettler, R. L. (1987), *Past Trials and Present Tribulations: A Muslim Fundamentalist's View of the Jews*, Oxford: Pergamon Press.

Nirenberg, D. (2013), *Anti-Judaism: The History of a Way of Thinking*, New York: Head of Zeus.

Nolte, E. (1966), *Three Faces of Fascism*, New York: Holt, Rinehart and Winston.

Parsons, T. (1966), *Societies: Evolutionary and Comparative Perspectives*, Englewood Cliffs, NJ: Prentice-Hall.

Payne, S. G. (1995), *A History of Fascism, 1914–1945*, Madison: University of Wisconsin Press.

Pfahl-Traughber, A. (1998), *Konservative Revolution und Neue Rechte. Rechtsextremistische Intellektuelle gegen den demokratischen Verfassungsstaat*, Opladen: Leske & Budrich.

Pierce, R. (2019), 'Black Antisemitism Is Not Inherently "Left-Wing"', *Jewish Currents*, 20 December, https://jewishcurrents.org/black-antisemitism-is-not-inherently-left-wing (accessed 7 November 2022).

Postone, M. (1980), 'Antisemitism and National Socialism: Notes on the German Reaction to "Holocaust"', *New German Critique*, 19 (1): 97–115.

Postone, M. (1985a), 'Bitburg: May 5, and After. A Letter to the West German Left', *Radical America*, 19 (5): 10–17, https://libcom.org/files/Rad%20America%20V19%20I5.pdf or here https://repository.library.brown.edu/studio/item/bdr:89274/ (accessed 4 January 2020).

Postone, M. (1985b), 'Theses on Fassbinder, Anti-Semitism and Germany: A Frankfurt Autumn, 1985', *Radical America*, 19 (5): 24–33, https://libcom.org/files/Rad%20America%20V19%20I5.pdf (accessed 4 January 2020).

Postone, M. (1986), 'Anti-Semitism and National Socialism', in A. Rabinbach and J. Zipes (eds), *Germans and Jews since the Holocaust: The Changing Situation in West Germany*, 302–16, New York: Holmes & Meier.

Postone, M. ([1979] 1992), 'Antisemitismus und Nationalsozialismus', in Redaktion diskus (ed.), *Küss den Boden der Freiheit*, 425–37, Berlin-Amsterdam: Diskus – Texte der Neuen Linken.

Postone, M. (1993), *Time, Labor, and Social Domination. A Reinterpretation of Marx's Critical Theory*, Cambridge: Cambridge University Press.

Postone, M. (2003), 'The Holocaust and the Trajectory of the Twentieth Century', in M. Postone and E. Santner (eds), *Catastrophe and Meaning: The Holocaust and the Twentieth Century*, 81–114, Chicago: University of Chicago Press.

Postone, M. (2006), 'History and Helplessness: Mass Mobilization and Contemporary Forms of Anticapitalism', *Public Culture*, 18 (1): 93–110.

Rohkrämer, T. (1999), 'Antimodernism, Reactionary Modernism and National Socialism: Technocratic Tendencies in Germany, 1890–1945', *Contemporary European History*, 8 (1): 29–50.

Ross, A. R. (2017), *Against the Fascist Creep*, Chico, CA: AK Press.

Sahgal, G., and N. Yuval-Davis (1990), 'Refusing Holy Orders', *Marxism Today*, March: 30–5, available at: https://banmarchive.org.uk/marxism-today/march-1990/refusing-holy-orders (accessed 14 April 2023).

Sahgal, G., and N. Yuval-Davis (eds) (1992), *Refusing Holy Orders*, London: Virago.

Saintin, A. (2013), 'L'intellectuel socialiste révolutionnaire Daniel Guérin en Allemagne avant et après la catastrophe', *Vingtième Siècle. Revue d'histoire*, 119: 15–28.

Schlembach, R. (2013), 'Alain de Benoist's Anti-political Philosophy beyond Left and Right: Non-emancipatory Responses to Globalisation and Crisis', Working Paper Series of the Centre for the Study of Social and Global Justice, University of Nottingham, WP022, available at: http://sro.sussex.ac.uk/id/eprint/50230/1/CSSGJ_Working_Paper_Series.pdf (accessed 7 November 2022).

Schroeter, D. J. (2018), '"Islamic Anti-Semitism" in Historical Discourse', *American Historical Review*, 123 (4): 1172–89.

Sieyes, E. J. (1963), *What Is the Third Estate?* (trans. M. Blondel; ed. with historical notes by S. E. Finer), London: Pall Mall Press.

Solty, I. (2015), 'Links/rechts', in W. F. Haug, F. Haug, P. Jehle and W. Küttler (eds), *Historisch-Kritisches Wörterbuch des Marxismus*, 1153–68, Hamburg: Inkrit.

Song, H. Y. (2011), 'Theorising the Korean State beyond Institutionalism: Class Content and Form of "National" Development', *New Political Economy*, 16 (3): 281–302.

Stangler, C. (2017), 'The Red and the Rainbow: The Life and Work of Daniel Guérin', *Dissent*, Spring, available at: www.dissentmagazine.org/article/red-rainbow-life-work-daniel-guerin-french (accessed 28 June 2023).

Stoetzler, M. (2004), 'Postone's Marx, a Theorist of Modern Society, Its Social Movements and Its Captivity by Abstract Labour', *Historical Materialism*, 12 (3): 261–83.

Stoetzler, M. (2007), 'Antisemitism, the Bourgeoisie, and the Self-Destruction of the Nation-State', in R. King and D. Stone (eds), *Hannah Arendt and the Uses of History, Imperialism, Nation, Race, and Genocide*, 130–46, Oxford: Berghahn.

Stoetzler, M. (2012), 'On the Possibility That the Revolution That Will End Capitalism Might Fail to Usher in Communism', *Journal of Classical Sociology*, 12 (2): 191–204.

Stoetzler, M. (2016), 'Karl Marx (1818–1883) and Imperialism', in I. Ness, Z. Cope and S. Maty Bâ (eds), *Palgrave Encyclopaedia of Imperialism and Anti-Imperialism, Vol. 1*, 167–74, London: Palgrave Macmillan.

Stoetzler, M. (2018), 'Critical Theory and the Critique of Anti-imperialism', in B. Best, W. Bonefeld and C. O'Kane (eds), *The Sage Handbook of Frankfurt School Critical Theory*, vol. 3, 1467–86, London: Sage.

Stoetzler, M. (2019a), 'Capitalism, the Nation and Societal Corrosion: Notes on "Left-Wing Antisemitism"', *Journal of Social Justice*, 9: 1–45, available at: http://transformativestudies.org/wp-content/uploads/Marcel-Stoetzler.pdf (accessed 14 April 2023).

Stoetzler, M. (2019b), 'Learning from the Power of Things: Labour, Civilization and Emancipation in Horkheimer and Adorno's Dialectic of Enlightenment', *Marxism 21*, 16 (2): 210–35.

Stoetzler, M. (2020), 'For a Dialectical Concept of Culture', *Cured Quail*, 2: 8–22.

Stoetzler, M. (2021), 'Capitalismo, nación y corrosión social: notas sobre el "antisemitismo de izquierda"', *Bajo el volcán, revista del posgrado de sociologia de la Benemérita Universidad Autónoma de Puebla*, 2 (4): 327–59.

Stoetzler, M. (2022), 'Capitalisme, la nació i corrosió social. Apunts sobre l'antisemitisme d'esquerres', in A. Baer, B. Herzog, M. Stoetzler, K. Stögner and S. Salzborn (eds), *Escrits sobre Antisemitisme*, 57–82, Valencia: talón de Aquiles.

Volkov, S. (2006), 'Readjusting Cultural Codes: Reflections on Anti-Semitism and Anti-Zionism', *Journal of Israeli History*, 25 (1): 51–62.

von Braunmühl, C. (1978), 'On the Analysis of the Bourgeois Nation State within the World Market Context', in J. Holloway and S. Picciotto (eds), *State and Capital: A Marxist Debate*, 160–77, London: Arnold.

Wallerstein, I. (1990), 'Culture as the Ideological Battleground of the Modern World-System', *Theory, Culture & Society*, 7: 31–55.

Weber, M. ([1912] 2003), 'Authority and Autonomy in Marriage', *Sociological Theory*, 21 (2): 85–102.

Women Living under Muslim Law (2005), 'WLUML Statement to the World Social Forum – Appeal against Fundamentalisms', available at: www.wluml.org/node/1850 (accessed 4 January 2020).

Yuval-Davis, N. (1997), *Gender and Nation*, London: Sage.

Zubaida, S. (2011), *Beyond Islam: A New Understanding of the Middle East*, London: Tauris.

Part 2

Extensions

6

'Pathic' identification in populist movements: The spectre of antisemitism in right and left protest

Patrick Ahern

The murder of George Floyd by Minneapolis police officers inspired one of the largest protest movements in US history. Along with these protests came not only the calls for the end of state violence against people of colour but also a broader call to resist white supremacy and authoritarianism in favour of a more democratic order. Unfortunately, amidst the enthusiasm of the protests, there also appeared a re-emergence of antisemitic rhetoric in the terms of both 'coded' forms of antisemitism and more explicit forms of antisemitic conspiracy theories. The impetus to research the role of antisemitism in left and right protest groups emerged out of the rise in violence and rhetoric from right-wing extremist groups, and also from the rise in antisemitic rhetoric in an ostensibly antiracist movement on the left. At the height of the protests in the summer of 2020, former National Basketball Association star and close friend of George Floyd, Stephen Jackson, became an outspoken voice against the racial violence and inequity that created the conditions that led to the murder of his friend. Unfortunately, in the midst of this spirit of justified outrage, while defending professional football player DeSean Jackson's fake Hitler quote in an Instagram post, he turned to common antisemitic conspiratorial tropes, stating: 'You know who the Rothschilds are? They own all the banks', exclaiming: 'I haven't said one thing that is untrue' (Owens 2020). What was alarming was not necessarily that he would make such a claim, but rather the reaction by many supposed advocates for racial justice who responded by lauding him for 'speaking truths' or, more commonly, with silence.[1] In the following week in June of 2020, he spoke in Kalamazoo, Michigan, a town that had recently suffered a spate of instances of police violence against protesters.[2] It was striking that the organizers of the public speaking engagement decided to remain silent in the face of such antisemitic comments that would seem to not have any place in promoting solidarity in the fight

---

[1] A notable exception was the initial pushback that he received from Mark Sheperd, a nineteen-year-old described as a 'seasoned antisemitism combat artist' who confronted Jackson in an exchange on Jackson's Instagram live feed (Keene 2020).

[2] Kalamazoo was also the site of a Proud Boys rally in August of 2020, marked by inadequate response by public safety to prevent the rally from devolving into street violence (Lando 2020).

for racial justice. Unfortunately, this was not an isolated event, and there is a long history of 'left-wing antisemitism' that seems to feed into an uncritical form of populist unity. Even if many of the expressions are not as explicit as the words of Mr Jackson, and certainly not as explicit or vitriolic as the antisemitic rhetoric and violence that is encountered in right-wing populist protest, it does open up the question of how a self-reflexive and critical form of solidarity, resistant to the allure of conspiracies and hateful antagonism, could be fostered in the fight against racist and undemocratic forces.

The deployment of antisemitism expressed in self-contradictory yet persistent ways has found a place within the political rhetoric of the 'agitators' of the right for generations. The antisemitism of the right is a more visceral and aggressive expression of hatred, promoting an atmosphere in which conspiracy, stereotypes and resentment are realized in actual violence against Jewish people. Contemporary harangues against 'Hollywood' and a so-called cabal of 'elites' or 'intellectuals' can trace their roots to the agitators of previous generations to devastating effect. While cognitively incoherent, the appeal and repetition of political agitators necessitates psychological, social and political analyses. Rather than providing the psychological, social and political outlets to transform the causes of a disaffected populace's resentment in the direction of emancipation, the agitator offers up conspiratorial stereotypes, redirecting the individual's rage against the objective conditions towards the supposed embodiment of this frustration in 'the Jew'. The consequence of this redirection of resentment becomes actual violence and rage against Jewish people.

One of the key challenges to those committed to the values of the fundamental principles of human rights in the current sociopolitical climate comes from the appeal to forms of populism that are often resistant to critical self-reflection and quite often are authoritarian in nature and harbingers to hate and violence. It follows that any critical resistance to racist and undemocratic impulses must understand the psychological, social and political conditions that promote, as well as the mechanisms that activate, the appeal of right-wing antisemitism as well as other forms of hatred based in social identifications. For those involved in activism or advocacy in opposition to these undemocratic forces, there must be a mode of self-reflection that does not respond to one delusional and pathic identification with another. Beyond looking to resources for understanding the appeal of antisemitism in populist movements, the question that I wish to pose is: what might it take to develop a critical form of solidarity that does not carry along the baggage of self-defeating, 'pathic' forms of identification?[3]

Contextualizing the rise of populism

The polarization of politics, not only in the United States but notably in many places in South America, Europe and Asia, has precipitated the concerns that come

---

[3] The use of the term 'pathic' is following its use in Theodor Adorno's lecture titled 'Aspects of the New Right-Wing Extremism' (2020).

with the proliferation of antagonistic and fractured political rhetoric and also the emergence of a new brand of undemocratic, authoritarian elements moving into the mainstream of political discourse and activity. The well-founded critiques of the limitations of democratic self-determination in liberal democracies, let alone neoliberal frameworks, have provided ample evidence of the failure of so-called democracies to live up to their promise as inheritors of the French Revolution, for liberty, equality or fraternity. Political participation in the neoliberal context was to be modelled after the economic marketplace, where political parties modelled themselves after goods in the market, appealing to the real or imagined interest of the populace while serving the bottom line in the hierarchical economic system. The consequences of this transformation can be felt in the increased concentration of capital, ultimately opening the space for the increase in authoritarianism, whether it is expressed in professedly democratic or undemocratic frameworks. In his reflection on right-wing extremism, presented in 1967 but perhaps even more relevant today, Theodor Adorno (2020: 2) identifies the dangers of the objective conditions in which we live today when he wrote that 'the conditions for fascist movements are still socially, if not politically, present. Here I am thinking especially of the still prevailing tendency towards concentration of capital.' While the concentration of capital has escalated, what appears to be the most alarming and demanding of an urgent response is that the political conditions would seem to be more, and not less, susceptible to authoritarianism than when Adorno was writing in the postwar years.

The rise of neoliberal expressions of authority has revealed a weakened and vulnerable model of democracy that appears to be moving towards an even more troubling state of affairs with increased polarization and the rise of populism. Populist movements have arisen from both corners of the political spectrum, but what they share is a general outlook towards politics that assumes that the possibility for democratic deliberation has passed. Rather than a competition of political views, interests and policies, politics is seen as a battle between forces that are reduced to 'us versus them', good versus evil, the 'people' versus the 'elites'. In describing this phenomenon, Samir Gandesha (2018: 50–1) contrasts parliamentary democracy with populist politics, when he writes: 'Indeed, in place of parliamentarianism, debate and discussion and compromise between opposed parties and groups, populism suggests that politics hinges on the existential confrontation between "the people" and the "elite" or the "powerful".'

The rise of populist movements and populism is not a monolith, and it can clearly be debated whether or not there can be emancipatory populist movements. For example, it can, in some instances, be argued that populist movements have perhaps widened political discourse in calling for political responses to the needs of the masses concerning issues such as epidemic levels of opioid abuse, healthcare, childcare and poverty. However, such political conditions, especially when accompanied by the social and economic conditions created by the increased concentration of capital, provide a fertile ground for the manipulation of the masses and the expansion of authoritarianism and social division which finds manifestation in, among other ways, the rise of antisemitism within these populist movements.

Pathic identification and right-wing antisemitism

In attempting to understand the attraction of right-wing extremism, it is striking how the work of the early Frankfurt School writers on extremism and antisemitism resonates for contemporary observers. In the section of *Dialectic of Enlightenment* titled 'Elements of Antisemitism: Limits of Enlightenment', Horkheimer and Adorno (2002: 142) identify many of the ways antisemitism serves the interests of the ruling class when they wrote that 'bourgeois antisemitism has a specific economic purpose: to conceal domination in production'. This iteration of the purpose of antisemitism is helpful for understanding how antisemitism can serve those in power, but alone it does not provide the observer with a better understanding of how right-wing 'agitators' find a broader appeal and following. To understand this appeal, one must look to what the adherent supposedly 'gains' from such ideology and what are the mechanisms used by right-wing agitators.

In their text *The Prophets of Deceit* (released in abridged form in English as *False Prophets: Studies in Authoritarianism: Communication in Society, Volume 3*), Leo Lowenthal and Norbert Guterman (2017: 11) contrast the right-wing 'agitator' from reformers or revolutionaries of various stripes. Unlike the traditional activist, the agitator appeals to his audience without either looking to the socioeconomic structures or political reflections that are the source of their frustration, or providing a vision of emancipation from real-world problems. 'The reformer or revolutionary concentrates on an analysis of the situation and tends to ignore irrational or subconscious elements', they write. 'But the agitator appeals primarily to irrational or subconscious elements at the expense of the rational and analytical.' Rather than mediating an analysis of a social form (such as capitalism for the socialist), the agitator proceeds by appealing to a world that is hopelessly rigged by mysterious forces beyond their control in the press, culture and science. This opens up an apocalyptic vision that does not offer respite to the weary. Ambiguous references to conspiracy prevent the possibility for embarking upon a rational analysis of the objective conditions that are the source of their frustration.[4] Lowenthal and Guterman (2017: 27) observe that 'the agitator proceeds in exactly the opposite way. He refers to popular stereotypes only to encourage the vague resentments they reflect … On a social scale, he stirs reactions similar to those of paranoia on an individual scale, and his means of doing this is by indefinitely extending the concept of conspiracy.' Rather than providing an outlet for a greater understanding, the agitator 'cheats them of their curiosity', and rather than providing constructive models for emancipation, the agitator plays upon the satisfaction of unconscious and infantile desires.

What, then, is offered by the crude nature of right-wing antisemitism and rhetoric, even if coded in terms that avoid using explicitly racial terms, such as 'elites', 'Hollywood' or 'intellectuals'? Since it is not emancipation from difficulties and frustrations being offered, then the source of satisfaction cannot be, strictly understood, political in nature.

---

[4] Reference by right-wing politicians and media in the United States of 'deep state' conspiracies draw upon such well-worn tropes of conspiratorial bureaucracy.

Lowenthal and Guterman (2017: 38) diagnose the situation as one that exacerbates unconscious impulses, rather than working through frustrations to constructive ends, in what they term 'psychoanalysis in reverse'. They write: 'It may be conjectured that by his reference to rape, incest, and plunder, the agitator evokes sadistic fantasies that add a connotation of promise to the warning: his followers may vaguely hope that when the deluge comes they, too, may be allowed to perform the acts that are attributed to the enemy.'[5] What is offered, then, is the satisfaction of unconscious and infantile desires for destruction.[6] Since understanding of, or escape from, the conspiratorial condition is hopeless, all that is left is the apocalyptic vision of destruction and the enticement of the satisfaction of sadistic, unconscious desires.

The unique position of antisemitic elements in right-wing agitation draws upon well-worn stereotypes and tropes that are cognitively incoherent and able to maintain the flexibility to insert 'the Jew' as the source of danger and derision. Some of the most iconic images of recent right-wing activism have included the images of 'the Jews' as vying for world domination – as when the tiki torch-wielding crowds in Charlottesville shouted, 'The Jews will not replace us' – and that of the dominated and helpless, as exemplified by the famous image of the 6th January insurrectionist wearing a 'Camp Auschwitz' t-shirt. 'The Jew' who cannot get in line with the 'pathic' nationalism of the audience becomes an object of resentment and, ultimately, violent expressions of rage. The right-wing agitator 'transforms the stereotypes into a logically self-contradictory but psychologically consistent image of the Jews, who appear both weak and strong, victim of persecution and persecutor, endowed with unchangeable racial characteristics and irrepressible individualism' (Lowenthal and Guterman 2017: 75). The fungibility for the Jew to provide a source of derision that undercuts the capacity for self-reflection becomes manifested as the enemy on all sides, whether that is in the form of the free-thinking and unrepressed individual or the powerless victim. The image of the Jew as the 'communist banker' epitomizes the fantastical nature of the role 'the Jew' plays in right-wing ideology, for 'the Jew' represents both the dark cloud of state-centred communism and the 'bad' capitalist who engages in usury.

To be sure, this leaves little room for rational reflection, and the depths of the pathological identification of 'nation' and 'race' may not allow for breaking free from the ideological force of such prejudices. However, as such identifications have moved from the so-called lunatic fringe towards the centre of mainstream political discourse, and since resignation is not an option, one is compelled to look to what is required in response to such delusions and prejudices, namely, independent thought. In *Dialectic of Enlightenment*, Horkheimer and Adorno (2002: 165) speak to this aspiration in writing: 'Only the liberation of thought from power, the abolition of violence, could

---

[5] One can find echoes of this rhetoric in Donald Trump's discussions of immigrants as well.
[6] One can see the irrationality and infantile rage in practice when considering the role that various symbols play for right-wing groups, where any perceived slight to the symbol (such as national flags) calls for ruthless, unmediated rage. It is unsurprising to find the importance of imageboards and memes to spread their message. As Adorno (2020: 29) remarked: 'So the unconscious tendencies that feed the authority-bound personality are not brought to light by this propaganda; on the contrary, they are forced even deeper into the unconscious. Consider the excessive significance of so-called symbols that characterizes all these movements.'

realize the idea which has been unrealized until now: that the Jew is a human being.' The 'split in people's consciousness', where they are able to see concrete benefits to themselves despite their pathological identifications with right-wing populist movements, such as can be seen in recent resistance to the dissolution of the 'Affordable Care Act'[7] or in response to the opioid crisis, provides some insight into the possibility that, despite the irrationality of beliefs and rhetoric, there is a space in which rational reflection of concrete interests can take hold (Adorno 2020: 37).

Antisemitism and the left

Antisemitism on the left, while sharing some features of the conspiratorial satisfactions of the right, traditionally does not have the same visceral maliciousness as that found in right-wing antisemitism. However, if the left is understood, unlike the right-wing agitator, to be providing an account of the objective social, economic and political conditions that prevent emancipation, as well as political models of emancipation that follow from the values of the French Revolution, then any model of solidarity in favour of democratic principles would have to resist the urge to dichotomous and prejudiced thinking that has infiltrated populist movements on the left as well. The appeal of antisemitism on the left takes various forms, but these forms of antisemitism are also driven, especially in their conspiratorial form, to blind the advocate from confronting the complexities of social, political, economic and even national power. I will briefly look to the historical nature of left antisemitism that arises in both socialist and liberalist traditions in the form of 'the Jewish question'; then I will look to the role of antisemitic conspiracies and the debates surrounding discussions of Israel and Zionism before turning to the complicated relation of Black and Jewish emancipation.

The so-called Jewish question arose within the context of the Enlightenment and the values of the French Revolution that inaugurated a call for 'universal' human rights, albeit in the context of the early forms of the modern nation-state. 'The Jew' served as the fundamental other of national identity on the one hand and, contradictorily, the rootless cosmopolitan who was perceived as not 'earning' the right to have rights. Robert Fine and Philip Spencer (2017: 2) sum up the origins of the modern 'Jewish question' when they write that

> one of the peculiarities of the 'anti-Judaic' tradition has been to represent Jews in some important regard as 'other' of the universal: as the personification either of a particularism opposed to the universal, or of a false universalism concealing Jewish self-interest. The former contrasts the particularism of the Jews to the universality of bourgeois civil society; the latter contrasts the bad universalism of the 'rootless cosmopolitan Jew' to the good universalism of whatever universal is advanced – be it nation, the race or the class.

---

[7] The 'Affordable Care Act' refers to 'The Patient Protection and Affordable Care Act', often colloquially referred to as 'Obamacare'. This refers to the comprehensive healthcare reform law enacted in March 2010 that significantly expanded public access to healthcare.

Marx famously addressed the 'Jewish question' in his rejection of Bruno Bauer's claim that Jews should be excluded from having rights. The nuance of Marx's writing in this essay as well as in other treatments of the topic is often misunderstood, in terms of both his critique of 'bourgeois' manifestations of human rights and his rejection of antisemitic arguments in liberal and socialist circles that sought to exclude Jewish emancipation from the scope of human emancipation. The tradition of left antisemitism purports to view the Jew as the enemy of the values of liberty, equality and fraternity while undermining the very revolutionary force of such a call. The criticism of 'bourgeois' rights given in Marx's essay is not that these values should be abandoned, but rather that their manifestations within the confines of capitalist power are self-defeating, preventing human emancipation that would provide for liberty or equality, let alone fraternity. The premise of these images of 'the Jew', while coded in contrast to the overt antisemitism of the right, still preys upon the conspiratorial ideologies that prevent a critical reflection of the objective conditions that undermine emancipation. Marcel Stoetzler (2019: 36) succinctly diagnoses the self-defeating nature of left antisemitism when he writes:

> By far most instances of what is commonly perceived to be 'antisemitic anticapitalism' is not anti-capitalism at all, but rather the antisemitic version of the conservative-reformist search for a way of politically *framing* capitalism that does not threaten pre-existing societal hierarchies of power, including those of nation, race, caste, creed, sex and sexuality.

The moral repugnancy of antisemitism should go without saying, but when one looks closer at the manifestations of antisemitism on the left, it becomes evident that it entails a turning away from rational analysis and reflection regarding objective conditions and, to that extent and more, from the promise of human rights and human emancipation.

The tenor of antisemitism on the left is most of all filtered through the lens of anti-Zionist and anti-Israel rhetoric. The complexities and historical forces at work in the tensions and violence in the Middle East lend themselves to reductive understandings. In some sense, this is understandable since it is so difficult, especially for those who are not immersed in the multiplicity of forces and interests at stake. To be sure, the state of Israel has perpetrated excessive violence against its neighbours, maintained an illegal occupation of Palestinian lands that led to continuous violations of international human rights law, and organized a society based in institutionally discriminatory practices. A commitment to the value of human rights would compel any observer to critique and call for a change to these objective conditions. There is, however, a uniqueness to the tenor of the criticisms of Israel on the left that, rather than looking at the Israeli civil and political society in its complexity, addresses Israel as if it were a reified, homogenous and immutable entity in ways that are not reserved for the crimes and failures of other nations. The fervour against an individual nation (and not an individual leader, party, etc.) borders upon the sort of unreflective rage that is usually the signature of the worldview presented by 'pathic' nationalists. Rather than analysing what is unjust and undemocratic in Israeli society in order to resist these forces continuing to perpetuate actual injustice, there is often a quick turn to the notion of Zionist global conspiracies and at times a call to wipe out the Jews. Rather than promoting justice and calling those responsible to task, such approaches are blinding and self-defeating in the pursuit of a peaceful and just Middle East.

Since I began this reflection on the infiltration of antisemitic views within the context of the Black Lives Matter protests, I think it is important to note the complex relations historically and socially between Jews and African Americans. It is beyond the scope of this essay to provide a detailed history of this relation, but I think it is worth pointing out that often this relation has been both fraught by the underlying injustices within American society and enhanced by a shared commitment to emancipation, as evidenced by the relatively considerable number of Jewish contributors to the struggle for African American civil rights. However, the wounds of a society fractured by racial injustice have also had understandable consequences in fomenting tension. James Baldwin ([1967] 1998: 744), when reflecting upon his community's ambivalent relation to Jewish people, writes:

> In the American context, the most ironical thing about Negro anti-Semitism is that the Negro is really condemning the Jew for having become an American white man – for having become, in effect, a Christian. The Jew profits from his status in America, and he must expect Negroes to distrust him for it. The Jew does not realize that the credential he offers, the fact that he has been despised and slaughtered, does not increase the Negro's understanding. It increases the Negro's rage.

Baldwin here identifies not only the feelings of rage or resentment, but importantly reflects upon the causes of this rage. Rather than turning away from the social, historical and political conditions out of which this rage emerges, Baldwin provides a critical perspective that self-reflectively looks to the sources of rage and outwardly turns towards its causes. He is identifying the source of frustration in the white power structure in the United States, causing resentment against those who benefit from this structure, including Jews. Baldwin directs his frustration towards the socioeconomic conditions that allow for greater opportunities for white Americans as a source of this frustration. Baldwin's analysis stands in stark contrast to the political agitator who harnesses the rage and directs it outwardly in hate and violence that leaves the unjust structures that are the source of this rage untouched by critique. Unlike right-wing agitation, or conspiratorial ideological thinking of right and left, such critical reflections open the possibility of emancipation that would otherwise be stifled.

Critical solidarity

The challenge of developing critical solidarity is central to the possibility of fighting against oppressive and violent hierarchies of race, gender, sexuality and class, as well as imperialistic and militaristic forces that are mobilized in preserving or deepening the divides within the status quo. There is an unmistakeable appeal in providing simple, satisfying responses to complex problems, especially those that overwhelm the subject. Pathological conditions reach the point of no return at the moment when prejudice blocks the capacity for experience and thus reflection. Antisemitic conspiracies are a product of pathological states and only serve to deepen those pathological conditions. As historical evidence shows, such responses lead to the outward and self-defeating expressions of rage and violence. The challenge is, of course, to develop a more robust model of solidarity. At the very least, the recurrence of antisemitic rhetoric, often at the most urgent moment of political action, calls for strenuous resistance and self-reflection for those committed to a more just and humane world.

The affective pull of the divisive rhetoric of left populism carries with it the danger of cutting off the possibility of developing critical solidarity, carrying with it the perils of unreflective identification, in what Horkheimer and Adorno (2002: 172) referred to as 'ticket thinking'. They correctly warn that the dangers of the irrational mob lurk in supposedly progressive circles as well as in right-wing protest if the need for critique and self-reflection is not persistently fostered. They write:

> To be sure, the psychologically more humane are attracted to freedom, but the advancing loss of experience is finally turning even the supporters of the progressive ticket into enemies of difference. It is not just the antisemitic ticket which is antisemitic, but the ticket mentality itself.

Critical solidarity can only be developed out of a resistance to all forms of irrational affects of hate and from an affirmative and self-reflective coordination that allows for difference and dissent. For when cohesion is formed only insofar as passions are stirred, there is only a mob and not a mass movement. As Spinoza (1986, IVP32D) points out, 'insofar as men are subject to passions, they cannot be said to agree in nature ... For things that agree only in negation, or in what they do not have, really agree in nothing.' In other words, the mobilization of mobs by means of directing rage towards prejudicial hate cuts off the possibility for developing critical solidarity. This critical solidarity is required for a social movement that aims towards emancipation. Following Spinoza's insight, solidarity can only properly be developed through the shared power to act, and not through the release of rage through prejudicial hate.

The source of critical solidarity can only be developed within a shared commitment to a justice and dialogical framework of self-reflection and contestation regarding means and, in some cases, even ends. There must be a resistance to constructing a false solidarity that comes with models of communitarianism formed out of the 'pathic' connections to in-groups and out-groups, but is rather built upon the understanding that the strength of a movement arises from its capacity to incorporate and sustain difference while pursuing a cosmopolitan notion of solidarity.[8] The universalism promoted by such a critical solidarity can come not from an assumption of sameness

---

[8] Fuyuki Kurasawa provides an analysis of the various models of solidarity that range from the 'false' forms of provincial solidarity to cosmopolitanism in his text, *The Work of Global Justice: Human Rights as Practices* (2007: 160).

but from the commitment to a model of emancipation that not only allows for difference but also takes as its strength the capacity for rational self-reflection that can come with the incorporation of diverse perspectives. Along with the recognition that identifications that divide according to nationality, race, gender and so on create an impediment to the pursuit of a more just world comes the understanding that exclusionary identifications, such as those proposed by the antisemite, leave the concrete structures of oppression in place. The call for a critical solidarity that rejects such 'pathic' models of identification is not only a moral injunction. Rather, it is a call that emerges out of a rational reflection upon the structures and causes preventing a just world, as well as the practical needs for the realization of social transformation towards collective emancipation.

The development of a critical solidarity calls for the rejection of the definition of interest in terms of either liberal individualism or collectivist models. The atomistic model of interest prevents the possibility of solidarity and, at worst, provides ample ground for authoritarian tendencies to flourish, as seen in recent right-wing protests. Collectivist models that view solidarity as arising from similitude can ultimately only reinforce the structures of oppression by turning away from social and economic causes in favour of affective, and often infantile, satisfactions and pathic identifications. Solidarity cannot be bound to the premise of 'in' or 'out' groups that demand assimilation from their allies. The lessons and dangers that accompany the assimilationist model have long been evident to observers of and activists engaged in movements for emancipation. W. E. B. Du Bois (1990: 12) came to this realization in writing that the African American engaged in the struggle for freedom 'began to have a dim feeling that, to attain his place in the world, he must be himself, and not another'. Assimilationist compulsions or exclusions based on ideological constructs, such as those found in the 'Jewish question', where Jews were excluded from universal rights because they were seen as particular or external to the false universality of the Enlightenment, only offer the promise of group identification that will conflict with the aims of emancipation. In other words, critical solidarity calls for a dialectical coordination in which difference is not subsumed in identity.

The rise of right-wing authoritarian populism comes with the alarming threat of violence and the breakdown of even formal democratic structures. These conditions present a real danger for violence and the dissolution of even the nominal preservation, let alone the advancement, of human rights. The false belief that the resonance of such authoritarian populism was restricted to a fringe group of 'deplorables', as Hillary Clinton famously referred to this movement, only serves the self-gratification of those hoping to maintain an untenable status quo. Since those words about the 'deplorables' were uttered, the real breadth of the appeal of authoritarian variants of populism in the United States has become undeniable. In the period after the Second World War, when the fascist movements were far less mainstream, or at least pushed underground, Adorno (2020: 9) referred to these movements 'as the wounds, the scars of a democracy that, to this day, has not yet lived up to its own concept'. If one is to accept this premise regarding the objective conditions that promote the rise of collective irrationalism in the form of populist rage, the resistance to this phenomenon would not be served either by name-calling or by reassuring oneself that its appeal is limited to some fringe element in society. Resistance to this phenomenon can only come with careful and sustained analyses of the social, historical, economic and political causes that create the political arena of a mob mentality that infiltrates not only right-wing but also left-wing populism. Whether it is possible for a left-wing populism to advance rigorously democratic principles is murky at best, but any movement that is weighed down by exclusionary ways of thinking, such as misogyny, racism, nationalism and, indeed, antisemitism, abdicates the capacity for transformation from the status quo to a more democratic and humane world. It should be noted that this entails not drawing divergent perspectives 'into line', but rather developing a model of critical solidarity that is structured around rational reflection and democratic principles of unity in difference.

References

Adorno, T. (2020), *Aspects of the New Right-Wing Extremism* (trans. W. Hoban), Cambridge, MA: Polity Press.

Baldwin, J. (1998), 'Negroes Are Anti-Semitic because They're Anti-White', in T. Morrison (ed.), *James Baldwin: Collected Essays*, 739–48, New York: Library of Congress Press.

Du Bois, W. E. B. (1990), *The Souls of Black Folk*, New York: Vintage Books.

Fine, R., and P. Spencer (2017), *Antisemitism and the Left: On the Return of the Jewish Question*, Manchester: Manchester University Press.

Gandesha, S. (2018), 'Understanding Right and Left Populism', in J. Morelock (ed.), *Critical Theory and Authoritarian Populism*, 49–70, London: University of Westminster Press.

Horkheimer, M., and T. Adorno (2002), *Dialectic of Enlightenment* (trans. E. Jephcott), Stanford, CA: Stanford University Press.

Keene, L. (2020), 'Meet Mark Shepard, the Jewish College Student Who Talked Stephen Jackson Off the Ledge of Anti-Semitism', *Forward*, 9 July, available at: https://forward.com/news/450540/the-kid-who-went-toe-to-toe-with-stephen-jackson-on-antisemitism/ (accessed 9 September 2022).

Kurasawa, F. (2007), *The Work of Global Justice: Human Rights as Practices*, Cambridge: Cambridge University Press.

Lando, B. (2020), 'Kalamazoo Was Ready for the Proud Boys. Then We Weren't', *Now Kalamazoo*, 9 August, available at: https://nowkalamazoo.com/2021/08/kalamazoo-was-ready-for-the-proud-boys-then-we-werent (accessed 9 September 2022).

Lowenthal, L., and N. Guterman (2017), *False Prophets: Studies in Authoritarianism*, London: Routledge. (Facsimiles of the entire series *Studies in Prejudice*, including *Prophets of Deceit* and *The Authoritarian Personality*, can be found on the online archive of the American Jewish Committee: https://ajcarchives.org/main.php?GroupingId=1380.) (Lowenthal used the spelling Lowenthal since his move to the United States; Löwenthal is the name he was born with.)

Owens, J. (2020), 'Stephen Jackson Doubles Down after Supporting DeSean Jackson's Hitler Post: "Haven't Said One Thing That's Untrue"', *Yahoo!*, 9 July, available at: www.yahoo.com/lifestyle/stephen-jackson-doubles-down-after-supporting-de-sean-jacksons-hitler-post-havent-said-one-thing-thats-untrue-191952252.html?guccoun ter=1&guce_referrer=aHR0cHM6Ly93d3cuZ29vZ2xlLmNvbS8&guce_referrer_sig =AQAAAAOPCu2AnkkXwxfI0kQgRF18yBecLI7QoU1YHE0Vn2ZclwmJhq6uDCh KdUP6OrkFLNu58MZKiYoTs8pKzhdHwfi8NgOv7xmqJnEwS-KALe7J66ZEmma9 tjfY4Twnuttq5rERMQWrQYS2U9hBmJ0lxwoTtJu0LlvLCpHTp3IPln6u (accessed 9 September 2022).

Spinoza, B. (1986), 'The Ethics', in E. Curley (ed. and trans.), *Collected Works of Spinoza*, 85–265, Princeton, NJ: Princeton University Press.

Stoetzler, M. (2019), 'Capitalism, the Nation and Societal Corrosion: Notes on Left-Wing Antisemitism', *Journal of Social Justice*, 9: 1–45.

7

Ancient aliens down to earth: Conspiracy theories, antisemitism and 'anonymous authority'

Joan Braune

The Frankfurt School's work has been crucial for understanding fascism and antisemitism. A particularly important driving factor in fascist recruitment in the current period is conspiracy theories, especially antisemitic ones targeting Jews, although other minority groups are also targeted with conspiratorial claims of being secret controllers (or secretly controlled). Conspiracy theories can be popularized in various ways and exist in a symbiotic relationship with mainstream opinion, policies and structures as well as popular culture. Furthermore, conspiracy theories appeal to deep human desires, providing everything from the hunger for intellectual excitement to a unifying vision of the world, to a paradoxical sense of being a victim of powerful malevolent forces, and an insider 'in the know' about those forces. While conspiracy theories can attract people at the fringes of society who are sceptical of a power structure that they rightly sense is harming them, conspiracy theorists seek to mainstream their ideas and gain ground through subcultures.

Some of the most whacky conspiracy theories, and the ones that are easiest to laugh off, concern extraterrestrial life. But conspiracy theories about aliens need to be taken seriously, especially because of how they are growing in 'conspiritual' spaces. One of the ways conspiracy theories are gaining ground today is through what some are calling 'conspirituality', the mixture of New Age spirituality with far-right conspiracy theories. The term was coined in 2011 by Charlotte Ward and David Voas to describe 'a hybrid of conspiracy theory and alternative spirituality' they saw gaining ground on the internet (2011: 103). The term has grown in recent usage, in part through a popular podcast called *Conspirituality*, which tracks the phenomenon in contemporary cults, the work of wellness influencers and political movements. Although the far right and fascists have always dabbled in the occult and alternative health and spiritual practices, these blendings often surprise people who tend to associate New Age spirituality and holistic wellness practices with femininity and the left, while associating right wing conspiracy theories with masculinity and the right (Ward and Voas 2011). Today, this toxic brew is contributing to the growth of far-right antisemitic movements like QAnon. New Age online spaces and communities, devoted to anti-vaxxer politics, organic foods, 'natural birthing' and – the theme of this chapter – the belief in extraterrestrial interference with humanity, are gateways to the far right. These fringe spaces and movements are leading to real-world violence and stoking reactionary social movements, as seen, for example, in the presence of 'QAnon shaman' Jake Angeli, dressed in horns and a fur mantle, among those storming the US Capitol on 6 January 2021.

In this chapter, I turn to Frankfurt School Critical Theory, and especially to Theodor Adorno's essay on the *Los Angeles Times* astrology column, to understand conspiracy theories that are influencing the far right through the History Channel's *Ancient Aliens* television series. I show how the pseudo-archaeological and paranormal theorizing of *Ancient Aliens* contributes to growing violent movements and more fringe theories like those of David Icke, who believes a secret sect of evil 'reptilian' extraterrestrials, a notable number of whom are apparently Jewish, controls the world.

Ancient Aliens is influencing fascist and far-right movements (Norris 2022), but the show is probably widely viewed as harmless, apolitical fun. The television series generally features theories about alien involvement in past human historical events, without attempting too hard to provide anything like proof or documentation, but in an amusing way that sometimes includes some historical education along the way, although muddied by its synthesis with misinformation and paranormal theorizing. However, the show generates interest among fascists and white nationalists who have discussed it on websites like *Stormfront* and *Counter-Currents* (Norris 2022). The show is used as a discussion topic to consider the possible role of white people in constructing the achievements of ancient people of colour, or to speculate about white people having special alien DNA, or about Jewish people being malicious extraterrestrials. This is not an accident, as we shall see, nor are the makers of the television show innocent of the show's involvement in fascism and white supremacy.

Likely benefiting from the increased normalization of racist alien theories popularized by *Ancient Aliens*, David Icke is a fringe figure but has a sizeable following – in 2012, one of his talks attracted an audience of 6,000 people (Mesure 2012). Once a famous soccer player and sports commentator, Icke in the 1990s proclaimed himself to be a divine figure and began publishing a series of books based on conspiracy theories, including the core claim for which he has become best known – that the world is secretly controlled by shape-shifting 'reptilian' aliens, many of whom hold positions of political power or celebrity. Although not all of Icke's reptilian elite are presumed to be Jewish, the conspiracy theory is antisemitic, for a number of reasons that I will address later.

The rich intellectual and empirical resources of Critical Theory are beneficial to the project of understanding the 'conspiritual' turn to alien conspiracy theories and the influence of these theories on the far right. In particular, I will be making use of Adorno's study of the *Los Angeles Times* astrology column in the 1950s, and I will draw from his claims there to help us understand *Ancient Aliens* and David Icke's conspiracy theories.

All three – the *Los Angeles Times* astrology column, *Ancient Aliens* and David Icke – warn of possible dangers and appeal to mysterious extraterrestrial forces or entities as determining human affairs. In the face of these inscrutable forces, however, there are frequent New Age-y or conspiritual suggestions to attempt to control reality through one's mind and the power of one's beliefs – one's personal 'charm' or 'magnetism' can 'attract' the results one wants from the universe – although the 1950s astrology column and David Icke say this more explicitly than *Ancient Aliens*, which offers few concrete suggestions for human behaviour in response to the 'information' it presents.

This chapter has four sections. The first section addresses Adorno's study of the *Los Angeles Times* astrology column, pointing to the main themes he addresses that may be relevant for an understanding of contemporary conspiritual phenomena, and especially the people and theories coalescing around the belief in extraterrestrial interference in earthly events. Although not all aspects that I discuss here will be clearly evident in both *Ancient Aliens* and David Icke, there will be an array of connections and affinities between all three and the wider milieu of their influence. In the second section, I will address the *Ancient Aliens* television show, especially its connections to racist ideology and its deployment of the phenomenon of 'anonymous authority' critiqued by Adorno in his study of the astrology column. The third section addresses David Icke and his influence, in particular his antisemitism and the dehumanizing properties of his 'reptilian' conspiracy theory, as well as how he believes that the world is both controlled by malevolent forces and also mystically controllable by the individual's personal attitude and beliefs. The fourth and final section of the chapter looks at how extraterrestrial theorizing contributes to violence, and why a rejection of spirituality in favour of science is not a solution to the dilemma of contemporary conspirituality about purported alien visitors.

'The stars down to earth': Adorno's analysis of the *Los Angeles Times* astrology column

Adorno's essay 'The Stars Down to Earth: The *Los Angeles Times* Astrology Column' is a study on the *Los Angeles Times* astrology column in the years 1952–3. Adorno proposes to study what he calls 'secondary superstition' – not 'the individual's own primary experience of the occult', but the 'social phenomenon' through which 'the occult appears rather institutionalized, objectified, and to a large extent socialized' (1994: 48).

Adorno's title is a play on words: the astrology column not only brings the stars 'down to earth' by applying an interpretation of celestial cycles to earthly happenings, but it also neutralizes, tames and adjusts the practice of astrology to serve a 'down to earth' function – a defence of the capitalist status quo in 1950s America. The *Los Angeles Times* astrology column turns the sacred or terrifying *mysterium tremendum* into something mundane, specifically to adjust people to obedient functioning in 1950s American roles as housewives, bureaucrats and salesmen. Not indulging in astrological predictions of death and apocalypse – although the prospect of an apocalyptic nuclear disaster was very much on the horizon – astrology in the *Los Angeles Times* exhorts readers to a synthesis of a Puritan work ethic and American consumer culture 'fun', a synthesis that enables them to survive psychologically in mid-twentieth-century America. The column advises readers to manage their finances carefully, submit to their boss's whims, get along with family members, attend church, purchase 'gadgets'

(Adorno 1994: 100) and balance their views safely between the 'conservative' and the 'modern' (122). It urges them to take pride in their 'family background' (122) and allows the reader to imagine themselves as a successful business leader rather than a proletarian pawn, but still a business leader who must get along with others – a kind of company 'vice president' (85).

According to Adorno, the typical reader of the 1950s astrology column takes astrology for granted, as just part of the set of things that compose reality, just as commodities on the capitalist 'market' are presumed to constitute basic components of reality, as Adorno notes following Marx. As with commodity form and 'market', the astrology column speaks with a fetishized 'abstract authority'. Something else, outside and independent from ourselves – the 'stars', our astrological 'sign' – has authority and power over us, and we are alienated from its power. However, while casually assuming it constitutes part of 'reality', the astrology column reader is also likely to encounter the column with a mixture of seriousness and unseriousness (Adorno 1994: 49). Asked whether she really believes in all that stuff, she might in fact laugh. But it nevertheless influences her life and decisions: perhaps later in the day, for example, she feels tempted to tell off her supervisor at work – remembering that the column warned that this day would be inauspicious for conflict, she swallows her pride and keeps quiet. (And if someone urges her to vote to go out on strike? Nope – Gemini were warned to guard against trouble today, she vaguely remembers, and she is a Gemini.)

Although the author of the astrology column was a man named Caroll Righter, whom Adorno names repeatedly in his analysis, the astrology column, of course, professes to convey information from 'the stars', not from Righter. The column also urges the reader to rely on 'the expert'. The expert is seen as having 'know-how' and 'as being above vested interests, solely motivated by his objective knowledge' (Adorno 1994: 146–7).

> The idea of the expert itself has gradually obtained a quasi-magical connotation … Through universal division of labor and extreme specialization he is not solely someone who has gathered special knowledge of some matter but this also involves that it is knowledge which other people, the non-expert, cannot master and in which he nevertheless has to trust implicitly since expertness is supposed to be based exclusively on rational processes. (147)

Adorno, in fact, sees the column as positivistic – it presumes to speak of scientific laws, capitalizing on the degree to which many people find science is inaccessible to the 'uninitiated' (157–8). In fact, he sees astrology not as a return to 'transcendent faith' but rather as a sign of the disenchantment of the world (157–8).

However, more importantly, the voice of the stars stands in for capitalism and 1950s American society. The column presumes that the reader is angry, volatile, narcissistic (72), feels slighted and has a raging id – and it exhorts the reader to calmness, humility and cooperation through a variety of means that flatter the reader and assure the reader that the problem is other people's insecurity, to avoid incurring the reader's defensiveness and resultant wrath. The reader is presumed to be a relatively powerless person – Adorno suggests many may be women, in fact (82) – but is threatened, flattered, appeased and promised future success. Criticizing or disagreeing would be hard, since the column is simply the voice of reality – astrology speaks with the force of the universe's authority, a sort of cold, scientific officialdom.

Among the influences on Adorno's discussion of 'abstract authority' is probably Erich Fromm's similar description of 'anonymous authority', in his best-selling *Escape from Freedom* (1969, originally 1941), which warned of the possibility of fascism in America. Fromm argued that fascism was possible in America given the tendency of people to flee from the burdens of freedom under capitalism, the limited 'negative freedom' offered by capitalism coupled with loneliness and alienation. Fromm wrote that 'the structure of modern society affects man in two ways simultaneously: he becomes more independent, self-reliant and critical, and he becomes more isolated, alone, and afraid' (1969: 124). The experience of freedom created by the modern world is incomplete, leaving the individual with many negative freedoms – for example, the freedom from the state's encroachment on speech or religion – but without a sense of 'positive freedom', a sense of what freedom can be *for*. Modern humanity, according to Fromm, has gained freedom of religion but 'lost to a great extent the inner capacity to have faith in anything which is not provable by the methods of the natural sciences', and has gained freedom of speech but 'has not acquired the ability to think originally', submitting instead to the 'anonymous authorities' of 'public opinion and "common sense"' (1969: 125; Braune 2019). Righter's astrology column is clearly just another example of this anonymous authority. The individual who lacks faith is assured of a vague connection with some transcendent but physical, inscrutable, vaguely 'scientific' source, and the individual who lacks the ability to think originally is assured that she can have an insight into the nature of reality and the interconnectedness of things via the anonymous authority of astrology. For those more passionate for a vision of unity grounded in what Adorno calls a social 'climate of semi-erudition', fringe 'astrology magazines' offer more (1994: 61). Adorno writes:

> [In the astrology magazines] primary naivete, the unreflecting acceptance of the existent has been lost whereas at the same time neither the power of thinking nor positive knowledge has been developed sufficiently. The semi-erudite vaguely wants to understand and is also driven by the narcissistic wish to prove superior to the plain people but he is not in a position to carry through complicated and detached intellectual operations. To him, astrology, just like other irrational creeds like racism, provides a short-cut by bringing the complex to a handy formula and offering at the same time the pleasant gratification that he who feels to be excluded from educational privileges nevertheless belongs to the minority of those who are 'in the know'. (61)

The desire to be an elite initiate, to be 'in the know', is also addressed by Leo Lowenthal's study of the American antisemitic agitator, *Prophets of Deceit*, which Adorno also cites in the essay. Lowenthal writes of being 'in the know' as not only a trope of the agitator but as part of the appeal of antisemitic ideology to the listener:

> Equally gratifying to listeners may be the fact that such revelations help satisfy their curiosity, a universal feature of contemporary mass culture. It may be due to the prevalent feeling that one has to have 'inside information' that comes 'from the horse's mouth' in order to get along in modern society. Perhaps, too, this curiosity is derived from an unconscious infantile desire to glimpse the forbidden life of the grown-ups – a desire closely related to that of revealing and enjoying scandals. When the listener is treated as an insider his libido is gratified ... He has been allowed to become one of those 'in the know'. (Lowenthal and Guterman 2016: 139–40)

Another element of Adorno's analysis of the astrology column that is also addressed by Lowenthal is the issue of 'unseriousness'. Lowenthal writes the antisemitic agitator's 'approach to values is often revealed by an undercurrent of unseriousness in his statements, the effect of which is to dismiss ideals as mere bunk, hogwash, lies' (Lowenthal and Guterman 2016: 34). 'It is difficult to pin [the agitator] down to anything and he gives the impression that he is deliberately playacting' (7). Fascism itself, of which Lowenthal's 'antisemitic agitators' are fundamentally proponents, is characterized by a mixture of half-joking, bullying snark and ardent fanatical seriousness, the latter of which paradoxically also rests on a great deal of lying and self-deception (Finchelstein 2020; Braune 2021). The 1950s astrology column, while absent perhaps this element of bullying, is greeted with a similar combination of insincerity and belief. The reader both laughs it off and believes it.

As American politics has acutely reminded us for the past six years, laughter is by no means a sure protection against far-right ideology. The reader of the astrology column can both laugh at it and believe in it. Some have written on 'irony poisoning' as a significant factor in the inculcation of people into the alt-right (Varis 2019). People may start by laughing at memes, move to sharing them 'ironically', then defending them when they face criticism and ultimately believing the ideology. In fact, this is no accident but is part of a white nationalist recruitment strategy. For example, the 'Style Guide' to the neo-Nazi *Daily Stormer* website suggested:

> The tone of the site should be light. Most people are not comfortable with material that comes across as vitriolic, raging, non-ironic hatred. The unindoctrinated should not be able to tell if we are joking or not. There should also be a conscious awareness of mocking stereotypes of hateful racists. I usually think of this as self-deprecating humor – I am a racist making fun of stereotype[s] of racists, because I don't take myself super-seriously. This is obviously a ploy and I actually do want to gas kikes. But that's neither here nor there. (Feinberg 2017)

Similarly, Adorno suggests, the informality with which the *Los Angeles Times* astrology column is greeted specifically assists in its acceptance.

In fact, underlying the light and down-to-earth tone of the astrology column, Adorno sees more sinister forces lurking. At the same time that it seems to urge a lack of 'seriousness', the column presents the reader with a bizarre mix of personal agency and external control and manipulation. On the one hand, the column severely circumscribes the individual's arena of decision-making. It is suggested that most of the events of the individual's life are controlled by the stars, and that the individual can only worsen the outcome for herself by any attempt at bucking this 'fate'.

On the other hand, in the astrology column, semi-magical powers are ascribed to the individual, whom it suggests can bend the world to her will through the exertion of 'charm' and 'magnetism' (Adorno 1994: 84, 111). In addition to this personal magical power, the *Los Angeles Times* astrology column feeds the narcissism of the reader by letting the reader feel privy to secret knowledge, of being 'in the know' about the secret laws of the universe and the stars' determination of earthly affairs.

Adorno also compares more fringe astrological publications with the sanitized *Los Angeles Times* astrology column. Here Adorno briefly surveys early 1950s 'astrology magazines', noticing their tendency to apocalyptic predictions (a nod to the Cold War nuclear build-up) and their accusation that societal disintegration would be accelerated by 'disruptive minorities' (1994: 62).

The distance between these magazines and the newspaper column is not as far as it may at first appear. The 'secondary superstition' of the astrology column – down-to-earth, institutionalized superstition that supports contemporary power structures – may be greeted with a lightness that combines humour with acceptance, yet Adorno also understands that it can feed a kind of *fanatical seriousness* that rises to the assistance of anonymous authority. Alongside this sanitized 'secondary superstition' lie more virulent and overt versions of 'superstition' that can enforce with greater (vigilante/paramilitary) violence the maintenance of the system from which these generalized superstitions arise. That is, how do we get from the *Los Angeles Times* astrology column to 'astrology magazines' … or QAnon? From Norman Vincent Peale (*The Power of Positive Thinking*) and the 'law of attraction' (the magic of believing your way to success) to Donald Trump? From the History Channel's slightly sanitized conspiracy theories to David Icke's reptilians running the United Nations?

Although astrology and alien theorizing are rather separate realms, it makes sense that they would share some common themes. Not only does each seek to explain an occult connection between the earth and the heavens – each deals with the mysterious in a way that renders it mundane, seeks to bring the stars 'down to earth' and enforces social control by this means. Next I will explore the impact of *Ancient Aliens* followed by David Icke's conspiracy theories.

'Ancient astronaut theorists suggest': *Ancient Aliens*, racism and anonymous authority

Hosted by the perplexingly named History Channel, *Ancient Aliens* recently completed its eighteenth season since it began to air over a decade ago in 2010. The premise of the show is that many historical achievements were the product not of human beings but of extraterrestrial visitors. In addition, the show suggests that earthly human life itself might be an alien creation, that aliens are continuing to visit earth today and that aliens are colluding with (or are) sinister controlling forces that might do harm to humans.

Many have pointed to the show's inherent racism, most notably its frequent tendency to deny the past cultural achievements of non-white civilizations, attributing their great architectural and artistic achievements to the work of extraterrestrials (Bond 2018; Halmhofer 2021; Zaitchik 2018). Among the show's racist tropes that have been critiqued are its participation in the 'mound-builder myth', which posits that the ancient land sculptures[1] of North America were not made by Native Americans (Bond 2018; Colavito 2020; Zaitchik 2018).

Although the show does not ascribe alien communication or involvement exclusively to non-white people, the ways in which it deploys tropes of alien involvement both reinforce racist tropes and bolster white supremacy. Defenders of the show would probably be quick to point out that the show also ascribes cultural achievements by white people, like ancient Greek architectural feats, to alien involvement. The show also describes some historical white people as possessing special access to alien communication, as it does for some non-white people. For example, the show suggests that Leonardo da Vinci (Season 4 Episode 8), the American Founding Fathers (Season 3 Episode 11) and Edward Turing (Season 11 Episode 5), among many others, may have been in touch with aliens through special powers they possessed. However, the presence in the show of alien-influenced white people does not disprove its racism. In fact, in some cases, these narratives seem designed to bolster a justification for greatness and supremacy, though not explicitly of racialized whiteness – for example, the episodes portraying early American history seem to suggest an American exceptionalism, and specifically imply that the United States (whose founding, of course, involved slavery and indigenous genocide) may have had some form of special extraterrestrial, transcendent blessing.

The show's racism is also found in the way that it exoticizes non-white cultures, including engaging in Orientalist tropes and suggesting that various non-white peoples may have mystical powers enabling them to communicate with extraterrestrial forces. While this could be mistaken for a form of respect, it reinforces prejudices by linking non-white civilizations to the *alien*, both as extraterrestrial and as 'other'. The show does make use of people of colour as among its 'experts', although the authority within their identities they claim is often questionable. For example, one of the show's Native American guests employs the title 'Chief' but is chief not of his tribe but of the New Age 'Galactic Federation of Light' group (Colavito 2013).

The racist othering of *Ancient Aliens* is, like the fortune-telling of the 1950s astrology column, backed up by anonymous authority and appeals to 'experts'. In *Ancient Aliens*, abstract authority is ever present: the aliens themselves – mysterious and in varying cases malevolent and benevolent, though never easily to be trusted – and the 'theorists', who are always raising various 'questions': 'Ancient astronaut theorists suggest … .' 'Some ancient astronaut theorists ask … .'

---

[1] These sculptures, often called 'Indian mounds', are large 'earthwork' carvings of the land into designs and drawings and are found especially in the eastern and southern United States. Some were burial mounds, while others had festival or ritual purposes.

Ancient Aliens is also, despite the bizarre details that strike a different note from the 1950s astrology column's advice to 'work hard' and 'seek amusements', deeply 'down to earth' in Adorno's sense of the term: it is undergirded by a certain sort of positivism. For one, there is a highly literalist interpretation of all the statements of ancient peoples and indigenous groups. If people saw a light in the sky, or drew a strange being that is half-animal half-human, or spoke of gaining wings and being lifted up on high, all of these things refer to literal physical and natural happenings that, since they cannot be explained by contemporary science and earthly technologies of the time, require the presence of extraterrestrial visitors.

Imagination and metaphor are entirely erased. In the worldview of the show, all ancient peoples are believed to have been literalists, with all their stories being journalistic accounts of events and with all their art being realist depictions of objects and events of their world. This attitude resembles the stolid atheism of the New Atheist demanding empirical proof, or the analytic philosopher demanding a clearer definition of a word, not the liberationist atheism of Ludwig Feuerbach and Karl Marx. For Feuerbach, religious yearnings point us to the depth of human potential. We find this same Feuerbachian yearning in Marx's 1843 letter to Arnold Ruge: 'The world has long since dreamed of something of which it needs only to become conscious for it to possess it in reality' (Marx n.d.). This conscious awakening, of course, implies a material act for Marx; it is through revolution that the unconscious or repressed 'dream' is made reality. By contrast, *Ancient Aliens* diverges into myth not to transform reality in accord with the repressed 'dream' of human liberation, but to reinforce the sense that the world is controlled by mysterious transcendent forces. These forces can certainly be 'investigated' with the help of 'experts', but they always remain ineffable and beyond our control (perhaps, it is even suggested, as they are even the creators of the human race). *Ancient Aliens* quite literally reinforces the power of fetishism, which is the exact opposite of the perspective of the Marxian Critical Theory.

The show's storyline also draws from a reactionary, mythic milieu, rather than recovering the stories ('dreams') of the oppressed. *Ancient Aliens* (as does Icke) reveals its racism as it draws upon the five 'root races' of nineteenth-century 'Theosophist' Helene Blavatsky: Polarian, Hyperborean, Atlantean, Lemurian and Aryan. At least, while it stays away from emphasizing the Aryans and Hyperboreans, emphasized by the Nazis, it comfortably speaks of these (fictional) lost Atlantean (e.g. Season 12 Episode 6) and Lemurian (e.g. Season 17 Episode 4) civilizations (History Channel 2018, 2021). Blavatsky's theories about ancient races, the only one remaining being the 'Aryans', were further developed later by Rudolf Steiner, the founder of the Waldorf education model, among others (Staudenmaier 2008: 9–10). These 'root races' appear in the neo-Nazi and fascist theorizing of others. Hitler-era Nazis were unsurprisingly interested in theories of ancient 'root races' that placed themselves, the Indo-European 'Aryans', at the pinnacle, and theories concerning the 'root races' continued to be propagated in postwar fascist and Nazi theorizing.

Along with the Aryans, Blavatsky's theory of an ancient white Hyperborean 'root race' preceding the Aryans also fascinated the Nazis. Savitri Devi, the founder of postwar esoteric Hitlerism, carried on the Hyperborea legend (Devi 2022). Chilean 'esoteric Hitlerist' Miguel Serrano also believed that the Hyperboreans had survived – they had attempted to preserve racial hierarchy through the implementation of the caste system, but after intermarriages diluted their 'divine blood', racially 'pure' Hyperboreans retreated to Antarctica, where 'the continent of Hyperborea became invisible and vanished into the hollow earth, where other Hyperboreans reestablished their divine order in … secret underground cities' (Goodrick-Clarke 2002: 181). Numerous Nazi-era and postwar fascists also theorized about secret alien bloodlines or Hitler's extraterrestrial origins. Prominent Canadian neo-Nazi and Holocaust-denier Ernst Zündel believed that Hitler had survived and travelled to Antarctica, where he theorized that Nazis had found an 'Inner Earth' and were developing UFOs with the help of extraterrestrials (161).

These theories are also being used to recruit to neo-Nazism and fascist movements today. Conspiracy theory and disinformation researcher Abbie Richards has tracked the promotion of the 'Hyperborea' theme on TikTok, notably a platform popular with teens and young adults. She produced a TikTok video warning of the use of these conspiracies to recruit into Nazi ideology (Richards 2021). Through the allure of conspiracy theories and myths about underground civilizations and secret Nazi bases in Antarctica, Nazis are using the Hyperborea myth, as they are using similar material across the internet, to lure in and recruit curious youth.

Enlisting the use of 'root races' is not the only tool of conspiracy theorists for recruitment; ancient gods are also added to the mix. A key premise of Erich von Däniken's *Chariots of the Gods* was that the ancient gods of the Sumerians, the Anunnaki, were actually aliens. Theories about the Anunnaki were further developed by Zecharia Sitchin in the 1970s. Sitchen's 1976 book *The Twelfth Planet* posited that the Anunnaki were visitors from the (made-up) planet of Nibiru. Sitchin's book was popular in the 1970s and influenced some cults. But in David Icke's formulation, as we shall see in a moment, the Anunnaki are malevolent 'Reptilians' – allied to the Illuminati, the Rothschilds, the British royal family and others.

Ancient Aliens stops short of promoting the openly antisemitic versions of these conspiracy theories. They dabble in Antarctic Nazi bases and hollow earths (History Channel 2019). They also posit a 'reptilian' alien race. In fact, *Ancient Aliens* devoted a number of episodes to 'the reptilians' (see in particular Season 8 Episodes 1 and 5, and Season 14 Episode 8). In 2019, the show featured a young woman who claimed to be a 'reptilian–human hybrid' named Charmaine D'Rozario Saytch (with dazzling green eye shadow and green nail polish, which seem to be doing a lot of the persuasive work), who claims she was forcibly taken into an underground world by Reptilian aliens, who converted her into a 'reptilian–human hybrid' and explained their power. 'They have not manipulated all of humanity, but certain groups', D'Rozario Saytch tells us (History Channel 2020). Which groups? We are left to decide for ourselves, as *Ancient Aliens* quickly cuts away to a different 'expert', sidestepping the scapegoating and far-right implications, leaving them for the viewer to determine.

I will now turn to a more overtly 'fringe' and antisemitic alien conspiracy theorist, David Icke. Although Icke's theories are much more direct in their assertions than the sanitized, soothing, 'down to earth' anonymous authority of the *Los Angeles Times* astrology column and the pseudonymous 'ancient astronaut theorists' who are always 'suggesting' and 'asking questions', Icke's conspiracizing has more in common with the

1950s astrology column than we might expect, and more in common with *Ancient Aliens* than a belief in extraterrestrial intervention into earthly affairs.

David Icke's Jewish space lizards and the law of attraction

Icke's central thesis is that a 'Luciferian' 'cabal' associated with the Rothschild and Rockefeller families controls global political and economic systems; Icke also believes they are 'obsessed with ritual' and engage in child sacrifice (Icke 2004). And it turns out, these world controllers are also lizards from space, a 'reptilian' alien race. (He has been asked many times if *the lizard thing was a metaphor* and has asserted he is completely serious.)

Icke's propaganda is antisemitic, although not in a straightforward way. Michael Barkun refers to Icke's and other UFO theorists' 'refracted antisemitism' (2013: 141, 143–4). While many UFO theorists like Icke disclaim antisemitism and abhor Hitler, they rely on antisemitic tropes to describe the 'conspiracy' in which aliens or their terrestrial supporters are engaged, or the physical features of the aliens themselves.

The chief problem that arises concerning classifying Icke's theories as antisemitic is that his 'reptilians' and Jews are not concurrent sets – there are people that he classifies as 'reptilians' (the Rockefellers and Bill Gates, for example) who are not Jewish; and there are Jews (the 'ordinary' Jews who are not in control of the world) that he does not classify as reptilians. This can cause some confusion, because, after all, there are considerably bad people in any sizeable group of human beings, and if Icke is simply describing bad people in such bombastic terms as to equate them with lizards from space, that would be over the top – certainly eccentric – but not necessarily antisemitic. However, proving Icke's promotion of antisemitic ideas does not depend on proving that 'reptilians' are his personal code word for 'Jews'. There are several reasons for this.

First, antisemitism often relies on a theory of 'Jewish control' by the 'Jewish leaders', and it does not require a belief that all Jews are part of this leadership or 'in on it'. There is no 'leader of the Jews', and there are no 'Elders of Zion' and so on. (To be clear, it does not follow that criticism of Israeli political leaders is antisemitic; Israeli government leaders are not the leaders of 'the Jews', and treating them as such can, in fact, be a form of antisemitism.) Secondly, Icke also says some problematic things about Jews in general and about the Holocaust, not just about the specific Jews whom he thinks are reptilians. So, the fact that he does not believe all Jews are reptilians does not exempt him from charges of antisemitism.

Finally, the dehumanizing character of the 'reptilian' trope also needs to be considered. Although not all Jews are 'reptilians', and not all of Icke's 'reptilians' are Jews, using a dehumanizing language to describe a powerful group of people can have an element of antisemitism when that language overlaps with common antisemitic tropes or racist imagery. As David Livingstone Smith points out in *Making Monsters: The Uncanny Power of Dehumanization*, caricatures can be dehumanizing even if they ascribe superior ability to the other.

The reptile would be ranked rather low in a traditional Western 'Great Chain of Being' (Smith 2021). The reptilian includes not only the lizard but also the snake, which (as the 'serpent') is classified by Christianity as symbolic of the devil. Medieval antisemitism equated Jews with the devil and consequently spawned antisemitic caricatures of Jews as snake-like, with the snake and devil being likewise seen as 'sly', sneaky and cunning (Smith 2021). Modern antisemitism was heavily influenced by the infamous *Protocols of the Learned Elders of Zion*, which describes the Jews as characterized by a 'symbolic snake' representing a centuries-long Jewish plot for world domination, and the *Protocols* were often published with a cover showing 'a snake or an octopus coiling around the globe' (Bronner 2019: 30, 58).

Christian Identity, a white supremacist movement that emerged in the early twentieth century in the United States as an outgrowth of British Israelism and which rose to prominence in the 1980s–2000s organizing through churches like the Aryan Nations, again identified Jews as a snake-like race (Zeskind 2009: 177). The Christian Identity movement believed that the 'fall' was actually an act of intercourse between the serpent and Eve, creating a race that combined the demonic with the human, and that the Jews belonged to this race, which Christian Identity seeks to eradicate (Zeskind 2009: 180).

Xenophobic cartoons in American history sometimes depicted immigrants in dehumanizing reptilian caricatures, as in the case of a famous anti-Catholic immigrant cartoon that shows Catholic bishops arriving in the United States as vicious alligators, their tall mitres (hats) depicted as jaws with gleaming fangs. More recent in the American imagination is the reading of 'The Snake'[2] by Donald Trump on the 2016 campaign trial. Used by Trump as a nativist allegory that casts immigrants as threats to the homeland, the poem tells the story of a woman whose empathy for a wily snake leads her to let him into her home, whereupon the snake bites her:

'I saved you', cried that woman,
'And you've bit me heavens why?
You know your bite is poisonous and now I'm going to die!'
'Oh shut up, silly woman', said the reptile with a grin.
'You knew damn well I was a snake before you took me in.' (Hinton 2021: 3)

This poem features prominently in Alexander Hinton's *It Can Happen Here: White Power and the Rising Threat of Genocide in the U.S.*; as Hinton argues in the introduction, it is indicative of the political and rhetorical shifts that set the stage for genocide of minorities.

Dehumanization is also often linked to discussions of blood. In the case of antisemitism, there is a fascination with blood in relation to blood libel conspiracy theories. Blood libel and theories about Jewish blood converge in contemporary antisemitic conspirituralism, where in QAnon, for example, people both theorize about Jewish bloodlines and worry about a secret 'cabal' of paedophiles drinking the blood of children. Among the alien theorists, we often find talk of 'bloodlines' – the 'bloodlines' behind various alien races, including those deemed noble and those deemed evil and

---

[2] The poem was adapted by Trump from a 1968 song by African American soul singer Al Wilson, who did not intend this political message (Hinton 2021: 2).

conniving. Michael Barkun points out that even among alien theorists who denounce racism, a familiar pattern unfolds, with 'Nordics' with Aryan features, and malicious 'greys' being depicted as evil and conniving and described with stereotypically Jewish features (Barkun 2013: 143).

To return again to those who might say Icke is not antisemitic because he does not hate every Jew: antisemitism allows for exceptions – like any form of racism or prejudice, really, which always allows for exceptions to the effect that someone is 'one of the good ones', 'not like most of them'. In her book about the flat-earther conspiracy movement, Kelly Weill documents significant antisemitism. In one case, she interviews a Jewish flat-earther as another conference speaker's booming voice can be heard condemning Jews down the hall. 'You know, people call me the Jewnicorn because I'm a rare Jew', he tells her. 'There's not a lot of Jewish people like me that don't get easily offended at some of these things' (Weill 2022: 188). How some Jews resolve the cognitive dissonance of antisemitism in certain subcultures is beyond the scope of what I wish to address here. My point is only: many an antisemite is willing to allow for 'Jewnicorns'.

Furthermore, Icke dabbles in Holocaust revisionism and makes use of the infamous antisemitic forgery, *The Protocols of the Learned Elders of Zion*, which he suggests does not describe a conspiracy involving all Jews, but involving the Illuminati and Zionist leaders (Icke 2004, 1994). He also blames Jews for antisemitism, suggesting that a feeling of 'guilt' 'attracts' antisemitic attacks. Notice how his language holds affinities with the *Los Angeles Times* astrology column's claims of the individual's power to control events through 'magnetism' and 'charm' – as though the individual can direct the course of events merely through the power of belief. Icke (2004) writes:

> The conditioned thought patterns in the collective Jewish mind have repeatedly created the physical reality of oppression, prejudice, and racism which matches the pattern – the expectation – programmed into their collective psyche. They expect it; they create it. When Jewish people as a whole break free from the mind control of their hierarchy and start to let go of those feelings of fear and expectation of prejudice, they will stop attracting such experiences to them. When they openly reject the inherited view of racial superiority, those patterns will disperse from their magnetic cape/aura, and they will cease to attract racism to them.

This kind of 'advice' is also reminiscent of the film and book *The Secret*, which preaches the 'law of attraction', according to which one can acquire anything one wants by believing hard enough and following a series of steps including visualizing already possessing it. The film version employs the story of a gay man who was fearful of encountering homophobic harassment until he adopted the methods of the 'law of attraction' and then became popular, safer and more socially accepted. The belief that believing hard enough creates one's reality never lies far from victim-blaming. In the tradition of the *Los Angeles Times* astrology column, *The Secret* offers an element of choice within a largely deterministic universe – by believing hard enough, like the 'charm' and 'magnetism' (Adorno 1994: 112) of the astrology column, the individual can become healthy, wealthy, powerful and well-liked. Failure, according to this New

Age Calvinism, is a sign of your lack of faith. Interestingly, Donald Trump was deeply influenced by one of the progenitors of 'the law of attraction', the pop preacher Norman Vincent Peale (Blair 2015; Steinberg 2017).

Violent outcomes and the limits of positivist responses

As with *Ancient Aliens*, it would be tempting to laugh off David Icke. In the initial television interview that made him famous, in which he announced he was the reincarnation of Jesus himself, he attempted to capitalize on the laughter of the audience, encouraging their joyfulness, until host Terry Wogan pointedly explained, 'They're not laughing with you – they're laughing at you' (Vice 2012). But as with *Ancient Aliens* and other conspiracy theories (flat earth, etc.), people can laugh their way into believing. Presenting these beliefs with a veneer of seriousness, on the History Channel in the case of *Ancient Aliens*, and with footnotes and recommended reading lists of other conspiracy-minded texts (including publications of the Liberty Lobby, founded by Holocaust-denier Willis Carto) in the case of Icke, these ideas may initially capture humour or imagination, but those who spend long enough in this world will acquire a new understanding of the specific capacities and limits of their own agency and new theories about the mysterious alien 'others' who attempt to curtail it – new enemies to scapegoat for their own feelings of loss or impotence.

Further, Icke gains in the appearance of legitimacy as he is platformed, for example, through his participation in Gaia, a Netflix-like New Age streaming subscription service. Paid ads for Gaia on YouTube and social media platforms often feature Icke – others often feature a young man named Matías de Stefano, who claims to be a reincarnated ancient Atlantean. De Stefano spins a complex tale that includes the 'creation of the races', including the 'Atlantean' peoples, who came from a hybrid of earthly and extraterrestrial origins (Gaia 2020), and, unsurprisingly perhaps, Gaia also hosts dozens of interviews with *Ancient Aliens*' Erich von Däniken and documentaries about his life.

The growing embrace of these theories on large platforms could feed not only far-right subcultures and movements but also acts of violence in particular. Noteworthy in this context is the influence on Icke of William Cooper's *Behold a Pale Horse* (1991), which suggested the US government was under alien control and proposed before Icke that the *Protocols of Zion* referred to an 'Illuminati' conspiracy (Barkun 2013: 36; Icke 1994). Cooper's work may have influenced the Oklahoma City bombing – Cooper stirred up conspiracy theories about Oklahoma City and was tied to the militia movement that influenced Timothy McVeigh and his accomplice, Terry Nichols (Anon. 1997).

More recently, a militia member who spent time with the Proud Boys, Buckey Wolfe, killed his brother with a sword, having read David Icke and believing his brother to be a shape-shifting reptilian (Neiwert 2020: 27). And on Christmas 2020, Anthony Quinn Warner set off a bomb in Nashville, Tennessee, that brought down internet and cell phone service for many. Warner may have been worried by misinformation that

5G internet was killing people (Loadenthal), and he allegedly believed that numerous politicians and celebrities were reptilian aliens (Winter, Kosnar and Wong 2020). During the Covid pandemic, dozens of 5G internet towers were vandalized in the UK, possibly some in connection with Icke's theorizing that 5G was causing Covid (Langfitt 2020).

Alien theorizing feeds on 'anonymous authority' – Adorno suggests the appeal is partly masochistic, the submission to authority. Recently, discussions of extraterrestrial life have obtained a greater veneer of credibility, especially in light of hearings led by the US Congress, and also due to the influence of right-wing public figures such as Fox News' Tucker Carlson, who has also appeared on *Ancient Aliens* (Season 14 Episode 21), pushing for the government to reveal its files on UFOs. The Congressional hearings have, in turn, sparked wider, more 'legitimate' discussions of extraterrestrial interference in human affairs.

If we believe we are being malevolently 'watched' or benevolently 'watched over' from above, this provides an occult explanation for something the *Los Angeles Times* astrology column also accounts for: the individual's sense of powerlessness in late capitalism. The anonymous authority of these benevolent or malevolent aliens, who perhaps created us, watch over us and will one day return, or to whom we can one day ascend, however, is not one of sheer disempowerment of the individual handed over to fate, just as the *Los Angeles Times* astrology column was not found to be such in Adorno's study (1994: 60). The aliens may not care about you – in fact, they may even wish to harm you – but if positing their existence constructs a worldview in which you can be a hero fighting a subhuman enemy, then what they provide is less like shallow consolation and perhaps an occasion for violence.

Before concluding, I will offer a caveat: I have nothing against astrology in itself, nor about theorizing concerning alien visitors (although if you think aliens are responsible for the greatest achievements of ancient civilizations of colour, you might be racist and might want to take a look at that). My impulse here is not debunking – this is not a scientistic or positivist attempt to clean up the messiness of human assumptions and superstitions and to tell people how to get the facts or how to do science, history and archaeology the 'right way', with proper understandings of trustworthy data and 'peer review'.

I am the sort of Marxist Critical Theorist who would, in fact, like to keep socialism strange. I want a broad and expansive and *weird* socialism, with room for what Margaret Cohen and China Miéville call 'gothic Marxism', which sees 'a culture's ghosts and phantasms as a significant and rich field of social production' and valorises 'a culture's detritus and trivia as well as its strange and marginal practices' (Cohen 1993: 11; Turl 2015). Likewise, I am drawn to what Michael Löwy calls the Romantic socialist tradition, agreeing that not all backward-looking nostalgia or yearning for lost spiritual communion is a form of political reaction (1992: 1–3; 2020: 45). The yearning to recover or sustain a historically unfolding but gravely endangered 'spirit of utopia' (Ernst Bloch) or 'prophetic messianism' (Fromm) is far from being a counter-revolutionary impulse. I want room on the left for religion, spirituality, 'superstition', communion with nature and wild aesthetics. I want room for all kinds of strange manifestations of exploration and struggle. Capitalism disenchants the world, and the world is forever resisting this disenchantment. In fact, as nature itself is further disenchanted, we seem to be approaching the threat of planetary death. Something at the heart of reality resists positivistic reduction. Life and enchantment are inseparable.

However, *Ancient Aliens* and David Icke's reptilians do not represent a progressive revolt of enchantment against capitalism, and they lack the sincerity that might characterize the popular spirituality of workers and peasants. Rather than seeking to 'pluck the imaginary flowers from the chain so that man may shall bear the chain without fantasy or consolation' – as Marx reassures us in 'The Contribution to the Critique of Hegel's Philosophy of Right' that he does not wish to do through his critique of religion – alien conspiracy theories chain us in synthetic plastic flowers, preventing us from plucking the real, living flower (1964: 44). They unsettle one set of illusions, perhaps, but they replace them with a new set of illusions which cannot be defeated merely by the presentation of facts, despite the conspiracy theories' scientific framing. After all, the conspiracy theories are presented with an appeal to the audience's desires, not evidence, and relying on shifting the burden of proof by posing questions in a form that is virtually impossible to deny: '*Is it possible* that aliens could have helped ancient civilizations?' '*Could* this symbol be a spaceship?' Ancient aliens theorizing, both the show and the wider genre, represents a fundamentally reactionary impulse, as does the *Los Angeles Times* astrology column, manipulating the individual's sense of atomization and alienation with false promises of agency, while in fact controlling them for reactionary or mainstream ends.

The promises of these conspiracy-minded worldviews are bleak, and their offer grim. Rather than being met with trembling awe or joyful surprise, these visions inspire illusions of victimization ('the Jewish space lizards are after us!') or supremacy ('we come from a great white alien race!') in relation to the mysterious forces they describe. Their answer to this false narrative of victimization likewise rings hollow.

That the problem is not a fluffy spiritualism – that in fact, like the *Los Angeles Times* astrology column and many conspiracy theories, *Ancient Aliens* is positivistic, preaching the value of 'experts' and '[doing your own] research' – also suggests that scientific debunking might not be sufficient to counter *Ancient Aliens*' toxic influence. Nor, however, should we simply seek to rescue people from conspiratorial worldviews through recruiting them to either rival spiritualisms or scientism. We need to understand which psychological or cognitive processes are necessitated for the individual to then switch to alternative sources of meaning. We also need to uncover which social and individual conditions facilitate the shift in those psychological or cognitive processes.

Perhaps it is in returning to Critical Theory – to work of Frankfurt School theorists like Adorno, Lowenthal and Fromm – that we can confront the latest synthesis of the reactionary occult and the 'down to earth' voice of the expert who urges us to get along, to passively wish for the best and to 'attract' a desired outcome with our upbeat, positive attitude. The flip side of the breezy, down-to-earth voice of the astrology column is the dark, foreboding warning of the 'astrology magazines', just as the ominous conspiracism of David Icke rests behind the more cheerful veneer of alien theorizing projected by the History Channel and, to some degree, by Icke himself. The cheery positivism of the 'ancient astronaut theorist' should induce not our laughter but our ongoing investigation of how to counteract the growing power of dangerous conspiritual forces.

References

Adorno, T. (1994), *The Stars Down to Earth: And Other Essays on the Irrational in Culture* (ed. S. Cook), London: Routledge.
Anon. (1997), 'New Trial May Solve Riddle of Oklahoma Bombing', *The Guardian*, 3 November, available at: www.theguardian.com/world/1997/nov/03/mcveigh.usa (accessed 26 August 2022).
Barkun, M. (2013), *A Culture of Conspiracy: Apocalyptic Visions in Contemporary America*, Berkeley: University of California Press.
Blair, G. (2015), 'How Norman Vincent Peale Taught Donald Trump to Worship Himself', *Politico*, 6 October, available at: https://www.politico.com/magazine/story/2015/10/donald-trump-2016-norman-vincent-peale-213220 (accessed 24 August 2022).
Bond, S. E. (2018), 'Pseudoarcheology and the Racism behind *Ancient Aliens*', *Hyperallergic*, 13 November, available at: https://hyperallergic.com/470795/pseudoarchaeology-and-the-racism-behind-ancient-aliens/ (accessed 16 August 2022).
Braune, J. (2019), 'Void and Idol: A Critical Theory Analysis of the Neo-Fascist "Alt-Right"', *Journal of Hate Studies*, 15 (1): 11–37.
Braune, J. (2021), 'Review Essay: Fascism and Eluded Truths', *Free Associations: Psychoanalysis and Culture, Media, Groups, Politics*, 84: 85–96.
Bronner, S. E. (2019), *A Rumor about the Jews: Conspiracy, Antisemitism, and the Protocols of Zion*, 2nd edn, Cham: Palgrave.
Cohen, M. (1993), *Profane Illumination: Walter Benjamin and the Paris of Surrealist Revolution*, Berkeley: University of California Press.
Colavito, J. (2005), *The Cult of Alien Gods: H. P. Lovecraft and Extraterrestrial Pop Culture*, Amherst: Prometheus Books.
Colavito, J. (2013), '*Ancient Aliens*' Native American Contributor Objects to Using the Word "Aliens" to Describe Visitors from the Stars', Jason Colavito, 3 June, available at: www.jasoncolavito.com/blog/ancient-aliens-native-american-contributor-objects-to-using-the-word-aliens-to-describe-visitors-from-the-stars (accessed 7 August 2022).
Colavito, J. (2020), *The Mound Builder Myth: Fake History and the Hunt for a 'Lost White Race'*, Norman: University of Oklahoma Press.
Devi, S. (2022), 'Hitlerism and Hindudom', in R. G. Fowler (ed.), *The Savitri Devi Archive*, available at: https://savitridevi.org/savitri_devi_works/hitlerism-and-hindudom (accessed 24 August 2022).
Feinberg, A. (2017), 'This Is the Daily Stormer's Playbook', *Huffpost*, 13 December, available at: www.huffpost.com/entry/daily-stormer-nazi-style-guide_n_5a2ece19e4b0ce3b344492f2 (accessed 23 August 2022).
Finchelstein, F. (2020), *A Brief History of Fascist Lies*, Oakland: University of California Press.
Fromm, E. (1969), *Escape from Freedom*, New York: Avon Books.
Gaia (2020), 'Atlantis and the Creation of the Races – Matías de Stefano', *YouTube*, 8 June, available at: www.youtube.com/watch?v=Yvdr9LasPBA (accessed 20 June 2022).
Goodrick-Clarke, N. (2002), *Black Sun: Aryan Cults, Esoteric Nazism, and the Politics of Identity*, New York: New York University Press.
Halmhofer, S. (2021), 'Did Aliens Build the Pyramids? And Other Racist Theories', *Sapiens*, 5 October, available at: www.sapiens.org/archaeology/pseudoarchaeology-racism (accessed 16 August 2022).

Hinton, A. L. (2021), *It Can Happen Here: White Power and the Rising Threat of Genocide in the U.S.*, New York: New York University Press.

History Channel (2018), '*Ancient Aliens*: Forgotten Kingdoms (Season 12, Episode 6)', *YouTube*, 29 August, available at: www.youtube.com/watch?v=tFTFFmWZ5Zw (accessed 24 August 2022).

History Channel (2019), '*Ancient Aliens*: The Hollow Earth Theory (Season 10)', *YouTube*, 6 May, available at: www.youtube.com/watch?v=M7vt5paORIc&t=9s (accessed 16 August 2022).

History Channel (2020), '*Ancient Aliens*: Alien Reptiles Manipulate Human DNA (Season 14)', *YouTube*, 5 May, available at: www.youtube.com/watch?v=q30UFr_5ltA&t=95s (accessed 24 August 2022).

History Channel (2021), '*Ancient Aliens*: The Mystery of Mount Shasta', 17 September, available at: www.history.com/shows/ancient-aliens/season-17/episode-4 (accessed 24 August 2022).

Icke, D. (1994), *The Robots' Rebellion: The Story of the Spiritual Renaissance*, Bath: Gateway Books.

Icke, D. (2001), *Children of the Matrix: How an Interdimensional Race Has Controlled the World for Thousands of Years – And Still Does*, Wildwood: Bridge of Love.

Icke, D. (2004), *… And the Truth Shall Set You Free*, Ryde: David Icke Books.

Langfitt, F. (2020), '5G Conspiracy Theories Trigger Attacks on Cellphone Towers', *NPR*, 19 April, available at: www.npr.org/2020/04/19/838195056/5g-conspiracy-theories-trigger-attacks-on-cellphone-towers (accessed 15 August 2022).

Loadenthal, M. (2021), 'Anti-5G, Infrastructure Sabotage, and Covid 19', *Global Network on Extremism & Technology*, 19 January, available at: https://gnet-research.org/2021/01/19/anti-5g-infrastructure-sabotage-and-covid-19 (accessed 15 August 2022).

Love, S. (2020), '"Conspirituality" Explains Why the Wellness World Fell for QAnon', *Vice*, 16 December, available at: www.vice.com/en/article/93wq73/conspirituality-explains-why-the-wellness-world-fell-for-qanon (accessed 15 August 2022).

Lowenthal, L., with N. Guterman (2016), 'Prophets of Deceit: A Study of the Techniques of the American Agitator', in L. Lowenthal (ed.), *False Prophets: Studies on Authoritarianism*, 3–171, New Brunswick: Transaction Publishers. (Facsimiles of the entire series *Studies in Prejudice*, including *Prophets of Deceit* and *The Authoritarian Personality*, can be found on the online archive of the American Jewish Committee: https://ajcarchives.org/main.php?GroupingId=1380.) (Lowenthal used the spelling Lowenthal since his move to the United States; some publications use the spelling Löwenthal which is the name he was born with.)

Löwy, M. (1992), *Redemption and Utopia: Jewish Libertarian Thought in Central Europe: A Study in Elective Affinity* (trans. H. Heaney), Stanford, CA: Stanford University Press.

Löwy, M. (2020), 'Jewish Messianism and Revolutionary Utopias in Central Europe: Erich Fromm's Early Writings (1922–1930)', in K. Durkin and J. Braune (eds), *Erich Fromm's Critical Theory: Hope, Humanism, and the Future*, 43–51, London: Bloomsbury.

Marx, K. (1964), *Karl Marx: Early Writings* (trans. and ed. T. B. Bottomore), New York: McGraw-Hill.

Marx, K. (n.d.), 'Letter from Marx to Arnold Ruge', *Marxist Internet Archive*, available at: www.marxists.org/archive/marx/works/1843/letters/43_09-alt.htm (accessed 16 August 2022).

Mesure, S. (2012), 'David Icke Is Not the Messiah. Or Even That Naughty. But Boy, Can He Drone On', *The Independent*, 27 October, available at: www.independent.co.uk/news/

uk/home-news/david-icke-is-not-the-messiah-or-even-that-naughty-but-boy-can-he-drone-on-8229433.html (accessed 16 August 2022).

Neiwert, D. (2020), *Red Pill, Blue Pill: How to Counteract the Conspiracy Theories That Are Killing Us*, Lanham, MD: Prometheus.

Norris, M. (2022), 'Episode 18 – Steph Halmhofer on *Ancient Aliens*, Pseudoarcheology – and the Far-Right', *Enemies of the People*, available at: https://podcasts.apple.com/us/podcast/episode-18-steph-halmhofer-on-ancient-aliens pseudoarchaeology/id1581679731?i=1000548886027 (accessed 16 August 2022).

Richards, A. (2021), 'Antarctica', *TikTok*, 8 September, available at: www.tiktok.com/@tofology/video/7005695895693970693?is_from_webapp=1&sender_device=pc&web_id=7014592059626227206 (accessed 24 August 2022).

Rothschild, M. (2021), *The Storm Is Upon Us: How QAnon Became a Movement, Cult, and Conspiracy Theory of Everything*, Brooklyn, NY: Melville House.

The Secret (2006), Dir. Drew Heriot, Australia/United States: Prime Time Productions.

Sitchen, Z. (2007), *The 12th Planet*, New York: Harper.

Smith, D. L. (2021), *Making Monsters: The Uncanny Power of Dehumanization*, Cambridge, MA: Harvard University Press.

Staudenmaier, P. (2008), 'Race and Redemption: Race and Ethnic Evolution in Rudolf Steiner's Anthroposophy', *Nova Religio*, 11 (3): 4–36.

Steinberg, A. (2017), 'Religion: Donald Trump and the Law of Attraction', *Huffpost Religion*, 16 February, available at: www.huffpost.com/entry/religion-donald-trump-and_b_9243272 (accessed 24 August 2022).

Turl, A. (2015), 'A Thousand Lost Worlds: Notes on Gothic Marxism', *Red Wedge*, 4 June, available at: www.redwedgemagazine.com/evicted-art-blog/a-thousand-lost-worlds-notes-on-gothic-marxism (accessed 16 August 2022).

Varis, P. (2019), 'On Being Diagnosed with Irony Poisoning', *Diggit Magazine*, 14 March, available at: www.diggitmagazine.com/column/being-diagnosed-irony-poisoning (accessed 16 August 2022).

Vice (2012), 'David Icke: Conspiracy of the Lizard Illuminati (Part 1/2)', *YouTube*, 24 August, available at: www.youtube.com/watch?v=1w2dMekIJLw (accessed 24 August 2022).

Von Däniken, E. (1999), *Chariots of the Gods* (trans. M. Heron), New York: Berkley Books.

Ward, C., and D. Voas (2011), 'The Emergence of Conspirituality', *Journal of Contemporary Religion*, 26 (1): 103–21.

Weill, K. (2022), *Off the Edge: Flat Earthers, Conspiracy Culture, and Why People Will Believe Anything*, Chapel Hill, NC: Algonquin Books.

Winter, T., M. Kosnar and W. Wong (2020), 'Feds Probing Whether Nashville Bomber Believed in Lizard People Conspiracy', *NBC*, 30 December, available at: www.nbcnews.com/news/us-news/girlfriend-nashville-bomber-warned-police-he-was-building-explosives-2019-n1252536 (accessed 16 August 2022).

Zaitchik, A. (2018), 'Close Encounters of the Racist Kind', *Southern Poverty Law Center*, 2 June, available at: www.splcenter.org/hatewatch/2018/01/02/close-encounters-racist-kind (accessed 16 August 2022).

Zeskind, L. (2009), *Blood and Politics: The History of the White Nationalist Movement from the Margins to the Mainstream*, New York: Farrar, Straus, Giroux.

8

Antisemitism, antiblackness and the nation in the storming of the US Capitol

Christopher D. Wright

Fascination with the radical direct actions of the Nazis led some on the German communist left to believe the Nazis were potentially revolutionaries, but it merely led them to fascism.[1] There are disturbing echoes of such delusions among some self-described communists and socialists in the United States today who want to perceive some objectively radical content in the 6 January 2021 coup attempt. Instead of losing ourselves in poorly disguised sympathy for these attempts at authoritarian rebellion and in wet dreams of macho-proletarian insurrection, we must rather try and grasp why almost 40 per cent of the population of the United States, necessarily including a large portion of the working class, believe that what was overall a very normal, unimpeded election was stolen from Donald Trump and thus from these Americans themselves, despite all evidence to the contrary and even the repeated rejection of such claims by Republican judges and official bureaucrats. It should be asked why the ideas and symbols on display at every level of this milieu are fascist but lack anything anti-capitalist or anti-state whatsoever.[2]

This (dis)orientation signals a general incapacity to think in the present, rooted in the same transformation of capitalist society which has radically changed the forms of appearance of capital and labour and undermined the traditional notion of revolution. Much of the left continues to hold a Lukácsian idea of 'the Proletariat' as the Subject of World History in all of its irremediably nineteenth-century senses, despite the absence of a single revolution corresponding to that idea since 1936.[3] Further, with few exceptions, it continues to treat antisemitism, racism, sexism and anti-queerness as 'ideologies' but class as 'reality', and pays little, if any, attention to the actual transformations of capitalist valorization and its materialization in the labour process. The exceptions to this history of intellectual and political failure provide the means of making sense of the present and of the events of 6 January 2021.

---

[1] An earlier version of parts of this chapter was posted in *Cured Quail* (Wright 2021).
[2] The only flags flown aside from the American flag were the Confederate Battle flag and the Nazi flag.
[3] We could bicker about 1956 in Hungary and 1968 in France, but to say that even those struggles did not achieve the scope and scale of 1917–23 or 1936 ought to be self-evident, and further that the character of social struggles from the 1950s onward took on aspects hitherto unseen.

In order to grasp various elements of the consciousness of the participants and passive supporters of the event, we have to grasp the centrality of antisemitism and antiblackness, how they inform a very particular sense of the nation-state and the impact of transformations of the labour process on the formation of actual social relations, forms of organization and kinds of consciousness.[4] The events up to and including 6th January cannot be grasped without addressing why, despite the broad appeal these days of conspiracy theories among all 'racial groups', the milieu partaking in and passively supporting the events is overwhelmingly white, Christian, nationalist, authoritarian and opposed precisely to the social welfare dimensions of the state. Antiblackness and antisemitism are constitutive elements of these politics of *ressentiment*, the revanchist opposition to dislocation within the changing social order.[5] I will work through Moishe Postone's conceptualization of antisemitism and Hylton White's novel appropriation of Postone and Franz Fanon for an analysis of antiblackness in order to conceptualize how the categories of abstract and concrete labour, use-value and exchange-value, money and capital, industry and finance constitute the determinate unconscious structures productive of the fetishistic forms of consciousness we think of as antisemitism and antiblackness.

Populist outrage: Antisemitism, antiblackness and the discontent with the current form of capitalism

Conceptualizing the centrality of antisemitism and antiblackness to the logic, motifs and tropes of this revanchist politics allows us to grasp what is otherwise dismissively treated as 'madness', 'irrationality', 'self-sabotage' and so on. In fact, it is precisely this dismissal that lends itself to some leftists believing there is the possibility of a Red–Brown alliance, that violent frustration with being on the losing end of some aspects of capitalist society constitutes a potentially revolutionary rejection of capitalism. On the contrary, I do not see in revanchist politics a rejection of capitalism but a demand that Others suffer for their loss, that Others are to blame for capitalism not working the right way and therefore that Others should pay the price for rectifying the order of things.

Antisemitism and antisemitic tropes are heavily present among many that participated in or passively supported the 6 January events: anger over the power of global finance; international conspiracies of supranational 'globalist' powers against the nation-state (the United Nations, the EU, and mysterious cabals centred on Davos and the like); belief in widespread paedophilia, one of the oldest of antisemitic tropes; even blood libel, which was already used by Sarah Palin back in 2011 when these people still

---

[4] In this chapter, 'antiblackness' is spelled without a hyphen, following the established practice of spelling 'antisemitism' without a hyphen, for the same reason: like there is no such thing as 'semitism' that one could be opposed to, there is no such thing as 'blackness'. These words are mere names, by convention, for groups of phenomena.

[5] My use of the term 'revanchist' is captured by Merril Perlman (2018). It is a unity of the desire for revenge and recovery of a lost status.

seemed somewhat fringe, now finds a certain frequency (Epstein 2011; James 2011). All of this is core to QAnon and many of the other alt-right groups at the heart of mass revanchist politics. If, especially in the United States, antisemitism has not historically been the major animating force of politics it has been in Europe, and if the relationship with Israel and affinities between the Israeli far right and the US far right has made for strange bedfellows, nonetheless, explicit antisemitism and violent attacks on Jewish people grew considerably during Trump's administration (Walters 2020).

Understanding why antisemitism has become more and more central to revanchist milieus *globally* requires more than empirical data. It requires an adequate grasp *conceptually* of the centrality and peculiarity of antisemitism to modernity and its discontents. Moishe Postone's work precisely grounds modern antisemitism in the categorial determinations of capital, those determinations forming the unconscious structure modern antisemitism takes that marks it as different from an antisemitic prejudice. Antisemitism is a fetishistic form of consciousness flowing from the quasi-autonomy of money, from money as the fetish form of the commodity, of money which, seemingly *ex nihilo* begets more money via interest and a host of financial mechanisms, in which the abstract forms of capital that become quasi-independent of capital's *concrete* forms of appearance, are then fetishistically embodied in 'the Jews'. 'The Jews' embody the independence and 'parasitic' power of money capital from productive capital, from the 'real' economy of production. This is especially present in the tropes of 'the Jew' as various kinds of infinite or universal: cosmopolitan, ungrounded in a nation; sexually infinite lecher; inassimilable to any other nation or community, only capable of being predatory or vampiric; of *universal law* as sovereign; and the threat of world money decoupled from the nation-state.

Modern antisemitism, with its most complete expression in Nazism, therefore, can express a 'foreshortened' form of critique of capitalist society, a kind of anti-capitalism with a romanticist, utopian element. Instead of grasping the source of oppression as capital as a whole, it hypostatizes the problem in one moment of capital, in money and finance, and identifies it with a specific, *finite* group of people, 'the Jews'. Antisemitism, unlike how other racisms depict the racialized, does not reckon 'the Jews' as inferior, but as a supremely powerful group that seeks to impose its domination over everything. It believes that liberation from domination can only be achieved through the annihilation of 'the Jews'. Following this line of thought, Postone draws the conclusion that Auschwitz is not the fulfilment of capitalism, but the fulfilment of Nazi anti-capitalism. Unlike with a mere prejudice, it allows us to comprehend why, in the midst of Germany's impending military defeat by the Soviet army, all manner of resources were redirected to make sure that the annihilation of the Jews was completed. Victory in war was less important than the victory over the Jewish threat.

Postone presents a striking analysis of how antisemitism constructs the Jewish Other, but says less about the self-consciousness of the antisemite, the finite being of the nation, and the concrete national-racial community of 'blood and soil', those who can only be who they are because their blood is one with *this* soil, *this* nation. As such, if antisemitic racism reckons the infinite as *abstract*, as the pure power of money to command, as infinite appropriation of the productive wealth of others through M-M', the non-Semite cannot but present themselves as that *concrete being* which has to destroy that power, destroy the embodiment of the infinite in order to bring it back under the control of 'productive' capital, the 'real' economy, the national economy. This is the ground of antisemitism as a finite critique of capitalism, the *ressentiment* of productive capital against finance, the small property owner against the 'money lender', and therefore as a *generalized* genocidal impulse against 'the Jews' as a collective parasite on the real, as opposed to an ideology used by this or that class or party to protect capitalism.[6]

Importantly, Postone does not equate fascism with Nazism. Rather, Nazism is fascism which conceives its utopian dimension, its 'national socialism', as only realizable through the annihilation of 'the Jews', conceived as bearers of a corrupt cosmopolitan capitalism. The depth of this difference was expressed in the utter lack in Germany of any anti-fascist revolt at the end of the war, any welcoming of the Allied forces – unlike in Italy where both took place, and also where antisemitism and the annihilation of the Jews did not play a central role[7] – and instead a need to act as if nothing special had taken place.[8] The characterization herein of the elements supporting Trump and the coup attempt as fascist and as antisemitic is not per se, despite the flags, equivalent to Nazism precisely because one of the peculiar features is that the Trumpian revanchist milieu lacks the utopian element that would see a new 'Final Solution' as inaugurating the overcoming of capitalism. Rather, it finds itself inherently antisemitic in its complaint about capitalism *without* any traces of anti-capitalism, without pretending to aim at anything more than a return to a fantastical past of a white, Christian, masculine, heteronormative order, violent and murderous but, at least for now, not genocidal precisely because of its mundane and anti-utopian aspirations.

Antisemitism is not the only moment of the conceptual core of this revanchist politics, however: antiblackness is as essentially constitutive of the revanchist consciousness, and here we must go beyond Postone who correctly grasps the uniqueness of antisemitism but not the radical particularity of antiblackness. This

---

[6] Hylton White's summary is worth quoting at length: 'Postone's approach is to show how features of antisemitic discourse gain political purchase by offering partial, fetishised representations of the functioning of capital. Three things stand out. The first is that antisemitism represents Jews as agents possessing extraordinary social power. This in itself is remarkable: a racism that comprehends its targets as possessors of control. The second is that antisemitism depicts this Jewish power as invisible. It operates through conspiracy, from behind the scenes, by manipulating the interventions of concrete representatives. The third is that this influence is unhealthy: Jewish power is a disease within the national body politic, parasitically twisting its dynamics to fulfil purposes that are foreign to its nature. In all these ways, for Postone, antisemitic imagery provides a potent symbol for the fetish form of capital. Not capital comprehended as a totality of complex social relationships that sustain accumulation, but capital as a fetishised congelation: as the apparent power of money, in particular – the power that money seemingly has to dissemble, to commensurate, to control the world from behind a hidden distance. In this fetishised appearance, money is the body of the abstract dimensions of capital, and antisemitic imagery makes the Jew into the racial body of money' (2020: 28–9).

[7] There are varying views on the matter, which cannot be gone into in depth here, but few people have claimed that antisemitism was the unifying anti-capitalist, utopian element in Italian fascism, especially before 1938, despite Mussolini's party being in power since 1922 and his own avowed antisemitism. For examples of varying views, see Ben-Ghiat (2017), Bernardini (1977) and Anon. (2020).

[8] Postone develops this most completely in Postone (1990).

failure limits his grasp of the internality of racialization to the nation-state, and thus the dynamics of antiblackness as a wholly capitalist social form which itself is generative and not 'mere ideology'. Postone's relative quietude on the dynamic of state and nation, may in part be comprehended by this limitation. Therefore, we must find an adequate concept of antiblackness and work out the centrality of both antisemitism and antiblackness to populist nationalism.

In taking up antiblackness as another essential element of revanchist populism, most notions of racism fail because they are unwilling or unable to grasp the constitution of racism as internal to capitalist society.[9] Hylton White's work brings together Postone's Critical Theory of antisemitism with Frantz Fanon's Critical Theory of racialism, grasping antiblack racism as caught up in its own fetishistic dynamic, but here not at the level of the fetishistic consciousness of capital, but the fetishistic aporias of labour. Antiblackness fetishizes the black body as the embodiment of pure potency, of *abstract labour* in its pure representation, as infinite capacity, as infinite drive, but also in this purity as mindless, as inert, which cannot be *active and productive* without the guiding consciousness of the master, of concrete productive capital turning it into concrete labour, into mindful, purposeful activity.[10] Fanon grasps the fetishization of the black body thus:

> The Jew is attacked in his religious identity, in his history, in his race, in his relations with his ancestors and with his posterity; when one sterilizes a Jew, one cuts off the source; every time that a Jew is persecuted, it is the whole race that is persecuted in his person. But it is in his corporeality that the Negro is attacked. It is as a concrete personality that he is lynched. It is as an actual being that he is a threat. (Fanon 1986: 125–6; published originally in 1952)

Hylton White presents antiblackness as essentially the opposite of the infinite power of monetary intellect, of money as a will of its own secretly controlling of us, 'the Jew' as the sorcerer behind the invisible hand. For antiblack racism, 'blackness' is the pure potentiality of biological energy, 'humanity in its most vital yet its most brutish,

---

[9] It is impossible here to cover the range of theories of the *causes* of racism, Marxist or not, but most of them rely on some combination of essentializing race, reducing it to an effect of competition within the working class, or as some form of localized, historically specific ideology with a largely contingent relation to capital. Postone's and White's concepts show the way in which Marx's *Capital* allows us to grasp the fundamental *determinations* that structure forms of consciousness and social relations understood as *racial*, that is, as determinations of a process of *racialization* immanent to capitalist society and its discontents. The distinction between causes and determinations is central to my argument here: searching for *causes* calls for narratives and is basically empiricist and historicist (Marxist or otherwise); *determinations* relate to social forms and require conceptual-theoretical argument. The former asks why racism or antisemitism appears here or there, but not elsewhere, whereas the latter asks why a certain social practice takes the *form* of racism or antisemitism. My argument sees racism and antisemitism as structured forms of practice and consciousness determined by the social forms of capital as such. Why racism or antisemitism arose in this place at this time is important but secondary to asking why the response to capitalist society takes those forms, and not just once but repeatedly.

[10] In this chapter, black is spelled in lower case in keeping with the usage by radical black scholars such as Jared Sexton (cf. Barber 2017).

biological expression: animal vigour ... Money is a power of control, but the biological body is a power that requires control' (White 2020: 31).

However, this does not mean that antiblackness is a 'generic racism', a mere ideology of difference in general.[11] On the contrary, if 'antisemitism ... has a direct relationship with "modernity's" attempt at reconciling its constituting contradiction, that is the class antagonism between capital and labour', it does so from the side of capital, whereas antiblackness is also an attempt at reconciliation from the side of labour (Bonefeld 1997: 61–2). The failure rests upon the conflation of *labour*, as concrete and abstract, with *wage-labour*, its mode of existence. Labour materialized in the wage-labourer is doubly free wage-labour: the owner of labour power is free to sell it as they see fit to whomever they see fit, and is also free from any other form of property or means of production, and therefore free also to live under a bridge or go without bread. Once sold, however, this labour power is consumed in production as an object, variable capital, property of the capital which has purchased it. Precisely in production the freedom of the wage-labourer ends.

But wage-labour is not the only form labour can take. Labour has also taken the form of capitalist slave labour. In the case of the wage-labourer as doubly free, labour takes the form of variable capital and the source of value, while as the slave labourer, it is wholly unfree and takes the form of constant capital.[12] Slave labour is not merely something that happened during so-called primitive accumulation. Rather, following Werner Bonefeld's critique of the concept of 'so-called primitive accumulation', slave labour is subsumed by fully developed capitalism, which reduces the labourer's life force, through the production process, to mere capital, as something the labourer no longer owns and which the production process under the control of capital consumes. The moment of labour as enslavement is sublated within wage-labour, vanishing in one moment into the form of the 'free' exchange of labour power for a wage, and yet subsisting in the wage-*labourer* as mere object, as one more *means* of the production process, as a moment of capital (Bonefeld 2001, 2011). Antiblackness posits 'blacks' as the fetishizing embodiment of this unfree dimension of labour power as a racial group, as the purely abstract power of labour without subjectivity, and in asserting the condition of racial superiority, the fundamental equality of all whites as possessors of property, as the self-possessed, self-determining persons of concrete labour.[13] Antiblackness takes the reduction of the labourer to merely being 'time's carcass' and ascribes it to 'the blacks', to a fundamental property of 'blackness', against the dignity of labour which belongs to 'non-blacks'.[14] Precisely in this fashion, antiblackness and the claims of the dignity of labour go hand in hand. The non-black wage-labourer

---

[11] The claim of the necessity of grasping antisemitism in its particularity is fair, but to claim that it has a particularity from all other racisms which are relegated to 'racism in general' or 'ideologies of difference' fundamentally misunderstands the particularity of antiblackness. For typical examples, of the 'racism in general' argument, see Postone (1990: 234–5) and Bonefeld (1997).

[12] On this, see Nesbitt (2022).

[13] The notion of personhood as deriving from the pre-institutional 'property in oneself' that we all have found its quintessential expression in John Locke's *Two Treatises of Government* (1988): 'Every Man has a *Property* in his own *Person*. This no Body has any Right to but himself. The *Labour* of his Body, and the *Work* of his Hands, we may say, are properly his (ST §27)'.

[14] 'Time is everything, man is nothing; he is, at the most, time's carcase' (Marx 1982: 54). 'Carcase' is old-fashioned for 'carcass'.

thus asserts, within labour as form of domination *pace* Postone, their fundamental reconciliation with this form of domination and demands not the abolition of wage-labour, but the removal of the unfairness which turns it into 'wage-slavery'. In this sense, we might say that if calling wage-labour wage-slavery was on one level an injustice to the actuality of the conditions of slaves whom slavery reduced to constant capital, to mere objects, to machine-animals, it at least, at another level, grasped labour under capitalism for what it was: a form of domination with which one should not become reconciled.

This is why it is completely incorrect to imagine that antiblackness is 'racism in general' or a mere 'ideology of difference'. Antiblackness is instead a fetishized form of discontent with the infinite indignity of labour, the truth of which is not concrete labour, but abstract labour, value's substance. To put a finer point on it, 'concrete labour' in *Capital*, is not concrete, is not 'the concentration of many determinations'[15], but it is precisely a pseudo-concrete, the immediate form necessarily taken by labour in the abstract, which is that same labour as infinite, as sheer temporality and quantity. Marx's usage in *Capital* is precisely that here, 'concrete' labour is finite, while 'abstract' labour is infinite, and as infinite is the truth of labour in capitalism. Concrete labour is thus the appearance of labour in the immediate, and is essentially untrue, but it is precisely this untrue, finite immediacy taken as the truth of labour in a politics of the fundamental dignity of capitalist labour, that constitutes the unconscious structure of antiblackness.

Excursus 1: On the Hegelian concepts of the finite and the infinite

Readers might be puzzled by my frequent use of the categories 'finite' and 'infinite' in this chapter. While I use these concepts as they are developed in Hegel's *Logic*, their usefulness, I'd like to suggest, lies in illuminating the meaning of the concepts of 'abstract' and 'concrete' as used by Marx, which in turn link to the concepts of 'essence' and 'appearance'.

Since my argument, following Hylton White, that antiblack racism is a fetishistic form of consciousness arising specifically from the hypostatization of concrete labour (against, say, the hypostatization of money capital pace antisemitism), we must address the fact that, in *Capital* Vol. 1, labour is first discussed as abstract and concrete (Marx 1990). However, as used there these terms have a very particular, and in some sense, counterintuitive meaning. Whereas Marx defines (in the *Grundrisse* 'Introduction') concreteness as 'the outcome of many determinations', the concreteness of 'concrete labour' as in *Capital* vol. 1 is the pseudo-concreteness of immediacy rather than that of a complex, mediated concreteness. Concrete labour is the immediate, material and therefore *inessential* dimension of capitalist labour. Abstract labour, in turn, is

---

[15] 'The concrete is concrete because it is the concentration of many determinations, hence unity of the diverse' (Marx 1993: 101).

not abstract in the sense of 'ideal but lacking a concrete existence', or 'theoretical as opposed to actual', but rather the *essential*, determinate dimension of capitalist labour. Abstract labour is the dimension of capitalist labour that is the substance of value, with labour time indicating the magnitude of value.

If we consider which of these is the truth of capitalist labour, abstract labour is that which allows us to speak of labour in general, labour as sheer quantum, that is, *infinite* in the sense of the adequate concept of labour in capitalist society (and also as quantitatively infinite). 'Concrete' labour always entails incommensurate, particular and therefore *finite* activities.

For the buyer of labour power (capital), the use-value of labour is that it produces value. Labour power which cannot be used for the expansion or capture of abstract social wealth (whether as money, commodity capital or productive capital) has no use-value for capital. For the seller of labour power, labour is only useful if it can be sold for a wage with which to support their existence. In fact, the same activity completed on one's own time, for one's own ends and pleasure is not only not labour in the capitalist sense, it is frequently not even considered labour by the worker, but a form of leisure or enjoyment.

These uses of 'concrete' and 'abstract' labour are actually closer to Hegel's conception of 'finite' and 'infinite' than Hegel and Marx's more developed uses of 'abstract' and 'concrete'. In Hegel, the infinite is the fundamental perspective of philosophy, that is, interest in and commitment to truth: that which expresses something *as its concept*. When Hegel says that the infinite is the true, he expresses this in a variety of ways, such as his point that 'the truth' of the natural sciences does not consist in this or that fact or statistic, but the discovery of *laws* of nature. By comparison, while the infinite needs the finite (similar to how essence needs appearance because an essence that does not have a form of appearance is nothing), the finite (the immediate) is at the same time what is ephemeral and passing. Hegel's discussion of finite and infinite allows us to think both the qualitative and the quantitative dimensions in which what seems qualitative is actually quantum's own qualitativeness. Concrete labour is precisely the qualitative dimension as a finite activity that is given its actual truth only by its abstract, temporal, quantitative moment.

Hegel's discussion of the finite and the infinite in *The Science of Logic* brings to attention the fetishization of one moment over the other, and the untruth in particular of the emphasis on the superiority of the finite over the infinite:

> The qualitative and quantitative infinite are distinguished inasmuch as in the former the opposition of the finite and infinite is qualitative, and the transition of the finite into the infinite, or the reference of each to the other, is present only in the in-itself, in their concept. Qualitative determinateness is immediate; it refers to otherness essentially as to a being which is other than it; it is not posited as having its negation, its other, in it. By contrast, magnitude is as such sublated determinateness; it is posited as being unlike and indifferent to itself, and hence as something alterable. The qualitative finite and infinite, therefore, stand opposed to each other absolutely, that is, abstractly; their unity is the inner connection underlying them; hence the finite continues in its other only in itself,

not in it. By contrast, in the infinite in which the quantitative finite has its absolute determinateness, this finite refers to itself in it. (Hegel 2010: 190–1)

Hegel has taken up the finite-infinite in both the section on quality and on quantity, and it is on the qualitative that we will focus in taking up antiblack racism, antisemitic racism, the nation and state, and masculine-feminine.[16] Hegel's engagement with these categories helps illuminate the nature of the fetishistic consciousness which arises necessarily from the categories of capital. The qualitative moment of finite and infinite informs a number of couplets relating to the critique of political economy: the state as nation-state/capitalist state, commodity as use-value/value, labour as concrete/abstract. For Hegel, there is no finite without infinite and vice versa, a seemingly trivial point. But Hegel's insistence that truth is on the side of the infinite is at once also Marx's insistence that the truth of the commodity is value, rather than use-value; the truth of labour is abstract labour, not concrete labour; the truth of exchange-value is the equivalent form or money, not the relative form. Yet for Hegel, as much as for Marx, the infinite cannot *be* without the finite, nor does it precede the finite. Instead, the infinite posits the finite as in itself. If the infinite is the truth, it is the truth of each moment as a moment of its other. However, it is to the preponderance of one side *at the expense of the other* that Hegel's analysis helps illustrate the mystifications involved in both antisemitism and antiblack racism. Racialism elevates this finite concrete, this immediate and ephemeral concreteness, to being truth, that is, it elevates immediacy, in its domination by capital, to the truth of labour. It conceives of labour not as exploitation and domination but a form of dignity that belongs to the elect, and these elect are construed as a superior race opposed to the inferior racial other who embodies precisely the truth and terror of labour in capitalist society. Those who construe themselves as the elect race thus side with capital against its negation.

The production of 'the white man'

As with antisemitism, it is important to tease out not merely the fetishistic production of 'the Other', but the racial superior, *homo albus*, 'the white man'. Precisely as the fetishistic appearance of productive capital entails its own fetishistic self-consciousness as 'good' and 'real', so too does antiblack racialism posit a self-consciousness grounded in concrete labour. This concrete labour is 'knowledgeable', 'skilful', a power that expresses itself in productive activity as its own self-realization. This is the fetish of the importance of useful labour, of a finite labour, against merely abstract labour as infinite potency, whether as a self-determining subject of the labour process in concert with

---

[16] In an earlier section, Hegel makes a point of emphasizing that 'this applies to philosophy just as much as to religion, for religion also, no less than philosophy, will not admit finitude as a true being, an ultimate, an absolute, or as something non-posited, uncreated, eternal. The opposition between idealistic and realistic philosophy is therefore without meaning. *A philosophy that attributes to finite existence, as such, true, ultimate, absolute being, does not deserve the name of philosophy*' (2010: 124, emphasis added).

capital, seeking the recognition of labour, or as something revolutionary, but conceived as able to replace the unproductive capitalist (as the capitalist claimed to replace the unproductive landed aristocrat) who exists merely by exploiting the intelligence, hard work and skill of the worker. This notion of the relation of the worker to work was inherently *racialized as white*, as whites having property in themselves, as a property owner insofar as they could put that property into action. However, Hylton White's argument also opens up the non-entitlement of the black body to property qua capital because, conceived as brutish and animalistic potency, no 'black' can claim ownership of themselves nor therefore of any other property. Antiblackness marks 'blacks' as in need of a master in general and therefore as unfit for mastery of themselves or of property as such. Hylton White's argument opens up the possibility of asking not merely why the white *worker* is racist, but why there are *whites* constituted by antiblackness along the entire class continuum.

The importance of Postone, Fanon and White cannot be overestimated insofar as it becomes clear that antisemitism and antiblackness are neither non-capitalist particularities as the outcomes of empirical historical trajectories (phenomenological historicism passing itself off as Marxism), nor anachronisms of pre-capitalist history nor even of 'primitive accumulation' as a now-surpassed time of yore. Instead, they are fetishistic forms of being and consciousness constituted in and through capital's own categories and dynamics. Revanchist politics congeal around this revolt of the finite against the infinite, the belief that the infinite must be brought under the control of, must serve, must be mastered by, the finite. It should be unsurprising then that antisemitism and antiblackness, being specific moments of finite revolt against, and reconciliation with, the infinite power of capital and the infinite indignity of labour, constitute essential determinations of revanchist, fascist populism.

It is worth noting here some of the historical trajectories of antisemitism and antiblackness. Postone notes that traditional antisemitic prejudice which had associated 'the Jews' with usury, money-lending, expansion of wealth by the charging of interest, established in pre-capitalist Europe, provided a historical precondition of modern antisemitism in the context of dislocation of traditional social forms and views when German society exceedingly rapidly industrialized. Similarly, trans-Mediterranean (fourteenth to sixteenth centuries) and trans-Atlantic enslavement of Africans played an essential part in the global accumulation not merely of wealth, but of the shaping and spread of the capitalist *form* of wealth.[17] If 'the Jew' was the figure of illicit gain, of money untethered and irresponsible and all-powerful, so 'the black' represents labour as sheer enslavement, as the absence of property in oneself, as property to be set to work and consumed like any machine or animal. Just as early financial and merchant capital on one side and slave labour on the other, in the so-called primitive accumulation of capital, are eventually subsumed to accumulation as such in the industrial mode of production relying on wage-labour, nonetheless the seeming autonomy of money does not disappear, nor does the labourer as appendage to the machine, as mere raw

---

[17] Cf. Nesbitt (2022) and Solow (2016).

material to be used up. The subordination of everything to the power of money and the enslaving nature of labour do not disappear, and further remain identified with their fetishistic embodiments.

Lars Fischer expresses well why we should not think of antisemitism, and therefore also antiblackness, as forms of 'prejudice' in the sense of miscomprehending pre-judgement, but rather as something far more destructive and dangerous. He writes,

> As Horkheimer and Adorno pointed out in their 'Elements of Antisemitism', the crucial issue is therefore not that antisemitic notions regarding 'the Jews' are based on projection. In that respect they are no different from any other form of human perception. What radically sets them apart is the fact that they are predicated on a radical exclusion of the reflective and critical faculties from the process of projection. Hence they amount to a false projection that blurs the distinction between the projecting subject and the object. The object is reduced to a mere foil on which the projecting subject can see only what it has projected there in the first place. This is not a process, then, in which the subject's interaction with the object is cut short and the subject therefore passes premature judgement on the basis of incomplete knowledge. Instead, the subject refuses all interaction with the object from the outset in order to render it a suitable foil for the projection of an established set of stereotypes. (Fischer 2007: 9)

Critically, each finds further expression in the constitution of the nation which tends to go unexamined in typical Marxian notions of the state, and which finds continuous expression in the revanchist right that expressed itself on January 6th at the Capitol building.

Excursus 2: State and nation as the infinite and the finite of the political

Marxian thought takes the state as essentially capitalist. It appears as universality above social differences, the infinite mediator posited by capital that 'needs' the state because generalized exchange relations are inherently generalized contractual relations, and in order for those relations to be relations of equality of exchange, there must be a power above buyer and seller (and above the classes selling and buying labour power, not to mention within the classes) to guarantee that both parties fulfil the contract. (Every exchange is contractual in nature, whether or not formalized by a contract as a document.) This is the uniquely and universally capitalist separation of the political from the economic as separate spheres and the quasi-autonomy of the state from both the economy and classes. At this universal level, the state is posited through the adjudication and preservation of these social forms against any finite or particular interests. This is the simple reason that communists cannot take over the state to use it against capital because 'the state' as 'the capitalist state' is a mode of existence of capitalist social relations and has no existence outside or beyond (or before) them. As encompassing all individuals within the state as abstractly equal persons before the law, as citizens, the state is genuinely universalizing and infinite. There is, at the formal-logical level of the state, that is to say, abstractly, no limit to who can be a citizen or person before the law of a state and we may even reasonably grasp many social struggles as precisely the struggle to extend the universality of citizenship and the benefits that follow from it (to workers, to women, to Jews, to black people, to LGBTQ people, etc.). This is what Gáspár Miklós Tamás (2000) refers to as 'the Enlightenment tendency to assimilate citizenship to the human condition'. Revanchist politics, what Tamás calls 'post-fascism', are the drive to reverse this tendency and its actual achievements.

However, the capitalist state only has its *finite being* as actual, particular states, more specifically, as nations. When one thinks of what constitutes this or that nation – each of whose coming to be constitutes a much more contingent, incoherent process than is generally grasped – it does so not only through the constitution of 'the people', but also through the constitution of '*not* the people'. Other states form the most obvious 'not us' which comprise the limit, an explicit boundary demarcating an other people, an other nation. Less obvious however than the other as an excluded outsider, the foreigner as such, are the others who are 'excluded in'. Those 'excluded in' constitute all manner of others who are first and foremost subject *to* the state, objects of its law and, at the same time, not legitimately viewed as subjects *of* the state. This othering is the formal-legal element of racialization. The state as nation is thus doubly finite insofar as it identifies other states (and their people) as not *this* state (and this people), but also as who within this state qualify as constitutive of the nation, 'the people' and who are not of 'the people'. The capitalist nation-state is in this sense always racialist (broadly conceived, whether the word 'race' is used or not) because there is no nation-state without some group(s) 'excluded in', not merely 'excluded out', made external as members of another nation-state.

The state is the infinite as law applying to all persons as equals before the law, as abstract monads emptied of unequal particularity, but also as what constitutes all those persons as a *One, a nation*, rather than merely an aggregate in the social contractarian notion. However, if the state lacks finitude, if it takes itself as a universality free of its actuality expressed in a finite element, it will become the state of absolute terror, the law of the guillotine and 'gulps of water'.[18] It is not the individual who constitutes this finitude, however. The individual citizen cannot demand the state give up its life for them, but the state can most certainly command the individual citizen to give up their life for it, *willingly*. The finite of the state is the nation, the particular spirit of a people. For what we now (in ideal-typical manner) think of as 'political liberalism', the truth of the nation-state lies in its infinite aspects – law, liberty, freedom, the possibility of the respect for individuals – but in fact it is always grounded in the 'spirit of the people', the unity of state and nation. The position opposed to that of 'political liberalism' (as its equally one-sided mirror image, as it were) is that taken by Carl Schmitt, for whom law and universality must be subordinated to the nation as sovereign, whereby the nation is constituted by the elect, the *Volk*. Notions of personhood, equality of all citizens before the law, of all members of the state as citizens, violate the sovereignty of the *Volk*

---

[18] Cf. Hegel's discussion of the infinite state as 'Absolute Freedom and Terror' in para. 590 of *Phenomenology of Spirit* (2019).

as *nation-state*. The *volkish* state exerts the infinite power of violence to instantiate itself as sovereign, to show itself as sovereign.

Antisemitism and antiblackness answer the questions, 'who is excluded in?' and 'why are they excluded?' Antisemitism tells us that the Bolshevik-financier threat from the outside is also an invisible threat from within. (This is why antisemitism was always simultaneously anti-communist and anti-financier, seeing in the two of them the secret, hidden One of the Janus-faced Jew.) Antiblackness, by contrast, speaks of a brutish body unfit for personhood, useful for labour but in need of being mastered and incapable of self-determination. The problem of the liberal conception that imagines an eventual happy unity of nation and state is the critique which recognizes the inherently self-contradictory dynamic, that infinity and universality, that the state is in fact a limited universality both as posited by capital, but also as necessarily a *nation*-state, a particularity constituted against other states and a nation constituted by those who within it are also out of it. The universality of the state is short-circuited by its particularity as a nation, externally vis-à-vis other states and internally by the pressure to express who is a citizen, a subject of the law, in reference to populations of the nation who are *de jure* or *de facto* objects of the law, moments of the nation, but not fully persons, the Others who constitute the negative determination of the 'true' citizens.

The state is more finite than infinite, or rather, it is only as infinite as capital allows it to be. The true infinite is capital itself, self-valorizing value. This is, though, an infinite which is self-destructive. In the face of a financialized global economy, money certainly is perceived as the infinite, and all states seem to be subordinate to global flows of money.[19]

---

[19] Modern Monetary Theory (MMT) is the expression of this seeming autonomy of money. In brief, MMT holds that 'countries like the U.S., U.K., Japan, and Canada, which spend, tax, and borrow in a fiat currency (https://www.investopedia.com/terms/f/fiatmoney.asp) that they fully control, are not operationally constrained by revenues when it comes to federal government spending' (www.investopedia.com/modern-monetary-theory-mmt-4588060). Another way to put it is that they can print as much of their own fiat as they want to meet their spending goals. Despite the claim that it applies to several countries, it has a peculiar problem: the only currency which can function as world money from an MMT perspective is the dollar, and the dollar functions as world currency because of the US sovereignty. This sovereignty is in part military, but also the fact that the dollar is the only accepted currency for oil and is accepted globally as a means of payment of debts. In the present, as challenged on several sides, the crisis of the dollar is thus a crisis of sovereignty and vice versa. The infinite power of money that seems to be capable of being used for Keynesian social-democratic aims in any country with a 'sovereign currency' winds up being possible only for one sovereign currency. The sovereignty of the dollar is predicated on the domination of the world through US debt. Social-democratic/welfare state policies have always relied on colonialism and nationalist policies. This is said as a provocation and also as a wager but, beyond some suggestive hinting, cannot be cached out in full here.

As Michael Hudson shows in *Super-Imperialism*, the policies of Roosevelt went hand in hand with the impoverishment of Europe, the treatment of the British and French debts from the First World War as an infinite obligation which forced them to effectively loot Germany, which in turn helped create the conditions that paved the way for Nazism. This stood in direct contrast to the European tradition of the forgiveness of military aid debt to the Allies, that is, the debt as a finite obligation that could be forgiven. If this was the case in the 1920s and 1930s, how would a renewed social-democratic-Keynesian programme not involve a nationalist turning inward? And can we be certain that this would not still be implemented in ways fundamentally structured by antisemitism and antiblackness? Many black supporters of Bernie Sanders have raised the problem that Medicare for All, for example, does not mean more hospitals in black neighbourhoods, non-racist treatment

The revanchist revolt of the finite nation against the infinite state, and Memmi's concept of the consciousness of the colonizers

We do not have to go much further to grasp the meaning of the ever-present co-mingling of the American flag with the Nazi and Confederate flags at revanchist right rallies and of course on January 6th. The Trump supporters are not against the state. They are very much *for* the state, as long as it is wholly subordinated to the nation. They are opposed to any claims to primacy of the infinite aspects of the state, any registration of all citizens equally as persons before the law regardless of any finite 'qualifications'. For them, the finite 'qualifications' are overriding determinations of membership in the nation, to which the state owes ultimate fidelity. The nation must be master of the state and anyone not 'of the nation' is not entitled to the power of the state, and this 'not of the nation' is clearly conceived through the lenses of antisemitism and antiblackness. The 'excluded in' have no inherent right to be treated as equals before the law, a law which is to be enforced both by the police-military-prison apparatus, but also supplemented by the prerogative of (mostly) white, straight, Christian men to exercise extra-state violence. This is why any activity by the state that emphasizes the infinite-universal elements of the state threatens them, but they have an infinite thirst for the extension of the police-military-prison elements of the state and financial support of industries and small businesses to ensure the complete freedom to profit. Trump's supporters cannot imagine, any more than Southern segregationists could before them, a state not utterly subordinate to their nation. This loss, at this moment, is apparently a loss they cannot accept, and that it might be fair, untainted by corruption, vouchsafed by many Republican politicians and judges within the confines of bourgeois democracy, is incomprehensible to them. It introduces a reality as utterly bizarre to them as their claims are to anyone not them.

Contemporary complaints about the state from revanchists are always the same, a nostalgic longing for the 'good old days' when being white and/or male and/or straight, and so on, allowed you to not only have a better chance at getting ahead in the world, but at feeling powerful, in control, an identity between yourself and the powerful. Contrary to some on the left who would see this revolt in light of out-of-context quotes from the *Communist Manifesto*,[20] the petty bourgeois social elements which predominated in the

---

of black patients, more access to medical education and professional opportunities for black people and so on. For example, historically, Rooseveltian agricultural subsidies were deployed in the US South in the 1930s and 1940s in such a way as to destroy independent black farmers and support the expansion of white farmers, employing machinery to replace black labour, and to increase the number of white sharecroppers and tenant farmers so that they could buy their own farms outright.

[20] A variety of comments on 6 January referenced this section from the 'Bourgeois and Proletarians' section of the *Manifesto*, suggesting that despite themselves, the participants were 'objectively radical': 'The lower middle class, the small manufacturer, the shopkeeper, the artisan, the peasant, all these fight against the bourgeoisie, to save from extinction their existence as fractions of the middle class. They are therefore not revolutionary, but conservative. Nay more, they are reactionary, for they try to roll back the wheel of history. If by chance, they are revolutionary, they are only so in view of their impending transfer into the proletariat; they thus defend not their present, but their future interests, they desert their own standpoint to place themselves at that of the proletariat'

mob that took action on January 6th are not, even accidentally, following the lead of the proletariat. (Some of them may indeed try to avoid proletarianization, though, against the background of an utter failure to manage the Covid-19 pandemic which is killing small businesses as fast as people.) Further, the far larger passive base that supports them neither revolts against their impending slide into the working class nor against being wage-labour. Quite the opposite. They are desperately trying to remain valid and valued sellers of their labour power precisely as they experience the diminishing role of living labour in the production of material wealth. After all, what good is property in oneself as seller of the commodity labour power when no one wants what you are selling, or only at a heavily discounted rate?

Antisemitism and antiblackness are not the only possible answers to this crisis, of course, but when these are the answers people reach for, the question then becomes how they structure the dissatisfaction and how resistance to this crisis is expressed: as liberatory, reconciliatory or revanchist. Revanchism answers by steadfastly looking backwards engaged in a fascistic politics in a vain attempt to not be destroyed by capital's infernal churning, which they then blame on any and all attempts at social, economic and political egalitarianism within and through the state. Even for those of us who recognize that the state cannot cash out those promises because it must always manage those demands as subservient to the extended reproduction of capital, it should be clear that there is no going back. Rather pathetically, no small part of the left objectively desires the strong state and holds out for a (re)turn to social-democratic social policy, just as the revanchist right seeks a return to a Magical White Christmas-land America. This consciousness has striking similarities to the consciousness of the colonialist expressed almost six decades ago by Albert Memmi (1974). Memmi's recounting of the self-consciousness of the colonialist, as in the following quotation, reads like an extraordinarily prescient analysis of our current situation if only we replace the words 'colonialist' with 'Trump Supporter' and Memmi's various terms for 'citizens back in the home country' with 'coastal urbanites' and so on:

> Furthermore, the colonialist ... presents himself as one of the most perceptive members of the national community, for he is grateful and faithful. He knows, as compared to the citizens back home whose happiness is never threatened, what he owes to his origin. His faithfulness is, however, abstract ... . It is not soiled by all the trivialities of the daily life of his fellow citizens back home who must gain everything by ingenuity and electoral schemes. His pure fervor for the mother country makes him a true patriot, a fine ambassador, representing its most noble features ... . He loves the most flashy symbols, the most striking demonstrations of the power of his country. He attends all military parades and he desires and obtains frequent and elaborate ones; he contributes his part by dressing up carefully and ostentatiously. He admires the army and its strength, reveres uniforms and covets

(Marx and Engels 1970: 25). The Trumpist revanchists are adequately described by the first part of this statement – they are conservative or reactionary – not by the second part in which Marx and Engels somewhat optimistically suggested there *might be* some exceptions who are 'by chance' revolutionaries (such as Marx and Engels themselves).

decorations .... [This ostentatiousness] corresponds to a deep necessity of colonial life; to impress the colonized is just as important as to reassure oneself. (Memmi 1974: 102–3)

It is necessary, then, not only that the home country constitute the remote and never intimately known ideal, but also that this ideal be immutable and sheltered from time; the colonialist requires his homeland to be conservative. He, of course, is resolutely conservative. It is on just that point that he is most rigid, that he compromises the least ... he is seized with worry and panic each time there is talk of changing the political status. It is only then that the purity of his patriotism is muddled, his indefectible attachment to his motherland shaken. He may go as far as to threaten – Can such things be! – Secession! Which seems contradictory, in conflict with his so well-advertised and, in a certain sense, real patriotism.

But the colonialist's nationalism is truly of a special nature .... A homeland which became democratic, for example, to the point of promoting equality of rights even in the colonies, would also risk abandoning its colonial undertakings. For the colonialist, such a transformation would challenge his way of life and thus become a matter of life or death. In order that he may subsist as a colonialist, it is necessary that the mother country eternally remain a mother country. To the extent that this depends upon him, it is understandable if he uses all his energy to that end. Now one can carry this a step further; every colonial nation carries the seeds of fascist temptation in its bosom. (Memmi 1974: 105–6)

Memmi's description of the frame of mind of the colonialist hints at a way in which one might unironically refer to the mentality of the colonizer today without collapsing into racialist and culturalist essentialisms, which reify the oppressed as pure and authentic, asserting a politics not of the abolition of relations of domination, but of the naturalistic affirmation of race and nation and community difference whose politics is the recognition of 'their' equality.

This consciousness of the colonialist has been internalized in the nation-state itself *sans* colonies as an internal aporia because the secular tendencies in the development of capital itself has reflected the relations of colonial citizen (or frontiersman), colonized subject, and the 'Mother Country' citizen back into the nation-state itself. The splitting of the nation internally into liberal, metropolitan centres and reactionary, ex-urban and rural peripheries expresses in the material organization of labour and production the secular crisis of valorization with its increasingly uneven flows of global money and finance and dependence on the state as the consumer of fictitious capital delaying any reckoning with that crisis. This split is different from earlier periods with large rural populations engaged in agriculture being driven off the land into wage-labour, a process that continued in the American South until the 1960s. The current situation is one in which capital has subsumed everyone and instead of a process of proletarianization, we are seeing marginalization, precaritization, deindustrialization, alongside increased dependence on the state.

The consciousness Memmi describes as that of the colonialist has re-emerged from these overall changes, but in a context where white supremacy, antisemitism, et al, are increasingly viewed publicly as ignorant, immoral and politically unacceptable. We should not forget the utterly novel and historically unprecedented breadth and depth of this questioning, and even rejection, of any claims of any group to natural, inherent or even cultural superiority, and the world-historical importance of the fact that those who continue to believe in such superiority are seen by many in the present as being morally wrong, intellectually bankrupt and politically reactionary. And yet the revanchist ('colonialist') consciousness precisely locates their decline and loss of cultural cache, after decades of defeats and the obliteration of any progressive class institutions, in the elevation of 'the Jews' and 'the blacks' (and women, homosexuals, etc.), through the devaluation of work, nation, whiteness, Christianity and so on. In this context, any hint of universalism, of a universal equality of human beings with no pregiven claims of superiority or entitlement, even in the guise of the 'radical centrism' represented, for example, by Joe Biden, triggers a panic-stricken response and must be decried as 'socialism'.[21]

We should recognize that expulsion of living labour from the valorization process does seem to present to many in this internalized periphery, that is, those simultaneously in the homeland, but outside the global flows of capital, a mortal threat.[22] On the one hand, severe loss of certainty and stability in a world turned upside down, where membership in the 'white race' is no longer such good protection from falling into the abyss (an abyss long familiar to and reserved for black people collectively in many different forms).[23] On the other hand, despite the antisemitic fantasy that the 'Final Solution' would abolish finance capitalism, industry and production appear superseded by financialization and globalization, and not least by complete dependence on constant injections of money from the central banks.[24] Further, a combination of highly skilled technical jobs, often serving to get rid of more industrial jobs or serving finance, and the overwhelming quantitative predominance of low-skilled, low-paying, insecure service industry jobs, have superseded traditional industrial labour.

---

[21] 'Radical centrism' is a phrase used by Yannis Varoufakis, who refers by this to a liberalism that is blindly hostile to any sensibility that finds the current state of society terrible, terrifying, hopeless, miserable, anxiety-inducing and so on. 'Radical centrism' denies the traumatic core of the present in the name of a more or less socially liberal neoliberal capitalism (see Varoufakis 2020).

[22] If, to some extent, these hinterlands are indeed geographical, as outcomes of suburbanization and then ex-urbanization of populations and manufacturing in the United States, for example, after the Second World War, I am also referring to the expulsion of workers from the labour processes associated with value-producing industries, the so-called de-industrialization that is more a replacement of living labour by dead labour, variable capital by constant capital (see, e.g., Brynjolfsson and McAfee 2016; Ford 2016: 1–12).

[23] If my focus is on antiblackness and antisemitism, a more rounded view of racialization would address the specificity of the Native American peoples, in which those populations have been treated as a kind of natural impediment unable to be harnessed by capital, and therefore to be clear-cut, that is, moved, removed and annihilated. There is no grasping the racialization of the Native American peoples without grasping this foundational genocidal programme.

[24] Bloomberg, a Wall Street market and finance data analytics and news agency, has compiled data from the US Federal Reserve, European Central Bank and the Bank of Japan showing how they have used bonds, buying securities, and loaning money to banks and businesses to inject trillions of dollars into the world economy since 2009, a trend which almost doubled in the face of the Covid pandemic (Scott, Jackson and Wu 2021).

In other words, antisemitism is ascendant not because of anything Jewish people do, or the state of Israel, but of actual transformations of capital and a profound discontent that identifies the negative aspect of these transformations with 'the Jews' and the solution as a return to the finite, 'real' economy and the suppression of globalism and global finance by the nation-state. Nor is the resurgence of antiblackness because lower-income black people are closing the wealth or income gap through rapidly increasing incomes and wealth or extensive increases in political power, but because lower-income white households experienced greater losses since the 2007 crash, compared to middle-income households where racial inequality *increased*. This slight increase in equality, largely brought about by the declining economic situation of working-class white people is actually a moment of the production of the greatest wealth gap between the top 5 per cent and the bottom 95 per cent since these measures began being recorded (Kochhar and Cilluffo 2017). The increasing inequalities of incomes and wealth are but moments of a secular crisis of valorization.

The secular crisis of capital and revanchist populism as the revolt of the finite against the infinite

The rise of revanchist populism and the end of twentieth century workerist class radicalism are two moments of the same crisis. Capitalist society overcomes its crises by the transformation of both the valorization process and the labour process as its materialization, leading to an increasing integration of the whole of society into these processes, eliminating what it cannot internalize. This transformation does not merely restructure the relationship of workers to the labour process, but all social relations and social forms. We are socialized in new ways that produce new forms of consciousness, new forms of organization and disorganization, new forms of domination and new forms of resistance.

If the fascist impulse fixates on the finite as the good and the infinite as that which must be subordinated, we must avoid the opposite tendency: to eschew the finite and fixate one-sidedly on defending, or taking the side of, the infinite. Even though capitalist society remains predicated on the valorization of value and crises of valorization, the infinite of valorisation is *made manifest* through and materialized as transformations of the finite labour process. If capital points beyond itself in its own crises, it does not do so in the same way each time. The organization of capital, labour and money and their crises in Marx's time were no more a template for the period between the World Wars than the struggles at the end of Fordism were comprehensible in the schemas of Leninism, Social Democracy and left communism. None of them have much to say about today.

We confront today the political dilemma that working-class identity has dissolved, its universalizing tendencies giving way on one side to its liberal aspect, that is, the formal-legal side associated with unions as legal bargaining entities which accept the fundamental legal framework and pose no ethical challenge to capital as such, versus the communitarian side in which 'blue collar' becomes a cultural category associated with revanchist populism that elevates work to life's prime want, who enjoy the right to work of every individual, who 'earn' their money, who are 'responsible and law-abiding' patriots, generally religious and wedded to common sense. The power of labour organized around an antagonistic class identity, in forcing capital to accommodate the worker as consumer, negated that very working-class identity and formed one associated with having 'made it': home owner, car owner and so on. The formal-legal side of this bifurcation has been shrinking, as its predicate was a workers' movement and an antagonistic working-class identity that does not quite match the transformation of the actual conditions of the capital–labour relation, that is, of the labour/valorization process. The communitarian side, in the meantime, having shed its universalizing aspects, has adopted the Southern conception of the worker: anti-union, individualistic, uneducated, conservative Christian, provincial, paternalistically tied to the company, and militantly opposed to state intervention which disrupts any of the aforementioned moments.[25]

Unlike the various Marxisms, Marx's critique of political economy remains at the forefront of the capacity to think against this society because it provides a way to continually grasp the aporetic unity of the finite and the infinite: the infinite of *capital* as the truth of this society, and yet wholly attentive to its finite forms of being. Insofar as what constituted whiteness was always grounded in this identification with concrete labour against the pure potency and animal overproductiveness of the black body as embodiment of abstract labour, a lot of this disconnect and irrationalization governs the consciousness of those whites whose position is most unstable, most at risk, most reliant on the state as subordinated to the nation.

There are long-run aspects to the increasing organic composition of capital, which leads to the increasing superfluity of living labour in the production of material wealth and problems of the valorization of value. This is the increasing contradiction between the material production of wealth and the social form of that production, in which an increasingly large amount of unvalorizable surplus must be absorbed by unproductive consumption, especially by states and

---

[25] This is not only true of class. Identity politics oriented towards fixation of gender and racial divisions have superseded the universalizing tendencies which sought to undermine the very validity and foundation of gender and race, that is, identity politics want to 'empower' groups *as minorities*, in effect accepting as real and rational the very gender and race divisions that were rejected as social relations of domination. Where people like Martin Luther King, Jr and Gloria Steinem, to simply make use of archetypal public figures, explicitly did not seek a reversal of roles with whites and men, nor an accommodation with a system of racialized or gendered relations, but the deracializing and degendering of all levels of society (not only the state and civil society, but the most notoriously private domain in bourgeois society: the family), contemporary politics in both of these dimensions have tended to devolve into their liberal and communitarian dimensions as well. For example, in the wake of the Civil Rights and Black Power movements, the demand for formal-legal recognition in terms of representation along racial lines leads to situations in which American cities with majority black populations are reproducing equally racialized political apparatuses to those found in majority white cities, with the expectation that a 65 per cent black population *should mean* that 65 per cent or more of the politicians are black, under the assumption that only black can represent black, just as white racial politics always assumed that 'only like can represent like' in a system of formal racial parity which is also a system re-enforcing racial identity. If such racialized regimes of power were tragedy the first time around, they appear the second time as farce, that is, as a pauperized and diminished version of the urban racial regime.

massive financial markets, supported by constant injections of money by central banks. This diremption is not only increasingly intense, but also makes living labour more and more superfluous from the point of view of the production of value compared to dead labour. In particular and in light of this, one way of understanding the role of the US government here is that it spends vast sums of money in unproductive sectors (military, carceral, direct subsidies) to absorb unrealizable value. The US government can do this on a level other states cannot because the dollar is world money. *For now*, US massive deficit spending is a form of control over the world. Internally, the portion of this spending that does not go to various capitals has overwhelmingly gone to the population which makes up the base of this revanchist politics in the so-called red states and rural and ex-urban areas, a population which is simultaneously more and more superfluous from the point of view of valorization, and increasingly dependent on the state. In the United States, the decomposition of the working class since the 1970s has led to extensive dependence of the white rural and ex-urban populations on this government spending – especially the spending that goes into the military–industrial complex (arms industries, military bases and personnel, policing), the carceral complex (federal prisons and state prisons are very important sources of income in rural and ex-urban areas), agricultural subsidies and dependence on jobs in the Finance-Insurance-Real Estate (FIRE) sector, such as credit card company call centres, insurance company call centres and so on. And of course the bigger ticket jobs not only rely heavily on government spending but also on the most militaristic, police-state aspects of that spending. Further, the material and productive dependence of agriculture, livestock and meat packing on cheap and precarious illegal immigrant labour constitutes another kind of 'excluded in'. The call to defund the police or reduce military spending, to replace incarceration with social policy, to remove immigrants from a status of precarity, or to implement a new kind of farming, all implicitly attack the material and psychological grounds of this decomposed pool of labour now tied to the military-carceral state for its existence.

It is not accidental that the element most supportive of this revanchist politics is proportionately much larger and more influential in ex-urban and rural areas, made clear by the least discussed voting outcome: Biden overwhelmingly won metropolitan areas, even in rural states, whereas Trump overwhelmingly won the ex-urban and rural areas. These are the spaces of the greatest superfluous labour expenditure: military production plants, military bases, federal and state prisons, heavily government-subsidized agriculture. There is not only a dependence of jobs on the repressive apparatus but also of Starbucks workers, the Walmart employee and so on in these areas on the military and carceral complexes – fostering a tertiary identification with the punitive state. The majority of these people depend on industries whose superfluous labour expenditure would *consume* both use-values and exchange-values but *create* an object that had neither use-value nor exchange-value. The government subsidizes these areas and the areas that receive the most are (1) overwhelmingly white and (2) rely on industries that are nationalist, anti-immigrant, anti-Native American and antiblack. All this supports a population that considers itself anti-government and anti-immigrant, but which is wholly dependent on both. Dependence on what one despises is likely to create all kinds of psychological effects, especially if one considers that no one is the bad guy in their own story. These populations cannot but find it difficult at best to admit their complete dependence on immigrants, the government, a system of mass incarceration that keeps the jails full and their people employed, on military spending and so on. These populations are living on government handouts and the police state, hoping that 'being white' will protect them from diseases, bankruptcy and so on. Trump is the epitome of these takers, someone who has turned serial bankruptcy, illiteracy, illogic and mediocrity into wealth.

I wager that the increasing superfluity of labour to the production of wealth, leaving fewer and fewer workers actually engaged in value producing labour, alongside the disconnection of the workers' intellect and capacity for self-recognition from the labour process, softens the working class to antiblackness, antisemitism, but also all manner of conspiracy theories and generalized irrationality.[26]

In summary, Trumpism, as a particular form of the current global wave of revanchism, has a foundation in political, psychological and material transformations of the actual relations of production, changes in the labour process that reflect transformations in the valorization process and the global crisis of valorization in which the US government intervenes at a global level through its spending and control of global currency.

It is not a great exaggeration to describe white rural and ex-urban America as drug-addicted, un(der)employed, and government-dependent, which psychologically is the root of the break with even minimal elements of reality. This break has to be grasped structurally in the transformation of capital, not merely psychologically or empirically (poverty, inequality, lack of education, etc.). This also helps explain why revanchist populism is *global* in scope: albeit working itself out in different ways in different places, that is, unevenly, this secular crisis of valorization and the subsequent transformation of the labour process is global.[27]

If antisemitism is structured by the diremption of capital as abstract and concrete, what happens if industry, production of commodities as use-values, the entirety of the economy that appears to us as concrete, solid, tangible, has become subordinated, in its secular crisis of valorization to money, credit and debt, interest and financial instruments and to their seeming autonomization?

In this situation, where income is far more dependent on ownership and manipulation of financial assets and wages have been at best stagnant overall, wealth inequality has reached historically unprecedented levels alongside constant cuts to social services in the state. The major demands from revanchist circles are simple: cuts in government services and benefits that the bottom 90 per cent are most dependent

---

[26] I have addressed the decline of the working class as a Third Estate, that is, 'as a self-aware, independent political actor' within capitalist society, in Wright (2010, 2015).

[27] Because of the different particularities of Europe, it finds its expression there in fiercely renewed antisemitism and anti-Zyganism, alongside exploding anti-immigrant racism. Anti-Zyganism is the term for what most Americans would call 'anti-Gypsy' or 'anti-Roma' racism. The Nazis murdered somewhere between 250,000 and 500,000 Roma, somewhere between one-sixth and half of the Roma peoples in Europe (*Holocaust Encyclopedia* n.d.).

on, tax cuts (which always favour the wealthiest), and the wholesale privatization of public services and benefits.[28] However, there is always more money for (1) prisons, police, arming the police and so on and (2) the military. A real situation of economic insecurity, widespread austerity, instability and massive increases in inequality exists, but also as we noted earlier, a creation of material dependency on the military-carceral state on one side and corporations on the other, with, nonetheless, blame laid squarely on 'financial elites', 'globalizers', code words for 'the Jews'.[29]

The abolition of living labour by capital within capitalism is therefore the abolition of the self-identity of a certain kind of racialism, gendering and so on. Quite a few of those who are determined as white/male/heterosexual/and so on, but who are positioned to 'succeed' in this new capitalism, can accept and even welcome the rejection of the supremacy of whiteness, masculinity, heterosexuality and so on. To the extent that they have a better position within the reorganization of capital's valorization, they do not feel obliged to hold on to the more toxic forms of whiteness, masculinity and so on.[30] Not so for the majority of Trump supporters. They are staring into the abyss and it is staring back. This is what drives revanchist populism, rather than alleged ignorance, stupidity or lack of education. They are willing to destroy everything they always claimed to hold dear because what they always held dear was the nation. So when Trump promised his administration would create new industrial jobs, the return of the coal industry, stop other countries' 'unfair trade practices', reign in the power of finance, drain the swamp, stop handouts to the unworthy, he was promising them a programme that would simultaneously restore the dignity and order and security of a fantastical prior time ('Make America Great Again') and lead a revaluation of values in which white, Christian, male, heterosexual and so on, will be restored as *virtuous*, not deplorables.[31]

Except, there is no restoration. There is no escape from the abolition of labour by, and within the confines of, capital. As capital goes about abolishing itself, bringing

---

[28] The appeal of this privatization to especially the white working class is bound up with greater access to individual home ownership, better access to cheap credit, higher income and wealth (tied to housing in most cases), all of which were already a driving part of white-flight suburbanization, which married home ownership with low residential taxes and racial and class purity. Suburbanization helped condition a large part of the white working class towards revanchist politics.

[29] It is not an accident that the unions, Bernie Sanders and Donald Trump all put forward various kinds of nationalistic trade and tariff policies as a solution (Bradner 2015). When NAFTA was first passed, the Teamsters organized against allowing Mexican truckers into the United States, not quite an action of class solidarity, but anti-NAFTA, pro-protectionist, sheerly nationalistic sentiment was widespread in the unions (Richman 2009). Of course, it was workers in the much more typically progressive UAW who smashed, at times with official sanction, Japanese cars parked at GM, Ford or Chrysler production plants in the late 1970s and early 1980s.

[30] Though I have not attempted to address it here, there is also an obviously heteronormative-misogynist *ressentiment* against the feminization of capitalist social relations in which white, male, Christian heterosexuality is treated as privileged and inherently toxic, especially if left unchecked. Here antisemitism and antiblackness overlap with anti-feminism in the sense that both 'the Jew' and feminists want the emasculation of the strong, Christian man and the threat to white masculinity represented by the phallic dominance of symbolic black male sexuality (requiring castration).

[31] In her 9/9/2016 fundraiser speech in New York City, Hillary Clinton had notoriously, and in keeping with 'radical centrist' contemptuousness, said 'you could put half of Trump's supporters into what I call the "basket of deplorables"' (Clinton 2016).

about its own existential crisis, it by no means abolishes its own fetish forms of existence, but can generate new forms and intensify existing ones.

Infinite violence, the labourism of fools and how capital's circle might be broken

Revanchist politics radically reinforce the state as infinite violence subordinated to the finite nation, in all of the most brutal, militaristic, punitive and communitarian, and therefore antisemitic, antiblack, misogynist and other ways. Left fantasies of a Red–Brown alliance resound of a recycled German National Bolshevism, with its deluded hope that underneath fascism there is an objective radicalism waiting to challenge capitalism. It is worth noting, however, that unlike Strasserism or other elements in the historical National Socialist Party, Trump supporters absolutely, positively *never* espouse anything that even sounds like anti-capitalism. Any wager that these events are implicitly anti-capitalist rests entirely on their mouthing something that seems like anti-statism, but which is merely their willingness to destroy the universalist and redistributive elements of the state in a futile effort to turn back time, which will do nothing more than strengthen the state against all of us. In other words, antisemitism is the 'socialism of fools' not on the revanchist right but only among those Leftists and Progressives who idolize the labour movement, blame the banks and financialization for all our woes, support nationalist 'fair trade' tariff policies (whether of the Sanders or the Trump variety), and combine antisemitic anti-Israel politics with support of 'progressive' nationalisms (including in the US Black Nationalism), as if the last fifty years had not demonstrated the bankruptcy of supposedly progressive or 'socialist' nationalism.

Identification with some element or elements of domination does not actually secure one in this society and no individual is beyond being consumed and expelled. We live in a present in which so much is at risk that most people's spontaneous reaction is to hang on to whatever fetish we believe will work for us, even if to do so seems to require the worst of us. Righteousness, left, right or 'radical centre', is complicit with a system predicated upon abstract domination (Marx's and Postone's 'Capital as Subject') because it blames bad people with bad ideas, letting the society that has autonomized itself from us off the hook. The left, as completely as the right, believes that in identifying the bad groups, it has grasped the problem and only need wage *the right war*.

Then again, some of those who recognize the actuality of the injury to many of those backing this revanchist politics, believe that these are simply 'working-class people who are duped'. They misconstrue fascism as just another option along a continuum of progressive-liberal-conservative when it is in fact a complete breakdown of reason in its demand for order, hierarchy, obedience and the punishment of the Other. Its violence attacks the notion of even a minimal, universal human dignity, of the very ability of individuals to have even minimal trust in one another, to treat them as individuals meriting basic respect (Bernstein 2020). Fascism is the mass destruction of dignity in which one population is expected and willing to play the role of torturer of the Other and of anyone who steps out of line against that dignity-destroying violence.[32]

When some leftists say that 'politics is over', they mean politics understood as social-democratic reformism or liberal centrism.[33] When some revanchists use the same kind of phrase, they mean, however, that there is no society (universal human connection, despite capitalism having created the conditions for it), there is no alternative (no socialism/communism, despite capitalism having created the conditions for it), there is no universal acceptance of human difference as good (universal human dignity, despite capitalism having created the conditions for it); that there is only hierarchy (nature-given), heteronomy (inscribed in human nature), superiority (inscribed by nature in their race as the superior form of human being), and no law but the law of the tribe (their legitimate right to use force to claim their place). Further, when the revanchists blame 'globalists' or 'elites', they mean 'the Jews'. And when they are saying 'the Jews', they are not even saying 'capitalism is to blame', they are saying that 'the Jews' are ruining their chances *within* capitalism, stealing their opportunity and their joy.

Against a leftism that is itself anachronistic, reduced to a caricature of its former self, only Critical Theory can grasp the idea that the true infinite at the problematic heart of this society is not labour, the commodity, value, money or the state, but capital itself. The fetishistic incomprehension arises not merely from the hypostatization of the dualisms of abstract versus concrete labour, or use-value vs. value, or value vs. exchange-value, but of the inability to grasp capital itself as the essential infinite because commodity, money, labour, means of production are merely momentary forms taken by capital as the infinite self-valorization of value. The cycle of capital that preserves and expands itself through its changes of form turns money, commodity and labour into other things than what they are in other forms of human society. It turns itself into a process that becomes autonomous from the human beings who enact it. With regard to both the competition between individual capitals and the struggle of wage-labourers and capitals over the share of the social wealth, the only answer open

---

[32] Specifically on this point, the acquittal of all charges in the case of Kyle Rittenhouse, the seventeen-year-old who brought an assault rifle to a Black Lives Matter (BLM) demonstration nominally in order to 'preserve order and protect property' and who subsequently shot three and killed two white pro-BLM demonstrators, is an especially regressive precedent.

[33] Many of those who call themselves leftists today do not identify with social-democratic or Leninist statism and are closer to the anti-politics of anarchism. I am neither 'anti-political' nor 'political' in any of these senses, but rather lean towards Gillian Rose's notion of politics in her book *Mourning Becomes the Law: Philosophy and Representation*: 'Politics begins not when you organise to defend an individual or particular or local interest, but when you organise to further the "general" interest within which your particular interest may be represented' (1996: 4). This formulation points to the Hegelian and Marxian critique of representation, whereas the fascist revanchists critique representation on libertarian and communitarian grounds, claiming that the individual is beyond representation and that at the same time the group is beyond representation. They sever the singular and the particular, the finite, from the universal and the infinite. The critique of representation can lead to the rejection of the state, but it can also lead to the rejection of the possibility of a general interest, potentially of universal self-governance. The latter denotes the refusal to take responsibility for such a general (infinite) interest as opposed to (finite) individual or communitarian group (or 'community') interests.

to capital, trapped on its treadmill,[34] is to increase productivity, producing more for less. This requires increasing the organic composition of capital to create short-term competitive advantages for more productive capitals. And so the solution aggravates the problem it means to solve.

The present age has seen the exponential expansion of automation and automation of control, and the continuing transformation of work such that the labour process is more and more a direct product of the application of the natural sciences, and less and less anything reflecting the mechanization or automation of workers' own knowledge and activity as had been the case with earlier generations of machinery. The result is an increasing disconnect between individuals and their work, which leads to a disconnect between what we do and our sense of control and self-certainty. One further expression of this loss is the collapse of any form of independent working-class culture with its own institutions and sense that it could, as a class, take control of a world that is produced by its own efforts. This does not mean that capital has won but that we have to be willing to think about how to overcome capital in terms that arise in the conditions of the present, rather than through Romantic hopes for some kind of a rerun of the past.

And in fact other possibilities did arise in 2020. If capital, in its infinite command for valorization, left tens of millions unemployed almost overnight, it showed that freedom from labour time can genuinely turn us from cogs in its machinic logic into something better, something braver. Instead of denouncing Black Lives Matter as supposedly 'petty bourgeois' left populism, we should think about how negative growth and mass unemployment pointed towards freedom. In 2020, the freeing of human beings from the domination of the temporality of capital coincided with millions becoming militants in a few months. Compare that to the failure of the left to make a millimetre of headway in decades. The collapse of 'growth' showed that a meaningful reversal of our headlong rush into ecological catastrophe was not only possible, but possible in an unprecedentedly short amount of time. Instead of the demand for full employment at forty hours/week, the growth of the welfare state, restrictions in trade and more state control over finance and the banks, all of which direct us back to the state and reinforce the power of capital over us, we should recognize that all of us could work far, far fewer hours and still provide abundantly for our needs, and furthermore, have more time to do as we will. If the left cannot recognize the future because it still believes, despite Auschwitz, that work makes us free, so much the worse for the left.

References

Anon. (2020), 'Joseph Goebbels Complains of Italians' Treatment of Jews', *History Channel*, 10 December, available at: www.history.com/this-day-in-history/goebbels-complains-of-italians-treatment-of-jews (accessed 19 November 2022).

---

[34] Postone develops his idea of this treadmill effect in *Time, Labor and Social Domination* (1993: 289–91).

Barber, D. C. (2017), 'On Black Negativity, or the Affirmation of Nothing: Jared Sexton, Interviewed by Daniel Barber', available at: www.societyandspace.org/articles/on-black-negativity-or-the-affirmation-of-nothing (accessed 24 June 2023).

Ben-Ghiat, R. (2017), 'We Are Evidently Aryans', *Slate Magazine*, 20 January, available at: https://slate.com/human-interest/2017/01/jews-in-fascist-italy-and-anti-semitism-in-an-italy-that-saw-itself-as-a-backwater.html (accessed 19 November 2022) (excerpted from *Fascist Modernities: Italy, 1922–1945*, Berkeley: University of California Press).

Bernardini, G. (1977), 'The Origins and Development of Racial Anti-Semitism in Fascist Italy', *Journal of Modern History*, 49 (3): 431–53.

Bernstein, J. M. (2020), *Torture and Dignity: An Essay on Moral Injury*, Chicago: University of Chicago Press.

Bonefeld, W. (1997), 'Notes on Antisemitism', *Common Sense*, 21: 60–76.

Bonefeld, W. (2001), 'The Permanence of Primitive Accumulation: Commodity Fetishism and Social Constitution', *The Commoner*, 2, available at: https://thecommoner.org/wp-content/uploads/2019/10/The-Permanence-of-Primitive-Accumulation-Bonefeld.pdf (accessed 19 November 2022).

Bonefeld, W. (2011), 'Primitive Accumulation and Capitalist Accumulation: Notes on Social Constitution and Expropriation', *Science & Society*, 75 (3): 379–99.

Bradner, E. (2015), 'Here's How Donald Trump Could Spark a Trade War with Mexico and China', *CNN*, 26 August, available at: www.cnn.com/2015/08/26/politics/donald-trump-bernie-sanders-free-trade-2016 (accessed 19 November 2022).

Brynjolfsson, E., and A. McAfee (2016), *The Second Machine Age: Work, Progress, and Prosperity in a Time of Brilliant Technologies*, New York: W. W. Norton.

Clinton, H. (2016), 'Campaign Speech', *Time*, 10 September, available at: https://time.com/4486502/hillary-clinton-basket-of-deplorables-transcript (accessed 19 November 2022).

D'Souza, D. (2022), 'Modern Monetary Theory (MMT): Definition, History, and Principles', *Investopedia*, available at: www.investopedia.com/modern-monetary-theory-mmt-4588060 (accessed 19 November 2022).

Epstein, J. (2011), 'Palin Charges Critics with "Blood Libel"', *Politico*, 12 January, available at: www.politico.com/story/2011/01/palin-charges-critics-with-blood-libel-047477 (accessed 19 November 2022).

Fanon, F. (1986), *Black Skin, White Masks*, London: Pluto Press.

Fischer, L. (2007), *The Socialist Response to Antisemitism in Imperial Germany*, Cambridge: Cambridge University Press.

Ford, M. (2016), *Rise of the Robots: Technology and the Threat of a Jobless Future*, New York: Basic Books.

Hegel, G. W. F. (2010), *The Science of Logic* (trans. and ed. G. di Giovanni), New York: Cambridge University Press.

Hegel, G. W. F. (2019), *Phenomenology of Spirit* (trans. T. Pinkard), New York: Cambridge University Press.

Holocaust Encyclopedia (n.d.), 'Genocide of European Roma (Gypsies), 1939–1945', *United States Holocaust Memorial Museum*, available at: https://encyclopedia.ushmm.org/content/en/article/genocide-of-european-roma-gypsies-1939-1945 (accessed 19 November 2022).

Hudson, M. (2003), *Super-Imperialism: The Origin and Fundamentals of U.S. World Dominance*, London: Pluto Press.

James, F. (2011), 'Sarah Palin's "Blood Libel" Charge Stirs New Controversy', *NPR*, 12 January, available at: www.npr.org/sections/itsallpolitics/2011/01/12/132861457/sarah-palins-blood-libel-use-stirs-new-controversy (accessed 19 November 2022).

Kochhar, R., and A. Cilluffo (2017), 'How Wealth Inequality Has Changed in the U.S. since the Great Recession, by Race, Ethnicity and Income', *Pew Research Center*, available at: www.pewresearch.org/fact-tank/2017/11/01/how-wealth-inequality-has-changed-in-the-u-s-since-the-great-recession-by-race-ethnicity-and-income (accessed 19 November 2022).

Locke, J. (1988), *Two Treatises of Government* (ed. P. Laslett), Cambridge: Cambridge University Press.

Marx, K. (1982), *The Poverty of Philosophy*, New York: Progress.

Marx, K. (1990), *Capital*, vol. 1, London: Penguin Classics.

Marx, K. (1993), *Grundrisse*, London: Penguin Classics.

Marx, K., and F. Engels (1970), *The Communist Manifesto*, New York: Pathfinder Press.

Memmi, A. (1974), *The Colonizer and the Colonized*, Boston, MA: Souvenir Press.

Nesbitt, N. (2022), *The Price of Slavery: Capitalism and Revolution in the Caribbean*, Charlottesville: University of Virginia Press.

Perlman, M. (2018), 'Exploring the Meaning of "Revanchist" Amid Trump-Putin Coverage', *Columbia Journalism Review*, 16 July, available at: www.cjr.org/language_corner/revanchist.php (accessed 19 November 2022).

Postone, M. (1990), 'After the Holocaust: History and Identity in West Germany', in K. Harms, L. R. Reuter and V. Duerr (eds), *Coping with the Past: Germany and Austria after 1945*, 233–51, Madison: University of Wisconsin.

Postone, M. (1993), *Time, Labor and Social Domination*, Cambridge: Cambridge University Press.

Richman, E. (2009), 'The NAFTA Trucking Provisions and the Teamsters: Why They Need Each Other', *Northwestern Journal of International Law & Business*, 29 (2): 555.

Rose, G. (1996), *Mourning Becomes the Law: Philosophy and Representation*, illustration edn, Cambridge: Cambridge University Press.

Scott, M., P. Jackson and J. W. Wu. (2021), 'A $9 Trillion Binge Turns Central Banks into the Market's Biggest Whales', *Bloomberg*, 7 July, available at: www.bloomberg.com/graphics/2021-central-banks-binge (accessed 19 November 2022).

Solow, B. (2016), *The Economic Consequences of the Atlantic Slave Trade*, reprint edn, Plymouth: Lexington Books.

Tamás, G. M. (2000), 'On Post-Fascism', *Boston Review*, Summer: 42–6, available at: www.bostonreview.net/articles/g-m-tamas-post-fascism (accessed 24 June 2023).

Varoufakis, Y. (2020), 'Joe Biden, We Are Happy That You Beat Trump. But Here Is Why We Shall Oppose You, Starting Today', 11 September, available at: www.yanisvaroufakis.eu/2020/11/09/joe-biden-we-are-happy-that-you-beat-trump-but-here-is-why-we-shall-oppose-you-starting-today-video (accessed 19 November 2022).

Walters, Q. (2020), 'Anti-Semitic Crime in the U.S. Reaches Record Levels', *WBUR*, 12 May, available at: www.wbur.org/news/2020/05/12/antisemitic-crime-record-level (accessed 19 November 2022).

White, H. (2020), 'How Is Capitalism Racial? Fanon, Critical Theory and the Fetish of Antiblackness', *Social Dynamics*, 46 (1): 22–35.

Wright, C. (2010), 'Night without End: Notes from the Vanguard of Retrogression', a talk presented at *Historical Materialism NYC 2010*, available at: www.academia.edu/7136818/Night_Without_End_Notes_from_the_Vanguard_of_Retrogression (accessed 19 March 2023).

Wright, C. (2015), 'Its Own Peculiar Decor: Capital, Urbanism, and the Crisis of Class Politics in the U.S.', *Endnotes 4*, available at: https://endnotes.org.uk/articles/its-own-peculiar-decor (accessed 19 March 2023).

Wright, C. (2021), 'The Infinite and the Finite in the Storming of the US Capitol', *Cured Quail*, 14 February, available at: https://curedquailjournal.wordpress.com/2021/02/14/the-infinite-and-finite-in-the-storming-of-the-us-capitol (accessed 19 November 2022).

9

Antisemitism and racism 'after Auschwitz': Adorno on the 'hellish unity' of 'permanent catastrophe'

Jonathon Catlin

This chapter reconsiders the Frankfurt School of Critical Theory's, and particularly Theodor W. Adorno's, theories of antisemitism and racism in light of recent debates about global memory of the Holocaust vis-à-vis other genocides and forms of racialized and colonial violence. It reconstructs how the first-generation critical theorists came to recognize the significance and distinctiveness of modern antisemitism through their own experience of persecution as Jews in the 1930s and 1940s, but by the 1960s came to see 'Auschwitz' in a global and comparative framework of history, memory and social theory. This chapter thus contests interpretations of Adorno as defending an exclusive focus on the Holocaust and antisemitism at the expense of other historical events with which he repeatedly claimed they were joined in a 'hellish unity' as part of the 'permanent catastrophe' of the same modern capitalist social order, including the Armenian genocide, the bombing of Hiroshima, war atrocities in Vietnam and 'torture as a permanent institution'. Instead, it argues for reading Adorno as advancing what Michael Rothberg (2009) has called 'multidirectional memory' of antisemitic violence and the Shoah, and for using the understanding of social pathologies arising from these traumatic histories to advance 'differentiated solidarity' between contemporary forms of oppression in order to move beyond national, ethnic and identity-based 'competitive memory' that Adorno would have rejected as provincializing the truly *universal* significance of the Holocaust and the 'new categorical imperative' he coined in its aftermath: for 'unfree mankind ... to arrange their thoughts and actions so that Auschwitz will not repeat itself, so that nothing similar will happen' (1973: 365).

From the proletariat to the Jew: Orienting Critical Theory around antisemitism

In the early 1940s, while in exile from Nazi Germany in the United States, Adorno, Max Horkheimer and a number of their colleagues formerly associated with the Institute for Social Research in Frankfurt radically reconceptualized Western civilization, Enlightenment and modernity around the thesis that the ongoing Nazi domination of Europe and persecution of European Jewry was not a barbaric exception to the civilizing process but evidence of its hyper-intensification through the valorization of power and instrumental rationality.

Soon after the Nazi regime came to power in 1933, both Adorno and his senior colleague Horkheimer lost their professorships in Frankfurt under laws prohibiting Jewish public employment. In the years that followed, Adorno went into exile in Oxford and then New York and Los Angeles, thanks to visas and academic invitations from across the Atlantic. Adorno's aged parents were not so lucky. His father was wounded and imprisoned in the November Pogrom in 1938, and 'Adorno must have feared that he would never see his parents again' (Claussen 2008: 241). With Adorno's assistance, his parents were finally granted visas to Cuba and were later able to join him in New York (Claussen 2008: 58–9, 241). In August 1940 Adorno wrote to Horkheimer:

> Thanks also to the latest news from Germany, I am less and less able to free myself from having to think about the fate of the Jews. It often seems that everything that we used to see under the aspect of the proletariat has been concentrated today with frightful force upon the Jews ... I ask myself whether we should not say what we really want to say in connection with the Jews, who are now at the opposite pole to the concentration of power. (Adorno and Horkheimer 2004: 84)

'These lines', Rolf Tiedemann has written, 'provide us with a key to Adorno's thinking from 1940 on' (2003: xix). Horkheimer replied in September 1940, 'I am convinced that the Jewish Question is the question of contemporary society – in this we agree with Marx and with Hitler' (Adorno and Horkheimer 2004: 103). In such passages, we see that even before the full extent of the mass murders we now call 'the Holocaust' had taken place, Horkheimer and Adorno were reorienting their Critical Theory of modern society around understanding new forms of violence and oppression that targeted Jews with particular intensity.

That same month in 1940, Adorno and Horkheimer's German-Jewish colleague Walter Benjamin took his own life at the Franco-Spanish border after failing to escape from occupied France. In the collaborative text that was to become their fundamental work *Dialectic of Enlightenment: Philosophical Fragments*, as Adorno wrote to Horkheimer on 12 June 1941, they were inspired above all by Benjamin's last essay before his untimely death, 'On the Concept of History' (1940), which imparted them with the key theses of 'the conception of history as permanent catastrophe, the critique of progress and mastery of nature, and the place of culture' (quoted in Wiggershaus 1995: 311). Anson Rabinbach has similarly written that Benjamin's last text provided '"a guiding star" around which the constellation of themes – the fate of exile, the fate of the Jews, and the catastrophe of civilization – that ultimately make up *Dialectic of Enlightenment* could be organized' (1997: 174). Personal experience of antisemitism and persecution and intellectual reorientation away from class-determinist Marxian theories of fascism still held by others in their Frankfurt milieu went hand in hand as Adorno and his colleagues in exile increasingly turned their attention to understanding the racialized antisemitism then taking an unprecedented genocidal turn.

During their American exile, the theorists' research agenda pivoted to addressing the problem of antisemitism becoming more manifest to them by the day (Jay 1986), as Nazi persecution of European Jews changed, in 1941, from a programme of forced emigration and expulsion to one of confinement and mass murder, first in the so-called 'Holocaust by bullets' during the invasion of Eastern Europe, then in overcrowded ghettoes and finally in killing centres and death camps. By 1944, the year the first edition of *Dialectic* was published, the theorists in exile would have been well aware of the Nazi Judeocide, if not its full extent (Claussen 2008: 121). During the Institute's exile period, theoretical texts like *Dialectic* were accompanied by Adorno's 1951 essay on fascist propaganda (1991), studies of 'the individual under terror' by Leo Lowenthal (1946) and the Nazi regime in Franz Neumann's *Behemoth* (1942/4), while Neumann and Herbert Marcuse worked for the US government's Office of Strategic Services (OSS) producing intelligence reports on Nazi Germany (Neumann et al. 2013).

Scholars have long debated the connection between these thinkers' theoretical works and empirical social-scientific studies, the latter of which were partly produced to appeal to funding agencies such as the American Jewish Committee (Jacobs 2014; Rensmann 2017; Catlin 2020). Suffice it to say that the exile period dramatically shaped the questions motivating their research, while also pushing them to pioneer new social-scientific methodologies. Eric Oberle (2018) has shown how Adorno in particular arrived in the United States with a dismissive attitude towards the notion of 'race', which he once saw as merely a Nazi myth rooted in pseudo-scientific eugenics. However, he left the United States in 1949 considering race a *reality* as a social fact (if resolutely not a biological one). As he wrote in *Minima Moralia* in an aphorism dated to 1945, 'the most compelling anthropological proofs that the Jews are not a race will, in the event of a pogrom, scarcely alter the fact that the totalitarians know full well whom they do and whom they do not intend to murder' (1974: 102). As for other German-Jewish exile thinkers such as Hannah Arendt, the experience of everyday antisemitism and racial segregation in the United States imparted the insight that race was not merely a myth to be dismissed as an invention of the *völkisch* worldview. After they experienced the violent force of race in history, it could no longer be wished away by naïve liberal universalistic or cosmopolitan aspirations, and had to be recognized as a social fact of modern Western societies. Indeed, the first thesis of Horkheimer and Adorno's 'Elements of Antisemitism' takes direct aim at toothless liberalism that falsely presumes human differences to have already been overcome, calling it 'an apology for the existing order' of stark racial divisions and even genocide (138). Genuine analysis of modern antisemitism, then, was going to require a deeper understanding of how racialized differences are produced and can be used for social and political control.

During the exile period, several of the Frankfurt theorists' own historical experiences of persecution began to challenge some of their earlier theories (Jacobs 2014; Catlin 2017). In Adorno's letters, one can trace his doubt and worry build in months leading up to his dismissal from Frankfurt University in September 1933 as a result of anti-Jewish laws. As Müller-Doohm describes this period of realization: 'Overwhelmed by his shame and his impotence in the face of the bestial events unfolding before him, Adorno felt paralyzed' (2005: 169). Martin Jay writes that while Horkheimer had relocated the Institute to Geneva in 1933, and then to New York in 1934, 'Adorno, in fact, seems to have naively hoped that the Nazis were a passing phenomenon and he might still salvage his career', and thus continued to publish music reviews under a false non-Jewish name (1984: 31), an act for which some like Hannah Arendt never forgave him (Jacobs 2014: 56). As Adorno admitted that same year, 'I looked for a way to remain in Germany regardless of the cost' (cited in Jacobs 2014: 56). This was partly due to Adorno's half-Italian birth and Christian upbringing; he simply did not identify as a Jew until he was persecuted as one. It also reflected his naïve view that antisemitism was 'at least as present' in the United States as in Germany, and on account of despair: 'I am convinced that one is hopelessly trapped, regardless of where one may be. And it was this conviction that was the root of my resistance against emigration' (56–7). Adorno ultimately fled the Third Reich and took up a research post at Oxford. Yet, according to a letter Adorno wrote to Horkheimer the day before he left England for America in February 1938, six months before the November Pogroms, he anticipated the dismal fate of Germany's Jews at a time when many still held his earlier naiveté: 'Adorno predicted that there would be no country that would admit Jews who remained in Germany, and that those Jews would, therefore, be extirpated [*ausgerottet*]' (53).

These biographical experiences are worth considering because they contextualize some of the Frankfurt School's most influential writings on antisemitism in a period of uncertainty amidst unprecedented events. They defamiliarize for the contemporary reader 'the twisted road' to what we now call 'the Holocaust' and thereby enrich our understanding of the tremendously difficult personal and intellectual circumstances under which the Frankfurt theorists began to study Nazi antisemitism. As Dan Diner (2000) has argued in his influential analysis of Nazi 'counter-rationality', the Holocaust could not have been intuited or grasped before it took place – it was 'beyond the conceivable' even for many of the era's most perceptive social thinkers. This context is also important for understanding a number of early missteps in the theorists' analysis. For example, in 1939, before it was widely understood that Nazi persecution would end in genocide, Horkheimer's essay, 'The Jews and Europe' (1939: 135), which employed a number of tropes from Marx's 'On the Jewish Question', attributed 'guilt' to Jews complicit with bourgeois capitalism for their later persecution at the hands of the Nazis; and this was an essay on which Adorno claimed he had 'intensively collaborated' (Adorno and Benjamin 1999: 313). It was around this time, in December 1938, that Benjamin wrote to Adorno from Paris about 'the situation of the Jews in Germany, from which none of us can dissociate ourselves' (294). The palpable urgency of the 'Jewish question' and personal concern for the deteriorating situation of German Jews was not yet matched by adequate concepts to understand the way they were about to be persecuted to the point of extermination.

Dialectic of Enlightenment and the 'Elements of Antisemitism'

As Lars Rensmann (2017) has explicated, the central claim of *Dialectic's* analysis of antisemitism is that its pathology lies in the antisemitic subject and not their Jewish objects, which is to say that antisemitism is a form of 'false projection' or 'pathic projection' within the antisemitic subject: What is attributed to Jews – brutality, power, world domination, etc. – is instead often a quality or aspiration of antisemites and their own movements. The antisemite, wrote Adorno and Horkheimer, 'creates everything in his own image' (2002: 200). Antisemitism is thus essentially detached from 'real' historical Jews; the rejection of perceived Jewish difference occurs at a more fundamental social-psychological level. As one scholar explains this basic thesis shared by Jean-Paul Sartre's *Anti-Semite and Jew* and *Dialectic* (both, interestingly, from 1944): The

> purely contingent relationship between antisemitic perceptions and actual Jewish behavior, between antisemitic convictions and the real world of Jewish-Gentile interactions, is a fundamental characteristic of antisemitism *per se* ... antisemitism is an ideology about Jews that is autonomous from and only tangentially related to the true conditions of Jewish existence. (Staudenmaier 2012: 173–4)

The abstraction inherent to antisemitism partly explains the variety of sometimes contradictory 'elements' of antisemitism the authors present in an unsystematic way. Perhaps most influentially, thesis III of the 'Elements' argues that centuries of exclusion from other trades made Jews appear as conspicuous agents of petty commerce and capitalist exploitation. Their exclusion from other forms of livelihood made them even more despised and outcast, reinforcing antisemitic stereotypes about their greed, power, rootlessness and parasitical social effects. Moishe Postone's theory of antisemitism as a fetishized revolt against the abstract domination of modern industrial capitalism centres on this paradoxical distortion resulting from the complexity and abstraction of capitalist domination: 'The Jews were not seen merely as representatives of capital ... They became the *personifications* of the intangible, destructive, immensely powerful, and international domination of capital as a social form' (1980: 112). Going beyond Horkheimer and Adorno, Postone argues that 'modern antisemitism involves a biologization of capitalism ... as International Jewry' (112; also see Rensmann and Salzmann 2021). Yet emphasis on the abstraction inherent to modern antisemitism also informs Adorno and Horkheimer's insight about 'ticket thinking' in thesis VII of the 'Elements', whereby hatred of Jews is so often joined by hatred of other groups such as women, queers, people of colour, etc. These hatreds have taken different forms throughout history, yet are socially determined by capitalist society, which enforces homogeneity, conformism, commodification and the sacrifice of individuality and genuine subjectivity to the imperatives of instrumental rationality and economic productivity.

This insight from *Dialectic* also reinforces the often misunderstood conclusions of Adorno's contributions to *The Authoritarian Personality* (1950). Some theorists such as Zygmunt Bauman have at times inaccurately dismissed this study as suggesting that fascism is the product of individual 'bad apples' or fascist actors with individual sadistic intentions and antisemitic prejudices: 'To Adorno and his colleagues, Nazism was cruel because Nazis were cruel; and the Nazis were cruel because cruel people tended to become Nazis' (Bauman 2000: 153). Nothing could be further from Adorno's own conclusion, which was only published in recent years. In Adorno's 'Notes' to *The Authoritarian Personality*, he claims explicitly, 'We are convinced that the ultimate source of prejudice has to be sought in social factors which are incomparably stronger than the "psyche" of any one individual involved' (Adorno et al. [1950] 2019: xlii). Even in the 1950 published version of the study, Adorno and his co-authors suggested that the ubiquity of the potentially fascist personality could perhaps be ameliorated through reforming education and authoritarian parenting; but since this widespread disposition was the product of 'the total organization of society', it was ultimately 'to be changed only as that society is changed' (xxxv). While we may find fault with particular theories based on their inevitably partial historical and sociological analysis, what remains valuable still today is the Frankfurt theorists' ambition to explain antisemitism through materialist analysis of the functions it has served in modern societies at particular times.

The Frankfurt School's theory of antisemitism offers a number of general insights about authoritarian subjectivity and racialized othering in modern societies. However, after the realization after 1945 of the particularity of Jewish persecution in the Holocaust, these universal theories became linked to the particular site and symbol of Auschwitz, which, for Adorno, in its concreteness, irrationality and horror, resists any kind of rationalization.

The Frankfurt School 'after Auschwitz'

Beginning with Adorno's 1949 essay 'Cultural Criticism and Society', the phrase 'after Auschwitz' figured prominently in Adorno's writing and characterizes the fate of millions of Europe's Jews as a turning point in the understanding of modernity. Michael Rothberg (1997) has theorized 'after Auschwitz' as a *chronotope*, or time-place, that serves as a metonym for the Holocaust. As Adorno himself once clarified, 'by Auschwitz I mean of course the entire system' (2006: 7). Adorno is perhaps best known for the line, 'to write poetry after Auschwitz is barbaric' (1983: 34); yet the phrase 'after Auschwitz' has implications that go far beyond literature or aesthetics. He repeatedly uses this phrase to posit a metaphysical rupture that Dan Diner (1988, 2000) called a *Zivilisationsbruch*, after which not only art but also philosophy, morality, education and life itself can never be the same. As Adorno remarked in a 1965 lecture course, 'There can be no one ... for whom the world after Auschwitz, that is, the world in which Auschwitz was possible, is the same world as it was before' (2000: 104). The historical experience of Auschwitz thus contains for Adorno a 'compelling universality' – the universal possibility of future genocide.

On the other hand, in that very same 1965 lecture Adorno speaks of 'Auschwitz' as a '*sign*' that represents a greater system of domination (2000: 101). When he uses the word Auschwitz, he says, 'I mean not only Auschwitz but the world of torture which has continued to exist after Auschwitz and of which we are receiving the most horrifying reports from Vietnam' (101). The historical experience of catastrophe of his generation, which he emphasizes 'is also experienced by those on whom it was not directly perpetrated', has been shaped 'not only through Auschwitz but through the introduction of torture as a permanent institution and through the atomic bomb – all these things form a kind of coherence, a hellish unity' (104). While these events are historically distinct, they were also produced by the same capitalist social order, and sometimes by the same perpetrators and related ideologies of racial othering. This is the meaning of the provocative view of history as 'one single catastrophe' or a 'permanent catastrophe' Adorno adopted from Benjamin.

Such reflections serve as a point of entry into the Frankfurt School's understanding of the relationship between antisemitism and racism generally. Already in the exile period, these issues were for Adorno hardly separable. Writing in *Minima Moralia* in 1945, he saw the enlightened liberal ideal of 'tolerance' as not only an ideal yet unrealized practice but in fact an ideological lie concealing the reality of deep inequality and ineradicable differences in modern societies: 'To assure the black that he is exactly like the white man, while he obviously is not, is secretly to wrong him still further' (1974: 103). The very notion of 'equality' had been distorted into the 'bad equality' which, as in the concentration camps, homogenizes its victims as objects of domination. In both liberal and Stalinist conceptions of equality Adorno saw the proto-totalitarian destruction of all that is different: 'The melting-pot was introduced by unbridled industrial capitalism. The thought of being cast into it conjures up martyrdom, not democracy' (103). Adorno also describes the 'unitary tolerance' he identified in 1940s America as less motivated by the particular identity of its targets such as Blacks or Jews than by the general desire to punish those groups who remain 'refractory' or unassimilated. Adorno would later develop this idea into his reflections on Auschwitz in *Negative Dialectics*: 'Genocide is the absolute integration .... Auschwitz confirmed the philosopheme of pure identity as death' (1973: 362). For Adorno, Auschwitz serves as an extreme example of general tendencies towards total social integration and the eradication of difference.

In the aphorism on race we have considered from *Minima Moralia*, Adorno also offers one of his clearest prescriptions for a less repressive society: 'An emancipated society, on the other hand, would not be a unitary state, but the realization of universality in the reconciliation of differences' (1974: 103). We should thus, he elaborates, 'conceive the better state as one in which people could be different without fear'. Thereafter, difference without domination became the desideratum of Adorno's philosophy, and Eric Oberle (2018) has argued that reflection on social questions of racial identity in turn informed Adorno's later philosophical work on 'non-identity' in *Negative Dialectics* (1973). Oberle offers the notion of 'negative identity' to describe the problem of enforced identities and social punishment surrounding identity, without reifying identities like 'Black' or 'Jewish' since they are time-bound categories produced by capitalist societies and can be used to enforce social domination. Oberle's notion of 'negative identity' is also helpful for understanding Adorno's conflicted coming to terms with his own hybrid German-Christian-Jewish identity. Adorno's philosophy resisted reifying positive identities yet recognized both the violence that can be done in the name of identity categories and the real social effects of racialized differences.

Provincializing Critical Theory: From anti-antisemitism to anti-racism

In the intellectual portrait sketched thus far, I have considered Adorno's personal experiences and theoretical insights about antisemitism alongside other forms of racialized violence. In this process, I have attempted to weave together strands of Adorno's philosophical, social-scientific, and aphoristic work not often considered together, and to show that Adorno's corpus and biography offer rich examples for thinking them together. The attempt to bring antisemitism into dialogue with other forms of social violence reflects contemporary insights from philosophy and social theory to which we will now turn.

Elad Lapidot's book *Jews Out of the Question* (2020) offers a provocative 'critique of anti-anti-Semitism', asking why philosophy has attended to the 'Jewish Question' so intently while remaining wilfully ignorant and silent about other social questions, such as other racial ideologies, that remain closely linked to it and arguably deserve similar consideration as fundamental pathologies of modern society. Lapidot provocatively identifies actual Jews as being 'out of the question' – so far removed are they as 'real' social and historical subjects of analysis, and so persistent has the figure of 'the Jew' and 'the Jewish' been as a fundamental abstract concept in Western thought, including in Frankfurt School Critical Theory.

The challenge Lapidot raises is to chart a course between several ultimately unsatisfying accounts of antisemitism. First, Sartre's theory whereby the antisemite 'invents' the Jew, which raises and leaves unanswerable the question of why Jews in particular have been so specifically persecuted in Western history. This argument, and its flaws, are partly shared by Horkheimer and Adorno's projective theory of antisemitism; hence their attempt to supplement it with various other historical factors throughout the 'Elements'. Recognizing this problem, Hannah Arendt in her *Origins of Totalitarianism* (1951) dismissed theories of 'eternal antisemitism' as offering little explanatory power with regards to the novel exterminatory antisemitism of the Nazi regime; purely 'scapegoat' or 'projective' theories raised the question, 'Why the Jews? Why not the bicyclists?' This led Arendt, at the other extreme, to insist in the first section of *Origins* that circumstances in 'real' Jewish history led to Jews becoming the conspicuous representatives of modernity, nation-states, liberalism and capitalism, all while lacking the actual political power and institutions to ensure their rights, citizenship and protection. Such accounts run the risk of victim-blaming, and impute an implausible rationality and consciousness to antisemites. The epilogue to David Nirenberg's landmark 2013 book *Anti-Judaism* evaluates these two leading theories against each other, finally granting the upper hand to Horkheimer and Adorno for grasping the essentially *projective* and *irrational* nature of antisemitism, with 'the Jew' serving for thousands of years as a foil through which the (Christian) West thinks itself, even with little experience or knowledge of 'real' Jews. These accounts agree that even if antisemitism depends upon irrational, individual, psychological mechanisms these are activated in historical moments according to changing social-political contexts. For example, in her important studies of Imperial German culture, Shulamit Volkov (1978) developed the notion of antisemitism as a 'cultural code' that served particular functions for distinguishing new and old social classes. Recognizing the social, political and cultural functions of antisemitism, the question always remains as to why antisemites target Jews and not some other social group.

As we have already seen, though, Horkheimer and Adorno recognized that antisemites often also target other marginal groups, and this is one reason they considered antisemitism alongside other forms of 'barbarism' in 'enlightened' civilization. Of course, monolithic notions of 'civilization' or 'culture' have long been challenged by postcolonial theorists, and it is helpful to see the *Dialectic* as challenging the unreflective valorization of Western civilization even while Adorno in particular remained wedded to its elite cultural forms. The notion of Auschwitz as a '*Zivilisationsbruch*', an interpretation championed since the 1980s by Diner, captures what for Adorno was an absolute 'metaphysical' as well as cultural rupture in post-Auschwitz civilization. For this reason, throughout his 'after Auschwitz' writings, Adorno rejected the naïve idea of resurrecting the 'good' (pre-Nazi) German culture, as the prominent liberal historian Friedrich Meinecke (1963) advised in 1946 to denazify Germany and restore its vaunted culture of *Dichter und Denker* through 'Goethe circles'. Adorno sharply criticizes this idea of restoring Western culture in *Minima Moralia*:

> The idea that after this war life will continue 'normally' or even that culture might be 'rebuilt' – as if the rebuilding of culture was not really its negation – is idiotic. Millions of Jews have been murdered, and this is to be seen as an interlude and not the catastrophe itself. What more is this culture waiting for? (1974: 55)

In this biting, almost cynical line, Adorno suggests that the Holocaust is rooted in such deep and fundamental structures of Western modernity that it cannot be overcome by rebuilding the very same civilization that produced such horror. He elaborates later in the same work:

> He who registers the death camps as a technical mishap in civilization's triumphal procession, the martyrdom of the Jews as world-historically irrelevant, not only falls short of the dialectical vision but reverses the meaning of his own politics: to hold ultimate calamity in check. (1974: 234)

Adorno saw Auschwitz as a stumbling stone that stood in the path of postwar Allied policies which urged Germans to move quickly past the Nazi era towards rebuilding, thereby minimizing the moral stain it would leave on all levels of German society (see Olick 2005).

As much as Adorno's view of the singular significance of Auschwitz and the antisemitism that contributed to its creation was important to stress in the postwar years in a society that had hardly even begun to reckon with its complicity in genocide, today the notion of a singular 'civilizational rupture' has become highly problematic. The historian Dirk Moses and others have stressed the Eurocentrism of the term – as if the pre-Auschwitz status quo ante of Western civilization were not built upon myriad forms of violence and exclusion, indeed the extreme violence of many European empires conducted not 'against' civilization but in the very name of a 'civilizing mission' towards black, brown and indigenous peoples around the world. Enzo Traverso (2017) and others have thus called out the Frankfurt School as insufficiently attuned to problems in the civilization concept; only Herbert Marcuse, in Traverso's view, recognized the problems of Eurocentrism, empire and racial domination through his outspoken advocacy against the Vietnam War, a war the conservative aging Horkheimer actually supported. No doubt this is a blind spot, but not, I would argue, as damning a critique of Horkheimer and Adorno's theory as Traverso claims; for it could also be suggested that a missing but implied chapter of *Dialectic*, falling somewhere between the Odysseus chapter on 'enlightened' man's violence against nature and himself and the final chapter on antisemitism, is a chapter on colonial violence – the historical progression found in Arendt's *Origins*. Amy Allen's *The End of Progress: Decolonizing the Normative Foundations of Critical Theory* (2016) has gone a long way towards opening up Frankfurt School Critical Theory to postcolonial critiques of notions such as progress and civilization without abandoning their original emancipatory projects. Part of this 'provincialization' of Critical Theory as a particular European tradition entails considering antisemitism alongside other forms of projective othering, including racism, sexism, ableism and sexual and gender-based violence. Rooted as the Frankfurt theorists thought antisemitism was in the 'pathic projection' of authoritarian subjects, rather than in the behaviour of actual Jews, the work of political, social, and educational interventions concerning all of the above-mentioned forms of violent 'othering' remain closely interconnected, even while antisemitism as an ideology retains a specificity and power that suggests it cannot be reduced to or conflated with them.

Adorno, antisemitism and Holocaust memory in a global age

It is striking to observe in contemporary debates the persistence of many of the same questions about singularity and universalism that characterize Adorno's reflections from decades ago about the relationship between Auschwitz and the general 'permanent catastrophe' of capitalist modernity. Traverso wrote in 2022 that in the now-hegemonic German memory culture 'the Holocaust became a pathological deviation from a linear Western path': overemphasizing the Holocaust's uniqueness as part of a German 'special path' allows it to be treated as an exception or anomaly, which appeared 'comfortably uncharacteristic and sociologically inconsequential' (Postone 2003: 86, paraphrasing Bauman). Historically and conceptually isolated in this way, Auschwitz fails to implicate the rest of modernity; characterizing it as a unique deviation became part of the effort to resurrect and reinforce the earlier liberal-democratic European civilization that had enabled the rise of fascism and the path to Auschwitz, rather than challenging its inner tendencies towards violence and exclusion. As Traverso rightly concludes, 'all genocides are "caesurae of civilization"', and thus 'the Jews annihilated by the Nazis ... deserve neither more nor less compassion and recollection than the Armenians destroyed in the Ottoman Empire on the brink of collapse, the Soviet citizens who died in the Gulags, the Ukrainian peasants extinguished in the Holodomor, the Congolese killed in Leopold II's rubber plantations' etc. As the global historian Sebastian Conrad (2021) has argued, the task facing Germany today is not *whether* to recognize the memory of the Holocaust or colonial violence, but *how* to recognize both.

As we have seen, the mature Adorno of the 1960s referred to Auschwitz as forming 'a hellish unity' with Hiroshima, Vietnam, 'torture as a permanent institution', and catastrophic global histories. In one of his very last texts, 'Marginalia to Theory and Praxis', Adorno expanded the phrase 'after Auschwitz' to 'after Auschwitz and Hiroshima' (2005: 268). In his magnum opus *Negative Dialectics*, he even approached Aimé Césaire's well-known reflections on the double standards of outrage towards violence within Europe versus violence in faraway colonies with his remark that moralistic claims like 'torture ought to be abolished; concentration camps ought not to exist' are 'true as impulse' since 'they register, that somewhere torture is occurring', for 'all this continues in Africa and Asia and is only repressed because civilized humanity is as inhuman as ever against those which it shamelessly brands as uncivilized' (1973: 285). One year later, in his 1967 lecture, 'Aspects of the New Right-Wing Extremism', Adorno similarly invokes a historical link between 'gruesome' European colonialism in Africa, Nazi atrocities and anti-democratic aspects of Cold War anti-communism (Adorno 2020: 19). I would thus argue that Traverso overstates his critique when he claims that unlike Marcuse, who in the 1966 'Political Preface' to the second edition of *Eros and Civilization* explicitly linked colonial crimes in Africa and Vietnam and the domestic American ghettoes of Mississippi and Harlem with Nazi crimes in concentration camps, 'The idea of such a comparison never crossed the minds of Adorno and Horkheimer', whose Critical Theory he charges, along with their predecessor Marx, of harbouring a 'colonial unconscious' (Traverso 2017: 175). Adorno returned again and again to Auschwitz as a negative moral foundation due to its concreteness and irrefutable horror. Yet overemphasizing the uniqueness of Auschwitz vis-à-vis other global atrocities would be to entirely miss the point of Adorno's decades of philosophical, moral and political reflection upon it, which is emphatic in its attempts to connect Auschwitz to longer histories of domination, instrumental rationality and racial othering. As Jay Bernstein aptly put it, 'Auschwitz is not metaphysically or epistemically privileged; even as negative theodicy, Auschwitz is not unique but, horrifyingly, exemplary' (Bernstein 2001: 395).

This understanding of Auschwitz as historically particular yet universally implicating is reflected in Adorno's New Categorical Imperative against the repetition of Auschwitz *or anything 'similar' to it* in his 1966 *Negative Dialectics* (1973: 365). In his 1966 radio lecture 'Education after Auschwitz' from that same year, Adorno proposes 'never again Auschwitz' (2005: 191) as a the most important ideal of postwar education, but at the same time also mentions the Armenian genocide of 1915 as a precedent for the Holocaust, among other reasons because parts of the German military was informed about it and condoned it (192). By situating 'Auschwitz' in relation to other catastrophic histories and explicitly making the New Categorical Imperative universal and applicable to other 'similar' events, Adorno makes clear that the prohibition includes other genocides (Skirke 2020). But as Dirk Moses has argued, we should also not restrict our moral concern for actions that 'shock the conscience of mankind' (2021a: 13) according to the uniquely 'transgressive' category of genocide when so much more endemic violence continues to be done in the name of achieving 'permanent security', including politically motivated violence and ongoing 'humanitarian' or 'targeted' wars. Adorno's imperative 'Never Again' extends not only beyond Auschwitz and antisemitism, but also beyond the category of genocide.

At the same time, an interesting document in Adorno's archive points to the limitations of his proximity to the explicit relativization of the Holocaust undertaken by many of his left-wing students in the 1960s (see Kundnani 2009).[1] When Adorno was invited to meet with a socialist student association in Bremen in 1967, they sent him in advance the questions they wished for him to answer: What did he think about Kurt Georg Kiesinger, a former member of the Nazi party, becoming chancellor of West Germany? Wasn't this evidence of ominous continuities between the Third Reich and the Federal Republic? Didn't it seem to suggest 'that a radical overthrow of fascism in West Germany did not take place'? Hadn't West Germany changed from a 'post-fascist' to a 'pre-fascist' state? Their final questions lay bare the limitations of their Marxist frameworks, which seem to understand all violence and imperialism as rooted in capitalism, as well as the crude analogies between Nazi and American imperialism for which the student movement was notorious: 'Can Auschwitz be understood as the ultimate consequence of late capitalism?' 'Can Vietnam be compared to Auschwitz? Is there a potentially crucial difference?' Unfortunately, the archive does not contain Adorno's responses. However, from his many other writings and lectures on such topics we have considered, we can reconstruct the complex responses he might have given. In his powerful 1959 radio lecture, 'The Meaning of Working through the Past', Adorno had boldly claimed that 'National Socialism lives on' in Germany '*within*' its democracy and urged a more intensive public reckoning with the legacies of Nazism for a nation in which 'the willingness to commit the unspeakable survives in people as well as in the conditions that enclose them' (2005: 89–90). Adorno did not admit of *equivalence* between Auschwitz and atrocities like the Vietnam War that seemed to animate the political ire of the Bremen students, yet he insisted on recognizing both as moral outrages and holding them together as products of the same catastrophic late capitalist social order.

This fundamental ambivalence about 'Auschwitz' in Adorno's thought crystallizes, characteristically, in a dialectical 'constellation': the figure of 'hellish unity' Adorno claimed united such modern atrocities. This connection occurs at the conceptual level

---

[1] This document is accessible in the Walter Benjamin Archiv at the Akademie der Künste, Berlin, signature TWAA_Ge_206 Bremer Studenten mit TWA, 1967.

of social theory: similar processes of othering, instrumentalization and state violence play out across different groups of victims and perpetrators. Yet Adorno stops short of advancing what Dirk Moses and other genocide studies scholars today call 'entangled histories', emphasizing, for example, the Holocaust in Eastern Europe as a product of German colonial expansionism with certain continuities in racial attitudes and personnel from Germany's colonial genocides in Africa – the suggestion of a path 'from Windhoek to Auschwitz' (Zimmerer 2011).

Adorno's claim that Auschwitz stands in a 'hellish unity' with the 'permanent catastrophe' of other forms of modern violence suggests that we can only understand the historical particularity of the Nazi Holocaust in light of longer-term social and political processes that enabled it and connect it to other catastrophic histories. Adorno and Horkheimer's contributions to the theory of antisemitism have been productively developed by a number of leading theorists of contemporary antisemitism (Claussen, Ziege, Rensmann and Postone, among others) and mobilized for decades, especially by parts of the German left, to emphasize the unique characteristics of modern antisemitism as distinct from other forms of racism: that for antisemites Jews are not simply inferior, but are singled out as uniquely powerful and threatening, and therefore subject to particular violence and genocidal extermination. Too often, however, this focus on the distinctiveness of antisemitism has entailed a 'competitive' framework that establishes and defends a hierarchy of prejudice and victimization rather than identifying common patterns and political solidarities in the more constructive intersectional framework the remainder of this chapter will propose.

Revisiting the Frankfurt School's theory of antisemitism in light of current debates

The relationship between antisemitism and racism has been a matter of much debate in recent years, culminating in a clash between the widely adopted International Holocaust Remembrance Alliance's (IHRA) definition of antisemitism, which includes the so-called new antisemitism rooted in critiques of the state of Israel, and the alternative Jerusalem Declaration on Antisemitism, which instead emphasizes connections between antisemitism and other forms of racism (see discussion in Penslar 2022). The Jerusalem Declaration states in its very first point that 'What is true of racism in general is true of antisemitism in particular', and its authors elaborate that 'while antisemitism has certain distinctive features, the fight against it is inseparable from the overall fight against all forms of racial, ethnic, cultural, religious, and gender discrimination'. Between these two influential definitions, the first endorsed by many states and officials, the second by a smaller group of progressive scholars, lies the intractable issue of the Israel–Palestine conflict. Whereas the IHRA definition defends the legitimacy of Israel as a Jewish state and links specifically Jewish suffering in the Holocaust to contemporary antisemitism, the Jerusalem Declaration suggests that the 'universal lessons of the Holocaust' can also be legitimately applied to other victimized groups including Palestinians.

Fitting with its roots as a nineteenth-century political *Kampfbegriff*, 'antisemitism' today is not a neutral social-scientific term, but often a term of dispute, accusation and abuse. In the scholarly arena, the usefulness of the antisemitism concept has been criticized by the Holocaust historian David Engel, whose influential 2009 essay 'Away from a Definition of Antisemitism' argued that the concept creates more conceptual blinders than it does insights into why anti-Jewish violence happens where and when it does. Engel rightly characterizes antisemitism as 'a socio-semantic convention created in the nineteenth century and sustained throughout the twentieth for communal and political ends, not scholarly ones' (2009: 53).

It was one such debate, about the boundary between legitimate critique of Israel and antisemitism, that led to calls for the disinvitation of the prominent Cameroonian theorist Achille Mbembe from a German culture festival in the spring of 2020 on charges of antisemitism and 'relativizing the Holocaust', setting off what has been called the 'Historians' Debate 2.0' (for an overview, see Catlin 2021 and the interview Catlin 2022). This debate reactivated for a much more diverse and globalized German society some of the central questions of the first 'Historians' Debate' (*Historikerstreit*) from 1986–7, which concerned the particularity of the Holocaust vis-à-vis Stalinist atrocities. But more than that, the recent debate centred on effects of the official German programme of 'anti-antisemitism', in whose name many prominent thinkers have been effectively cancelled from German public life, ranging from the progressive Jewish-American philosopher Judith Butler (who supports BDS – Boycott, Divestment and Sanctions of Israel) to postcolonial theorists like Mbembe, and voices from the Global South such as the Indonesian art collectives at the 2022 documenta art festival in Kassel, some of whose artwork in fact included antisemitic caricatures (for nuanced discussion see Rothberg 2022a).

The perceived closing of freedom of expression led prominent public intellectual Susan Neiman, a self-described 'cosmopolitan Jewish intellectual' who identifies with the 'tradition of universalistic Judaism' of her parents who campaigned for African American civil rights in the 1960s (Führer 2021), to worry that such German-Jewish luminaries as Albert Einstein and Hannah Arendt would not be allowed to speak in Germany today owing to their critical views on Israel (Neiman 2020). Neiman thus led an initiative calling for '*Weltoffenheit*' (openness to the world) in German society, after official programmes of anti-antisemitism had begun to provincialize the German public sphere by cutting it off from even Jewish artists and intellectuals who violated the official position declared by Angela Merkel in 2008 that 'Israel's security is part of German *Staatsraison*'. One of the first consequences of the Bundestag's 2019 anti-BDS resolution was the shutting down of a reading group on 'Unlearning Zionism' led by Jewish-Israeli art students in Berlin – the beginning of a campaign some have likened to a 'witch hunt' (Mashiach 2020). In a cutting 2021 essay written in an 'Arendt-inspired tone' (Stone 2022), genocide scholar Dirk Moses (2021b) criticized the way official German Holocaust memory, which once 'served an important function in denazifying the country', had 'outlived its usefulness' and hardened into a 'catechism' rigidly upholding Israeli policy and often wielded against Muslims and other minorities deemed 'the new antisemites'. The catechism positions morally redeemed philosemitic Germans as the Jews' new protectors, while Holocaust guilt is 'subcontracted' to migrant groups (see Özyürek 2023, also discussed in the interview Catlin 2022).

Because Adorno has often been invoked as a source of inspiration for contemporary German Holocaust memory culture (Scholl 2017), it is worth reconsidering how his work might contribute to the latest debates. As the German-Israeli philosopher Omri Boehm has written, 'The central point [of the 1980s *Historikerstreit*] was Germany's commitment to ethical universalism – a commitment that, [Jürgen] Habermas argued, Germany could only make by acknowledging the uniqueness of its crime' (2021). But today, Boehm writes, we see 'Germany putting its obligation to the Jewish state above its obligation to international law'. Boehm thus calls for a truly radical universalism that, like Adorno's thought, incorporates the lessons of Auschwitz but rather than reifying them into a rigid maxim continues to reflexively adapt their meaning for an ever-changing society. As Enzo Traverso writes in a similar vein: 'Thirty-five years after the *Historikerstreit*, the German state has replaced Nazi "redemptive" antisemitism (Friedländer) with a sort of "redemptive" philosemitism which means not the struggle against racism, but Israeli security inscribed into law'. 'Today', Traverso concludes, 'philosemitism has become the "cultural code" of a reunified, post-national Germany, considering Jews as special friends and defending Israel as a moral duty'.

Habermas, a former assistant to Adorno, seems to have learned from the excesses and calcification of the Holocaust memory culture he was instrumental in establishing as the moral foundation of postwar Germany decades ago. Responding to the latest *Historikerstreit*, he stressed that as a form of communicative rationality and ongoing social learning process, historical memory should not become 'frozen' but must change as German society has become far more diverse than it was in the 1980s: 'The memory of our colonial history, which was suppressed until recently, is an important extension', he said, concluding that 'the immigrant acquires a fellow citizen's voice, which from now on counts in public and can transform and develop our political culture' (2021: 11). It is with such a consciousness that the German state in recent years has begun to formally apologize for its colonial genocide in Namibia and that President Steinmeier's 2021 speech at the opening of the Humboldt Forum similarly recognized the need for German society to open itself up and effectively adopt 'multidirectional memory' of its colonial crimes *and* the Shoah. As Peter E. Gordon (2020) has written in an American context, 'If every crime is unique and the moral imagination is forbidden from comparison, then the injunction "Never Again" itself loses its meaning, since nothing can ever happen "again"'.

Amidst these ongoing debates, the writings of the Frankfurt School theorists offer a more complex and intersectional picture than is suggested by their appropriation as theorists of the specificity of antisemitism. These debates lead us back to an old problem. In Adorno and Horkheimer's 'Elements', they argued that according to their theory of antisemitism as 'false projection', 'there is no authentic antisemitism, and certainly no born antisemite' (2002: 140). Hence 'the blindness of antisemitism, its lack of intention' means that to a certain extent its 'victims are interchangeable' (140). While in the final 1947 edition of the text they wrote 'vagrants, Jews, Protestants, Catholics', in the first 1944 edition instead of 'vagrants' they wrote 'Negroes, Mexican wrestling clubs' (272). In its most radical form, the projective theory of antisemitism as rooted in the authoritarian subject (and not actual Jews) means that the victims are interchangeable: antisemitism, like other forms of othering violence, functions as a 'release valve' whereby 'rage is vented on those who are both conspicuous and unprotected' (140).

Such passages raise the question of the relationship between racism in general and antisemitism in particular. In a 2017 essay, Steven Aschheim sharply criticized *Dialectic* for retaining such ambivalence about the singularity of antisemitism and Jewish victims even in their revised 1947 version in light of what by then was well known about the singularly exterminatory genocide of Europe's Jews. To Aschheim, 'Elements' offers an 'a-historical shopping cart of possibilities' that employs 'generalized and often vague notions' instead of specific historical and social analysis (2017: 441). Lars Rensmann (2017: 290) has also argued that the authors 'blur' the specificity of antisemitism and can seem to suggest 'a false universality in which everything is arbitrarily interchangeable: human beings, perpetrators, victims, prejudices' (see critical discussion in Catlin 2020). In his essay 'Blindness and Insight' (2012) on 'the conceptual Jew', Jonathan Judaken goes even further in criticizing the authors for developing a philosemitic figure of 'the Jew' as a source of resistance to domination or a positive site of critical rationality that risks being just as mythic and stereotyped as the negative figure the authors criticize. In other words, Horkheimer and Adorno at times adopt what Zygmunt Bauman (1998) called an 'allosemitic', othering, portrait of the Jew that ambivalently wavers between stereotypes and a kind of mythic valorization that is nonetheless fetishistic.

While this ambiguity can be seen as a shortfall in Horkheimer and Adorno's work, it is also possible to read it as a potential strength as a site of theoretical openness and prescient intersectionality. The occasional lack of distinction between Jews and other victims of projective prejudice offers a theoretical opening through which to connect Adorno and Horkheimer's insights about antisemitism and antisemitic subjects to other cases of racism and the struggles against them. The lens of the 'authoritarian personality', backed up by more recent research, demonstrates that indeed, violent antisemites are often also racists, misogynists, homophobes and transphobes, etc. The manifestos of mass killers like Anders Brevik polemicize against both Jews and people of colour, while conspiracy theories about 'the great replacement' like those held by the shooter of the Tree of Life Synagogue in Pittsburgh link these two hatreds together by suggesting that non-white immigration is funded by liberal Jewish financiers like George Soros. Owing to the risks of conflating racism and antisemitism, this more global and intersectional side of these theorists' reflections has yet to be sufficiently developed in contemporary Critical Theory. However, in light of contemporary debates and evolving historical scholarship about connections between the Holocaust and earlier forms of scientific racism and colonialism, the time is ripe to articulate the connections Adorno and Horkheimer already suggested. On both the conceptual level of the projective nature of antisemitism and racism and on the level of historical entanglements between the perpetration of modern atrocities, the frame in which we view the Frankfurt School's writings on antisemitism can and should be expanded well beyond the Holocaust.

Historians of genocide including Dan Stone and Dirk Moses have deepened our understanding of the 'entangled histories' that led up to the Holocaust by developing and correcting the historical sketch first given in Hannah Arendt's *Origins* connecting, in its three parts, the rise of modern antisemitism, European colonialism and the Nazi dictatorship and its persecution of Jews and other groups. The work of Michael Rothberg (2009) has given us a 'multidirectional' framework in which to appreciate the mutual learning and cultural borrowings that can happen between the memory of historically distinct traumas, leading a way beyond the framework of 'competitive memory' and excessive worry about Holocaust 'relativization' that in fact limits understanding of the Holocaust and its continuing relevance for the contemporary world. For example, recent scholarship has shown that Nazi officials took inspiration from America's anti-Black anti-miscegenation laws in their drafting of the anti-Jewish Nuremburg Laws (Whitman 2017). There were also continuities in personnel, racial science, and population control techniques between Hitler's colonial war in Eastern Europe and Germany's earlier colonial violence in Southwest Africa, including the 1904–7 genocide of the indigenous Herero and Nama peoples (Erichsen and Olusoga 2010).

To claim, with the Jerusalem Declaration, that 'what is true of racism in general is true of antisemitism in particular', is not to claim the inverse and erase the specificity of antisemitism; rather, it is to illuminate the broader category of racial oppression through the particular experience of antisemitism. While highlighting important distinctions between these social pathologies, the penultimate section of this chapter aims to develop Adorno and Horkheimer's insights and to argue for the mutual illumination of these forms of projective othering in light of both some of their common features and their entangled histories.

Moving the study of antisemitism beyond 'Judeopessimism'

In a recent study of the far-right American-Israeli leader Meir Kahane, Jewish studies scholar Shaul Magid argues that Kahane's thought was premised on a thoroughgoing sense of 'Judeopessimism' – on positing an unbridgeable ontological divide between a fundamentally antisemitic world and the figure of the Jew as a permanent victim. From this perspective, Kahane's view of the persistence and centrality of antisemitism in history mirrors the way in which many so-called Afropessimists have understood the deep and seemingly intractable structure of anti-Black racism. In Magid's account, Kahane was an anti-assimilationist and a segregationist; he eschewed liberal projects of Jewish inclusion and assimilation because he believed there was no solution to either white–Black racism nor to antisemitism besides group separation and independence to be found in the Jewish state of Israel. For Kahane, antisemitism was an 'ontological hatred of the Jews that outweighs other forms of racism' (Magid 2021: 87).

On the other hand, Afropessimists such as Alexander Weheliye have criticized the Eurocentrism and Judeo-centrism of figures such as Giorgio Agamben, in his influential work *Remnants of Auschwitz* (1998), positing Auschwitz as 'the most absolute incarnation of modernity's politicization of *zoe*' – mere biological life, or bare life (Weheliye 2014: 53). Weheliye rightly criticizes the way 'Agamben's dogmatic insistence on a stringently juridical instantiation of the state of exception reinstitutes the holocaust as the most severe and paradigmatic manifestation of bare life' (85). As he quotes David Scott, 'Why should we be obliged to submit to the semiotic inflation that makes the Holocaust the primal scene of the original crime, and the extermination camp the fundamental paradigm, of modern Western power? What Western anxiety – what desire – drives this philosophico-political exorbitance?' (64). Weheliye goes on to conclude, 'we could just as well assert that racial slavery represents the biopolitical nomos of modernity, particularly given its historically antecedent status vis-à-vis the Holocaust and the many different ways it highlights the continuous and nonexceptional modes of physiological and psychic violence exerted upon black subjects since the dawn of modernity' (38).

What is at stake in this 'just as well'? What grounds the common desire for what Anson Rabinbach (2015) has called 'negative exceptionalism' at the core of both Afropessimist and Judeopessimist discourses and their exclusive claims to the 'foundational' violence of Western modernity? Wendy Brown (1993) persuasively criticized such grievance-based identity claims as ahistorical 'wounded attachments' whereby subjects and groups hold on to their past injuries rather than work to repair them in solidarity with more politically productive coalitions. In this spirit, it is troubling to see in some reception of Adorno up to the present, particularly in Germany, the use of his work on antisemitism to advance particular ideological agendas that betray the universalist, anti-nationalist and anti-identitarian thrust of his philosophy of non-identity articulated most clearly in *Negative Dialectics*.

As we have seen, Adorno hardly identified as a Jew until he was persecuted by the Nazi regime as one. While in exile in the United States he became part of a community of fellow Jewish émigrés, but not religiously observant; as Horkheimer explained Adorno's non-Jewish funeral, the extent of his Jewishness was that he 'identified with the persecuted' (quoted in Claussen 2008: 365). Eric Oberle (2018) has theorized this relation as 'negative identity', which is no less real for being imposed from outside, but which nevertheless resists positive identification and certainly national or group identity politics. As Adorno wrote in a note in 1963: 'Whoever belongs among the persecuted has ceased to possess any unbroken form of identification. The concepts of native land [*Heimat*], country, are all shattered. Only one native land remains from which no one is excluded: mankind' (quoted in Claussen 2008: 25).

Given the centrality and prominence of opposition to all forms of identitarianism and ethnonationalism in Adorno's thought following his traumatic experience of fascism, it is striking to see some prominent readers of Adorno present him as a supporter of Zionism. In a polemical essay published on the blog the rightward-leaning journal *Telos* in 2014 and then appended as the epilogue of his 2018 book on Adorno, *Wahrheit und Katastrophe*, Dirk Braunstein (2018), the current director of the Archive of the Institute for Social Research, quotes Adorno writing to his Viennese friend Lotte Tobisch in the midst of the 1967 war:

> We are terribly worried about Israel. In a corner of my consciousness I have always imagined that this would not go well in the long run, but I was completely surprised that this is happening so quickly. One can only hope that the Israelis

will still be militarily superior to the Arabs for a while so that they can hold the situation. (Cited in Braunstein 2018: 328)

In this passage, Adorno expresses solidarity with and concern for the plight of countless Holocaust survivors that were widespread among his generation of refugees – especially since he saw himself as 'one who escaped by accident, one who by rights should have been killed' (1973: 363). In 1956 during the Suez Crisis, Adorno similarly expressed his concern for Israel's safety in letters to Gershom Scholem and Julius Ebbinghaus (Adorno and Scholem 2015; Jacobs 2014: 137). Yet, as Peter Gordon has suggested, it is perhaps telling that Adorno never found the time to accept Scholem's invitations to visit Israel, and these passages of understandable concern do not support Braunstein's implied conclusion that Adorno was a Zionist or supported the Israeli state as such (Gordon 2016). Indeed, he surely would not have supported its various far-right governments in ensuing decades, nor ethnonationalist policies such as the 2018 Jewish Nation State Law, which codified Jewish superiority over Palestinians. 'The truth is that Adorno always bristled at communalism', Gordon writes. 'Whatever its historical longevity or political utility, ethnonationalism was for Adorno a surrender to the instincts of the horde, not a future ideal' (Gordon 2016).

Braunstein invokes this passage to criticize what he considers a 'misreading' of Adorno by Columbia University Iranian Studies scholar Hamid Dabashi. In an essay entitled 'Gaza: Poetry after Auschwitz' (2014), Dabashi suggested that Adorno's famous dictum about poetry after Auschwitz might also be applied to the 2014 war in Gaza, which resulted in Israeli bombing killing over two thousand Palestinians, while Palestinian militants killed seventy-two Israelis, most of them soldiers. Dabashi provocatively wrote, 'After Gaza, not a single living Israeli can utter the word "Auschwitz" without it sounding like "Gaza". Auschwitz as a historical fact is now archival. Auschwitz as a metaphor is now Palestinian'. Dabashi sees 'crystallized in Israel' the concerns about the violence of modern states 'that Adorno saw, diagnosed, and feared'.

Braunstein sharply contests Dabashi's rereading of Adorno 'after Gaza' as 'propaganda' and 'raging instrumentalism', claiming that 'the theme that concerned Adorno his whole life after Auschwitz' was not a universal aim of preventing future atrocities but specifically combatting 'antisemitism'. Surely Braunstein is right to denounce any simplistic inversion or 'vacuous analogy' in which 'Jews are the Nazis of today'. Yet Dabashi's essay was not a call to arms but a plea for the right to mourn Palestinian civilians crushed by the ruins of their own bombed-out homes – a right the large Palestinian diaspora in Germany is increasingly denied (Doughan and Toukan 2022). While Braunstein writes that Adorno 'resists this posthumous manipulation into an anti-Zionist', Adorno would clearly also not condone violence against civilians done in the name of Zionism. The most serious problem with Braunstein's polemic is that it defends 'Auschwitz' as the exclusive moral property of a provincial German perspective that privileges antisemitism over other forms of oppression that we have seen also deeply concerned Adorno. Here a particular German 'Judeopessimism' is said to monopolize legitimate interpretations of Adorno. Yet as Susan Neiman (2013) once quipped, glossing a maxim of the Bulgarian thinker Tzvedan Todorov: 'Germans should talk about the particularity of the Holocaust, the Jews about its universality'.

Anson Rabinbach has explored in depth why a generation of European Jews including Adorno, Arendt and Zygmunt Bauman did exactly that, advancing highly universalistic historical and social theories of the Holocaust out of a generational investment in making the Holocaust universally relevant rather than provincializing it as the exclusive domain of Jewish or German history (2003).

The Palestinian literary critic Edward Said once referred to himself as 'the last Jewish intellectual … the only true follower of Adorno. Let me put it this way: I'm a Jewish-Palestinian' (Shavit 2000). Said praised Adorno as exemplifying the intellectual as a 'permanent exile' who rubs their own society against the grain and remains a 'permanent outcast, someone who never felt at home, and was always at odds with the environment, inconsolable about the past, bitter about the present and the future' (1996: 56, 47). The Turkish-Jewish critical theorist Seyla Benhabib (2018) similarly argues that the Frankfurt School's work on exile and migration defies confinement to their particular history; the migrants of today are not the same as those of yesterday, yet the experience of Jews in the 1930s and 1940s inspired the human rights and anti-genocide conventions now essential for protecting other persecuted groups. Thus Hannah Arendt's 1943 essay 'We Refugees' about a particular experience of German-Jewish persecution and exile was reissued in German in a bestselling pocket edition in 2015 during the Syrian refugee crisis. Adorno once wrote that 'open thinking points beyond itself' (2005: 293); using his thought and life as a model, we would also have to add that Jewish experience and persecution points beyond itself. These cases show 'lived multidirectionality' at work (Sultan Doughan in Catlin 2022; see elaboration in Rothberg 2022b).

A further reason to revisit the Frankfurt School's work on antisemitism is that, to invoke Keynes, the facts have changed. The historiography of the Third Reich and the Holocaust has vastly expanded and transformed beyond models fixated on 'Auschwitz' as 'the very capital of the Holocaust' (Hayes 2003) and reflected in Saul Friedländer's (1997) Judeo-centric understanding of the Nazi regime as driven by the zeal of 'redemptive antisemitism' as a political religion. Alex J. Kay's *Empire of Destruction: A History of Nazi Mass Killing* (2021) begins this history in a much earlier and unexpected place: the systematic starvation of disabled Germans during WWI rationing. Continuities of personnel, eugenic racial-scientific ideology, and the criteria of 'unfitness for work', 'useless eaters', and 'life unworthy of life' later established direct links between Operation T4 against the disabled and the later genocide of the Jews. Here Kay echoes a claim made by Henry Friedlander decades ago: 'euthanasia was not simply a prologue but the first chapter of Nazi genocide' (Friedlander 1995: xii; Kay 2021: 40). In another chapter, Kay shows how the Nazis also held a 'blanket identification of Roma with partisans' (2021: 115) and killed them on this ground, just as the first murders of Jews in the East were justified on the grounds of 'equating Jews with partisans' (175) – even as these groups were in fact '*least likely* to be partisans' (182). Similarly, 'although economic motivations lay at the core of proposals to starve [about 7] millions of Soviet citizens to death, racial considerations shaped the discourse when it came to what was deemed possible or not' (126). In all these cases, racial 'supremacist ideology became the means by which allegedly superfluous human beings were identified' (127). In the lead-up to the genocide of European Jews, exterminationist racial thinking combined with the paranoid threat of partisanship Dirk Moses (2021a) has called the Nazi pursuit of 'permanent security' in the East. Decades ago, the historian Arno Mayer (1988), himself a former Jewish child refugee from Luxemburg, argued that only the novel threat of 'Judeo-Bolshevism' in the Nazi expansionist imperial war in the East, and not simply the age-old phenomenon of antisemitism as a prejudice or ideology, could explain the turn to extermination. Paul Hanebrink's *Judeo-Bolshevism* (2018) similarly emphasizes the power of this mythic concept in the Nazi imaginary, which explains why Jews were killed *as partisans* assumed to be associated, in Nazi ideology and imagination, with the Soviet war machine. As Enzo Traverso (2022) has more recently written in this tradition:

> During the war, these three dimensions of Nazism [anti-communism, colonialism and antisemitism] merged resulting in a unique process: the destruction of the USSR, the colonization of Central and Eastern Europe, and the extermination of the Jews became inseparable aims. For Nazi ideology, the USSR brought together two forms of otherness that had shaped Western history for two centuries: the Jew and the colonial subject.

This reassessment fits with other studies such Richard Overy's recent work *Blood and Ruins* (2022), which recasts the war not as a clash between democracy and tyranny or liberty and totalitarianism – frames that work better for European fronts than for the Pacific – but rather as a struggle between incumbent (Britain, France, the Soviet Union and the United States) and insurgent (Japan, Italy and Germany) empires over colonies, 'living space', and spheres of influence. In August 1941, after a tour through newly occupied Ukraine, Hitler praised 'the German colonist' and proclaimed, 'What India was for England the territories of Russia will be for us' (Lower 2005: 24). 'Starvation and colonization were German policy', Timothy Snyder has similarly written: 'discussed, agreed, formulated, distributed, and understood' (2010: 163).

These accounts amount to what Saul Friedländer, writing in 1985, called 'global interpretations of Nazism' built on universal historical frameworks such as 'fascism', 'totalitarianism', or, as is increasingly the case today, 'empire' (1989: 4). Against German proponents of writing the 'everyday' history of Nazism such as Martin Broszat, Friedländer insisted on the regime's '*sui generis* character', emphasizing 'the centrality of Hitler's anti-Semitic drives' in the Judeocide (31). Yet while Friedländer succeeded in distinguishing the particularity and significance of the genocide of the Jews from other Nazi atrocities, his single-pronged thesis of 'redemptive antisemitism' also obscured the essential broader context of ruthless anti-Soviet colonial war in the East whose conditions made it possible.

Even within Jewish history, Friedländer's emphasis on the uniqueness of Nazi antisemitism is complicated by Steven Zipperstein's (2018) work on the Kishinev (then part of the Russian Empire) Pogrom of 1903 and Jeffrey Veidlinger's (2021) work on Ukrainian pogroms of 1918–21, in which over a hundred thousand Jews were killed, both of which were fundamental 'catastrophes' (Yiddish, *khurban*) in their own right, with their own memorial practices and particular contextual factors that activated long-standing antisemitism into mass murder. Veidlinger shows that the overwhelming proportion of Holocaust victims from Eastern Europe experienced their persecution as a replay of these now largely forgotten precedents, and he even argues that we should see the Holocaust as having *begun* with these pre-Nazi traditions of antisemitic mass murder in Eastern Europe. The portrait that emerges from this recent historiography is neither one of undifferentiated 'eternal antisemitism' nor of the Holocaust as an exceptional, radical departure, but of contingent configurations of racial violence that form links and continuities across European history and beyond.

Conclusion: Towards a 'multidirectional' Adorno

Adorno wrote in his final, unfinished work, *Aesthetic Theory*, 'Even prior to Auschwitz it was an affirmative lie, given historical experience, to attribute any positive meaning to existence' (2002: 152). Nevertheless, 'after Auschwitz' the genocidal potential of modern societies became clearly manifest and identified with this death camp and the exterminatory antisemitic ideologies that led to the murder of its approximately one million Jewish victims, the most of any one site in the Holocaust. Thanks in part to the work of figures such as Adorno in his role as a public intellectual, Auschwitz continues to serve today as a uniquely universally powerful and recognized reminder of the brutality of which modern society is capable, and it continues to leave an indelible stain on that social form as a genocide that continues to 'shock the conscience of humankind' (Moses 2021a: 4) while many other horrors that this same order has produced have been ignored or forgotten.

Consistent with Adorno's general proscription on prescriptions for ethical living in a false society (see Judith Butler's 2012 Adorno Prize Lecture), his theoretical writings on antisemitism offer little in the way of answering the old question, 'what is to be done?' His lectures to students and public audiences, however, offer some practical insights. For all his doubts about the power of rationality to enable autonomous moral subjecthood in texts like *Dialectic*, he later often advocated cultivating morality through autonomy and rationality in the Enlightenment tradition: 'The single genuine power standing against the principle of Auschwitz is *autonomy*, if I might use the Kantian expression: the power of reflection, of self-determination, of not cooperating' (Adorno 2005: 195). In such a project, Adorno combined the power of critical rationality with psychoanalytic insights and Marxian-materialist ideology critique. In his still-untranslated 1962 lecture 'Combating Antisemitism Today', Adorno arrived at a remarkably Freudian conclusion: only 'militant Enlightenment' can break the 'spell' of antisemitic prejudice by bringing its unconscious mechanisms to the light of reason, reflection, and public debate (Adorno 1986: 382). Similarly, he said in a 1967 lecture that the propagandistic and ideological substance of antisemitic right-wing movements can only be counteracted with the 'penetrating power of reason, with the genuinely unideological truth' (Adorno 2020: 40). The myths on which projective antisemitism stands still today cannot be fought with further manipulation, but only with enlightenment and critical reflection that Adorno held ultimately required the radical transformation of late capitalist society.

Finally, antisemitism cannot be combatted independently of recognizing and addressing other forms of historical violence, discrimination, and persecution that form the 'hellish unity' Adorno identified between Auschwitz and other events in the 'permanent catastrophe' of modern society. The 'multidirectional' Adorno I have presented would support Michael Rothberg's call for 'differentiated solidarity' as the most fitting way to pursue an ethics and politics of non-identity for the contemporary world: 'In the face of complex implication' in various historical atrocities, 'a multidirectional politics of differentiated, long-distance solidarity has greater purchase than a politics premised on identification, purity, or the absolute separation between locations and histories' (2019: 203). The 'emancipated society' Adorno envisioned 'in which people could be different without fear' still requires 'the realization of universality in the reconciliation of differences' (1974: 103).

References

Adorno, T. W. (1973), *Negative Dialectics* (trans. E. B. Ashton), New York: Continuum.
Adorno, T. W. (1974), *Minima Moralia: Reflections from a Damaged Life* (trans. E. F. N. Jephcott), New York: Verso.
Adorno, T. W. (1983), *Prisms* (trans. S. Weber), Cambridge, MA: MIT Press.
Adorno, T. W. ([1962] 1986), 'Zur Bekämpfung des Antisemitismus Heute', in R. Tiedemann (ed.), *Vermischte Schriften I*, 360–83, Frankfurt am Main: Suhrkamp.
Adorno, T. W. (1991), 'Freudian Theory and the Pattern of Fascist Propaganda', in J. M. Bernstein (ed.), *The Culture Industry*, 132–57, London: Routledge.
Adorno, T. W. (2000), *Metaphysics: Concepts and Problems* (ed. R. Tiedemann, trans. E. Jephcott), Stanford, CA: Stanford University Press.
Adorno, T. W. (2002), *Aesthetic Theory* (trans. R. Hullot-Kentor), London: Continuum.
Adorno, T. W. (2005), *Critical Models: Interventions and Catchwords* (trans. H. W. Pickford), New York: Columbia University Press.
Adorno, T. W. (2006), *History and Freedom: Lectures 1964–1965* (trans. R. Livingstone), Cambridge: Polity.
Adorno, T. W. (2020), *Aspects of the New Right-Wing Extremism* (trans. W. Hoban), Cambridge: Polity.
Adorno, T. W., and W. Benjamin (1999), *The Complete Correspondence 1928–1940* (ed. H. Lonitz, trans. N. Walker), Cambridge: Polity.
Adorno, T. W., E. Frenkel-Brunswik, D. J. Levinson and R. N. Sanford ([1950] 2019), *The Authoritarian Personality*, New York: Verso.
Adorno, T. W., and M. Horkheimer (2002), *Dialectic of Enlightenment* (trans. E. Jephcott), Stanford, CA: Stanford University Press.
Adorno, T. W., and M. Horkheimer (2004), *Briefwechsel 1927–1969: Band II – 1938–1944*, Frankfurt am Main: Suhrkamp.
Agamben, G. (1998), *Remnants of Auschwitz: The Witness and the Archive* (trans. Daniel Heller-Roazen), Brooklyn, NY: Zone.
Allen, A. (2016), *The End of Progress: Decolonizing the Normative Foundations of Critical Theory*, New York: Columbia University Press.
Arendt, H. (1951), *The Origins of Totalitarianism*, New York: Schocken.

Aschheim, S. E. (2017), 'The *Dialectic of Enlightenment* Revisited', *Journal of Genocide Research*, 19 (3): 427–47.
Assmann, A. (2021), 'A Spectre Is Haunting Germany: The Mbembe Debate and the New Antisemitism', *Journal of Genocide Research*, 23 (3): 400–11.
Bauman, Z. (1998), 'Allosemitism: Premodern, Modern, Postmodern', in B. Cheyette and L. Marcus (eds), *Modernity, Culture, and 'the Jew'*, 143–56, Cambridge: Polity.
Bauman, Z. (2000), *Modernity and the Holocaust*, Cambridge: Polity.
Benhabib, S. (2018), *Exile, Statelessness, and Migration: Playing Chess with History from Hannah Arendt to Isaiah Berlin*, Princeton, NJ: Princeton University Press.
Bernstein, J. M. (2001), *Adorno: Disenchantment and Ethics*, Cambridge: Cambridge University Press.
Boehm, O. (2021), 'Die universalen Menschenrechte und die Fallen der Realpolitik', *Die Zeit*, 14 August, available at: www.zeit.de/2021/33/holocaust-erinnerung-israel-nahostkonflikt-antisemitismus-internationaler-strafgerichtshof (accessed 22 June 2023).
Braunstein, D. (2014), 'The Vigilant Jew as an Annoyance: How Hamid Dabashi Misreads Adorno', *TelosScope*, 27 August, available at: www.telospress.com/the-vigilant-jew-as-an-annoyance-how-hamid-dabashi-misreads-adorno (accessed 22 June 2023).
Braunstein, D. (2018), *Wahrheit und Katastrophe: Texte zu Adorno*, Bielefeld: Transcript Verlag.
Brown, W. (1993), 'Wounded Attachments', *Political Theory*, 21 (3): 390–410.
Butler, J. (2012), 'Can One Lead a Good Life in a Bad Life? Adorno Prize Lecture', *Radical Philosophy*, 176 (November/December): 9–18.
Catlin, J. (2017), 'Review of Jack Jacobs, *The Frankfurt School, Jewish Lives, and Antisemitism*', *Antisemitism Studies*, 1 (2): 415–23.
Catlin, J. (2020), 'The Frankfurt School on Antisemitism, Authoritarianism, and Right-Wing Radicalism', *European Journal of Cultural and Political Sociology*, 7 (2): 198–214.
Catlin, J. (2021), 'Wounds of Democracy: Theodor Adorno's Aspects of the New Right-Wing Extremism and the German Antisemitism Debate', *Radical Philosophy*, 2 (10): 11–20.
Catlin, J. (2022), 'A New German Historians' Debate? A Conversation with Sultan Doughan, Dirk Moses, and Michael Rothberg', *Journal of the History of Ideas*, 2 February. Part I: https://jhiblog.org/2022/02/02/a-new-german-historians-debate-a-conversation-with-sultan-doughan-a-dirk-moses-and-michael-rothberg-part-i; Part II: https://jhiblog.org/2022/02/04/a-new-german-historians-debate-a-conversation-with-sultan-doughan-a-dirk-moses-and-michael-rothberg-part-ii/ (accessed 22 June 2023).
Claussen, D. (2008), *Theodor Adorno: One Last Genius*, Cambridge, MA: Harvard University Press.
Conrad, S. (2021), 'Erinnerung im Globalen Zeitalter: Warum die Vergangenheitsdebatte Gerade Explodiert', *Merkur*, 75 (867): 5–17.
Dabashi, H. (2014), 'Gaza: Poetry after Auschwitz', *Al Jazeera*, 8 August, available at: www.aljazeera.com/opinions/2014/8/8/gaza-poetry-after-auschwitz/ (accessed 22 June 2023).
Diner, D. (1988), *Zivilisationsbruch: Denken nach Auschwitz*, Frankfurt am Main: Fischer Verlag.
Diner, D. (2000), *Beyond the Conceivable: Studies on Germany, Nazism, and the Holocaust*, Berkeley: University of California Press.

Doughan, S., and H. Toukan (2022), 'How Germany's Memory Culture Censors Palestinians', *Jacobin*, 16 July. https://jacobin.com/2022/07/germany-israel-palestine-antisemitism-art-documenta (accessed 22 June 2023).

Engel, D. (2009), 'Away from a Definition of Antisemitism: An Essay in the Semantics of Historical Description', in J. Cohen and M. Rosman (eds), *Rethinking European Jewish History*, 30–53, Liverpool: Liverpool University Press.

Erichsen, C. W., and D. Olusoga (2010), *The Kaiser's Holocaust. Germany's Forgotten Genocide and the Colonial Roots of Nazism*, London: Faber and Faber.

Friedlander, H. (1995), *The Origins of Nazi Genocide: From Euthanasia to the Final Solution*, Chapel Hill: University of North Carolina Press.

Friedländer, S. (1989), 'From Anti-Semitism to Extermination: A Historiographical Study of Nazi Policies toward the Jews and an Essay in Interpretation', in F. Furet (ed.), *Unanswered Questions: Nazi Germany and the Genocide of the Jews*, 3–31, New York: Schocken.

Friedländer, S. (1997), *Nazi Germany and the Jews, Volume 1: The Years of Persecution, 1933–1939*, New York: HarperCollins.

Führer, S. (2021), 'Philosophin Susan Neiman: "Ich bin der Typus kosmopolitische, jüdische Intellektuelle"', Deutschlandfunk Kultur, 25 May, available at: www.deutschlandfunkkultur.de/philosophin-susan-neiman-ich-bin-der-typus-kosmopolitische-100.html (accessed 22 June 2023).

Gordon, P. E. (2016), 'The Odd Couple', *The Nation*, 9 June, available at: www.thenation.com/article/archive/the-odd-couple (accessed 22 June 2023).

Gordon, P. E. (2020), 'Why Historical Analogy Matters', *New York Review of Books*, 7 January, available at: www.nybooks.com/online/2020/01/07/why-historical-analogy-matters (accessed 22 June 2023).

Habermas, J. (2021), 'Der neue Historikerstreit', *Philosophie Magazin*, 6: 10–11.

Hanebrink, P. (2018), *A Specter Haunting Europe: The Myth of Judeo-Bolshevism*, Cambridge, MA: Harvard University Press.

Hayes, P. (2003), 'Auschwitz, Capital of the Holocaust', *Holocaust and Genocide Studies*, 17 (2): 330–50.

Horkheimer, M. (1939), 'The Jews and Europe', *Studies in Philosophy and Social Science*, 8: 115–37.

Jacobs, J. (2014), *The Frankfurt School, Jewish Lives, and Antisemitism*, Cambridge: Cambridge University Press.

Jay, M. (1984), *Adorno*, Cambridge, MA: Harvard University Press.

Jay, M. (1986), 'The Jews and the Frankfurt School: Critical Theory's Analysis of Anti-Semitism', in *Permanent Exiles: Essays on the Intellectual Migration from Germany to America*, 90–100, New York: Columbia University Press.

Judaken, J. (2012), 'Blindness and Insight: The Conceptual Jew in Adorno and Arendt's Post-Holocaust Reflections on the Antisemitic Question', in L. Rensmann and S. Gandesha (eds), *Arendt and Adorno: Political and Philosophical Investigations*, 173–96, Stanford, CA: Stanford University Press.

Kay, A. J. (2021), *Empire of Destruction: A History of Nazi Mass Killing*, New Haven, CT: Yale University Press.

Kundnani, H. (2009), *Utopia or Auschwitz? Germany's 1968 Generation and the Holocaust*, New York: Columbia University Press.

Lapidot, E. (2020) *Jews Out of the Question: A Critique of Anti-Anti-Semitism*, Albany: State University of New York Press.

Lowenthal, L. (1946), 'The Crisis of the Individual: II. Terror's Atomization of Man', *Commentary*, January, available at: www.commentarymagazine.com/articles/the-crisis-of-the-individual-ii-terrors-atomization-of-man (accessed 22 June 2023).

Lower, W. (2005), *Nazi Empire-Building and the Holocaust in Ukraine*, Chapel Hill: University of North Carolina Press.

Magid, S. (2021), *Meir Kahane: The Public Life and Political Thought of an American Jewish Radical*, Princeton, NJ: Princeton University Press.

Mashiach, I. (2020), 'In Germany, a Witch Hunt Is Raging against Critics of Israel: Cultural Leaders Have Had Enough', *Haaretz*, 10 December, available at: www.haaretz.com/israel-news/2020-12-10/ty-article-magazine/.highlight/in-germany-a-witch-hunt-rages-against-israel-critics-many-have-had-enough/00000 17f-db0d-df0f-a17f-df4fa21b0000 (accessed 22 June 2023).

Mayer, A. (1988), *Why Did the Heavens Not Darken? The 'Final Solution' in History*, New York: Pantheon.

Meinecke, F. (1963), *The German Catastrophe: Reflections and Recollections* (trans. Sidney B. Fay), Boston: Beacon.

Moses, A. D. (2016), 'Anxieties in Holocaust and Genocide Studies', in C. Fogu, W. Kansteiner and T. Presner (eds), *Probing the Ethics of Holocaust Culture*, 332–54, Cambridge, MA: Harvard University Press.

Moses, A. D. (2021a), *The Problems of Genocide: Permanent Security and the Language of Transgression*, Cambridge: Cambridge University Press.

Moses, A. D. (2021b), 'The German Catechism', *Geschichte der Gegenwart*, 23 May, available at: https://geschichtedergegenwart.ch/the-german-catechism (accessed 22 June 2023).

Müller-Doohm, S. (2005), *Adorno: A Biography*, trans. Rodney Livingstone. Cambridge: Polity.

Neiman, S. (2013), 'History and Guilt', *Aeon*, 12 August, available at: https://aeon.co/essays/dare-we-compare-american-slavery-to-the-holocaust (accessed 22 June 2023).

Neiman, S. (2020), 'Hannah Arendt dürfte heute hier nicht sprechen', discussion with Jörg Biesler, *Deutschlandfunk*, 10 December, available at: www.deutschlandfunk.de/initiative-gg-5-3-weltoffenheit-neiman-hannah-arendt-100.html (accessed 22 June 2023).

Neumann, F., H. Marcuse and O. Kirchheimer (2013), *Secret Reports on Nazi Germany: The Frankfurt School Contribution to the War Effort* (ed. R. Laudani), Princeton, NJ: Princeton University Press.

Oberle, E. (2018), *Theodor Adorno and the Century of Negative Identity*, Stanford, CA: Stanford University Press.

Olick, J. K. (2005), *In the House of the Hangman: The Agonies of German Defeat, 1943–1949*, Chicago: University of Chicago Press.

Overy, R. (2022), *Blood and Ruins: The Last Imperial War, 1931–1945*, New York: Viking.

Özyürek, E. (2023), *Subcontractors of Guilt: Holocaust Memory and Muslim Belonging in Postwar Germany*, Stanford, CA: Stanford University Press.

Penslar, D. (2022), 'Who's Afraid of Defining Antisemitism?' *Antisemitism Studies*, 6 (1): 133–46.

Postone, M. (1980), 'Anti-Semitism and National Socialism: Notes on the German Reaction to "Holocaust"', *New German Critique*, 19, Special Issue on 'Germans and Jews' (Winter): 97–115.

Postone, M. (2003), 'The Holocaust and the Trajectory of the Twentieth Century', in M. Postone and E. Santner (eds), *Catastrophe and Meaning: The Holocaust and the Twentieth Century*, 81–114, Chicago: University of Chicago Press.

Rabinbach, A. (1997), *In the Shadow of Catastrophe: German Intellectuals between Apocalypse and Enlightenment*, Berkeley: University of California Press.

Rabinbach, A. (2000), 'Why Were the Jews Sacrificed? The Place of Anti-Semitism in Dialectic of Enlightenment', *New German Critique*, 81 (Autumn): 49–64.

Rabinbach, A. (2003), '"The Abyss That Opened Up before Us": Thinking about Auschwitz and Modernity', in E. Santner and M. Postone (eds), *Catastrophe and Meaning: The Holocaust and the Twentieth Century*, 51–66, Chicago: University of Chicago Press.

Rabinbach, A. (2015), 'In the Shadow of Catastrophe: An Interview with Anson Rabinbach'; 'Apocalyptic Thought in the Aftermath of the World Wars: An Interview with George Prochnik', *Cabinet*, 57 (Spring), available at: www.cabinetmagazine.org/issues/57/prochnik_rabinbach.php (accessed 22 June 2023).

Rensmann, L. (2017), *The Politics of Unreason: The Frankfurt School and the Origins of Modern Antisemitism*, Albany: State University of New York Press.

Rensmann, L., and S. Salzborn (2021), 'Modern Antisemitism as Fetishized Anti-Capitalism: Moishe Postone's Theory and Its Historical and Contemporary Relevance', *Antisemitism Studies*, 5 (1): 44–99.

Rothberg, M. (1997), 'After Adorno: Culture in the Wake of Catastrophe', *New German Critique*, 72: 48–81.

Rothberg, M. (2009), *Multidirectional Memory: Remembering the Holocaust in the Age of Decolonization*, Stanford, CA: Stanford University Press.

Rothberg, M. (2019), *The Implicated Subject: Beyond Victims and Perpetrators*, Stanford, CA: Stanford University Press.

Rothberg, M. (2020), 'Comparing Comparisons: From the "Historikerstreit" to the Mbembe Affair', *Rosa Luxemburg Stiftung*, 23 November, available at: www.rosalux.de/en/news/id/43395/comparing-comparisons-from-the-historikerstreit-to-the-mbembe-affair (accessed 22 June 2023).

Rothberg, M. (2022a), 'Learning and Unlearning with Taring Padi: Reflections on Documenta', *New Fascism Syllabus*, 2 July, available at: http://newfascismsyllabus.com/opinions/documenta/learning-and-unlearning-with-taring-padi-reflections-on-documenta (accessed 22 June 2023).

Rothberg, M. (2022b), 'Lived Multidirectionality: "Historikerstreit 2.0" and the Politics of Holocaust Memory', *Memory Studies*, 15 (6): 1316–29.

Said, E. W. (1996), *Representations of the Intellectual: The 1993 Reith Lectures*, New York: Random House.

Scholl, J. (2017), 'Deutsche Identität und Auschwitz: Das Schweigen der Intellektuellen', discussion with Peter Trawny, *Deutschlandfunk*, 27 January, available at: www.deutschlandfunkkultur.de/deutsche-identitaet-und-auschwitz-das-schweigen-der-100.html (accessed 22 June 2023).

Shavit, A. (2000), 'My Right of Return', interview with Edward Said, *Haaretz*, 18 August. https://lists.h-net.org/cgi-bin/logbrowse.pl?trx=vx&list=h-radhist&month=0008&week=e&msg=nY%2B/t%2BkE9pOqjTxZIFSnsw&user=&pw= (accessed 22 June 2023).

Skirke, C. (2020), 'After Auschwitz', in P. Gordon, E. Hammer and M. Pensky (eds), *A Companion to Adorno*, 567–82, Hoboken, NJ: Wiley Blackwell.

Snyder, T. (2010), *Bloodlands: Europe between Hitler and Stalin*, New York: Basic Books.

Staudenmaier, P. (2012), 'Hannah Arendt's Analysis of Antisemitism in *The Origins of Totalitarianism*: A Critical Appraisal', *Patterns of Prejudice*, 46 (2): 154–79.

Stone, D. (2021), 'Paranoia and the Perils of Misreading', *Centre for Analysis of the Radical Right*, 13 January, available at: www.radicalrightanalysis.com/2022/01/13/paranoia-and-the-perils-of-misreading (accessed 22 June 2023).
Tiedemann, R. (2003), 'Introduction: "Not the First Philosophy, but a Last One": Notes on Adorno's Thought', in Theodor W. Adorno, *Can One Live after Auschwitz? A Philosophical Reader* (ed. Rolf Tiedemann), xi–xxvii, Stanford, CA: Stanford University Press.
Traverso, E. (2017), *Left-Wing Melancholia: Marxism, History, and Memory*, New York: Columbia University Press.
Traverso, E. (2022), 'No, Post-Nazi Germany Isn't a Model of Atoning for the Past', *Jacobin*, 6 June, available at: https://jacobin.com/2022/06/post-nazi-germany-colonialism-holocaust-israel-atonement (accessed 22 June 2023).
Veidlinger, J. (2021), *In the Midst of Civilized Europe: The Pogroms of 1918–1921 and the Onset of the Holocaust*, New York: Metropolitan.
Volkov, S. (1978), 'Antisemitism as a Cultural Code: Reflections on the History and Historiography of Antisemitism in Imperial Germany', *Yearbook of the Leo Baeck Institute*, 23: 25–46.
Weheliye, A. G. (2014), *Habeas Viscus: Racializing Assemblages, Biopolitics, and Black Feminist Theories of the Human*, Durham, NC: Duke University Press.
Whitman, J. (2017), *Hitler's American Model: The United States and the Making of Nazi Race Law*, Princeton, NJ: Princeton University Press.
Wiggershaus, R. (1995), *The Frankfurt School: Its History, Theories, and Political Significance* (trans. M. Robertson), Cambridge, MA: MIT Press.
Zimmerer, J. (2011), *Von Windhuk nach Auschwitz? Beiträge zum Verhältnis von Kolonialismus und Holocaust*, Münster: LIT Verlag.
Zimmerer, J. (2022), 'Humboldt-Forum und Documenta: Wir sollten aufhören mit zweierlei Maß zu messen', *Berliner Zeitung*, 3 August. www.berliner-zeitung.de/kultur-vergnuegen/humboldt-forum-und-documenta-wir-sollten-aufhoeren-mit-zweierlei-mass-zu-messen-li.252352 (accessed 22 June 2023).
Zipperstein, S. J. (2018), *Pogrom: Kishinev and the Tilt of History*, New York: Liveright.

10

Antisemitism, centre-periphery dynamics and anti-Zionism in Poland today

Anna Zawadzka, translated by Maja Jaros

In this chapter I intend to present what happens when contemporary Western activist and academic anti-Zionism falls on the fertile soil of a country which is, firstly, semi-peripheral and, secondly, burdened with a history of antisemitism that is as intense as it is specific. Its specificity entails three postwar waves of Jewish emigration caused by antisemitic violence, primarily to Israel. The first two happened in 1946–9 and 1956–60, respectively. The third of these waves was triggered by what in Poland is generally referred to as 'March'. The repression of student youth protesting against censorship intensified in March 1968, but the antisemitic campaign with which the state authorities cracked down on opposition within the party and on the streets lingered on for much longer. It was unleashed under the banner of 'anti-Zionism'. I will first briefly outline the events of that period, since knowledge of them is essential to understanding the meanings with which the term 'Zionism' is imbued in Poland. Next I will outline the contemporary politics of remembrance of 'March' and, more broadly, the stakes of Polish historical politics, which are related to the collective manifestations of Poles' attitudes towards Jews. These three phenomena – March 1968, the management of its memory and contemporary historical politics reproducing antisemitic clichés – form, so I would like to suggest, the first context against which the functioning of anti-Zionism in Poland today should be considered.

The second, no less important, context is the semi-peripheral status of the former communist bloc countries in relation to the West. At the same time it should be remembered that the term 'West' here refers as much to the real cultural and economic dominance of so-called old Europe and the United States as it does to a phantasm. This phantasm is cultivated on the substrate of centuries-old stereotypes of the East as a region of savagery, barbarism, the opposite of Europeanness and anti-civilization, whose embodiment was to be first mythical Asia and then the Soviet Union (Zecker 2011; Hanebrink 2018: 122–62). Internalized, these stereotypes generate powerful neurotic dispositions in countries like Poland, and with them a compulsive need to prove that one is not Eastern. This compulsion also affects local progressive circles: activists, academics and leftist politicians. Among other things, it manifests itself in the unreflective assimilation of identities, as well as descriptive and critical categories incoming from the West, without taking into account the local contexts that redefine their connotations. I will try to demonstrate that this is what happens with anti-Zionism. I argue that the uncritical adoption of the anti-Zionist agenda of the contemporary Western left by Polish progressive circles has made the latter take an active part in reinforcing the nationalist status quo, contrary to their declarations (and probably their intentions).

History

'March' is usually regarded as a single event in Poland. However, it was the culmination of a long-term process. The events of 1967–8 could not have happened if it had not been for the antisemitic categories of perception and patterns of thinking ingrained in Polish culture and reproduced in its canon. In the political practice of the time, 'March' began in earnest in October. The term 'October' (as well as the term 'Thaw') is used in Polish historiography to describe the ending of Stalinism in 1956 which was to bring a loosening of the grip that the communist regime had over Polish society.[1] This period is remembered as a breath of freedom, and was greeted with enthusiasm and hope. However, to Jews, and to all those who had long ceased to self-identify as Jews, but were stigmatized as 'Jews' by the Polish majority, October brought fear (Machcewicz 1993, 1996; Węgrzyn 2016; Szajda 2018). This period is sometimes referred to as the 'dry pogrom' – 'dry' because allegedly without bloodshed, although Jewish testimonies clearly contradict this.[2] The fear felt by Jews at the time was accompanied by the painful eclipse of the hope for a Poland without top-down acquiescence to antisemitism.

October marked the beginning of the so-called Polish road to socialism. This was the term used by Władysław Gomułka, the new First Secretary of the Polish United Workers' Party, to define its course. The period of 1948–53 was a time of stabilizing the achievements of the communist revolution and consolidating the regime's still very weakly legitimized power. Today, as deeply demonized as it is still poorly researched, this period was nevertheless far from the terror of, for example, Thermidor (Fidelis 2010; Kozłowski 2019; Chmielewska and Wołowiec 2021). During October, the stereotype of 'Jewish Bolshevism' (Pol.: *żydokomuna*) was used to attribute responsibility for the events of this period, recently officially discredited by Khrushchev's paper,[3] to the Jews

---

[1] On 21 October 1956, a new First Secretary of the Central Committee of the Polish United Workers' Party was appointed. During the period of state socialism, this function corresponded to the contemporary rank of prime minister.

[2] I refer here to materials currently being collected during research conducted as part of the project 'Jewish Community in Poland in the Aftermath of the 1967–1968 Antisemitic Campaign. Biographical Experiences, Identity Transformations and Environmental Dynamics' (2020/39/D/HS3/02028). The biographical interviews we are conducting as part of the project provide numerous examples of antisemitic violence, up to and including physical violence, directed primarily against individuals from communist families during the post-October thaw.

[3] On 25 February 1956, three years after Stalin's death, at the Twentieth Congress of the Communist Party of the Soviet Union, its First Secretary Nikita Khrushchev delivered a speech in which he denounced the previous personality cult as incompatible with Leninist doctrine and exposed many of the crimes of Joseph Stalin's rule, primarily those related to purges within the party. The paper is considered the symbolic end of Stalinism in the Soviet Union and, more broadly, the

(Smolar 1986; Friszke 2004; Starnawski 2016; Węgrzyn 2016). This, in fact, was the message behind the slogan about the 'Polish road to socialism': Polish, that is, not Soviet, but also not Jewish. All the bad things are not on us, they're on them – this message, repeated over and over again, translated into an upsurge of violence against Jews and caused another wave of emigration of Holocaust survivors. Some 30,000 Jews left Poland at the time.

Equal rights for national minorities, including the Jewish minority, were introduced for the first time in Poland's history by the Polish People's Republic directly after the war (Aleksiun 2002; Grabski and Berendt 2003; Berendt 2009; Cała 2014; Datner 2016), starting from the Manifesto of the Polish Committee of National Liberation, allied with the Red Army, proclaimed on 22 July 1944, and the so-called Small Constitution of 22 February 1947. For the first time ever, Jews were able to hold state positions, enjoy public education and health care on an equal footing with others, and benefit from subsidies for Jewish culture: the Jewish press, theatre, associations, social, sports and aid organizations, including those of Zionist or religious backgrounds, or those connected to the Yiddish-speaking culture. The onset of communism in Poland also marked the first official recognition by the state of antisemitism as a problem and of antisemitic violence as a crime. Finally, the years 1945–8 saw one of the most inquisitive discussions of Polish antisemitism. It took place on the pages of the magazines *Kuźnica* and *Odrodzenie*, in which primarily communist intellectuals published (Chmielewska 2019; Datner 2021). The multifaceted participation of Poles in the Holocaust, the pogroms of 1945–6, the murders of Jewish survivors returning to their villages, the antisemitically motivated 'verdicts' of the postwar anti-communist partisans – all this revealed the scale of the phenomenon. Antisemitism was finally recognized as a fundamental problem, and attempts were made to diagnose its causes.

However, this discussion did not translate into state policy (Tych 1999). As in other countries of the region, antisemitism was somehow erased from the official vocabulary by encoding its history and its effects under the term 'fascism' (Bohus, Hallama and Stach 2022). In the name of fighting the distinction between Poles and Jews, which was said to be full of sinister meanings but was diagnosed as *racist* rather than *antisemitic*, everyone was posthumously subsumed to the category of Polishness (Zawadzka 2019). No distinction was acknowledged between Jewish and non-Jewish Poles. This kind of universalist anti-racism sacrificed a crucial aspect of the historical truth: the reality of this division determined first, in the interwar period, the violence experienced by Jews, and then extermination. During the war, Jews perished because they were Jews, not Poles. They also perished because non-Jewish Poles did not treat them as 'their own'. These facts, and with them individual and collective Jewish experiences and testimonies, were symbolically invalidated under falsely universalizing slogans about '6 million Polish victims' and the 'biological destruction of the Polish nation'. After 'October', this discourse was gradually intensified, promoting slogans about a fictitious

beginning of a new, post-Stalin era throughout the Eastern Bloc. Although it was classified, its secrecy was not guarded, and it quickly made its way into public opinion on both sides of the Iron Curtain.

Polish-Jewish 'brotherhood of arms', and over time promoting an equally fictitious image of Poles saving Jews en masse and with sacrifices (Datner, Keff and Janicka 2014; Żukowski 2013). From the 1940s to the 1960s, the communist idea of internationalism was gradually replaced in Poland by a national mythology, one of the pillars of which was to hide Polish participation in the Holocaust. A look at the contemporary politics of history, which have exploded in size (and budgets) makes clear that to a large extent the whole game has been about just that.

The second half of the 1960s is marked by three parallel processes. The first is the growing conflict within the Communist Party between the nationalist faction and the old-school communists, who had grown up on the communist ethos of the International and came from the pre-war structures of illegal activity. The second is the growing mood of rebellion among the intelligentsia, in particular the metropolitan student youth, against the restrictions imposed by the state, mainly in the cultural sphere: censorship of the press and arts performances. This rebellion was partly supported by the old party members, increasingly concerned about the 'Polish road to socialism', most of whom lost their party memberships in 1968. The third is the escalating anti-Israel campaign unleashed by the Soviet Union and countries in its orbit of influence. Only the synergy of the contexts and processes outlined briefly here made possible what is known in Poland as 'March'.

In June 1967, in response to the Six-Day War, following the example of the USSR, the Polish government broke off diplomatic relations with Israel and intensified its anti-Zionist propaganda campaign (Szaynok 2007: 394–444; Starnawski 2016: 316–19). At the same time, it launched obnoxiously antisemitic initiatives. Individuals categorized, for example, on the basis of the sound of their surname as Jews are removed from the army (Stola 2000: 69–78). (It is important to keep in mind that this is the working of a stigma, not of someone's voluntarily adopted and deliberately cultivated identity.) Editors of Jewish magazines, creators of Jewish culture, directors of Jewish institutions are forced to make public statements against Israel (Leszczyński 1996; H. Grynberg 2018; M. Grynberg 2018; Szajda 2018; Markusz 2020). Those who refuse to comply lose their jobs. The Polish press escalated the atmosphere of suspicion against 'people of Jewish descent', purporting that they may be 'disloyal' to the Polish state and secretly rooting for Israel (Głowiński 1991, 2009: 93; Osęka 1999). In response to the student protests, the government harnessed the already escalating antisemitic propaganda to tame the internal enemy. Not wanting to use overtly antisemitic vocabulary, because the country is, after all, officially against racism, politicians and journalists call them not Jews, but Zionists. Based on old antisemitic clichés, a pogrom atmosphere is being stoked, and the tool to do it in white gloves is anti-Zionism (Głowiński 2009: 25).

Stigmatized as 'false Poles', people mostly coming from fully assimilated, secular Jewish communist homes are summoned for interrogation, lose their job and experience harassment from police, security offices and neighbours (Mieszczanek 1989; Wiszniewicz 2008). The younger ones, born after the war, often don't even know they have Jewish origins until they hear antisemitic gossip or insults against them (Melchior 1990; Wiszniewicz 2008). In the Holocaust survivors, the worst memories are revived (Starnawski 2016; M. Grynberg 2018). They are more and more tightly encircled by the government's antisemitic propaganda indiscriminately broadcast by radio, television and the press. They see more and more clearly the emptiness around them, they lose their acquaintances, they look in vain for gestures of solidarity. They become *personae non gratae* in the circles in which they were previously active, because associating with them carries the risk of unpleasant consequences. The authorities strongly urge 'disloyal citizens' to leave the country by renouncing their Polish citizenship. The persecuted hear that they should leave for their own good, because there is no future for them in Poland.

Remembrance

The currently dominant politics of remembrance of March 1968 run along a three-pronged course. On the one hand, the events of the time are presented and commemorated as the heroic struggle of the democratic opposition against the 'totalitarian' regime's power. (The concept of 'totalitarianism' is applied in Poland to every aspect and every period of state socialism.). In this view, antisemitism is downplayed, presented as a marginal theme, just one more of the many nasty tools 'the communists' used against 'the democrats'. It is overshadowed by an anti-communist narrative whereby the victims of the antisemitic campaign are either relegated to the background or described as having been exiled because they fought against communism, not because they were stigmatized as Jews.

On the other hand, 'March' is the only aspect of Poland's multifaceted and rich history of state and grassroots antisemitism (including the university 'ghetto benches',[4] *numerus clausus*, pogroms and mass murders) that is readily discussed. No antisemitic 'episode' in Polish history has been treated in such an abundance of literature, especially from historians, and none has been as unequivocally diagnosed as antisemitic. This is because 'March' dovetails with contemporary history politics that are entirely built on anti-communism, and therefore fits seamlessly into the dogmatic assumptions of contemporary political discourse. By way of discussing 'March', one proves in Poland that one is not blind to antisemitism, that one is able to recognize this phenomenon, and that if there ever was any antisemitism here at all, it was the domain of the communists. Used in this way, and supplemented by the stereotype of 'Jewish Bolshevism' (Pol.: *żydokomuna*), 'March' turns out to be a factional struggle of the new communists against the old ones (i.e. Jews).

And this is the popular third narrative: reducing the antisemitic campaign to a feud within the party; an internal matter that the 'average Pole' had nothing to do with. At stake here is the innocence of the latter. But not only that. This type of remembrance of 'March' also avoids confronting an inconvenient fact: the lack of a thoughtful, coherent

---

[4] In the 1930s, ghetto benches (*getto ławkowe*) were introduced at many Polish universities by decision of their rectors, including the University of Warsaw, the University of Poznań and the University of Vilnius. Special benches for Jews were designated in lecture halls. Jewish students were not allowed to sit on other benches. The ghetto benches were lobbied for by nationalist political groups and their affiliated student associations. They were the ones who later policed its observance, bringing militias into lecture halls to terrorize Jewish students (Rudnicki 2008: 135–54; Krzywicki 2009: 9–122; Ogonowski 2012: 130–31).

or even partial, but solidarity-based response from the anti-communist opposition of the time to antisemitism which, after all, also affected their fellow students. The opposition did not treat the issue of antisemitism as a priority, but marginally, as an 'add-on' to the main issue: censorship. More: it removed from the committees representing the opposition people who could be perceived as Jews (e.g. due to their surnames), explaining that it was better not to give the authorities the opportunity to argue that the rebels were in fact 'Zionists'. In this way, a kind of blackmailer consensus prevailed on both sides of the barricade.

The contemporary ways of writing about and remembering 'March' are all linked by an approach according to which antisemitism was only a means, one of many, to other ends: to purge old communists from decision-making positions within the party, to fight the opposition or to demonstrate support for Soviet policy in the Middle East. I reject such depictions because they make antisemitism appear as a side issue. This resonates with the tradition of Polish historiography, within which 'Jewish affairs' are treated separately, so to speak: in a way that is not integrated into the mainstream of historical events. In my opinion, the antisemitic purge was the culmination of the 'Polish road to socialism', made possible by the *longue durée* of the categories of perception according to which it is the Jews who spoil Poland and are responsible for everything wrong with it. The structure of Polish collective identity is reflected in 'March' as if through a lens: the distinction between Pole and Jew is an integral part of this identity, which has manifested itself many times, and sometimes escalated, in the course of Polish history. In 'March', Jews were not accidental victims, like bystanders who are killed by stray bullets, but once more functioned as the default projection screen on which Polish tensions played out.

The example of Hersz Smolar aptly demonstrates that anti-Zionism was a pretext for an antisemitic purge, and that this purge consisted neither of removing the enemies of communism, nor of removing the old communists, but was strictly nationalistic in nature. His story is a good example of the trajectory of Jewish biography in the context of Polish communism. It illustrates what 'March' essentially was about, seen from the perspective of the local history of communism.

Born in 1905, Hersz Smolar was involved in communist activity in the interwar period. At the time, he was sentenced to prison time on several occasions for it. During the war he organized escapes from the Minsk ghetto, making it possible for some 10,000 people to flee to the surrounding forests. He also organized communist resistance: first in the ghetto, then outside. He created a network of seven partisan units joined by 2,000 Jews (Smolar 2021: 86). Even then he knew how important testimony and description would be, so he meticulously collected information. His accounts of the uprising, struggle and extermination of the Minsk ghetto would prove to be the most reliable and detailed. After the war, Hersz Smolar did not plan to leave the country. On the contrary: he proceeded to rebuild and animate secular Yiddish Jewish life in Poland. He was completely devoted to this cause until he was forced to emigrate in 1971.

In February 1967, during a visit to Israel, speaking to the editors of the Israeli communist newspaper *Kol-Haam*, the organ of the revisionist MAKI party (formed after the split of the Communist Party of Israel into two factions), Hersz Smolar expressed full support for the idea of 'absolute national and civic enfranchisement of

Arabs living in Israel' (Smolar 1967: 135–6). Referring to the escalation of tensions in the Middle East, he condemned what he saw as Western Europe's pro-Israeli foreign policy as imperialist. At the end of the meeting, Smolar said: 'Our sensitized hearts recoil with alarm when we hear that there is unrest at your borders, that here and there an enemy mine has taken Jewish lives. Is the cup of blood shed by our people not full yet?' Thereupon he wished his comrades peace with their Arab neighbours.

The final part of the speech caused an uproar in the ranks of the Rakah – the pro-Soviet faction of Israel's Communist Party – and subsequently in Poland. This one sentence about Jewish bloodshed led to Smolar being accused of favouring imperialism, colonialism and Israeli nationalism (Leszczyński 1996). It was deemed that by empathizing with the Jewish victims, Smolar expressed his support for Israeli politics. Later that year, in a rising tide of antisemitic purges, Hersz Smolar lost his job at the Jewish Social and Cultural Society, of which he was chairman, and his position as editor-in-chief of the most important Yiddish magazine in postwar Poland, *Fołks Sztyme*. He was forced into early retirement. Both of his sons, Aleksander and Eugeniusz, were imprisoned for their student opposition activities. Hersz then wrote a letter to the party's First Secretary, saying that if his emigration would save his sons' lives, he would leave (Smolar 2021: 149). He applied for a passport and was refused. In 1971, when both his sons were free, during a business trip to Paris, he fled to Israel with the help of a Jewish agency. There he remained a communist dedicated to saving Yiddish culture. He died in 1995 in Tel Aviv.

As a result of the 1967–8 campaign, some 15,000 people of Jewish background emigrated from Poland (Starnawski 2016: 160–1). Most of them with the status of stateless refugees, because in exchange for a travel document, offices deprived them of Polish citizenship before they left. A few thousand Jews, who for various reasons, such as family, could not or chose not to emigrate, remained in the country (Cała and Datner-Śpiewak 1999: 176). Most of them hid even deeper in the closet.

Politics

In Poland, antisemitism and how it is problematized, diagnosed and countered, which one might have expected are exact opposites, can be found in paradoxical harmony. As an example of the difficulties connected with the latter, I would like to point to a study of 'attitudes of Poles toward Jews' produced by the Center for Research on Prejudice that was presented as the most recent data on antisemitism in Poland in an event in November 2021.[5] The presentation showed that the centre has been using the same research tool for many years, dividing antisemitism into exactly, and only,

---

[5] The event was the inauguration of the programme 'Antisemitism in Poland: Definition, Monitoring, Effective Counteraction', initiated by Stowarzyszenie Otwarta Rzeczpospolita (Open Republic Association) (Wiszniewski 2021). The Center for Research on Prejudice is part of the Department of Psychology at the University of Warsaw. The centre's team has been conducting research since 2007. Relying on quantitative research, as well as cooperating with NGOs and the media, it has become a leading centre for antisemitism research in Poland. The CBU website is available in English at: http://cbu.psychologia.pl/en/.

three categories, 'traditional', 'conspiracy' and 'secondary' antisemitism. 'Traditional antisemitism' here refers to superstitions derived from Christianity (Jews killed God, Jews need Christian blood for their rituals, etc.), 'conspiracy antisemitism' is the belief that Jews, both behind the scenes and in an organized manner, seek to dominate politics and the economy, while 'secondary antisemitism' defines the attitude of those who believe that Jews feel too much self-pity and benefit from their martyrdom which they skilfully 'sell' to the world (Bulska and Winiewski 2017). Survey questions are formulated according to the research hypothesis implied in these categories and then asked to a representative sample of Poles. I argue that this dogmatic and rigid categorization is not appropriate to the ways antisemitism has evolved in the contemporary situation. Besides, it is also worth noting that the coding of the answers seems dubious: answering 'hard to say' to the questions 'do Jews seek to expand their influence on the world economy?', 'do Jews seek to rule the world?', 'do Jews often act behind the scenes, secretly?' is classified by the Center for the Study of Prejudice as *neutral*, and is therefore not counted in the statistics as antisemitic. Only the answer 'yes' was considered antisemitic. The supposedly 'neutral' answers amount to at least as many as the negative answers: 20 to 30 per cent. This is as if answering 'it's hard to say' to the question 'does being gay mean being a paedophile?' qualified as 'neutral'.

My main objection to surveys of this kind is that they still focus on *who* (is antisemitic) while they define the realm of *what* (is antisemitic) according to outdated categories. In Poland today, antisemitism is primarily the domain of history politics, namely the appropriation of the Holocaust to describe the experience of a generic, undifferentiated category of 'Poles'. In this context, antisemitism is closely coupled with anti-communism. It is upon these two that the Polish collective identity is built: they are the victims of communism unjustly overshadowed by the Jewish victims of Nazism; the heroes who liberated the world from communist evil; the victims of unfair accusations of antisemitic crimes when they 'just' saved the world from the (Jewish) communists; the heroes who once selflessly rescued Jews and then were 'betrayed' by them.[6] The relativization of the Holocaust by equating Nazism and communism (Kovács, Glöckner and Schoeps 2011; Shafir 2002; Subotić 2019: 30–41); the narrative of 'Jewish Bolshevism' legitimized by many historians; the effective promotion of the concept of the *double genocide* within the European Union (Katz 2017); the judicial threats against researchers of Polish participation in the Holocaust[7]; anti-refugee

---

[6] This conviction stems, again, from the stereotype of 'Jewish Bolshevism', extremely elaborate in Poland, according to which Jews working in the communist security apparatus treated interrogators with particular cruelty.

[7] In 2018, Polish President Andrzej Duda signed into law a bill providing for a fine or imprisonment for speaking publicly about Poles' participation in the Holocaust. This is an amendment to the Act on the Institute of National Remembrance, passed on 26 January 2018. On 27 June 2018, the parliament canceled this amendment, presumably under pressure from the US government (RMF FM 2018; Sommer, Sławiński and Zubel 2018; 'Uchwalili po dwóch latach. Skasowali w dwie godziny' 2020). In February 2021, the Holocaust Research Center at the Institute of Philosophy and Sociology of the Polish Academy of Sciences was attacked. The case concerned the book *Dalej jest Noc* (*It Is Night Still*), a detailed study of the course of the so-called third phase of the Holocaust – the period after the liquidation of the ghettos – in selected districts in occupied Poland (Engelking and Grabowski 2018). The book's editors, Barbara Engelking and Jan Grabowski, were sued by an individual. The court ruled that the plaintiff had been slandered not as a private individual but as a Polish

paranoia fuelled by reminders of Poland's former 'Jewish infestation'; dilapidated Jewish cultural sites for the restoration of which neither the state nor local governments are offering funds: these are the contexts where antisemitism is most intense today, and its temperature continues to rise. To grasp the scale of Polish antisemitism, therefore, we need new tools and new research questions to diagnose and analyse it. One does not have to believe that Jews rule the world or kidnap children for matzah in order to be deeply stuck in and reproduce an antisemitic culture. If we recognize that the culture that has shaped us is saturated with antisemitic patterns, and that the identity we have been raised in is based on antisemitic patterns of distinguishing between Pole and Jew, Polishness and non-Polishness, etc., it will be easier to see antisemitism in its current manifestations.

Anti-Zionism

In the Polish context, we deal with a multifaceted social situation consisting of: (1) an unprecedented local history of antisemitic purges carried out under the guise of anti-Zionism, as a result of which thousands of people had to flee and found refuge in Israel, among other places, (2) the instrumentalization of this history by contemporary history politics, whose *modus operandi* is anti-communism, (3) the failure to recognize this politics as a key antisemitic agent in contemporary Polish realities. We need to keep all this in mind when we try to understand what happens when we add a fourth element to this tangle: contemporary, anti-Israel anti-Zionism.

Anti-Zionism is not yet, as it is in Western Europe and North America, a prominent feature in the academic world, although I suspect it will become one in the next five to ten years. It is already, though, in the world of left-wing activism and left-wing political parties. Poland's location on the semi-periphery of the world system, combined with a centuries-old 'Easternness' hang-up, results in unreflective imitation of Western trends. As far as the radical left is concerned, the latter come primarily from Berlin – a place close enough to build social and political contacts with, and yet part of the mythical West. In Berlin, anti-Zionism has dominated the radical left to such an extent that BDS followers seek to paralyse activities (including those that have nothing to do with Israel) that are not legitimized by expressions of 'solidarity with Palestine', and are sometimes surprisingly effective in doing so.[8] The peripherality neurosis causes Polish

---

woman. When giving the reasoning for the judgement, the judge said, among other things: 'It must be accepted that publishing content attributing to Poles the crimes of the holocaust perpetrated by the Third Reich can be considered hurtful and detrimental to a sense of national identity and pride.' The court ruled that the editors of the volume must apologize to the plaintiff (Leszczyński 2021). Lithuanian journalist and writer Rūta Vanagaite faced similar reprisals after publishing, with Efraim Zuroff, the book *Our People: Discovering Lithuania's Hidden Holocaust* about Lithuanian participation in the Holocaust (Vanagaite and Zuroff 2020).

[8] An example is the Radical Queer March initiative. The annual alternative to the mainstream Pride march eventually disappeared from the German capital as it had come under increasingly fierce attacks from pro-Palestinian organizations year after year. An attempt to renew the initiative in 2019 ended in failure, for the same reason. The march was dominated by a group of anti-Zionist activists

left-wing activists to follow Hamas statements with bated breath because they feel that is what they do in the great metropolis of Berlin while knowing little or nothing about antisemitism – a case of the standard individual and group reproduction of culture assimilated in the process of unreflective socialization.

In fact, they do not want to discuss antisemitism because in their circles, dealing with antisemitism has become a sign of belonging to a political camp that is hostile to them, a sign of conservatism and being right wing (Schraub 2019: 395–6, 407; Stögner 2019, 2020). The burning of a Jewish puppet (MLZ 2020), the 'hanging of Judas' (TOKFM 2019), the 'March for Life of Poles' organized on the grounds of the Auschwitz-Birkenau camp (Walczak 2019), the chanting of 'death to Jews' by a crowd gathered in a city square (Walczak and Jaros 2021), or excrements on the fence of a Jewish cemetery (BAK 2021) elicit at best a shrug from the Polish left. In the reckoning of wrongs motivated by racism, chauvinism, nationalism and xenophobia, wrongs inflicted on Jews don't count (Baddiel 2021). Antisemitism has almost disappeared from the radar of those who monitor these wrongs, and this disappearance is another manifestation of antisemitism. The same left is outraged time and again by the 'spontaneous racist violence of Israel's Jewish population' (Pietrzak 2015) and the 'apartheid of the colonial-settler state of Israel against the Palestinian people' (Codziennik Feministyczny 2021).[9] The Polish public sphere provides ample evidence that antisemitism here is still an unmatched model of racist theory and practice. Meanwhile, organizations focused on countering various forms of racist violence downplay this or ignore it completely.

Three examples from 2021

In May 2021, the left (OKO.press 2021a) and the extreme right ('Nacjonaliści przeciwko żydowskiemu ludobójstwu, Narodowe Odrodzenie Polski (NOP) – Nacjonalistyczna Opozycja' 2021) protested outside the Israeli embassy in turns. One banner of the left-wing protesters, joined by members of the Polish parliament from the Razem (Together) left-wing party, read: 'STOP THE HOLOCAUST OF THE PALESTINIANS'. The far-right demonstration was adorned with a banner reading 'REAL PALESTINE HOLOCAUST. STOP JEWISH CRIMES'.

Also speaking in defence of the Palestinians were participants in a nationalist demonstration in Jedwabne, which took place on 10 July 2021, the eightieth anniversary of the murder of Jedwabne Jews by their Polish neighbours (OKO.press

---

who, contrary to the organizers' guidelines, showed up at the march with large symbols of the BDS movement and anti-Israel banners (Richter-Montpetit 2019). See discussion at: www.facebook.com/events/2356989967878298/?active_tab=discussion.

[9] When in 2016 – in response to a dramatic intervention by Polish queer activists against alleged Israeli 'pink-washing' – I wrote an article about how anti-Zionism in Poland should be approached with more caution, I received an immediate response entitled with a rhetorical sarcastic question: 'Did Palestinians help Poles murder Jews in Jedwabne?' (Qandil 2016). 'Oh, so I'm supposed to explain to my Palestinian friend, who is afraid that her children returning from school will be killed by Israeli soldiers, that it's ok because they don't like Jews in Poland?', an anarchist trade union activist sarcastically wrote on Facebook.

2021b).¹⁰ 'And what are you doing now, organizing a Palestinian Holocaust?', one of the demonstrators addressed the imaginary Jews. The main slogan of the demonstrators – 'I don't apologize for Jedwabne'¹¹ – was complemented by a banner referring to the stereotype of 'Jewish Bolshevism', 'Jews, apologize for the crimes of your fellow Jews'. It displayed, among other things, pictures of state functionaries from the communist period. Participants in the event carried Palestinian flags and keffiyehs, in Poland called 'arafatki'.

In June 2021, the Polish parliament passed a law according to which outstanding restitution claims that have not been resolved in the past thirty years will be halted or dismissed. New appeals against administrative decisions issued more than thirty years ago will also be prevented (Aderet 2021; *Report of the Extraordinary Committee for Amendments to Codifications on the Committee Draft Law on Amendments to the Law – Code of Administrative Procedure* 2021). On the face of it, the law is supposed to curb reprivatization abuses. It is primarily concerned with tenements that were nationalized under a Stalinist-era law. Today, on the basis of questionable credibility of the evidence, alleged heirs of the former owners make claims to them. Often, these are individuals put forward by development companies (Ślązak 2014; PAP 2017; Śpiewak 2017; Prokuratura Krajowa 2021). After taking over the tenements, the developers double the rents overnight or throw the existing tenants out on the street. The law also means, though, that Jews will not be able to claim back property seized from them by Poles during the Holocaust. The chances of recovering such property were already limited anyway. The Polish lawmaker could have inserted a proviso into the wording of the law to the effect that it did not apply to Holocaust-related cases. However, this was not done: no one even made such a proposal. Out of 460 deputies sitting in the Polish parliament, 309 voted in favour, including almost all of the extreme right, all of the ruling party and all of the left ('Vote No. 73 at the 33rd session of the Sejm – Sejm of the Republic of Poland' 2021). One hundred and twenty deputies, mostly conservative liberals, abstained from the vote, not because of the antisemitic nature of the bill, but because of doubts about respecting the property laws, sacred in their eyes.

---

[10] On 10 July 1941, under occupation conditions, but on their own initiative, Polish residents of Jedwabne, in the north-east of Poland, murdered Jews living in this and surrounding villages. They herded the victims into a barn, bolted the door and set the building on fire. This murder was described in the book *Sąsiedzi* (*Neighbours*) by Jan Tomasz Gross (2000). The Polish edition of this book sparked a wave of outrage, but it also began a new phase in Polish Holocaust research, taking into account the participation of local communities more broadly. Over time, Jedwabne became a symbol of the nationwide dispute over Polish attitudes towards Jews during the war. It is worth mentioning at this point that, based on the testimony of witnesses and survivors, murders and pogroms of this kind – including the one in Jedwabne – were described in detail by researchers of the Central Jewish Historical Commission in Poland immediately after the war. Their publications, however, never made their way into Polish public opinion. They were downplayed as internal affairs of the Jewish community and marginalized as biased. They were not translated from Yiddish into Polish.

[11] This popular slogan among nationalists refers to the fact that after the publication of the book *Neighbors*, a ceremony was held in Jedwabne to commemorate the victims of the crime, during which then President Aleksander Kwaśniewski, on behalf of the Poles, apologized to the Jewish community.

That the June 2021 law is antisemitic was revealed by a triumphant gesture by Młodzież Wszechpolska (All-Polish Youth), shown four days after the law was passed, when voices of outrage still resonated in Israel, and even more so their echoes that had reached Poland. Members of this far-right organization with pre-war fascist traditions dumped a tonne of rubble in front of the Israeli embassy in Warsaw and stuck a banner on it: 'Here is your property'. They posted a photo of this installation on Twitter, with the following comment:

> To be clear: Jewish circles don't even deserve a brick. But let it be, let them know our mercy, we decided to throw a whole ton of rubble in front of the Israeli Embassy, after all, only rubble was practically left of our country after the war. Here is your property! (Młodzież Wszechpolska 2021)

The proverbial pile of rubble sent to the symbolic Jews found many fans. The gesture was later repeated in the form of memes and even artefacts ('The Polish Government Has Launched a Nationwide Collection of Jewish Property Lost during the Holocaust' 2019). The rubble and the bricks allude to Jewish property in multiple ways: it is not only a symbol of looted Jewish belongings, destroyed Jewish homes, Jewish apartments occupied by Poles, but also of what Jewish property was left in Poland after the Holocaust: almost nothing. The brick rubble symbolizes ruins, in Warsaw – the ruins of the Warsaw Ghetto, meaning mass murder, total destruction. I read the dumping of rubble in front of the Israeli embassy as an act of derision, a gratifying reminder that Poland is 'Judenfrei'.

Two paradoxes

These examples illustrate the two paradoxes in which the Polish left has become entangled: one nationalist, one imperialist. The nationalist paradox is that the left, taking for granted the anti-Zionist dogma of its Western counterparts according to which the problem of antisemitism today is an issue only raised by conservatives and right-wingers, in fact stands side by side with the Polish far right in protests against Zionism. Shaped by reading Judith Butler and Jasbir Puar rather than Mordechai Canin (Canin 2019) and Mirosław Tryczyk (Tryczyk 2015, 2020),[12] Polish activists have been imbibed with American academic discourse: Jews are white, and therefore Jews are privileged. Nevertheless, they are not alarmed by sharing political goals with

---

[12] Immediately after the war, Mordechai Canin, claiming to be an English-speaking journalist, toured Poland in the footsteps of the exterminated Jewish communities. Reports from this trip were published by the American Jewish magazine *Forwerts*. In 1952, Canin's texts were published in Israel in the form of a book titled *Through Ruins and Rubble. A Journey through One Hundred Exterminated Jewish Communities in Poland*. Canin's book saw a Polish publication in 2019. Mirosław Tryczyk is a researcher of the participation of Polish local communities in the extermination of Jews. He has set himself the goal of disseminating the findings to date on this subject. Both of his publications on the subject – *Miasta śmierci* (*Cities of Death*, 2015) and *Drzazga. Kłamstwa silniejsze niż śmierć* (*Sliver. Lies Stronger Than Death*, 2019) – are written in an accessible language of non-fiction. Tryczyk, as he himself emphasizes, abandoned scientific jargon in fauvor of promoting knowledge.

overt racists draped in Celtic crosses and demonstrating under slogans: 'Europe will be white or uninhabited' (Mikołajewska 2017). Furthermore, they fail to ask whether the American diagnosis fits Polish reality (irrespective of whether it is accurate in its own context). They fail to ask whether its application in Eastern Europe might not be yet another manifestation of the cultural imperialism of the United States, against which the same activists often protest, for example, when they slander the state of Israel. The left seems happy to accept some categories in spite of, or perhaps even because of their 'Americanness' but rejects others because of the same 'Americanness', as an imperialist dark force this time. This includes intellectual fashions such as the career of the term *intersectionality* which has been adopted without any real reflection on how intersectionality would reformulate Polish discourses on minorities if it were really implemented.

Polish progressive circles have accepted the category of 'intersectionality' with everything that comes with it, including the notion that Israel represents white imperial domination. They have adopted it to such an extent that a few years ago one of the annual feminist Wrocław demonstrations went under the slogan 'Our demonstration is intersectional', which sounded obscure to onlookers. Approaches to antisemitism within contemporary intersectionality studies often define it as a form of racism, while at the same time, contrary to the original intent of intersectionality, reduce racism to the Black–white distinction, which qualifies Jews as the latter. The alleged whiteness of Jews functions as an alibi: by attacking Israel we attack the hegemony of Judeo-Christianity[13] and the West (Schraub 2019: 401). This is flawed reasoning, however, because antisemitism does not follow the colour divides and, consequently, is also not straightforwardly translatable into categories of privilege or lack thereof. 'In regard of antisemitism as a phenomenon, we can say that we will fail to grasp its complexity if we see it *only* as a form of racism; but we will not understand it if we do not *also* recognize it as a form of racism', writes Karin Stögner (2020). Unlike a stigma that is unambiguously visible, like skin colour, in the case of Jews the decisive aspect of racialization is instability. Jews, depending on the times and the need of the dominant group, are at one point too many, at another point too few, then white, then coloured, once capitalist, once communist. Moreover, the very fact that Jews 'pass as white' is sometimes the most racist argument against them: they are dangerous because they can impersonate 'us' (Kaye/Kantorowitz 2007: 12; Burton 2018). Thus, for example, assimilation into Polishness and the perfect fulfilment of its conditions became another 'proof' of the specificity of Jews – as a group particularly adept at impersonating others. Mimicry was attributed to the Jews as their feature. A dangerous feature, because it shows the instability of categories such as whiteness, class, nationality – since they can simply be imitated (Levine-Rasky 2008: 58). As David Baddiel jokingly put it, 'Jews are invisible, working their terrible magic behind the global scenes, and they don't even have a visual mark. Unless, of course, you're one of those specific racists with the superpower to spot that underneath, Jews are lizards' (Baddiel 2021: 50).

---

[13] For more on the history of the concept of Judeo-Christianity, see Hanebrink (2018: 200–36).

In the history of Poland, Jews have been racialized many times, not only culturally, but also biologically. Jews were seen as physiologically and anatomically different from Poles, Christians, non-Jews, and from the physical difference all others were to follow. An example is the 'corpse affair': Between the two world wars, medical faculties in Poland demanded that Jewish students study only the corpses of Jews (Andersz and Aleksiun 2020). The idea was that Jews should not 'profane' Christian bodies with their touch. It was argued, among other things, that future Jewish doctors should know the peculiarities of Jewish bodies, after all, they would be treating Jews first and foremost. The study of this form of antisemitic thinking gradually disappeared, replaced by more sophisticated and more veiled forms of racism. However, I think that biological racism is still firmly rooted in Polish society. The categories of perception it provides – that one's body, anatomical structure, blood, shapes one's psyche, mind, behaviour, morality, belonging – have not only not been deconstructed, but have been further reinforced by the sociobiological discourse triumphant in the mainstream, including the liberal mainstream, of Polish culture from the late 1990s until just recently. The stakes of the domestic rendition of sociobiology were primarily the maintenance of systemic sexism and the homophobic *status quo*, not racism, but nevertheless the pattern of thinking – physiology determines the social and cultural, and social violence is only a manifestation of that determination, unnecessarily politicized and validated – remains the same.

In Poland, Jews were and still are sometimes perceived as non-white, where white equals Polish. 'Bad looks', 'a Pole will always recognize a Jew', the orientalization of Jewish beauty in the case of women, the pointing out of the 'dark-skinned', circumcision as a bodily sign of non-Polishness – these are, after all, from the classic repertoire of racial passing. The matter is further complicated by the fact that precisely because of the hidden nature of the Jewish stigma, *recognition* was made into a kind of national sport, subject to a whole range of racist rules ('by appearance', 'by name', 'by look', 'by accent', 'by the manner of walking', etc.). Before the war, this game was crowned with physical violence by fascist militias, during the war, trips to the Gestapo station. The non-whiteness of the Jews highlights the absence of other Others with visible stigmas such as skin colour or eye shape. Thus, it is not my goal to abandon the category of race as overly American in Polish conditions. On the contrary: it can be helpful in diagnosing contemporary antisemitism. For this to happen, however, it is necessary to pose research questions that are appropriate to local specificities. How is race constructed in a region where racial others are not primarily, as in the States, African Americans and Latinos, but Jews, Roma, and more recently Arabs (Bobako 2017: 163–7)? What is whiteness in Second World conditions, since a Pole remains the quintessential white person in Poland, but may cease to be white when he or she migrates to the West for bread? What are the specifics of passing rituals in post-Holocaust territory?

Conclusion

An immediate effect of the 'Jews don't count' mechanism is the lack of regular monitoring of manifestations of antisemitic violence in Poland. It makes the scale of this violence – whether symbolic or physical – increasingly difficult to assess. Added to this are outdated definitions and inadequate tools for diagnosing contemporary antisemitism. A situation of this kind causes reality and its descriptions to increasingly diverge. The history of Polish antisemitism, including at the micro level, is being studied in more and more depth. With the development of this branch of historiography, critical reflection on the methodology of historical research is developing. Increasingly, voices are being heard that research approaches need to be revised if we want to hear the testimonies of individuals and groups hitherto persistently denied legitimacy (Fricker 2009: 1–5), including Jewish testimonies. I think we need a similarly critical look within sociology. We should put our toolbox in order. Especially since we are about to need it ever more. The academic world in Poland is not yet dominated by discussions of whether and how universities should 'boycott Israel' and lectures on 'Zionist genocide'. But, judging by the usual delay with which Western trends reach Poland, it soon will be. In the context of today's completely trivialized ghetto benches, *numerus clausus* and regular assaults on Jewish students and lecturers before the war, as well as 'March', when more than a dozen professors were fired from Warsaw University because of their alleged 'Zionism', it would be good to be prepared.

Acknowledgements

This research was funded in whole or in part by the National Science Centre, Poland, grant no. 2020/39/D/HS3/02028. For the purpose of Open Access, the author has applied a CC-BY public copyright licence to any Author Accepted Manuscript version arising from this submission.

References

Aderet, O. (2021), 'New Law in Poland Would End Property Restitution for Holocaust Survivors, Causing a New Crisis With Israel', *Haaretz*, 25 June, available at: www.haaretz.com/world-news/europe/jewish-poland/.premium-new-law-in-poland-to-end-property-restitution-for-holocaust-survivors-1.9940416 (accessed 24 April 2022).

Aleksiun, N. (2002), *Dokąd dalej? Ruch syjonistyczny w Polsce (1944–1950)* (*Where to Next? The Zionist Movement in Poland (1944–1950)*), Warszawa: Centrum Badania i Nauczania Dziejów Kultury Żydów w Polsce im. Mordechaja Anielewicza, Wydawnictwo TRIO.

Andersz, K., and N. Aleksiun (2020), 'Studenci żądają żydowskich trupów' ('Students Demand Jewish Corpses'), *Chidusz*, available at: https://chidusz.com/afera-trupia-natalia-aleksiun (accessed 30 April 2022).

Baddiel, D. (2021), *Jews Don't Count: How Identity Politics Failed one Particular Identity*, London: TLS Books.

BAK (2021), 'Kolejny akt antysemityzmu na cmentarzu żydowskim. W worku były fekalia' ('Another Act of Antisemitism at a Jewish Cemetery. The Bag Contained Faecal Matter'), *Bielsko Biala*, 3 July, available at: https://bielsko.biala.pl/aktualnosci/46309/

kolejny-akt-antysemityzmu-na-cmentarzu-zydowskim-w-worku-byly-fekalia-foto (accessed 25 April 2022).

Beck, E. T. (1988), 'The Politics of Jewish Invisibility', *National Women's Studies Association Journal*, 1 (1): 93–102.

Berendt, G. (ed.) (2009), *Społeczność żydowska w PRL przed kampanią antysemicką lat 1967–1968 i po niej* (*The Jewish Community in the People's Republic of Poland before and after the Antisemitic Campaign of 1967–1968*), Warszawa: Instytut Pamięci Narodowej.

Bobako, M. (2017), *Islamofobia jako technologia władzy. Studium z antropologii politycznej* (*Islamophobia as a Technology of Power. A Study in Political Anthropology*), Kraków: Universitas.

Bohus, K., P. Hallama and S. Stach (eds) (2022), *Growing in the Shadow of Antifascism*, Budapest: Central European University Press.

Bulska, D., and M. Winiewski (2017), 'Powrót zabobonu: Antysemityzm w Polsce na podstawie Polskiego Sondażu Uprzedzeń 3' ('The Return of Superstition: Antisemitism in Poland Based on the Polish Prejudice Survey 3'), *Centrum Badań nad Uprzedzeniami, Wydział Psychologii Uniwersytetu Warszawskiego*, available at: http://cbu.psychologia.pl/wp-content/uploads/sites/410/2021/02/Antysemityzm_PPS3_Bulska_fin.pdf (accessed 23 June 2023).

Burton, N. (2018), 'White Jews: Stop Calling Yourselves "White-Passing"', *Forward*, 2 July, available at: https://forward.com/opinion/404482/white-jews-stop-calling-yourselves-white-passing (accessed 20 April 2022).

Cała, A. (2014), *Ochrona bezpieczeństwa fizycznego Żydów w Polsce powojennej. Komisje specjalne przy Centralnym Komitecie Żydów w Polsce* (*Protecting the Physical Security of Jews in Postwar Poland. Special Commissions under the Central Jewish Committee in Poland*), Warszawa: Żydowski Instytut Historyczny.

Cała, A., and H. Datner-Śpiewak (1999), *Dzieje Żydów w Polsce, 1944–1968* (*History of Jews in Poland, 1944–1968*), Warszawa: Żydowski Instytut Historyczny.

Canin, M. (2019), *Przez ruiny i zgliszcza. Podróż po stu zgładzonych gminach żydowskich w Polsce* (*Through Ruins and Rubble. A Journey through One Hundred Exterminated Jewish Communities in Poland*) (trans. M. Adamczyk-Garbowska), Warszawa: Nisza, Żydowski Instytut Historyczny.

Chmielewska, K. (2019), 'Życie na niby czyli diagnoza na serio. Polski świadek Zagłady' ('Life as if or Diagnosis in Earnest. The Polish Witness to the Holocaust'), in M. Hopfinger and T. Żukowski (eds), *Lata czterdzieste. Początki polskiej narracji o Zagładzie* (*The Forties. The Beginnings of the Polish Holocaust Narrative*), 215–50, Warszawa: Instytut Badań Literackich PAN.

Chmielewska, K., and G. Wołowiec (eds) (2021), *Reassessing Communism. Concepts, Culture, and Society in Poland 1944–1989*, Budapest: Central European University Press.

Codziennik Feministyczny (2021), 'Sprzeciw pracownic_ków kultury wobec czystek etnicznych i strategii kolonialnych Izraela [LIST]' ('Cultural Workers' Opposition to Ethnic Cleansing and Israel's Colonial Strategies. A Letter'), 17 May, available at: http://codziennikfeministyczny.pl/sprzeciw-pracownic_kow-kultury-wobec-czystek-etnicznych-strategii-kolonialnych-izraela (accessed 6 July 2022).

Datner, H. (2016), *Po Zagładzie. Społeczna historia żydowskich domów dziecka, szkół, kół studentów w dokumentach Centralnego Komitetu Żydów w Polsce* (*After the Holocaust. Social History of Jewish Orphanages, Schools, Student Circles in Documents of the Central Jewish Committee in Poland*), Warszawa: Żydowski Instytut Historyczny.

Datner, H. (2021), 'Immediately after the War the Picture Was Complete: Szymon Datner's Narrations on the Holocaust', in I. Grudzińska-Gross and K. Matyjaszek (eds), *Breaking the Frame. New School of Polish-Jewish Studies*, 159–92, Pieterlen and Bern: Peter Lang.

Datner, H., B. Keff and E. Janicka (2014), 'Polska panika moralna. Czy upamiętnić Sprawiedliwych koło Muzeum Historii Żydów Polskich' ('Poland's Moral Panic. Whether to Commemorate the Righteous Near the Museum of the History of Polish Jews'), *Gazeta Wyborcza*, 30 May, available at: https://wyborcza.pl/magazyn/7,124 059,16065323,polska-panika-moralna-czy-upamietnic-sprawiedliwych-kolo-muzeum.html (accessed 5 July 2022).

Eisler, J. (2006), *Polski rok 1968 (The Polish Year 1968)*, Warszawa: Instytut Pamięci Narodowej.

Engelking, B., and J. Grabowski (eds) (2018), *Dalej jest noc. Losy Żydów w wybranych powiatach okupowanej Polski*, Warszawa: Centrum Badań nad Zagładą Żydów.

Fidelis, M. (2010), *Women, Communism and Industrialization in Postwar Poland*, Cambridge: Cambridge University Press.

Fine, R., and P. Spencer (2017), *Antisemitism and the Left: On the Return of the Jewish Question*, Manchester: Manchester University Press.

Fricker, M. (2009), *Epistemic Injustice. Power and the Ethics of Knowing*, Oxford: Oxford University Press.

Friszke, A. (2004), 'Miejsce Marca 1968 wśród innych "polskich miesięcy"' ('The Place of March 1968 among Other "Polish Months"'), in K. Rokicki and S. Stepień (eds), *Oblicza marca 1968 (Faces of March 1968)*, 15–23, Warszawa: Instytut Pamięci Narodowej.

'Głosowanie nr 73 na 33. posiedzeniu Sejmu – Sejm Rzeczypospolitej Polskiej' ('Vote No. 73 at the 33rd Session of the Sejm – Sejm of the Republic of Poland') (2021), available at: www.sejm.gov.pl/Sejm9.nsf/agent.xsp?symbol=glosowania&nrkadencji=9&nrposi edzenia=33&nrglosowania=73 (accessed 24 April 2022).

Głowiński, M. (1991), *Marcowe gadanie. Komentarze do słów, 1966–1971 (March Talks. Commentaries to Words, 1966–1971)*, Warszawa: Pomost.

Głowiński, M. (2009), *Nowomowa i ciągi dalsze (Newspeak and Further Sequences)*, Kraków: Universitas.

Grabski, A., and G. Berendt (2003), *Między emigracją a trwaniem. Syjoniści i komuniści żydowscy w Polsce po Holokauście (Between Emigration and Survival. Zionists and Jewish Communists in Post-Holocaust Poland)*, Warszawa: Żydowski Instytut Historyczny.

Gross, J. T. (1986), 'Ten jest z ojczyzny mojej …, ale go nie lubię' ('This One Is from My Country … But I Don't Like Him'), *Aneks*, 41–42: 13–35.

Gross, J. T. (2000), *Sąsiedzi. Historia zagłady żydowskiego miasteczka*, Sejny: Pogranicze.

Grynberg, H. (2018), Memorbuch, Wołowiec: Wydawnictwo Czarne.

Grynberg, M. (2018), *Księga wyjścia (The Book of Exodus)*, Wołowiec: Wydawnictwo Czarne.

Hanebrink, P. (2018), *A Specter Haunting Europe: The Myth of Judeo-Bolshevism*, Cambridge: Harvard University Press.

Herbert, Z. (2008), *Wiersze zebrane (Collected Poems)* (ed. R. Krynicki), Kraków: Wydawnictwo a5.

Katz, D. (2017), 'The "Double Genocide" Theory', *Jewish Currents*, 22 November, available at: https://jewishcurrents.org/the-double-genocide-theory (accessed 22 April 2022).

Kaye/Kantorowitz, M. (2007), *The Colors of Jews. Racial Politics and Radical Diasporism*, Bloomington: Indiana University Press.

Kovács, A. (2011), 'From Anti-Jewish Prejudice to Political Anti-Semitism? On Dynamics of anti-Semitism in Post-Communist Hungary', in O. Glöckner and J. H. Schoeps (eds), *A Road to Nowhere? Jewish Experiences in Unifying Europe*, 247–69, Leiden: Brill.

Kozłowski, M. (2019), 'Red Nationalism? A Brief Overview of the Origins of Polish Stalinism', *Studia Litteraria et Historica*, 8: 1–14, available at: https://doi.org/10.11649/slh.2034.

Krzywicki, L. (2009), *Ekscesy antyżydowskie na polskich uczelniach w latach trzydziestych XX w.*, Warszawa: Towarzystwo Wydawnicze i Literackie Sp. z o. o.

Leszczyński, A. (1996), 'Sprawa redaktora naczelnego "Fołks-Sztyme" Grzegorza Smolara na tle wydarzeń lat 1967–1968' ('The Case of the Editor-in-Chief of *Fołks-Sztyme* Grzegorz Smolar against the Background of the Events of 1967–1968'), *Biuletyn Żydowskiego Instytutu Historycznego*, lipiec 1995–czerwiec 1996: 131–4.

Leszczyński, A. (2021), 'Sąd: Można skazać historyków za naruszenie "poczucia dumy narodowej". Publikujemy uzasadnienie wyroku', *Oko.Press*, 23 April, available at: https://oko.press/sad-mozna-skazac-historyka-za-naruszenie-poczucia-dumy (accessed 24 April 2022).

Levine-Rasky, C. (2008), 'White Privilege. Jewish Women's Writing and the Instability of Categories', *Journal of Modern Jewish Studies*, 7 (1): 51–66.

Machcewicz, P. (1993), *Polski rok 1956 (The Polish Year 1956)*, Warszawa: Mówią Wieki.

Machcewicz, P. (1996), 'Antisemitism in Poland in 1956', *Polin: Studies in Polish Jewry*, 9: 170–83.

Markusz, K. (2020), *Polak nierdzennie polski. Antysemicka kampania z Marca '68 przeciwko szefowi Towarzystwa Społeczno-Kulturalnego Żydów (Non-native Polish. The Antisemitic Campaign of March '68 against the Head of the Jewish Social and Cultural Society)*, Kraków: Austeria.

Melchior, M. (1990), *Społeczna tożsamość jednostki (w świetle wywiadów z Polakami pochodzenia żydowskiego urodzonymi w latach 1944–1955) (The Social Identity of the Individual (in Light of Interviews with Poles of Jewish Origin Born between 1944 and 1955))*, Warszawa: Uniwersytet Warszawski.

Mieszczanek, A. (1989), *Krajobraz po szoku (Landscape after the Shock)*, Warszawa: Wydawnictwo Przedświt.

Mikołajewska, B. (2017), 'W Marszu Niepodległości szło wielu rasistów i neofaszystów. Policja nie reagowała. Apelujemy: przesyłajcie zdjęcia i filmy potwierdzające łamanie prawa' ('Many Racists and Neo-fascists Marched in the Independence March. The Police Did Not React. We Appeal: Send Photos and Videos Confirming Violations of the Law'), Oko.Press, 18 November, available at: https://oko.press/marszu-niepodleglosci-szlo-wielu-rasistow-neofaszystow-policja-reagowala-apelujemy-przesylajcie-zdjecia-filmy-potwierdzajace-lamanie-prawa (accessed 6 July 2022).

Młodzież Wszechpolska (2021), '*Młodzież Wszechpolska na Twitterze*' ('Młodzież Wszechpolska on Twitter'), *Twitter*, available at: https://twitter.com/MWszechpolska/status/1410259015116939271 (accessed 24 April 2022).

MLZ (2020), 'Film ze spalenia kukły Żyda pokazany podczas Światowego Forum Holokaustu. Pojawiły się też urywki z marszu niepodległości' ('Video of the Burning of a Jewish Puppet Shown at the World Holocaust Forum. There Were Also Excerpts from the March of Independence'), *Gazeta*, available at: https://wiadomosci.gazeta.pl/wiadomosci/7,114884,25626327,film-ze-spalenia-kukly-zyda-pokazano-podczas-swiatowego-forum.html (accessed 6 July 2022).

'Nacjonaliści przeciwko żydowskiemu ludobójstwu, Narodowe Odrodzenie Polski (NOP) – Nacjonalistyczna Opozycja' ('Nationalists against Jewish Genocide,

Narodowe Odrodzenie Polski (NOP) – Nationalist Opposition') (2021), available at www.nop.org.pl/2021/06/08/nacjonalisci-przeciwko-zydowskiemu-ludobojstwu/ (accessed 24 April 2022).

Ogonowski, J. (2012). *Sytuacja prawna Żydów w Rzeczypospolitej Polskiej 1918–1939: Prawa cywilne i polityczne*. Żydowski Instytut Historyczny.

OKO.press (2021a), 'Polacy i Żydzi solidarnie z Palestyńczykami. Protest pod ambasadą Izraela przeciwko przemocy' ('Poles and Jews in Solidarity with Palestinians. Protest against Violence in Front of the Israeli Embassy'), available at: www.youtube.com/watch?v=SMyNUrEwKwU (accessed 24 April 2022).

OKO.press (2021b), 'Sceny hańby. 80. rocznica Jedwabnego' ('Scenes of Shame. The 80th Anniversary of Jedwabne'), available at: www.youtube.com/watch?v=AAa74bxwLoI (accessed 24 April 2022).

Osęka, P. (1999), *Syjoniści, inspiratorzy, wichrzyciele. Obraz wroga w propagandzie marca 1968* (*Zionists, Instigators, Troublemakers. The Image of the Enemy in March 1968 Propaganda*), Warszawa: Żydowski Instytut Historyczny.

PAP (2017), 'Dzika reprywatyzacja. Liczne przypadki nieuczciwych zwrotów kamienic są w całej Polsce, Serwis Samorządowy PAP', available at: https://samorzad.pap.pl/kategoria/prawo/dzika-reprywatyzacja-liczne-przypadki-nieuczciwych-zwrotow-kamienic-sa-w-calej (accessed 19 July 2022).

Pietrzak, J. (2015), '"The Wall" Marlene Dumas' ('*The Wall* by Marlene Dumas'), *Jarosław Pietrzak*, 19 December, available at: https://jaroslawpietrzak.com/2015/12/19/the-wall-marlene-dumas-apartheid-izraelski-mur (accessed 6 July 2022).

'Polski rząd rozpoczął ogólnokrajową zbiórkę żydowskiego mienia utraconego podczas Holokaustu' ('The Polish Government Has Launched a Nationwide Collection of Jewish Property Lost during the Holocaust') (2019), available at: https://demotywatory.pl/4917435/Polski-rzad-rozpoczal-ogolnokrajowa-zbiorke-zydowskiego-mienia (accessed 24 April 2022).

Prokuratura Krajowa, D. P. (2021), 'Prokuratura Regionalna we Wrocławiu: zarzuty w związku z reprywatyzacją nieruchomości', available at: https://pk.gov.pl/aktualnosci/aktualnosci-prokuratury-krajowej/prokuratura-regionalna-we-wroclawiu-zarzuty-w-zwiazku-z-reprywatyzacja-nieruchomosci (accessed 19 July 2022).

Qandil, A. (2016), 'Czy Palestyńczycy pomagali Polakom mordować Żydów w Jedwabnem?' ('Did Palestinians Help Poles Murder Jews in Jedwabne?'), 15 August, available at: http://codziennikfeministyczny.pl/qandil-czy-palestynczycy-pomagali-polakom-mordowac-zydow-jedwabnem/ (accessed 6 July 2022).

Richter-Montpetit, M. (2019), 'You Can't Pink Wash This', *BDS Movement*, available at: https://bdsmovement.net/news/you-can%E2%80%99t-pink-wash (accessed 19 July 2022).

RMF FM (2018), 'Weszła w życie nowelizacja ustawy o IPN dotycząca kar za "polskie obozy śmierci"', 1 March, available at: www.rmf24.pl/raporty/raport-spor-ustawe-ipn/fakty/news-weszla-w-zycie-nowelizacja-ustawy-o-ipn-dotyczaca-kar-za-pol,nId,2551401 (accessed 24 April 2022).

Rosenfeld, A. H. (2019), *Anti-Zionism and Antisemitism*, Bloomington: Indiana University Press.

Rudnicki, S. (2008), *Równi, ale niezupełnie*, Warszawa: Biblioteka Midrasza.

Schraub, D. (2019), 'White Jews: An Intersectional Approach', *Association for Jewish Review*, 43 (2): 379–407.

Shafir, M. (2002), 'Between Denial and "Comparative Trivialization"': Holocaust Negationism in Post-Communist East Central Europe', *Vidal Sassoon International*

Center for the Study of Antisemitism, *Analysis of Current Trends in Antisemitism*, 19, available at: www.researchgate.net/publication/239549015_Between_Denial_and_Comparative_Trivialization_Holocaust_Negationism_in_Post-Communist_East_Central_Europe (accessed 21 April 2022).

Ślązak, R. (2014), 'Przekręty na reprywatyzacji – rozmowa z dr Ryszardem Ślązakiem', available at: www.tygodnikprzeglad.pl/przekrety-na-reprywatyzacji (accessed 19 July 2022).

Smolar, H. (1967), 'Dokument nr 1' ('Document No. 1'), *Biuletyn Żydowskiego Instytutu Historycznego* (*Bulletin of the Jewish Historical Institute*), lipiec 1995–czerwiec 1996: 135–52.

Smolar, A. (1986), 'Tabu i niewinność' ('Taboo and Innocence'), *Aneks*, 41–42: 89–130.

Smolar, P. (2021), *Zły Żyd* (*Bad Jew*), Kraków: Wydawnictwo Znak.

Sommer, M., M. Sławiński and M. Zubel (2018), 'Prezydent o nowelizacji ustawy o IPN: nie wolno się wycofać', *Polska Agencja Prasowa SA*, 29 January, available at: www.pap.pl/aktualnosci/news%2C1266633%2Cprezydent-o-nowelizacji-ustawy-o-ipn-nie-wolno-sie-wycofac-.html (accessed 24 April 2022).

Śpiewak, J. (2017), *Ukradzione miasto. Kulisy wybuchu afery reprywatyzacyjnej*, Warszawa: Arbitor.

Sprawozdanie Komisji Nadzwyczajnej do spraw zmian w kodyfikacjach o komisyjnym projekcie ustawy o zmianie ustawy – Kodeks postępowania administracyjnego (2021), available at: www.sejm.gov.pl/Sejm9.nsf/druk.xsp?nr=1210 (accessed 24 April 2022).

Starnawski, M. (2016), *Socjalizacja i tożsamość żydowska w Polsce powojennej. Narracje emigrantów z pokolenia Marca '68*, Wrocław: Wydawnictwo Naukowe Dolnośląskiej Szkoły Wyższej.

Stögner, K. (2019), 'Challenges in Feminism: Intersectionality, Critical Theory, and Anti-Zionism', in A. H. Rosenfeld (ed.), *Anti-Zionism and Antisemitism: The Dynamics of Delegitimization*, 84–112, Bloomington: Indiana University Press.

Stögner, K. (2020), 'Intersectionality and Antisemitism: A New Approach', *Fathom*, May, available at: https://fathomjournal.org/intersectionality-and-antisemitism-a-new-approach (accessed 19 April 2022).

Stola, D. (2000), *Kampania antysyjonistyczna w Polsce 1967–1968* (*The Anti-Zionist Campaign in Poland*), Warszawa: Instytut Studiów Politycznych PAN.

Subotić, J. (2019), *Yellow Star, Red Star. Holocaust Remembrance after Communism*, Ithaca, NY: Cornell University Press.

Szajda, M. (2018), 'Obraz Polski wśród Żydów w Izraelu. Narracje przedstawicieli aliji gomułkowskiej i emigracji pomarcowej' ('The Image of Poles as Held by Jews in Israel. Narratives of the Gomułka-time Aliyah and of Post-March Emigration'), *Wrocławski Rocznik Historii Mówionej*, 8: 143–80.

Szaynok, B. (2007), *Z historią i Moskwą w tle. Polska a Izrael 1944–1968* (*With History and Moscow in the Background. Poland and Israel 1944–1968*), Warszawa: Instytut Pamięci Narodowej.

TOKFM (2019), 'Palenie kukły Judasza w Pruchniku. "Zwyczaj nie został przerwany. Z roku na rok taki sąd się odbywał"' ('Burning of a Puppet of Judas in Pruchnik. "The Tradition Still Lives. Every Year This Trial Took Place"'), available at: www.tokfm.pl/Tokfm/7,103085,24694786,palenie-kukly-judasza-w-pruchniku-zwyczaj-nie-zostal-przerwany.html (accessed 6 July 2022).

Tryczyk, M. (2015), *Miasta śmierci. Sąsiedzkie pogromy Żydów* (*Cities of Death. Jewish Pogroms by Neighbours*), Warszawa: Wydawnictwo RM.

Tryczyk, M. (2020), *Drzazga. Kłamstwa silniejsze niż śmierć* (*Splinter. Lies Stronger Than Death*), Kraków: Społeczny Instytut Wydawniczy Znak.

Tych, F. (1999), 'Kilka uwag o Marcu 1968' ('A Few Remarks about March 1968'), in *Długi cień Zagłady. Szkice historyczne* (*The Long Shadow of the Holocaust. Historical Sketches*), 119–36, Warszawa: Żydowski Instytut Historyczny.

'Uchwalili po dwóch latach. Skasowali w dwie godziny', *TVN24*, 27 June, available at: https://tvn24.pl/wiadomosci-z-kraju,3/pis-chcial-karac-za-polskie-obozy-szybko-zmieniona-ustawa-o-ipn,849161.html (accessed 27 June 2020).

Vanagaite, R., and E. Zuroff (2020), *Our People: Discovering Lithuania's Hidden Holocaust*, Lanham, MD: Rowman & Littlefield.

Walczak, A., and J. Jaros (2021), 'Skandaliczny marsz nacjonalistów w Kaliszu. Spalili Statut kaliski, śpiewając hymn narodowy' ('Scandalous March of Nationalists in Kalisz. They Burned the Kalisz Status while Singing the National Anthem'), 11 November, available at: https://kalisz.wyborcza.pl/kalisz/7,181359,27795429,swieto-niepodleglosci-wiec-nacjonalistow-w-kaliszu-tu-jest.html (accessed 6 July 2022).

Waluś, M. (2019), 'Piotr Rybak i narodowcy przemaszerowali pod bramę Auschwitz. "Czas walczyć z żydostwem"' ('Piotr Rybak and the Nationalists Marched through the Gate of Auschwitz. "Time to Fight the Jewry"'], 27 January. available at: https://krakow.wyborcza.pl/krakow/7,44425,24404379,piotr-rybak-i-narodowcy-przemaszerowali-pod-brame-auschwitz.html (accessed 29 December 2020).

Węgrzyn, E. (2016), *Wyjeżdżamy? Wyjeżdżamy! Alija gomułkowska 1956–1960* (*Shall We Go? Let's Go! Gomułka-time Aliyah 1956–1960*), Kraków: Austeria.

Wiszniewicz, J. (2008), *Życie przecięte. Opowieści pokolenia Marca* (*Life Cut in Half. Tales of the March Generation*), Wołowiec: Wydawnictwo Czarne.

Wiszniewski, P. (2021), 'Otwarta Rzeczpospolita', available at: www.otwarta.org/jak-dzialamy/antysemityzm-w-polsce/ https://youtu.be/bjbXDfZI_UA (accessed 26 April 2022).

Zawadzka, A. (2019), 'Nie skłamać i prawdy nie powiedzieć. O uniwersalizacji Zagłady w polskiej literaturze i podręcznikach szkolnych z lat czterdziestych' ('Not to Lie and Not to Tell the Truth. On Universalization of the Holocaust in Polish Literature and Schoolbooks of the Forties'), in M. Hopfinger and T. Żukowski (eds), *Lata czterdzieste. Początki polskiej narracji o Zagładzie* (*The Forties. The Beginnings of the Polish Narrative on the Holocaust*), 81–116, Warszawa: Instytut Badań Literackich PAN.

Zecker, R. M. (2011), ' "A Slav Can Live in Dirt That Would Kill a White Man": Race and the European "Other" ', in *Race and America's Immigrant Press: How the Slovaks Were Taught to Think Like White People*, 68–102, London: Bloomsbury Academic.

Żukowski, T. (2013), 'Wytwarzanie "winy obojętności" oraz kategorii "obojętnego świadka" na przykładzie artykułu Jana Błońskiego "Biedni Polacy patrzą na getto" ', *Studia Litteraria et Historica*, 2: 423–51, available at: https://doi.org/10.11649/slh.2013.018.

Żukowski, T. (2018), *Wielki retusz. Jak zapomnieliśmy, że Polacy zabijali Żydów* (*The Big Touch-Up. How We Forgot That Poles Killed Jews*), Kraków: Wielka Litera.

Zuroff, E. (2011), 'The Equivalency Canard', *Haaretz*, 11 May, available at: www.haaretz.com/life/books/1.5010649 (accessed 21 April 2022).

11

Labour, antisemitism and the critique of political economy

Matthew Bolton and Frederick Harry Pitts

This chapter uses the critical theory of antisemitism (e.g. Postone 2006) to analyse the antisemitism crisis which erupted in the British Labour Party under Jeremy Corbyn's leadership (2015–20). Explanations for the seemingly sudden explosion of antisemitism within leftist milieus commonly focused on the idea of antisemitism as a 'virus' imported into the party from outside by extremists (see Gidley et al. 2020 for an account). This chapter challenges this narrative, developing our previous work (2018, 2020a) to argue that the roots of the crisis under Corbyn can be found in the 'truncated' or 'foreshortened' critique of capitalism (see Kurz 2007; Heinrich 2012) that has been a feature of the British socialist and liberal left since its formation, of which 'Corbynism' represented a concentrated form. This worldview regards capitalism as the corruption of an otherwise benign form of productive society by capitalists motivated by greed and personal immorality. The 'real economy' of productive national industry is valorised and opposed to unproductive, parasitical global finance, which is taken to fraudulently conjure money out of money (Bonefeld 2014).

We do not suggest that such ideas and rhetoric *inevitably* lead to the kind of conspiracist and often antisemitic worldviews that characterized parts of the Corbyn movement. But there is nonetheless a potential for them to do so. 'Truncated critiques' lack a properly articulated analysis of global capital and the nation-state as mutually constitutive expressions of capitalist society understood as a global form of generalized impersonal domination. Instead, such critiques understand capital and the state as externally related antagonists, each driven by rival moralities. In this, truncated critiques create a receptive environment for the reformulation of long-standing conspiracy theories about the role of 'international Jewish interests' in undermining national peoples through control of finance and the media. Thus what Adorno and Horkheimer (1972) described as the 'elements of antisemitism' are latently present in such a perspective, awaiting political activation. Such *activation*, we argue, happened in the Labour Party in the Corbyn years, as opposed to the *importation* of any kind of 'racist bug' from outside.

This chapter focuses upon how a latent constellation of 'elements of antisemitism' was activated under Corbyn's leadership. In particular, we seek to show how the

Manichean anti-imperialism and 'absolutist' anti-Zionism which Corbyn had been personally associated with for decades is itself a manifestation of the truncated critique of capital and the state that underpinned the movement's economic analysis at the geopolitical level. In the anti-imperialist/anti-Zionist worldview, Israel is depicted as a parasitical and illegitimate 'entity' undermining the global community of peoples, with many of the traditional anti-Jewish stereotypes – secretive global power, vengefulness, amorality – projected onto the Jewish state. While truncated critiques of capitalism have been a feature of the socialist and liberal strands of the Labour Party from its formation, it was their political activation by a leader from the anti-imperialist/anti-Zionist strand of the movement that rendered antisemitism a pronounced and highly visible phenomenon within the party.

Antisemitism in Corbyn's Labour Party

At the core of the British Labour Party's antisemitism crisis under Jeremy Corbyn's leadership was a series of allegations about his statements and associations made across a career-long preoccupation with the Israel–Palestine conflict. Prior to the announcement of his candidacy for the leadership in 2015, Corbyn had, despite being an MP since 1983, been a minor figure on the national political scene. Yet Corbyn had long been notorious for his equivocation over, and support of, groups engaged in political violence, in particular the IRA and Hamas (for a comprehensive summary see Johnson 2019).

Corbyn had been a leading member and Chair of the Stop The War Coalition (STWC). Stemming from the left opposition to the NATO intervention to prevent Slobodan Milosevic's genocidal assault on Kosovo, STWC was formally established in the wake of 9/11 to protest against the US invasions of Afghanistan and later Iraq. Its leadership having been sourced from quarters of the Leninist hard left like the Socialist Workers Party and British Communist Party, STWC's opposition to British foreign policy was grounded in a rigid, binary form of 'anti-imperialism' which bore the imprint of Cold War Stalinism (Bloodworth 2015; Randall 2021: chapter 4). STWC's sympathies lie with any state or movement opposed to Anglo-American foreign policy and the legitimacy and existence of the State of Israel, no matter how violent, reactionary, fundamentalist, antisemitic or indeed – as became very clear in the organization's vacillations over the Russian invasion of Ukraine (see Thompson and Pitts 2022) – imperialist. STWC members, including Corbyn, routinely appeared at public events supporting and even lauding Hamas and Hezbollah operatives and assorted British Islamists (see Hirsh 2017; Rich 2018).

STWC's success in securing leadership of opposition to the Iraq war – a movement which had attracted broad support from across the liberal left – sanitized their public reputation to the effect that criticism of their political alliances failed to gain traction. Thus when Corbyn ran for Labour leader in June 2015, and when he won that election three months later, he was generally presented by the media, supporters and opponents alike as a principled if idealistic lifelong campaigner for peace, standing on an 'anti-austerity' economic platform which sought to reverse the public spending cuts imposed by the post-crisis governments of 2010–15. Criticism within Labour focused almost entirely on his supposed lack of 'electability'. In those early days, it was left to a small number of observers, and in particular Jewish activists, to point to some of the more problematic aspects of Corbyn's political worldview that belied his gentle homilies to peace and harmony.

In August 2015, with his victory in the leadership election seemingly inevitable, the *Jewish Chronicle* (JC) published seven 'key questions' about Corbyn's past statements and associations (*Jewish Chronicle* 2015). One concerned Corbyn's relationship with Deir Yassin Remembered (DYR), a Palestinian solidarity organization strongly associated with open Holocaust deniers. Most notable among the latter was DYR founder Paul Eisen, who in 2008 had published a blog entitled 'My life as a holocaust denier', writing that 'I question that there ever existed homicidal gas chambers. I question the figure of six million Jewish victims of the Nazi assault and I believe that the actual figure was significantly less' (Dysch 2015a). The extent of this denial, well known within British Palestine solidarity circles, led to the 2011 exclusion of DYR from the Palestine Solidarity Campaign (PSC), of which Corbyn is a patron. Despite this, in the years following the revelations of Holocaust denial and DYR's exclusion from the PSC, Corbyn attended its events, donated it money and in 2014, a year before his election as Labour leader, even invited its leadership to a private meeting in Parliament (Mendick 2017). Another question posed by the JC focused on Corbyn's support for the Palestinian cleric Raed Salah. In speeches and writings Salah had propagated the blood libel about Jews baking the blood of children into bread, labelled Jews 'the bacteria of all times', and engaged in 9/11 conspiracy theories (Community Security Trust 2011). In 2011 this history led to Salah being refused entry to the UK. Along with other activists, including Green Party MP Caroline Lucas, Corbyn campaigned against Salah's exclusion, describing the accusations against Salah as 'hysteria' whipped up by 'the Zionist lobby' (Sugarman 2019a). In 2012 he appeared with Salah at a press conference, declaring him 'an honoured citizen' and inviting him 'for tea on the [House of Commons] terrace, because [he] deserve[s] it'.

Corbyn's response was one of aggressive indignation, immediately seeking to frame any critique of his political commitments an unseemly personal attack. Corbyn described the accusations of 'associating' with antisemites as 'ludicrous and wrong', in each case claiming that the stories were a transparent attempt to 'smear' him and by extension all who support the Palestinian cause (Mason 2015). He denied that he would ever tolerate antisemitism, contending that he had been an 'anti-racist' all his life, and that 'antisemitism and all other forms of racism' were abhorrent. Corbyn's position was that his lifelong commitment to the left, to anti-racist politics and to the moral principles that he felt himself to embody through that commitment, meant it was inconceivable that he could fail to recognize or tolerate antisemitism, let alone act in an antisemitic manner himself. This therefore reduced the need to deal with the questions raised concerning the political values, goals and orientations of the individuals he had consorted with.

This mobilization of his own perceived personal morality was quickly picked up by Corbyn's supporters. It was, in effect, an extension of the claim of moral supremacism that had been central to Corbyn's leadership campaign from the outset, in which

Corbyn was depicted as both channelling and personifying the hitherto-thwarted moral principles of 'the people'. Corbyn had, so his supporters claimed, been on 'the right side of history' throughout his career (Bennett 2016). As such, claims of antisemitism against him could only be 'mood music', as Unite leader Len McCluskey put it (Edwards 2017), accompanying the orchestrated campaign to discredit the left, personified by Corbyn, and to defend Israel from legitimate critique. Corbyn himself was filmed describing an even-handed 2016 critique by the Guardian journalist Jonathan Freedland as 'utterly disgusting, subliminal nastiness' – implying a nefarious coded message in support of another aim (see Freedland 2020).

These claims of antisemitism had little impact on Labour's unexpectedly strong performance in the 2017 General Election. National attention was drawn to the issue only when in March 2018, the Jewish Labour MP Luciana Berger reposted an old, and initially dismissed, *JC* story about a Facebook comment Corbyn had made in support of graffiti artist Mear One. Mear One had painted a mural in London depicting a group of men, some with exaggerated hooked noses, sat counting money on a table resting on the backs of bent-double naked bodies, and surrounded by Illuminati conspiracy insignia (Dysch 2015b). Mear One had complained that the mural was being removed by Tower Hamlets council on the grounds that it was antisemitic. Corbyn commiserated with Mear One, apparently without going to the trouble of asking himself whether the local council might have a point. Here Corbyn's failure to notice the antisemitism did not manifest itself in relation to Israel but to conspiracy theories about Jewish political and economic power more broadly. This made it impossible for the Corbyn-supporting left to attribute the furore solely to the malign influence of 'Zionists', and some acknowledged for the first time that Corbyn had erred. However, the error was widely excused as a one-off moment of inexplicable misrecognition by a man otherwise committed to anti-racist praxis, with no wider significance (Segalov 2018).

This set the tone for the subsequent years, in which the left not only comprehensively failed to get to grips with the elements of antisemitism in Corbyn's Labour Party, but often exacerbated the issue and emboldened the conspiracist atmosphere that in part underpinned it. One particular and persistent response was to posit a monetary link between individuals making claims of antisemitism and their personal political and economic interests. In June 2019, for example, the Corbynite MP Lloyd Russell-Moyle suggested that Margaret Hodge, a long-standing Labour MP of Jewish background, was only criticizing Corbyn over antisemitism because she 'want[ed] to roll out more neo-liberalism and austerity on our country' (Harpin 2019).

Other responses accepted some of the evidence of antisemitism in the Labour Party but suggested any such anti-Jewish prejudice on the left was due to a naive acceptance of an ideological narrative constructed by capitalists and political, financial and media elites to deflect attention from their activity. Antisemitism was thus understood as a function of elite or capitalist power, with Jews the targets of a consciously designed 'scapegoat' ideology which accuses them of bearing responsibility for the world's evils (see, e.g., Gilbert 2018; Momentum 2019). A functionalist theory of this kind treats antisemitism as if it was merely a disposable means for a higher end, an instrument to be wielded by the powerful when it is required, and discarded when not. While it is a truism that all forms of ideology can be utilized by different social groups, this says nothing about why a particular ideology is *available* for use in the first place (Postone 1980: 104–6). The advantage of functionalist theory for its leftist adherents is that it provides an infallible alibi against any possibility of their own antisemitism. If antisemitism is merely a strategy of class division used by the powerful, then anti-capitalist leftists cannot be antisemitic in any true sense, the occasional lapse aside, so long as they retain, like Corbyn, the requisite socialist morality (see Bolton 2020a).

A vital alibi for the avoidance of seriously reckoning with antisemitism was the notion of the so-called cranks (Azim 2018), supposedly ageing Israel-obsessed fanatics who had been attracted to Labour by Corbyn's leadership but were seen as occupying the fringes of party life. Their antisemitism was associated solely with a mistaken internet-addled conspiracism that was regarded an alien imposition upon otherwise innocuous currents of left thought. Leaving aside the question of whether Corbyn himself should be ranked as one of the 'cranks', the firewall between the swelling mass of social media conspiracy theorists on whom successive scandals centred, and the intellectual and political leadership responsible for setting the policy agenda for the party, was arguably much more fluid than this permits.

In February 2019, for example, grassroots web activists demanded Labour MPs sign a 'loyalty pledge' declaring they would 'work for the achievement of a Labour-led Government under whatever leadership members elect'. The pledge was written and disseminated in response to rumours that the aforementioned Luciana Berger was considering her position after facing antisemitic abuse from members of her local constituency party and Corbyn and Labour supporters online (Hope 2019). Berger faced such levels of animosity that she had to be provided with police protection at the 2018 Labour Party conference. Shortly after speaking out publicly about the abuse – and how the party had not informed her about violent threats made against her – local activists put forward a motion of no confidence, on the basis that 'our MP is continually using the media to criticize the man we all want to be prime minister'. One of the members who had proposed the motion had previously described Berger as a 'disruptive Zionist' (*Jewish Chronicle* 2019). The motion was eventually withdrawn, but not before Shadow Chancellor John McDonnell amplified the activists' call for Berger to pledge fealty to a Corbyn-led party by appearing on national radio to demand that she 'just put this issue to bed – to say very clearly, "no I am not supporting another party, I'm not jumping ship"'. The pledge was then signed and promoted by a series of Shadow Cabinet members (Pickard 2019) who, far from seeking to challenge or negate the narratives pushed by the supposed minority of 'cranks', elevated and legitimized them within the highest ranks of the party.

The 'rigged system' and liberal socialism

Closer inspection would have connected the Labour antisemitism crisis to a more comprehensive worldview pervading large chunks of the left. Corbyn's incapacity to comprehend the content of the antisemitic mural expressed, in an exaggerated manner, the continuing legacy on the left of what critical theorists describe as 'foreshortened', 'truncated' or 'personified' critiques of capitalism. This mode of critique was summarized in slogan form by the idea that contemporary capitalism constitutes a 'rigged system'.[1] The idea of the economy and political system as 'rigged' in this way was central to Corbynism's distinctive attempt to combine a traditional liberal-socialist denunciation of capitalism with more contemporary populist political strategies. What might be labelled the 'latent' antisemitic potential that inheres in this kind of anti-capitalism in any context was available and receptive to being turbo-charged by the anti-imperialist obsession with Israel's supposedly singularly malicious threat to 'world peace'. And, much like Corbyn's default response to accusations of antisemitism, such critiques hinge on questions of personal morality.

Corbyn first adopted the rhetoric of the 'rigged system' in 2016, having seen it being successfully used, in different ways, as a populist campaign slogan by both Bernie Sanders and Donald Trump (Bolton and Pitts 2018: 209–10). In Corbyn's rendition, the founding contradiction of capitalist political economy today lay in the contrast between 'the many' – a unified, productive community of 'ordinary working people' – and 'the few' – a corrupt and unproductive 'elite' who had 'rigged' an economic system that would otherwise work for the benefit of all. Corbyn thus launched Labour's 2017 election campaign with a fierce speech denouncing a system 'set up by the wealth extractors for the wealth extractors', and raging at the 'morally bankrupt' elite who 'extract wealth from the pockets of ordinary working people' by means of a corrupt 'racket'. Only a Corbyn government would 'take on the cosy cartels that are hoarding this country's wealth for themselves' (see Corbyn 2017).

Through the lens of the notion of the 'rigged system', the structures and functioning of capitalism appear as the manifestations of the immoral desires of those in power. The exploitation of the labour of the productive 'many' in pursuit of profit is understood as the result of the personal greed of capitalists and political leaders. Opposing capitalism thus becomes a matter of finding out who those malignant individuals are and removing them from power. Such a perspective entails constant vigilance against those suspected of bearing personal responsibility for the miseries and inequalities of capitalism. The core of this mode of analysis encapsulates what Moishe Postone (1993: 64–5) describes as 'productivism': 'a normative critique of non-productive social groupings from the standpoint of those groupings that are "truly" productive'.

In the decade leading up to Corbyn's election as Labour leader, this type of personalized critique of capitalism found fertile ground in the wake of the 2008 Global Financial Crisis. The analysis of the financial crash put forward by groups such as Occupy Wall Street suggested it had been caused by a chronic imbalance of power between the financial and banking sectors on the one hand, and the 'real' or 'productive' economy on the other. This disparity was the result of three decades of 'neoliberalism', in which a lack of state regulation of the global financial system was seen as having enabled those sectors to make vast amounts of profit from speculation on behalf of

---

[1] The word 'rigged' – in the sense of 'deceitful' or 'trick' – does not derive from a ship's 'rigging' as one might assume but rather the 'thimblerig' or 'shell game'. This was an early version of the three-cup trick in which a ball is moved from under one cup (or shell) to another, and spectators are encouraged to bet on the final location of the ball. The game has long been notorious as a swindle, often involving shills who are allowed to 'win' before the swindle of the public begins.

the top '1 per cent' – or 'the elite' – at the expense of the '99 per cent' – or 'the people'. The 'real economy' had been undermined – or 'rigged' – by the power, greed and mathematical trickery of unproductive global financial institutions, for whom money seemed to beget money, apparently of its own accord (see, e.g., Hudson 2015). The crash was the inevitable, calamitous consequence of allowing the unproductive few to gain the upper hand over the productive many.

A contrast was often drawn between neoliberal 'casino capitalism', driven by the speculation of international financiers, and the postwar era of welfare capitalism (see, e.g., Giroux 2016). During the latter, earlier period, capital controls and the Bretton Woods system meant that capital had far less freedom to roam the globe in search of profits, with industry the 'master' of finance rather than vice versa, and the gap between the '1 per cent' and the rest much less pronounced (Reuters 2018). The shift from this form of Keynesian welfare capitalism, in which workers received their 'fair share' of wealth, to the financialized precarity of 'neoliberalism' in the early 1970s was regarded straightforwardly as the result of the machinations of the rich and powerful, facilitated by international free trade deals and supranational institutions, distorting a benign economic order so as to place profits above social needs.

Given the numerical disparity between the productive 'many' and the unproductive 'few', this account suggests, the only way the system can retain this 'rigged' character is either through direct violence or ideological trickery. Thus in many cases it is not only the political and economic system which is regarded as 'rigged', but the 'mainstream media' and political and civic culture more broadly. The 'rigged system' as a whole is invariably regarded as monolithic, omnipotent, entirely oppressive and devoid of contradiction. This can often lend such analyses a conspiratorial edge, even at their most sophisticated.

For his supporters, the power and passion of Corbyn's denunciation of capitalism as a 'rigged system', drawing on the critiques of capitalism articulated by Occupy and the anti-austerity movement, exemplified a Year Zero moment wiping out the spin, corruption and right-wing rhetoric of the New Labour years, and returning the party to the 'true Labour values' of Clement Attlee, Aneurin Bevin and Keir Hardie. In a sense, Corbyn and his supporters were correct to see his moralistic mode of politics, and his depiction of capitalism as a battle between the 'many' who produce the nation's wealth through their labour, and an unproductive 'few' who illegitimately claim that wealth as their own, in this vein (see Bolton and Pitts 2020b). While Corbynism's STWC-style foreign policy ran against the grain of the Labour Party's political traditions, in this respect it was very much in tune with a long-standing pattern of economic thought within Labour and the British left, cutting across its factional divisions and the left-right spectrum.

As the Labour MP and former Policy Coordinator Jon Cruddas (2021) has argued, theories of value and its relationship with labour have 'defin[ed] the politics of the last few centuries' throughout the British liberal and socialist left. This has resulted in the pursuit of a 'fairer' distribution of the fruits of production, rather than a more fundamental reconfiguration of the architecture of work and economic life – that is, what Marxists call 'the mode of production'. Within the UK labour movement, the Fabian tradition has been the standard bearer of this understanding on Labour's centre-left. Policy-wise, this has rested on the assumption that capitalism would generate levels of growth capable of facilitating fair redistribution of the proceeds across class strata. The technocratic generation of social democrats that led Labour through the middle part of the twentieth century – the moment of 'true Labour values' to which Corbynism was taken to return – established this notion as a core part of the 'labourist' arsenal of policies that a large, bureaucratic state was meant to implement (see Edgerton 2019: chapters 11–12). This framing of the capitalist economy as a question of distribution was explicitly revived within the mainstream of the party by Ed Miliband's centre-left leadership, whose post-2008 'producers' vs 'predators' rhetoric unwittingly laid the groundwork for Corbyn's subsequent radicalization of this discourse (for a summary see Pitts 2022).

While a conception of capitalism as a 'rigged system' where the unproductive dominate the productive is commonly attributed to Marx – indeed, media attempts to label Corbyn a 'Marxist' rested on this misconception – the roots of this imaginary lie not in Marx's work but in classical political economy and the bourgeois, or liberal, critique of the aristocratic legacy of feudalism. In particular, it stems from an understanding of class inequality as relating to the different interests that arise from the ownership of different forms of property that first appears in systematic form in the work of Adam Smith (see Clarke 1992 for a summary). For Smith, the dissolution of feudalism laid bare the three 'factors of production' – 'stock' (or capital), land and labour – which are the natural constituents of wealth in all societies. Each factor is the property of a different class, and delivers a different 'reward' to its owner – profit, rent and wages respectively – so that each class has distinct interests resulting from how it can increase its own revenue. Class membership is determined by the relationship between an individual and their property. Classes in this 'classical' conception are not socially constituted, but rather are separate 'worlds' whose social interaction begins when they are brought together as factors in the production process.

Smith thought that through prudent management by the state, the interests of the three classes could be kept in balance to ensure the wealth of the whole society would increase, to the good of all. The state should counteract the dangers of 'concentrated social power' within 'commercial society', with the interests of the merchant (or capitalist) class in particular regarded as potentially running against those of the 'commonwealth'. The pursuit of profit on behalf of individual capitalists, unrestrained by competition, morality or public administration, would reduce the overall rate of profit and impede the development of the division of labour, to the detriment of society as a whole, Smith thought.

David Ricardo took inspiration from Smith but thought the latter's partitioned account of the production and distribution of wealth was flawed. He argued that wealth was ultimately produced by labour alone, with profit being what remained after wages and rent had been subtracted from the labour product. The implication of Ricardo's theory, although not one that he himself drew out, was that wages and profit existed in an inverse relation. His analysis meant that profits could easily be construed as an illegitimate deduction from what 'properly' belonged to the worker as the 'rightful' owner of labour, which many post-Ricardian thinkers, in particular within the early labour movement, considered the sole foundation of wealth. The explosive implications of this shift in theory are clear: the capitalist class and the working class could now be perceived as being locked in a struggle over the same source of wealth, the product of workers' labour, rather than each class being 'rewarded' through a separate revenue stream.

By revealing the tension at the heart of capitalist production, Ricardo established the framework which has structured left-liberal thought ever since. The idea of a parasitical, unproductive aristocratic class was central to the first articulation of the theory of 'class struggle', between the purportedly 'active' and 'idle' elements of society by liberal historians of the French Revolution (Comninel 1987). It became a common trope of the English radical-liberal critique of 'Old Corruption' by industrialist interests, a critique that was then extended to those industrialists themselves by the nascent nineteenth-century labour movement (Stedman Jones 1983) – in so doing laying the theoretical groundwork for the productivist perspective that shaped the 'traditional Labour values' Corbynism sought to recapture. To the extent that this liberal understanding of class struggle is carried over into analyses of capitalist social relations, there is no qualitative difference between the bourgeois critique of feudal society and the socialist critique of capitalism. While the persistence of aristocratic forms of landed property was once seen by the bourgeoisie as an illegitimate and outmoded hindrance to the full development of industry, so too are capitalist private property, profit and the market now regarded as an irrational imposition preventing workers from developing their productive capacity to its full extent.

This understanding of the anachronistic nature of capitalist property relations was well articulated in #WeDemand, a Labour June 2017 campaign video, which articulated the 'demand' for a society where production would be no longer 'subject to grand profiteering, but planned, transparent, executed in efficient fashion under democratic control' (Official Jeremy Corbyn Channel 2017).[2]

This kind of liberal socialism does not provide a critique of either classical political economy or liberal theories of history, but often merely re-presents them from the perspective of the class interests seen as most closely tied to the unfolding 'forces of production'. It has played a vital role on the left of the Labour Party, with Tony Benn, the central figure connecting Corbyn to the Labour left traditions of the twentieth century, advocating what his rival Denis Healey dismissed as a form of 'feudal socialism' – one of the 'types' of socialist ideology that Marx and Engels attack and ridicule in the third chapter of the *Manifesto* as examples of 'reactionary socialism'. According to Healey, Benn 'read Marx for the first time in his fifties and thought he was wonderful, [but] was

---

[2] The video, directed by Ken Loach and released 2 June 2017, begins with several statements of what 'we know', including: 'We know the health worker and the firefighter contribute no less than the stockbroker and merchant banker' (which seems surprisingly generous to stockbrokers and bankers). This is followed by several individuals stating: 'We have had enough', leading to a series of 'We demand' statements, beginning with: 'We demand health, work, home, education and care in time of need, not subject to grand profiteering, but planned, transparent, executed in efficient fashion under democratic control, using our intelligence and imagination. We demand the full fruits of our labour.' Perhaps not entirely by accident, the phrase 'not subject to grand profiteering' is spoken by a priest in a clerical collar, subtly hinting at the roots of this rhetoric in Christian social doctrine.

exactly the sort of feudal socialist, the upper-class socialist, who was satirised by Karl Marx himself in the *Communist Manifesto* as a man who could make the bourgeoisie cringe with the wit of his satire but [was] basically totally ineffective in politics because of the total failure to understand the way in which the world was changing' (BBC 1995).

This blend of the classical critique of capitalism with the liberal critique of feudalism was continued by Benn's disciple Corbyn, and reappears in the understanding of class that underpins the notion of the 'rigged system'. Rather than seeking to bring the category of class into question through a critique of its constitutive position in capitalist society (see Bonefeld 2014: chapter 5), this kind of positivistic socialism tends to naturalize and treat as transhistorical givens historically specific capitalist social forms – in particular the peculiar forms assumed by labour and production in capitalist society. The focus immediately shifts instead to the distributive level, and the question of how the competing class 'interests' associated with those assumed social forms play out across society. According to this analysis, in order to sustain their power in society, the capitalist class must continually and creatively work together to build coalitions and 'hegemonic blocs'. The working class – those whose only property is their labour power – must in turn act creatively to defend their own interests and seize power. Class struggle, it follows, is a contingent process between two entirely separate groups, heavily dependent on a certain level of class consciousness. It is seen as arising out of attempts by the owners of labour power and the owners of capital to defend their respective interests, with both sides attempting to reduce the power and agency of the other, and in this way become the 'ruling class'.

From this perspective, any successful hegemonic project on behalf of the capitalist class must therefore be seen as a mode of 'rigging' these social dynamics in such a way as to ensure the cessation of class struggle, with workers erroneously coming to see the interests of the capitalist class as their own. Likewise, socialism is here regarded as the result of a rival hegemonic project constructed by the working class, culminating in the seizure of control over the means of production and the abolition of private property. The historical development of capitalist society – such as the transformation from Keynesian welfare capitalism to financialized neoliberalism – is explained in these terms (e.g. Harvey 2005), with the failure of one previously dominant ruling-class hegemonic project and the successful construction of another, and so on.

Rather than a contradictory negative category of capitalist society, this presents the working class as existing outside of it – capitalist social relations being artificially imposed upon the working class by alien forces. This reduces the analysis of class membership to a shared common culture or the recognition of shared interests standing in opposition to an external power. In the hands of left and right alike this often ends up in a kind of regressive communalism, shaped around the nation as a bulwark against global capital flows. This was evident in Corbyn's promises to 'build it in Britain' (Corbyn 2018), manifesto commitments ending the free movement of people from the EU on the supposed grounds it 'forced down wages' in the UK (BBC 2018), and the protectionist proposal to extrapolate on a national scale the much-heralded 'Preston model' espoused in so-called Corbynomics, whereby local authorities would use a procurement policy based on local 'anchor institutions' to concentrate and retain wealth within communities (Guinan and O'Neill 2018). This programme of economic nationalism was founded on the conviction that nationally produced wealth was being appropriated by extractive global forces (see Blakeley 2018). A 2017 report on 'Alternative Models of Ownership' commissioned by McDonnell recommended the adoption of a form of municipal, and then national, protectionism, underpinned by so-called anchor institutions with UK-only procurement policies, to prevent locally or nationally produced wealth 'leaking' away from its place of origin, or being 'stolen' by the international financial sector (Labour Party 2017: 7). This proposed policy platform reproduced in contemporary guise elements of that put forward by Tony Benn in the mid-1970s. In Benn's vision, the British state, workers and trade unions should unite in building a 'siege economy', a national barrier against a banker-led 'international capitalism' seeking to hijack money that would otherwise be productively invested in 'the British economy' (Benn 1989: 621).

This policy agenda resonated in the party's positioning on Brexit under Corbyn. Both Corbyn and McDonnell argued that the mutually agreed limits imposed on 'state aid' to national industries by membership of the European Single Market mean that Labour should push for 'Lexit' – leaving both the Single Market and Customs Union in order to pursue a form of state-driven 'socialism in one country', as well as ending the free movement of European workers to Britain. Indeed, in the months immediately following the vote to leave the European Union, McDonnell echoed Brexiteer arguments by asserting that opposing Brexit would place Labour 'on the side of certain corporate elites, who have always had the British people at the back of the queue'. Labour's 2018 'Build It in Britain' campaign thus promised to repatriate the 'thousands of jobs' successive Conservative-led governments had 'sent overseas' (Labour Party 2018). The implication was that Labour intended to restore the glories of a lost golden age of British industry through a protectionist programme of national renewal which will throw off the restrictions imposed by the EU, international finance and global trade. Corbyn had previously made this point explicit in a 2010 speech where he claimed 'they – the world's bankers, International Monetary Fund, European Union – they are utterly united in what they want ... deflation, suppressing the economy and creating unemployment' (Watts 2019).

Truncated critiques and capitalist society

Like its liberal and classical political economy forebears, the Corbynite notion of capitalism as a 'rigged system' affirms and dehistoricizes capitalism's historically *specific* social forms and treats capitalist labour, class identities and the so-called real economy of concrete production as if they were merely the eternally same natural interactions between humans and their environment. It thus stands opposed to one of the central aims of Marx's critique of political economy, which led to his rejection of liberal and classical forms of class analysis: the identification of the *historical specificity* of capitalist production and its class relations.

Every society throughout history has had powerful groups of one sort or another, following their own perceived interests over those with less power, and seeking to capture and consume what is produced by the labour of others. Capitalism is separated from previous modes of exploitation through the particular social forms through which these relations of power and processes of labour and consumption are necessarily expressed (Postone 1993; Heinrich 2012; Bonefeld 2014; Kurz 2016; Bolton 2020b). Acts of concrete, physical labour still exist in capitalism, just as in every society throughout history. Peculiar about capitalism, though, is that labour is organized not for the direct satisfaction of the material needs of either the labourer or the owner of the means of production, but rather for the production of that which carries value. Value, here, is not the same thing as material wealth. It is not a physical thing but a social relation that exists between things. In the context of the capitalist mode of production, no one can access the necessities of physical survival other than through the production of commodities which are successfully exchanged with other commodities, and as such validated as value-bearing and a 'socially necessary' part of the total labour of society as a whole. This means that in capitalist society, the relation between a concrete act of labour and access to the means of subsistence is not direct and immediate, but indirect and socially mediated. If a commodity fails to sell, the concrete labour that produced it has been a waste of time, no matter how useful or valuable it may be as a physical object. Thus while only human labour can produce value, not all acts of human labour do so. In a system where the production of value, rather than wealth, is the goal of production, the specific qualities of concrete labour will always be determined by the value side, namely, the need to *realize* the value in exchange. The impossibility of avoiding social mediation of one's existence through the processes of buying and selling of labour power and other products of labour distinguishes capitalist society from all other known forms of society.

An analysis, like that based on the notion of the 'rigged system', which endorses the concrete side of labour and the production of wealth but maligns the abstract side is unable to grasp the essential characteristic of capitalism to which their dialectic is central. The fact that the material means of subsistence are accessed only through the socially constituted form of value leads to a competitive dynamic in which producers struggle to ensure their commodities can be sold at their socially determined value, cheapening the costs of production through technological innovation or reducing labour costs in order to produce more for less. Failure to keep up with this race for productivity risks economic crises and ruin, and it is this wholly rational fear which compels states, capitalists and workers alike to organize themselves in such a way as to facilitate the continual expansion of value. The problem for everyone living under this system, whether capitalist or worker, is that the movement of social validation – the movement of capital itself – is not possible to consciously control. Because the status of any individual act of labour depends on the entire system of social production and exchange, no single individual, group or state can alter its trajectory, no matter how powerful they are. Indeed, from the perspective of an individual or state, the capricious movement of this standard appears as a law of nature, with its own contradictory logic and temporal dynamic. It is experienced as something which is completely out of reach of human activity but to which that activity must adapt if one is to survive. Crucially, this is not an illusion, a form of 'false consciousness' enforced on one part of society through the 'hegemonic project' of another. It is how things really are in a society mediated by abstract labour, where survival depends on the movement of commodities, money and value. Poverty, inequality and economic crises are the result of the *internal contradictions* of this form of society, rather than any external impositions.

The fundamental problem with an analysis which contrasts the 'good' capitalism of the past, dominated by the productive, with the 'bad' or immoral capitalism of today, over which unproductive finance is said to hold sway, is the failure to grasp the internal connections between the two. Anselm Jappe (2016: 70) puts this well: 'The rise of neoliberalism after 1980 was not some devious manoeuvre on the part of the greediest capitalists, nor a *coup d'état* carried out in collusion with smug politicians, as the "radical" left would have it. Neoliberalism was, on the contrary, the only possible way to make the capitalist system last a bit longer.' The traditional left-liberal critique that underpinned Corbynism's portrayal of the 'rigged system' can focus only on the evils of 'neoliberalism' or 'finance' in isolation from capitalism as a whole. As such, it is unable to comprehend the underlying social dynamic which drove the turn from Keynesianism to neoliberalism, and seeks instead to blame the suffering caused by capitalist society on supposedly exceptionally greedy, immoral or corrupt individuals or groups. Lacking any concept of capital as a mode of social relations, this is a 'truncated' critique.

Anti-Judaism and anti-Zionism

This critical inadequacy is not merely an academic problem. The way critique construes its object determines what strategies it is able to construct to act upon it. As such, a flawed or partial conceptualization of capitalism is likely to lead to equally flawed or partial forms of 'anti-capitalism'. Critiques of capitalism come in many shades, and, as in the case of the notion of the 'rigged system', they are not always emancipatory. A critique which depicts capitalism as a struggle between a productive national people and an unproductive global elite, with the former producing all the wealth and the latter stealing it, is not unambiguously progressive. Without an adequate theoretical framework for grasping the strange, topsy-turvy dynamic of capitalist society, partial forms of anti-capitalism on the left leave themselves open to reactionary or regressive outcomes, including authoritarian nationalism, fascism, ultraconservative theocracy and antisemitism.

This potential is clearly indicated by Mear One's above-mentioned mural. Titled 'Freedom for Humanity', the complex totality of capitalist modernity is reduced to the image of big-nosed bankers playing what looks like a game of monopoly, one of them counting money, on a 'table' formed by the backs of dark-skinned, lifeless, apparently enslaved human shapes, representing a totally passive and fully dominated image of 'the poor', overseen by the symbol of the Illuminati, the all-seeing eye, and flanked by a kitsch image of a black woman holding a small child. An 'activist' holds a sign with the fascist slogan 'The New World Order is the Enemy of Humanity', whereby 'enemy of humanity' as much as the 'all-seeing eye' radiate with not-so-subtle antisemitic subtext. The artist, Mear One, argued that, far from being antisemitic, his mural was an attack on 'class and privilege' and that he was not depicting Jews but rather 'the ruling class elite few' (see Whitehouse 2012). A critique of capitalism which is unable to grasp the central forms of that society – value, capital and commodity – but rather limits itself to the idea that an otherwise benign productive society has been 'rigged' by an immoral 'elite few' is not, on its own, inherently antisemitic. However, it fails to have anything to answer to reactionary propositions like Mear One's imagery, and fails to distinguish itself from antisemitic anti-capitalism. Indeed, like Corbyn and most of his defenders, it may not even recognize it when it stares in their faces.

The idea that the development of the good society is being held back by the conscious actions of a small group of amoral people wielding a shadowy omnipotent power has been a staple of antisemitic thought for centuries, shapeshifting with the times. David Nirenberg has shown just how deeply rooted this kind of opposition between 'good' and 'bad' forms of economic activity and modes of property is in the long history of 'anti-Judaism' within Western – or Christian – culture. From the time of St Paul onwards, the Christian supersessionist tradition constructed itself around the distinction between a supposedly 'Jewish' literalism, legalism and vengeful 'justice' and a Christianity which regarded the moral 'spirit' to be above the 'letter' of the law, and which sought salvation in grace, love and inner faith rather than blind adherence to an external law (Nirenberg 2018: chapters 2–3).

As the capitalist world economy started to emerge across the seventeenth, eighteenth and nineteenth centuries, this pre-existing opposition was reformulated in critiques of economic activity and property ownership which were driven by strict enforcement of legal rights and contracts over the moral health of the commonwealth as a whole. In both Kant and Hegel, there is a contrast drawn between 'property' – understood as being an expression of inner moral character and 'personality' – and 'possessions' – 'temporary holdings' enforced by law alone, with no moral limitation or expression, and frequently characterized as 'Jewish' (Nirenberg 2018: 433). From this perspective, a moral and rational society requires leaving behind – or 'converting' – forms of extractive, non-productive economic activity supposedly associated with Judaism, and the triumph of an economics expressing the morality and love of the community. In the young Marx's *On the Jewish Question*, prior to his development of the critique of political economy, again the 'anti-social' aspects of capitalism – 'practical need, individual utility … haggling' and 'money' itself – are presented as being innately Jewish, although with the proviso that capitalism is making society as a whole 'Jewish' (Marx 1979: 236). Later British radical and liberal critics of capitalism – a tradition to which Corbyn and Benn explicitly aligned themselves – would also at times frame their differentiation of 'good' from 'bad' forms of property in terms of Jews and Judaism: the antisemitism of influential British radicals from William Cobbett to J. A. Hobson can be traced back to this long-standing conceptual structure (on Hobson, see Bolton, this volume). Moreover, this opposition posed between 'Christian' inner morality and 'Jewish' external literalism was central also to Corbynist denials of the very possibility that the great man might have spoken or acted in antisemitic ways: piling up textual and discourse analyses of the various antisemitic incidents counts as only so much typically Jewish pilpul, abstract, formalist and literalist nit-picking that can be gentlemanly shrugged off – one is tempted to say, gentile-ly – by pointing to the good heart and anti-racist spirit of the Man himself. Maddeningly for those who tried to engage as forensically as possible with the evidence, Corbyn's professions of faith in his own anti-racist identity regularly overrode all that lawyerly talk, contributing, in turn, to JC's martyrium and Golgatha.

Through this lens it becomes possible to see the connection between the truncated critique of capitalism as a 'rigged system', the phantasy of the nation-state as a bulwark against the global movement of capital, and the liberal, non-Marxian foundations of the anti-Zionism central to Corbyn's milieu. Central to the latter is the equation of Zionism with racism that became the central sticking point in the 2018 dispute over Labour's adoption of the International Holocaust Remembrance Alliance's (IHRA) 'working definition' of antisemitism.[3] In response to proposals for the adoption of the IHRA definition, Corbyn and his supporters argued that describing the founding of *a* State of Israel – a conceptual, rather than historical critique of a Jewish nation-state – as 'a racist endeavour' was necessary in the pursuit of Palestinian rights, and should not be classed as antisemitic (Sarkar 2018). To this end, during the wrangling over the definition, activists stuck up posters across London declaring that 'Israel is a racist endeavour' (Powell 2018). But this rejection of Israel's right to exist as a Jewish nation-state was not grounded in a general critique of the capitalist state form as such. Rather it regarded the Jewish state as being a uniquely malign and deformed distortion of the form of a 'true', ethical state – in contrast to a Palestinian nation-state, which was heralded as a vehicle for universal emancipation.

While 'true' states are regarded as providing the architecture for the defence of a productive people from the intrusions of global capitalism, Israel is here granted the same globe-spanning power and intangible, destructive influence over world affairs and domestic policy that the rhetoric of the 'rigged system' attributes to the global financial elite. The violence of the Israeli state is not understood in terms of the violence that is inherent in the capitalist state form as such, but regarded as this particular state's failure to live up to the inner moral spirit that exemplifies true national communities. Such a perspective is similar to the functionalist explanation of antisemitism which, as argued earlier, reduces antisemitism to a contingent ideological cover for supposedly deeper economic interests, but here the argument is inverted: here, *anti*-antisemitism is

---

[3] The first version of what would become the IHRA definition of antisemitism was formulated in the wake of the 2001 UN World Conference against Racism in Durban. The conference was overwhelmingly focused on the supposed evils of Israel and Zionism, with delegates equating Zionism with racism and accusing Israel of genocide and Nazism. Pamphlets were distributed showing hook-nosed Jews depicted as Nazis, dripping blood and spearing Palestinian children with pots of money nearby. A thousands-strong march featured placards equating Zionism and Nazism, with one reading 'Hitler Should Have Finished the Job'. Jewish delegates feared for their physical safety (see Hirsh 2017: 135–46). Fearing that attacks on Jews based on this kind of rhetoric and aggression would not be classed as antisemitic by security and legal institutions, the new definition sought to outline the areas where ostensibly anti-Israel statements could, in context, be classed as antisemitic. The result was a short – and by no means conceptually watertight – definition of antisemitism as 'a certain perception of Jews, which may be expressed as hatred toward Jews', including attacks on individuals, property, community institutions, religious facilities and the State of Israel 'conceived as a Jewish collectivity'. This core definition was accompanied by a set of eleven illustrative examples, the most contested being that it could, in context, be antisemitic to claim that 'the existence of a State of Israel is a racist endeavor' – in short that aspirations of a Jewish nation-state are by definition, and unlike other national claims, racist. The definition also made clear that 'criticism of Israel similar to that leveled against any other country cannot be regarded as antisemitic' (International Holocaust Remembrance 2016).

supposedly functional for economic interests. In the context of rebuttals of antisemitic polemics against the right of Israel to exist as a Jewish nation-state, the history of Israel and Zionism is severed from that of the foundational anti-Judaism which pervades Western culture, culminating in the Holocaust, and is itself reduced to another disguised expression of capitalist and imperialist 'interests'. Anyone seeking to make a connection between antisemitism and the critique of the *concept* of a Jewish state, as highlighted by the IHRA definition, is regarded as fraudulently 'instrumentalizing' anti-antisemitism in order to defend capitalist and imperialist 'interests'. This anti-antisemitism is not one, it is suggested, and therefore the alleged antisemitism cannot be that, either.

In the Corbyn years, this often led to Jewish leftists being portrayed as disaffected right-wingers, 'neoliberals', and imperialists (Sugarman 2019b). They were accused of confecting claims of antisemitism in order to both undermine Corbyn's domestic agenda and to deflect criticism of the Israeli state. At times, this focus on the supposedly true 'interests' of those who refuse to deny Israel's right to exist as such can go so far as to lead to a distortion if not outright denial of the Holocaust. As the existence of the State of Israel is often linked to the need to ensure the Holocaust can never happen again, the 'absolutist', that is, unconditional and categorical opposition to the existence of Israel and to (any tradition of) Zionism can become the starting point for a revisionist history which seeks to downplay the reality of the Holocaust itself (see Yakira 2010: chapter 1). This can be expressed either through 'casting doubt' on the extent or purpose of Auschwitz, or the ahistorical and relativizing equation of Auschwitz or the Warsaw Ghetto with the current conditions in Gaza. Both of these forms of Holocaust distortion were frequently found within Corbyn-supporting milieus; indeed, Corbyn himself hosted an event in Parliament explicitly comparing Auschwitz to Gaza on Holocaust Memorial Day in 2010 (Marsh 2018).

Conclusion: Activating the elements of antisemitism

The crisis over antisemitism in Labour was not merely the result of one particular individual's failings, or those of a 'few bad apples', but was rather the culmination of a long process of political, ideological and theoretical degeneration that has disfigured parts of the left for decades. It is our contention that a critique which depicts capitalism as a struggle between a productive people and an unproductive elite, with the former group producing all the wealth and the latter stealing it, contains reactionary potential, including the potential for a distinct mode of antisemitism on the left which can, in certain circumstances, expand the room for the right to make political gains.

We do not want to understate the importance of challenging forms of concrete domination and the unequal distribution of power across society. But the critique of political economy as we have presented it here suggests that no individual or group can be made wholly responsible for the poverty, inequality and alienation of capitalist societies. Left antisemitism springs, at least in part, from this failure to grasp the abstract, intangible side of capitalist social relations, the historically specific form of impersonal power that, as Marx noted, 'works behind the backs' of all who live in capitalist society, including capitalists (Marx 1976: 135). The impossibility of locating in individuals or groups the totalizing and omnipotent power underpinning a society completely shaped by capital is undoubtedly a recipe for a dangerous and ever-mounting frustration. The case will never be closed on these culprits, because the locus of this power cannot and will not be identified in individual or collective human actors. This produces unsustainable notions of what it is possible to do to remedy capitalism's ills, and the perilous environment for the cultivation and manifestation of antisemitism.

As Postone (2016) put it: 'One of the roles of theory, and this sounds very modest but it is very important, is to show which paths are clearly mistaken. You can put a lot of energy and effort into mistaken paths.' Corbynism was one such mistaken path. Its vision of a unified national community of hardworking people manipulated by an unproductive global elite only served to expand the rhetorical space within which Brexitism and Johnsonism could operate with much greater electoral effectiveness. This was a decisive factor in Corbynism's irrevocable defeat in the 2019 General Election. The centrality of personalized critique to the Corbyn worldview, and the gradual activation of its latent antisemitic potential throughout his leadership, ended up with Corbyn-supporting social media milieus seeking to explain his election loss by accusing the British Board of Deputies of British Jews, the Chief Rabbi, and a whole host of Jewish communal organizations of conspiring to bring him down in a concerted effort to destroy the left and protect the State of Israel from criticism (see, e.g., Finn 2019; Stern-Weiner 2020; Harpin 2020).

Understanding how the elements of antisemitism are inscribed within the foundational social forms of capitalist society as a whole renders inadequate attempts to explain antisemitism as a contingent function of class ideology. Treating antisemitism solely as an instrument consciously wielded by powerful groups allows leftists to reassure themselves that antisemitism is something alien imposed upon them by their political opponents. The oft-stated idea on the Labour left that identifying as 'antiracist' is enough to inoculate leftists from the power of this narrative is therefore a comforting fallacy. But it is precisely because antisemitism is often presented as an emancipatory response to oppression that it is so seductive (Postone 2006; Hirsh 2017).

In its response, the left absolves itself of the need to grapple with the uncomfortable possibility that antisemitic worldviews – including the belief that Jewish national self-determination is uniquely malign – might not be simply the result of manipulation by those in power. In this sense, it is important not only to recognize the limits of relating Corbynism's antisemitism problem to the prevalence of a 'rigged system' narrative constructed around economic issues alone, but also to recognize the imbrication of this narrative with a form of antisemitism more indebted to anti-Israel sentiment, anti-Zionism and anti-Judaism. These two core elements of left antisemitism activate one another where there exist those theoretical conditions foundational to Corbynism: a critique of global capital in the name of the national community, a critique of unproductive classes in the name of the productive, and a critique of Western 'imperialism', personified in the form of the State of Israel, in the name of a reactionary 'anti-imperialism'.

References

Adorno, T. W., and M. Horkheimer (1972), *The Dialectic of Enlightenment*, London: Verso.

Azim, J. (2018), 'The Real Battle for Labour's Soul? Lansmanites vs Cranks', *Labour List*, 8 August, available at: https://labourlist.org/2018/08/the-real-battle-for-labours-soul-lansmanites-vs-cranks (accessed 28 November 2022).

BBC (1995), '*The Wilderness Years*, Episode 1: Cast into the Wilderness', available at: www.youtube.com/watch?v=pb4Y-QHe3yw&t=0s (accessed 28 November 2022).

BBC (2018), 'Andrew Marr Show', 21 January, available at: http://news.bbc.co.uk/1/shared/bsp/hi/pdfs/21011802.pdf (accessed 28 November 2022).

Benn, T. (1989), *Against the Tide. Diaries 1973–76*, London: Hutchinson.

Bennett, R. (2016) 'Jeremy Corbyn has been on the right side of history for 30 years. That's real leadership,' *The Guardian*, 16 September, available at: https://www.theguardian.com/commentisfree/2016/sep/16/jeremy-corbyn-leadership-david-cameron-libya-labour (accessed 24 July 2023).

Blakeley, G. (2018), 'Financial Globalisation Has Been a Disaster. Brexit Gives Us a Chance to Resist It', *Novara Media*, 24 June, available at: https://novaramedia.com/2018/06/24/financial-globalisation-has-been-a-disaster-brexit-gives-us-a-chance-to-resist-it (accessed 28 November 2022).

Bloodworth, J. (2015), 'The Bizarre World of Jeremy Corbyn and Stop the War', *Politico*, 11 December, available at: www.politico.eu/article/bizarre-world-of-jeremy-corbyn-and-stop-the-war-coalition-galloway-rees-iraq-far-left (accessed 28 November 2022).

Bolton, M. (2020a), 'Conceptual Vandalism, Historical Distortion: The Labour Antisemitism Crisis and the Limits of Class Instrumentalism', *Journal of Contemporary Antisemitism*, 3 (2): 11–30.

Bolton, M. (2020b), '"Democratic Socialism" and the Concept of (Post)Capitalism', *Political Quarterly*, 91: 334–42.

Bolton, M., and F. H. Pitts (2018), *Corbynism: A Critical Approach*, Bingley: Emerald.

Bolton, M., and F. H. Pitts (2020a), 'The Rigged System and the Real Economy: Corbynism, Antisemitism and Productivist Critiques of Capitalism', in A. Alietti and D. Padovan (eds), *Racism & Antisemitism in the Era of Neo-nationalism*, 187–220, Milan: Mimesis.

Bolton, M., and F. H. Pitts (2020b), 'Corbynism and Blue Labour: Post-liberalism and National Populism in the British Labour Party', *British Politics*, 15 (1): 88–109.

Bonefeld, W. (2014), *Critical Theory and the Critique of Political Economy*, London: Bloomsbury.

Clarke, S. (1992), *Marx, Marginalism and Modern Sociology*, London: Palgrave Macmillan.

Community Security Trust (2011), '"Doctored Quotes" and CST', *CST Blog*, 7 October, available at: https://cst.org.uk/news/blog/2011/10/07/doctored-quotes-and-cst (accessed 28 November 2022).

Comninel, G. (1987), *Rethinking the French Revolution: Marxism and the Revisionist Challenge*, London: Verso

Corbyn, J. (2017), '"It Is a Rigged System": Jeremy Corbyn's Launch Speech – In Full', *Independent*, 20 April, available at: https://inews.co.uk/news/politics/rigged-system-jeremy-corbyns-launch-speech-full (accessed 28 November 2022).

Corbyn, J. (2018), 'Jeremy Corbyn's "Build It in Britain" Speech at the EEF Technology Hub', *Labour Party*, 24 July, available at: https://labour.org.uk/press/jeremy-corbyns-build-britain-speech-eef-technology-hub (accessed 28 November 2022).

Cruddas, J. (2021), *The Dignity of Labour*, Cambridge, MA: Polity.

Das, S. (2012), 'Yvonne Ridley: Says Zionists Should Be "Hunted Down"; "Loathes" Israel; Supports Hamas …', *Left Foot Forward*, 15 November, available at: https://

leftfootforward.org/2012/11/yvonne-ridley-respect-rotherham-hamas (accessed 28 November 2022).
Dysch, M. (2015a), 'Corbyn Attended Holocaust Denier's Event', *Jewish Chronicle*, 18 August, available at: www.thejc.com/news/uk/revealed-jeremy-corbyn-attended-event-hosted-by-holocaust-denier-s-group-in-2013-1.68163 (accessed 28 November 2022).
Dysch, M. (2015b), 'Did Jeremy Corbyn Back Artist Whose Mural Was Condemned as Antisemitic?', *Jewish Chronicle*, 6 November, available at: www.thejc.com/news/uk-news/did-jeremy-corbyn-back-artist-whose-mural-was-condemned-as-antisemitic-1.62106 (accessed 28 November 2022).
Edgerton, D. (2019), *The Rise and Fall of the British Nation*, 2nd edn, London: Penguin.
Edwards, P. (2017), 'Len McCluskey: Anti-Semitism Claims Are "Mood Music" Used to Undermine Corbyn', *Labour List*, 27 September, available at: https://labourlist.org/2017/09/len-mccluskey-labour-anti-semitism-claims-are-mood-music-used-to-undermine-corbyn (accessed 28 November 2022).
Finn, D. (2019), 'The Never-Ending Story', *Jacobin*, 11 July, available at: https://jacobin.com/2019/07/labour-party-antisemitism-corbyn-williamson (accessed 28 November 2022).
Freedland, J. (2020), 'What Did Corbyn Mean When He Insulted Me?', *Jewish Chronicle*, 22 January, available at: www.thejc.com/comment/columnists/when-corbyn-insulted-me-what-did-he-mean-1.495769 (accessed 28 November 2022).
Gidley, B., B. McGeever and D. Feldman (2020), 'Labour and Antisemitism: A Crisis Misunderstood', *Political Quarterly*, 91: 413–21.
Gilbert, J. (2018), 'Antisemitism, Cosmopolitanism and the Politics of Labour's "Old" and "New" Right-Wings', *Open Democracy*, 14 April, available at: www.opendemocracy.net/uk/jeremy-gilbert/antisemitism-cosmopolitanism-and-politics-of-labour-s-old-and-new-right-wings (accessed 28 November 2022).
Giroux, H. (2016), 'The Mad Violence of Casino Capitalism', *Counterpunch*, 19 February, available at: www.counterpunch.org/2016/02/19/the-mad-violence-of-casino-capitalism (accessed 28 November 2022).
Harpin, L. (2019), 'Labour MP Branded a "Disgrace" for Saying Dame Margaret Hodge Pursuing "Vendetta" against Jeremy Corbyn', *Jewish Chronicle*, 11 June, available at: www.thejc.com/news/uk-news/labour-mp-branded-a-disgrace-for-saying-dame-margaret-hodge-pursuing-vendetta-against-jeremy-cor-1.485240 (accessed 28 November 2022).
Harpin, L. (2020), 'Board Says Facebook Too Slow to Act over "Bomb the Bod" Threat', *Jewish Chronicle*, 6 May, available at: www.thejc.com/news/uk-news/board-says-facebook-too-slow-to-act-over-bomb-the-bod-threat-1.499539 (accessed 28 November 2022).
Harvey, D. (2005), *A Brief History of Neoliberalism*, Oxford: Oxford University Press.
Heinrich, M. (2012), *An Introduction to the Three Volumes of Marx's Capital*, New York: Monthly Review Press.
Hirsh, D. (2017), *Contemporary Left Antisemitism*, London: Routledge.
Hope, C. (2019), 'Moderate Labour MPs Object over Pressure to Sign Up to "Great Leader Jeremy Corbyn" Pledge Card', *Daily Telegraph*, 17 February, available at: www.telegraph.co.uk/politics/2019/02/17/moderate-labour-mps-object-pressure-sign-great-leader-jeremy (accessed 28 November 2022).
Hudson, M. (2015), *Killing the Host: How Financial Parasites and Debt Destroy the Global Economy*, Dresden: Islet.

International Holocaust Remembrance Alliance (2016), 'Working Definition of Antisemitism', available at: www.holocaustremembrance.com/resources/working-definitions-charters/working-definition-antisemitism (accessed 28 November 2022).
Jappe, A. (2016), *The Writing on the Wall*, Alresford: Zero Books.
Jewish Chronicle (2015), 'The Key Questions Jeremy Corbyn Must Answer', 12 August, available at: www.thejc.com/news/uk/the-key-questions-jeremy-corbyn-must-answer-1.68097 (accessed 28 November 2022).
Jewish Chronicle (2019), 'Luciana Berger Called "Disruptive Zionist" by Labour Member Proposing No Confidence Motion in Her', 8 February, available at: www.thejc.com/news/uk-news/luciana-berger-called-disruptive-zionist-by-labour-member-proposing-no-confidence-motion-in-her-1.479721 (accessed 28 November 2022).
Johnson, A. (2019), *Institutionally Antisemitic: Contemporary Left Antisemitism and the Crisis in the British Labour Party*, London: Fathom.
Kurz, R. (2007), 'Grey Is the Golden Tree of Life, Green Is Theory', available at: https://libcom.org/library/grey-golden-tree-life-green-theory-robert-kurz (accessed 28 November 2022).
Kurz, R. (2016), *The Substance of Capital*, London: Chronos.
Labour Party (2017), *Alternative Models of Ownership*, London: Labour Party.
Labour Party (2018), 'Build It in Britain', *YouTube*, 4 September, available at: www.youtube.com/watch?v=Ze_pa1RCW1s (accessed 28 November 2022).
Marsh, S. (2018), 'Corbyn Apologises over Event Where Israel Was Compared to Nazis', *The Guardian*, 1 August, available at: www.theguardian.com/politics/2018/aug/01/jeremy-corbyn-issues-apology-in-labour-antisemitism-row (accessed 28 November 2022).
Marx, K. (1976), *Capital*, vol. 1, London: Penguin.
Marx, K. (1979), 'On the Jewish Question', in *Early Writings*, 211–42, London: Penguin.
Mason, R. (2015), 'Jeremy Corbyn Says Antisemitism claims "Ludicrous and Wrong"', *The Guardian*, 18 August, available at: www.theguardian.com/politics/2015/aug/18/jeremy-corbyn-antisemitism-claims-ludicrous-and-wrong (accessed 28 November 2022).
Mendick, R. (2017), 'Jeremy Corbyn's 10-Year Association with Group Which Denies the Holocaust', *Daily Telegraph*, 20 May, available at: www.telegraph.co.uk/news/2017/05/20/jeremy-corbyns-10-year-association-group-denies-holocaust (accessed 28 November 2022).
Momentum (2019), 'Rothschild Conspiracy Exposed', *YouTube*, 4 March, available at: www.youtube.com/watch?v=wFGjIEcvP7Q (accessed 28 November 2022).
Nirenberg, D. (2018), *Anti-Judaism*, London: Apollo.
Official Jeremy Corbyn Channel (2017), '#WeDemand', *YouTube*, available at: www.youtube.com/watch?v=28-fC6_Byu0 (accessed 28 November 2022).
O'Neill, M., and J. Guinan (2018), 'The Institutional Turn: Labour's New Political Economy', *Renewal*, 26 (2): 5–16.
Pickard, J. (2019), 'John McDonnell Criticised for Seeking "Loyalty Pledge" from Jewish MP', *Financial Times*, 8 February, available at: www.ft.com/content/1434fe9e-2b95-11e9-88a4-c32129756dd8 (accessed 28 November 2022).
Pitts, F. H. (2022), 'The Politics of Work and the Politics of Value', *Futures of Work*, #23, available at: https://futuresofwork.co.uk/2022/05/26/the-politics-of-work-and-the-politics-of-value (accessed 28 November 2022).
Postone, M. (1980), 'Anti-Semitism and National Socialism: Notes on the German Reaction to "Holocaust"', *New German Critique*, 19 (1): 97–115.

Postone, M. (1993), *Time, Labor and Social Domination*, Cambridge: Cambridge University Press.
Postone, M. (2006), 'History and Helplessness: Mass Mobilization and Contemporary Forms of Anticapitalism', *Public Culture*, 18 (1): 93–110.
Postone, M., A. Hamza and F. Ruda (2016), 'An Interview with Moishe Postone: That Capital Has Limits Does Not Mean That It Will Collapse', *Crisis and Critique*, 3 (3): 500–17.
Powell, T. (2018), 'Posters Claiming "Israel Is a Racist Endeavour" Appear at London Bus Stops and Are Being Investigated by Police', *Evening Standard*, 5 September, available at: www.standard.co.uk/news/london/outrage-as-posters-claiming-israel-is-a-racist-endeavour-spring-up-at-london-bus-stops-a3928681.html (accessed 28 November 2022).
Randall, D. (2021), *Confronting Antisemitism on the Left*, London: No Pasaran Media.
Reuters (2018), 'Big Banks Must Never Again Be "Master of the Economy", John McDonnell to Warn', *The Guardian*, 15 September, available at: www.theguardian.com/politics/2018/sep/15/john-mcdonnell-financial-crisis-big-banks-must-never-again-be-master-of-the-economy (accessed 28 November 2022).
Rich, D. (2018), *The Left's Jewish Problem: Jeremy Corbyn, Israel and Anti-Semitism*, 2nd edn, London: Biteback.
Sarkar, A. (2018), 'The IHRA Definition of Antisemitism Is a Threat to Free Expression', *The Guardian*, 3 September, available at: www.theguardian.com/commentisfree/2018/sep/03/ihra-antisemitism-labour-palestine (accessed 28 November 2022).
Segalov, M. (2018), 'Jeremy Corbyn Is No Anti-Semite, But He Did Fuck Up', *Huck*, 26 March, available at: www.huckmag.com/perspectives/opinion-perspectives/jeremy-corbyn-anti-semitism-michael-segalov (accessed 28 November 2022).
Stedman Jones, G. (1983), *Languages of Class*, Cambridge: Cambridge University Press.
Stern-Weiner, J. (2020), 'We Need to Learn Lessons from Labour's "Antisemitism Crisis"', *Jacobin*, 21 February, available at: https://jacobin.com/2020/02/labours-party-antisemitism-crisis-corbyn-sanders (accessed 28 November 2022).
Sugarman, D. (2019a), 'Corbyn Blamed "Zionist Lobby" for Blood Libel Cleric's Expulsion from the UK', *Jewish Chronicle*, 2 April, available at: www.thejc.com/news/uk/jeremy-corbyn-blamed-zionist-lobby-for-blood-libel-cleric-raed-salah-s-expulsion-from-the-uk-1.482455 (accessed 28 November 2022).
Sugarman, D. (2019b), 'Corbyn's Aides Interceded to Reinstate "Jews in Gutter" Activist Glyn Secker', *Jewish Chronicle*, 13 May, available at: www.thejc.com/news/uk-news/corbyn-s-aides-interceded-to-help-jews-in-gutter-activist-glyn-secker-1.484093 (accessed 28 November 2022).
Thompson, P., and F. H. Pitts (2022), 'Ukraine and Progressive Foreign Policy', *Labour Campaign for International Development*, 14 February, available at: https://lcid.org.uk/2022/02/14/ukraine-and-progressive-foreign-policy (accessed 28 November 2022).
Watts, J. (2019), 'New Video Shows Jeremy Corbyn Vowing to "Defeat" the EU before He Became Party Leader', *The Independent*, 11 February, available at: www.independent.co.uk/news/uk/politics/brexit-jeremy-corbyn-video-eu-defeat-labour-party-speech-world-bankers-a8774426.html (accessed 28 November 2022).
Whitehouse, G. (2012), 'Mear One's Brick Lane Street Art: Class and Societal Inequality Not Racial Hatred', *International Business Times*, 10 August, available at: www.ibtimes.co.uk/mere-one-mural-east-london-politics-antisemitism-392209 (accessed 28 November 2022).
Yakira, E. (2010), *Post-Zionism, Post-Holocaust*, Cambridge: Cambridge University Press.

Index

abstract 9, 22, 41, 177, 181, 264
  antisemitism becomes 37
  concept 85, 210
  and concrete 182
  dimensions of capital 178
  domination 98–9
  economic logic 77
  equality 36, 94–5, 101
  labour 38, 193
  labour time made 79
  legal equality 8, 96–7
  mechanisms 37
  monads 186
  power of labour 180
  reasoning 8
  relations 86
  social mediation 100
  social wealth 182
  synthesis 96–7
  system-logic structures 80
  universalism 103
abstraction 7–9, 20, 23, 76, 83–6, 88, 136, 207
  economic 80, 81, 85
  real 38, 80
  real economic 21, 76–7
abstractions, Talmudic 20, 23
Adorno 2–3, 8, 10–12, 15–16, 18, 20–4, 26, 30–49, 75, 77–89, 93–4, 102, 104–10, 112, 116, 128, 132–3, 135, 137, 144–8, 151–3, 156–61, 163, 167, 169–71, 185, 203–15, 217–22, 224–9, 269
  Aesthetic Theory 224–5
  'better state … different without fear' 116, 132, 209, 225
  'hellish unity,' 22, 203, 209, 214–15, 225
  Minima Moralia 205, 209, 211
  Negative Dialectics 106–7, 209, 213, 220, 225
  'new categorical imperative,' 30, 203, 213–14

'permanent catastrophe,' 22, 203–4, 209, 212, 215, 224
Adorno and others, The Authoritarian Personality 6, 20, 24–5, 42, 48, 107, 137, 172, 208, 218, 225
African Americans 150, 152, 166, 216, 244
Afropessimists 219–20
Agamben, Giorgio 219, 225
alien 34, 38, 45, 63, 155–7, 161–2, 164–72, 257, 262, 269
alienating 103, 123
alienation 18, 97, 100–1, 159, 170, 268
allosemitism 218, 226
American Jewish Committee 172, 205
ancient astronaut theorists 161–2, 164, 170
anonymous authority 22, 155, 157, 159, 161–2, 164, 169
Anthias, Floya 100, 103, 106–7, 132, 135
anti-antisemitism 1, 210, 216, 268
anti-assimilationist 219
anti-authoritarian
  individuals 125
  movements 16
anti-authoritarianism 113–15
antiblack 194, 197
antiblackness 22, 175–201
anti-Bolshevik 16, 113
anti-bourgeois 120
anti-capitalism 8–9, 83–4, 89, 109, 111–39, 149, 177, 197, 258, 265, 273
  anti-modernization 117
  antisemitic 111, 135, 149, 266
  and emancipation 124
  fetishized 25, 76, 229
  Nazi 177
  partial forms of 265
anti-capitalist 112, 120–1, 134, 175, 178, 197, 257
  pretensions 114
anti-Catholic 166
anti-civilization 231

anti-communism 187, 223, 233, 235–6, 238–9
anti-egalitarian 114
anti-Enlightenment 127–8
anti-fascism 5, 178, 246
anti-feminism 132, 196
anti-financier 187
anti-genocide conventions 222
anti-identitarian 135, 220
anti-immigrant 194
anti-imperialism 3, 16–17, 23, 53, 62, 76, 89, 92, 109, 112, 117, 128–32, 135, 139, 254, 258, 269
   anti-Zionist 254
   nation state-centric 2
anti-Israel 16, 149, 197, 234, 240, 269
anti-Judaism 122, 210, 266, 268–9
anti-liberalism, patriarchal 130
anti-liberal liberals 26
anti-miscegenation laws 219
anti-modernism 136, 138
anti-nationalism 114, 220
anti-nature 26
anti-politics 198
anti-positivist 101, 105
anti-queerness 175
anti-racism 92–3, 136, 210, 255–6, 269
anti-refugee 238
antisemites, armed apocalyptic 121
   cultural-resentment 121
   garden-variety 121
   left-wing 118–19
   liberal 128
   the new 216
   nineteenth-century petty-bourgeois 115
   radical 123
antisemitism, Black 138
   bourgeois 39, 146
   definition of 3, 215, 227, 267
   eliminatory 121
   eschatological 121
   exterminatory 210, 224
   functionalist explanation of 267
   Islamic 132, 138
   Islamist 127
   left-wing 2, 25, 73, 111, 115, 118, 134, 139, 144, 154
   and racism 176, 179, 183–4, 188–9, 196, 203–29
   redemptive 217, 222–3
anti-universalist sentiment 22
anti-utopian 178
anti-urbanism 131
anti-Zionism 6, 16, 22, 108, 139, 231–2, 234, 236, 239, 250, 265, 267
   absolutist 23, 254
   academic 231
   antisemitic 22, 249–50, 269
   centre-periphery dynamics and 231
anti-Zyganism 195
Aquinas, Thomas 118
arafatki 241
'Arbeit macht frei' 77, 84, 86
Arendt, Hannah 3, 10, 15, 52, 68–9, 71, 73, 97, 107, 115, 135, 139, 205–6, 210, 212, 216, 218, 222, 225–9
   Origins of Totalitarianism 52, 71, 73, 107, 115, 135, 210, 225, 229
aristocracy 56, 117, 119
   European old-regime 119
   financial 118–19
   unproductive 184
Aristotle 118
Armenians 214
Aryan 9, 101–2, 123, 163, 166, 171
assimilation 14, 19, 30, 36, 95–6, 152, 219, 232, 243
astrology 156–62, 164–5, 167, 169–70
Atlantis 163, 168, 171
atomistic model of interest 152
atomization 40, 99, 170
Attlee, Clement 259
Auschwitz 9–15, 22, 24–5, 30–1, 46–7, 83–6, 133, 177, 199, 203, 208–9, 211–15, 217, 219, 221–2, 224, 226–30, 268
   after 15, 22, 203–29
   Birkenau 240
   centrality to critical theory 13
   education after 48, 213
   gate of 77, 85, 251
   t-shirt Camp 147
authoritarian 5, 16, 47, 123, 125, 130, 144–5, 152, 176
   nationalism 125, 265
   parenting 208
   personality 125
   populism 91, 152
   rebellion 175

subject 212, 217
subjectivity 147, 208
authoritarianism 23, 26, 143, 145–6, 153, 172, 226
authority 42, 139, 145, 158, 162, 169, 235–6
    abstract 158–9, 162
    benign 134
    heteronomous 125
    and power 158
    racism and anonymous 161
    the universe's 159
autonomization 38, 195
autonomy 97, 102, 139, 224
    of money 184, 187
Al-Azm, Sadiq Jalal 127, 135
Al-Azmeh, Aziz 127–8, 135

bacteria 255
bad apples, a few 208, 268
Badiou, Alain 19–20
Baldwin, James 150, 153
Balfour Declaration 69
Balibar, Etienne 93, 107, 116, 123, 135
Bank, European Central 191
bankers 22, 39, 80–2, 261
    big-nosed 265
    communist 147
    greedy 126
    immoral 122
    merchant 261
    parasitic 81
    world's 263
banks 58, 84, 87, 143, 191, 197, 199
    central 191, 194, 201
barbaric 83, 204, 208, 221
barbarism 47, 87, 102, 211, 231
Bauer, Bruno 115, 123, 149
Bauman, Zygmunt 208, 212, 218, 222, 226
BDS (Boykott, Divestment, Sanctions of Israel) 216, 239–40, 249
Beauvoir, Simone de 103–4
bench ghetto 235, 245
Benjamin, Walter 15, 171, 204, 206, 209, 214, 225
    'permanent catastrophe,' 22, 203–4, 212, 215, 225
Benn, Tony 261, 263, 266, 270
Beveridge, William 57, 71
biopolitics 220, 230

bisexuality, universal 101
Black Feminism 93, 107–8, 230
Black Hebrew Israelites 120
blackness 104–5, 176, 180, 184, 186, 188, 191–2
Black Power 193
black women 105, 108
Blavatsky, Helene 163
BLM (Black Lives Matter) 150, 198–9
Bloch, Ernst 15, 169
blood 8, 63, 80, 82–3, 85–6, 166, 173, 176–7, 200, 223, 228, 237–8, 244, 255, 267
    Jewish 166
    and soil 83, 85–6
    warm-as- 126
bloodlines 166
bloodsucker 82
Blue Labour 115, 270
Bobbio, Norberto 113–15, 136
body 85, 101, 103–5, 178, 180, 187, 244
    bent-double naked 256
    black 179, 184, 193
    Christian 244
    harmonic 55
    racial 178
body politic 57, 178
Boer War 52–3, 62, 64, 66, 72
Bois, W. E. B. du 152–3
Bolshevik-financier 187
Bolshevism 133
    Jewish 232, 235, 238, 241
    recycled German National 197
boundaries 100–4, 116–17, 136, 186, 216
boundary-transcending 126
bourgeois 2, 9, 95–6, 100, 130, 148, 260
    capitalism 206
    coldness 12
    critique 261
    democracy 188
    dungeons 97
    emancipation 35
    form 123
    freedom 78
    masculinity 98
    modern individuals 102
    nation 139
    norms 100
    order 14, 123
    petty- 188, 199

rationality 14
relations of pure identity 83
revolution 12, 36, 118
rhetoric 129
rights 149
self-controlled 100
subject 12, 36, 102
universality 36
bourgeois and proletarians (Manifesto) 188
bourgeoisie 122, 139, 188, 261
    modern 36
bourgeois-liberal world 29
bourgeois society
    critique of 75
    emerging 95
    liberal 36
bourgeois state and law 9, 149
boycott 216, 245
brain surgery 132
Bretton Woods 259
Brevik, Anders 218
Brexit 263, 269–70
British Israelism 166
British Jews, Board of Deputies of 269
bureaucracy 6, 146, 157, 175
bürgerliche Verbesserung 94, 107–9
Burke, Edmund 54
Butler, Judith 76, 88, 216, 224, 226, 242

capital, abstract forms of 177
    accumulation 64–5, 70
    casino 271
    circulation 12
    concrete productive 179
    constant 180–1, 191
    control of 180
    critique of global 269
    cycle of 198
    development of 190
    extended reproduction of 189
    fetish 76, 80–1
    fetish form of 178
    fetishism of 39
    fetishistic consciousness of 179
    fictitious 190
    finance 8, 16, 84–5
    form 38
    general formula of 79
    global 88, 191, 253, 262, 267, 269
    increased concentration of 145
    increasing organic composition
        of 193
    individual 198
    industrial 85
    infinite power of 184
    interest-producing 39
    interests of 8
    and labour 21, 175
    Marx's conception of 78
    merchant 184
    mobile 102
    organic composition of 199
    relation 38
    social forms of 179
    as subject 197
    value-appropriating (raffend) 124
    wasted 59
capitalism, advanced 47
    all-round enriching 123
    analysis of domestic 51
    anti-capitalist 120
    benign 113
    biologization of 9, 207
    casino 259, 271
    concrete side of 9
    Corbynite notion of 263
    corrosive 112–13, 122
    corrupt cosmopolitan 178
    cosmopolitan 122
    critical concept of 124
    critique of 22, 61, 76–7, 81, 136, 177,
        253, 257, 259, 265
    defining features of 129
    depiction of 259
    developed 180
    dialectical understanding of 123
    dialectic of 21, 111
    dimensions of 113
    domestic 51
    expansion of 127
    exploitative 113
    finance 64, 83, 191
    financialization of 83
    free market 120
    global 53, 89, 124, 127, 267
    good and bad 126
    hard-working 126
    hated forms of 84

homey 127
immoral 265
industrial 8, 51, 53, 58, 70, 209
inequalities of 258
international 263
is to blame 198
Jewish 68, 83, 85, 112, 123, 126
Keynesian welfare 259, 262
late 169, 214
late-nineteenth-century 56
liberal 126
metropolitan 129
national form of 85
neoliberal 191
new 196
non-corrosive 124
opposition to 71
partial conceptualization of 265
patriarchal 5
progressive nature of 122
quasi-state 8
racial 201
rejection of 176
revolutionary rejection of 79, 99, 176, 181, 258, 261
so-called Jewish 83
so-called neoliberal 82
state 123, 128
totalized 12
truncated critiques of 254, 263, 267
understanding 105
welfare 259
capitalism-as-imperialism 119, 127
capitalist, circulation 122
  class 260, 262
  cosmopolitan 59
  creative 81
  domination 37, 207
  economy 59, 81, 260
  everyday life 8
  exploitation 207
  foreign 65
  form 79, 112
  global 22
  individuals 76, 260
  industrial 59
  industrialization 7
  labour 181–2, 263

mode of production 1, 12, 21, 112–13, 116–19, 121, 123, 125, 128–9, 134, 264
nation state 125–6, 186
parasitic 81
plot 64
production 61–2, 261, 263
progress 117
society 2, 4–5, 7–8, 12, 21, 58, 60–2, 76–7, 81, 83, 92, 98, 117, 125–6, 175–7, 179, 182–3, 192, 195, 207, 209, 253, 262–5, 268–9
system 64, 265
unproductive 184
valorization 36, 175
wealth 76, 78–80
world economy 266
world market 99
capitalist modernity
  development 103, 124
  expansion of 106, 126, 129
capitalist order, emerging 36
Capitalist Realism 108
capitalist relations, the state as mode of existence of 185
capitalists
  conspiracy of a group of 22
  European 129
capitalist society, late 224
Capitol, US 22, 156, 175, 185, 202
Carey, Henry Charles 86
Carrel, Alexis 128
Casa Pound 114
CDAS (conservative-defensive antisemitism) 117, 119–21
Charlottesville 147, 201
Chicago Dyke March 94
children 166, 172, 240, 255
  Jews kidnap 239
  Jews spearing Palestinian 267
  production of 57
ciphers 85–6
circulation 12, 14, 35, 37, 39, 79
  Jewish 98
circumcision 244
  second 36
citizens 9, 13–14, 22, 95–6, 186–90, 213, 217, 222, 235, 237, 255
citizenship 9, 36, 67, 95–6, 186, 210
Civic Improvement 94

civilization 1, 3, 15, 30–4, 40–1, 46, 58, 63, 112, 121–4, 126–9, 131, 133, 135, 139, 163–4, 204, 211–13
    against 212
    ancient 169
    caesurae of 213
    capitalist 15, 123, 135
    catastrophe of 204
    critique of 3
    dialectical critique of 112
    enlightened 211
    failed 102
    gentile 34
    liberal-democratic European 213
    limitations of 15
    machine 56
    modern 15
    modern European 30
    non-white 162
    process of 31
    progress of 133
    rebellion against 31
    repressive 34
    ritual of 32
    salvation of 128
    secular 131
    Western 132, 204, 211–12
civilizational caesura/ rupture 10, 14, 212
civilizational coercion 32
civilization's triumphal procession 211
civilizing mission 212
civil society 9, 66, 95–6, 148, 193
Claussen, Detlev 2, 10–15, 18–20, 23, 29, 31, 36–7, 39–40, 48–9, 204–5, 215, 220, 226
Clermont-Tonnerre, Stanislas Marie Adélaïde, comte de 36
Cobbett, William 266
co-constitution, social 103
coercion 32–4, 40–1, 43, 54, 99
    social 41
coldness 12, 75, 100
colonialism 62–3, 68, 72, 97–100, 103, 106, 187, 189–91, 213, 215, 217–19, 223, 237, 246
    European 213, 215, 219
colonialism and antisemitism 223
colonialism and Israeli nationalism 237
colonial violence 11, 203, 212, 219

colonization 63, 223
colonized peoples 62
Combahee River Collective 93, 106, 107
commodities 7–9, 12, 36–9, 56, 64, 78–9, 100, 119, 126, 129, 158, 177, 183, 195, 198, 264–5
commodity form 7, 37, 116, 158
common sense 7, 88, 136, 159, 193, 200
    capitalist everyday 8
communism 102, 122–3, 139, 233, 235–6, 238, 247, 250
    state-centred 147
communist 60, 123, 125, 175, 185, 231–8, 241, 243, 247, 254
communitarian 52, 130–2, 151, 192–3, 197–8, 232, 241, 246
communities 131, 155
community 8, 36, 44, 46, 55, 57, 59–60, 63, 65, 78, 85–7, 95–6, 98, 111–39, 150, 155, 177, 198, 220, 241–2, 254, 262, 266
    concrete 97, 101
    concrete national-racial 177
    longing for 130
    national 71, 82, 98, 125, 189, 267, 269
    productive 22, 51, 258
    societal 126
compulsion, mute 36
Comte, Auguste 118, 135
concentration camps 15, 209, 213
concrete
    mediation 98
    personality 179
concrete nature, rebellion for 83
concreteness 9, 11, 20, 22, 40–1, 59, 76, 83–6, 96, 98–9, 111–12, 117, 121, 131, 134–5, 148, 152, 157, 165, 177–8, 181–2, 208, 213, 263–4, 268
    ephemeral 183
    mediated 181
conservatism 240
    enlightened 134
    revolutionary 130
    socially-minded 115
conservative 4, 54, 111, 113–15, 117–18, 129, 133–5, 149, 158, 193, 197, 241–2
conservative modernizer 114
Conservative Revolution 120–1, 127, 131, 135

conspiracy 22, 34, 65, 92–3, 122–3, 144, 146, 164–5, 167, 170–1, 173, 178, 238
  deep state 146
  international 7, 43, 150, 176
conspiracy theories 147, 150, 155–6, 164, 168, 170, 173, 176, 218, 253, 255–6
  allure of 164
  antisemitic 68, 71, 84, 143, 148, 151, 155, 238, 253
  blood libel 166
  far-right 22, 155
  and generalized irrationality 195
  reptilian 157
  sanitized 161
  whacky 155
conspiracy theorists 155, 164, 257
conspirituality 22, 155–7, 166, 170, 172–3
constellation 5, 21, 29–30, 44, 46, 52, 70, 91, 93, 102, 105–6, 112, 124, 204, 214, 253
constitution 31, 38, 77, 102, 105, 116, 176, 179, 185–6, 253, 260, 264
  basic 14
  contradictory 103
  mutual 105, 109
  objective 31
  psychic 31
  social 21, 37, 77–8, 80, 97, 136, 200, 262
constitutive relations, mutually 7, 70
consumption 56, 59–61, 63, 78, 263
  poor 56
  unproductive 193
Corbyn, Jeremy 22–3, 52, 71, 76, 114–15, 136, 253–63, 265–73
Corbynism 88, 115, 136, 253, 258, 260, 269–70
corrosion, societal 25, 73, 139, 154
corrosive
  journalism 102
  talk about class struggle 121
Covid-19 pandemic 169, 172, 189, 191
cranks 257, 270
CRAS (conservative-revolutionary antisemitism) 120–1
Crenshaw, Kimberlé 93, 105
crises, economic 59, 66, 192, 264
crisis 8, 21, 23, 59, 71–2, 76, 89, 138, 187, 189–90, 192, 227, 253–4, 268, 271–3
  capitalist 8, 70

dual 102
existential 197
financial 22, 81, 83
global 195
of modernity 101
opioid 148
recurring 134
structural 8
of valorisation 195
critique, liberal 1–2, 261–2
  Marx's 2, 39, 76
  normative 258
  personalized 21, 76, 82, 87, 257–8, 269
  postcolonial 212
  postmodern 118
  social 104
  socialist 261
  of society 2, 75–89
  standpoint of 103
  traditional left-liberal 265
  truncated 71, 253–4, 265, 267
critique of capitalism
  classical 262
  finite 178
  foreshortened 71
  moralistic 51
  personalized 258
critique of political economy, Marx's 76, 78, 81, 89, 193, 263
Cruddas, Jon 52, 71, 112, 259, 270
crypto-antisemitism 46
cultural code, antisemitism as 120–1, 211, 217, 230
'cultural Marxism' 23, 75, 88

denial 57, 95, 121, 249–50, 255, 268
deplorables 152, 196
Deutsche Arbeit 107
development, economic 86
Devi, Savitri 163, 171
devil 19, 166
dialectic, of capitalism and emancipation 22, 111
  of civilization 129
  of difference and equality 116
  of enlightenment 94
difference, biological 97
  concrete 95
  defence of 116

enemies of 151
equality by way of 117
eradication of 209
essentializing notions of 97
ethnic 96
gender 97
ideologies of 180–1
Jewish 96–7, 207
natural 119
naturalization of 97
pre-capitalist forms of 94
racialized 205, 210
social 185
unity in 153
dignity 116, 181, 183, 196–8, 200
  human 197–8
Diner, Dan 10, 14–16, 24–5, 206, 208, 211, 226
discontent, fetishized forms of 181
discrimination, intersectional 93, 105
Disraeli, Benjamin 66, 114
division of labour 158, 260
Dohm, Christian Wilhelm 94–8, 101, 107, 109
  domination, abstract 36, 98–9, 105, 197, 207
  by capital 130, 183
  by capital and state 130
  generalized impersonal 253
  international of capital 9, 207
  modern 122
  new forms of 37, 192
  old 33
  racial 212
  relations of 36, 190
  social 33, 36, 40, 72, 76, 89, 109, 138, 199, 201, 209, 273
  universal 126
  white imperial 243
Dühring, Eugen 123
DYR (Deir Yassin Remembered) 255

economic 35, 39, 47, 56, 60, 76–9, 81, 83, 86, 87, 99, 145–6, 196, 222
  competition 56, 95
  compulsion 78
  depression 59
  dominance 231
  downturn 81, 83

  fangs 68
  fateful phenomena 87
  functionality 61
  functions 44
  heresy 59
  hierarchical system 145
  inequality 54
  injustice 37
  interests 256, 267
  life 98, 259
  man 67
  modernizers 35
  nationalist ideas 86
  nexus 65
  non-productive activity 266
  objectivity 76–7, 82
  objects 75–6, 78, 136
  platform 254
  power 78, 256
  rationality 12
  resentment 133
  resources 56, 64
  sphere 53
  strategy 86
  structure 55
  system 37, 39, 62, 165, 258–9
  theory 63–4, 259
economic activity, good and bad forms of 266
economic objectivity, critique of 76
economics 137, 266
  imperialist 52
economy, financialized 187
  global 86–7, 271
  libidinal 41, 44
  master of the 273
  monetarized 35
  national 178
  productive 258
  psychic 34, 41
  real 253, 258, 263, 270
  rigged 258
  siege 263
égalité 21, 111, 113–16, 134
Eisen, Paul 255
emancipation 2, 11–14, 21, 29, 36–7, 95–7, 104, 111–12, 115–16, 124, 126, 130, 132, 134–5, 139, 144–6, 148–52, 212, 265

Black and Jewish 148
capitalism hinders 112
circumscribed 117
collective 152
failed 12, 21
female 94
human 119, 129, 134, 149
Jewish 94, 96, 123, 148-9
Jewish and female 94
legal 66
movements for 2, 152
near-complete 96
political 9
social 2
universal 267
vision of 146
emancipatory response to oppression 269
emancipatory expectations, modernity's 29
empire 53, 62, 66, 71-2, 119, 137, 212, 223
   British 17, 59
   Ottoman 66, 213
   Russian 223
empires, European 212
empiricism, concept-less 1
Engels, Friedrich 112, 122-3, 134, 136-7, 189, 201, 216, 227, 261
enlightened self-control 36
Enlightenment 1, 4, 10-11, 15, 19-20, 25, 29-30, 33, 36, 49, 75, 82, 89, 97, 102, 105, 108-9, 112, 128, 132, 134, 137, 139, 146-8, 152-3, 186, 204, 207, 224-26, 228, 269
   eighteenth-century 2, 7, 9, 11, 13, 36, 94-7, 106, 113-17, 119, 128-9, 134, 145, 149, 180, 185-6, 190, 192, 209, 224
   limits of 10-11, 21, 29
   militant 224
enlightenment and modern capitalism, dialectic of 132
enlightenment subjects 101
equality
   class 114
   legal 94, 96, 116, 190
   liberal and Stalinist conceptions of 209
   natural 114
   observable 96
   political 94
   social 114

solidarity and 2
universal 191
essence 7, 33, 95, 115, 126, 181-2
ethnonationalism 220-1
eugenics 57, 72, 222
Eurocentrism 131, 212, 219
European-Christian antisemitic tradition 22
European Union 238, 263
exchange value 38, 99, 176, 183, 194, 198
excluded in 186
excluded out 186
extermination 5, 30-1, 46-7, 85-6, 206, 223, 227, 233, 236
   camp 220
   of Jews 242

Fabian 57-8, 67, 259
fanatics, ageing Israel-obsessed 257
Fanon, Frantz 179, 184, 200-1
   Black Skin White Masks 200
fascism 1, 16, 24, 30-1, 34, 47, 115, 121, 124-5, 137, 156, 159-60, 171, 175, 178, 197, 201, 204, 208, 213-14, 223, 233, 265
   in America 159
   defeat of 46-7
   determinist theories of 204
   and imperialism 124
   Italian 178, 200
   left-wing 114
   in power 16
   theory of 16
   'third-positionist' 114
   in West Germany 214
fascist 15-16, 22, 41, 48, 114, 120-1, 124-5, 134, 145, 152, 155-6, 163-4, 171, 175, 178, 190, 192, 205, 208, 225, 244, 265
   antisemites 121
   ideology 114
   left 113-14
   personality 208
   populism 184
   postwar theorizing 163-4
   pseudo-anti-capitalism 120
femininity 97-8, 101-3, 106, 155
   racialized 103
feminism 107-9, 250
Fenichel, Otto 33, 40-2, 49

fetish forms 177–8, 197
fetishism 3, 39, 126, 178
   commodity 76–7, 79, 200
   of labour 119
fetishistic 176–7, 179, 181, 183–5, 198, 218
   production 183
fetishized
   appearance 178
   cognition 38
   representations 178
   revolts 207
   thought 8
fetishizing 2, 124, 126, 180
feudalism 118–19, 260, 262
Feuerbach, Ludwig 163
finance 8, 23, 58–9, 65, 67, 71, 81–2, 84–5, 157, 177–8, 191, 194, 199, 253, 259, 265
   international 21, 65, 69–70, 176, 190, 192, 253, 259, 263
   and Jews 52
   metropolitan 62
   unproductive 65, 70, 265
financial houses, international 52
financial sector, international 263
financiers 64, 81
   befanged Jewish 69
   foreign 64
   Jewish 21, 65, 68–9
   Jewish international 69
   liberal Jewish 218
finite and infinite (Hegel) 181–2
Floyd, George 143
Fordism 127, 192
form
   benign (of nationalism or capitalism) 2, 22, 253
   social 7, 9, 47, 62, 99, 146, 179, 185, 192–3, 207, 224, 262–3
   traditional social 129, 184
forms
   abstract 36, 84, 177
   foreshortened 177
   foundational social 269
   global 253
   impersonal 37
fragmentation 98, 126
fraternité 22, 111, 113–16, 134
fraternity 115, 134, 145, 149

freedom 36, 43, 54, 57, 75, 78–9, 81–2, 85, 88–9, 136, 151–2, 159, 171, 180, 186, 188, 199, 216, 225, 232, 259
   negative 51, 54, 159
free trade, international 259
French Revolution 10, 12–13, 22, 36, 112–13, 115–16, 145, 148, 261, 270
Freud, Sigmund 10, 33, 35, 40–1, 44–5, 49, 224
Freytag, Gustav 49, 98–102, 107–8, 124
Friedländer, Saul 217, 222–3, 227
Fromm, Erich 18–19, 136, 159, 169–71
functionalist theory 256–7
fundamentalism 127–8, 132, 137, 139, 254

gay liberation movement, French 120
Gaza 221, 226, 268
gender 20, 24–5, 93–4, 96–7, 103, 106–7, 110, 126, 128, 139, 150, 152, 193, 215
   constructions of 93, 97
   fluid nature of 20
   and Jewishness 93, 101
   and national identity 101
   and race 21, 94, 193
gender and race, foundation of 193
gender and racial divisions, fixation of 193
genocide 6, 12, 47, 120–1, 139, 162, 166, 172, 178, 191, 203, 205–6, 208–9, 212–14, 216, 218–19, 222–4, 226–8, 267
   Armenian 203, 214
   double 238
   Nazi 47
Gilroy, Paul 92, 108
globalization 83, 117, 129, 132, 191
God; gods 13, 77, 83, 164, 173
Golden International 134
Green, Thomas Hill 53–4
Guillaumin, Colette 92, 103, 108
Guterman, Norbert 43, 49, 130, 137, 146–7, 153, 160, 172

Habermas, Jürgen 3, 15, 19–20, 49, 89, 217, 227
Hegel, Georg Wilhelm Friedrich 10, 12–14, 22, 54–5, 76, 80, 83, 88, 124, 170, 181–3, 186, 198, 200, 253, 264, 266, 271
heterosexism 2
heterosexual 196

Hezbollah 76, 254
hierarchy 91, 98, 105–6, 119, 122, 167, 197–8, 215
   class 113
   natural 120
   of prejudice and victimization 215
   racial 164
   societal 135, 149
   traditional 134
   world system's 6
Hill Collins, Patricia 93, 105, 108
Hindu fundamentalism 132
Hippel, Theodor Gottlieb von 94, 96–7, 101, 108
Hiroshima 203, 213
Historians Debate 216, 226
Historikerstreit 216–17, 229
Hitler, Adolf 5, 12, 30, 71, 121, 124, 153, 163–5, 171, 204, 223, 229–30, 267
Hobhouse, Leonard Trelawny 51, 54–5, 57, 61, 71–2
Hobsbawm, Eric 133, 137
Hobson, John A. 21, 51–2, 54–72, 128, 132, 266
   antisemitism 53, 66, 70
   called a social fascist 60
   on capitalism and imperialism 51–3, 61–3, 68, 70–1
   critique of modern capitalism 56
   depiction of industrial society 53
   national economic interest 64
Holocaust 1, 4–6, 10–12, 15, 23, 25, 89, 98, 109, 121, 131–3, 138, 165, 167, 201, 203–4, 206, 208, 211–12, 214–16, 218–22, 224, 226–30, 233–4, 238–42, 245–7, 249–51, 268, 272
   by bullets 205
   denial 255
   deniers 164, 168, 255
   distortion 268
   memory 212, 216–17, 229
   Palestinian 240
Holocaust Memorial Day 268
Horkheimer, Max 10, 12–16, 18–20, 24–5, 29–30, 32, 35, 39–40, 43, 45–6, 48–9, 75, 81–2, 86, 89, 103, 105, 108–9, 134, 137, 139, 153, 203–7, 210, 212–13, 215, 217–20, 225, 227, 253, 269
   conservative aging 212

Horkheimer, Max and Theodor W. Adorno 11–12, 15, 20, 24, 29–37, 39–46, 48, 81–3, 86, 94, 103, 105, 108, 112, 132, 139, 146–7, 151, 185, 204, 207, 210–11, 215, 218, 253
   'culture industry' 4, 11–12, 105, 128, 130, 225
   'Elements of Antisemitism' 2, 10, 21–2, 29, 39, 75–7, 80, 83–4, 87, 116, 123, 146, 165, 185, 205, 207, 253, 268–9
humanity 2, 11, 34, 36, 40, 85–6, 96, 112, 122, 156, 164, 179, 265
   civilized 213
   enemy of 265
   freedom for 265
   modern 159
   types of ideal 116
human rights law, international 149
Hyperborea 163–4

Icke, David 156–7, 161, 163–5, 167–70, 172–3
idealism, British 53–4
   Hegel-inspired 53
identification 2–3, 5–6, 8, 14, 22, 31, 77, 82, 106, 144, 147, 151–2, 193–4, 197, 220, 222, 225, 263
   exclusionary 152
   group 152
   pathic 143–4, 146, 152
   pathological 147–8
   positive 220
   social 144
identities 2, 13, 91, 101–6, 108, 116, 123, 125–6, 131, 152, 162, 171, 188, 201, 232, 234, 236, 239
   class 193, 263
   group 3, 104, 220
   national 100, 148, 239
Identity, Christian 166
identity
   Jewish-national 13
   negative 209–10, 220, 228
   politics 2, 5, 21, 91, 171, 193
   racial 193, 209
identity claims, grievance-based 220
ideology
   agrarian 118
   anti-commercial 118

capitalist everyday 7
conspiratorial 149
racial 210
racial-scientific 222
racist 157
reactionary 2, 75
supremacist 222
IHRA (International Holocaust Remembrance Alliance), definition of antisemitism 215, 267–8, 272–3
Illuminati 164, 167, 256, 265
immigrants 58, 64, 67, 72, 132–3, 147, 166, 194–5, 217
  Jewish 66–7
imperialism 16, 19, 21, 51–3, 57–9, 62–4, 66, 68–73, 84, 119, 124, 126–32, 136, 139, 200, 214, 228, 230, 237, 242–3, 254, 268–9
  critique of 64
  economic theory of 63
  European 129
  financiers underpinning 65
  first economic analyses of 51
  liberal 62, 137
  so-called scientific defence of 58
  stock-jobbing 64
  underconsumptionist theory of 70
imperialisms, genocidal 20
income, unearned 58, 60
indifference 12, 46, 115
indifference to difference 115
indignity of labour, infinite 181, 184
industrial capitalists and workers, combining 59
industry, national 81, 85–7, 263
infanticide 34
infinite, universal 188
infinite appropriation 177
infinity 187
  bad 116
international
  business operations 69
  entanglements 53
internationalism 17, 72, 76, 119, 234
  liberal 62
  of nations 17
intersectionality 22, 51, 62–3, 71, 73, 91, 93, 104–8, 110, 215, 217–18, 243, 249–50, 253

invisible hand 21, 76, 78, 82–3, 179
ISF (Initiative Socialist Forum) 16–17, 24
Islam 120, 127–8, 131–2, 135, 137, 139
Islamism 127–8, 131, 135–6, 254
Israel 10, 13–14, 16–20, 24–5, 70–1, 75, 89, 126–7, 131, 133, 148–9, 177, 192, 215–16, 219–21, 228, 231, 234, 236–7, 239–40, 242–3, 245, 249–50, 254, 256, 258, 267–9, 273
Israelis 13, 17, 149, 165, 177, 216–17, 220–21

Jacobs, Jack 16–20, 24–5, 205–6, 221, 226–7
Jandl, Ernst 111, 137
Jedwabne 240–1, 249
Jerusalem Declaration on Antisemitism 215
Jesus 82, 126, 168
Jewish Nation State Law 221
Jewish Question, the so-called 17, 19, 24, 30, 66, 71, 136, 148–9, 152–3, 204, 206, 210, 247, 266
Jewnicorns 167
Jews
  the rumor about the 46, 75–6, 84
  as effeminate 103, 106
Judeo-Bolshevism 223, 227, 247
Judeo-Christianity 243
Judeopessimism 219, 221
Judeophobic 132

Kahane, Meir 187, 219, 228
Kant, Immanuel 10, 224, 266
Keynes, John Maynard 57, 80, 83, 89, 187, 222
Khomeinist ideology 131

labour 21, 38–9, 52, 56, 59–61, 79–80, 84–6, 98–9, 119, 126, 129, 139, 175–7, 179–85, 187, 190–6, 198–9, 253–73
  abolition of 196
  abstract 38, 88, 139, 179, 181–3, 193, 264
labour
  in capitalist society 182–3
  concrete 8, 99, 176, 179–83, 193, 198, 264
  concrete human 99
  dignity of 180, 270

enslaving 185
German 98
living 39, 79–80, 189, 191, 193–4, 196
material organization of 190
non-capitalist 8
productive 68, 85
slave 99, 180, 184
social 78–9
valorisation process 193
labour movement 134, 197
  Marxist 134
Labour Party 22, 52, 70–1, 76, 114–15, 253–4, 256–7, 259, 261, 263, 270, 272
labour power 39, 61, 78–80, 85, 180, 182, 185, 189, 193, 262, 264
labour time, social 79
Labour values, traditional 261
Lassalle, Ferdinand 61, 115
law, and universality 186
LDSAS (liberal democratic socialist antisemitism) 118–20, 124, 134
lecher, infinite 177
left-wing 2–3, 16–17, 19, 22, 52, 91, 93, 111, 113, 115, 117–20, 134–5, 138, 214, 229, 239–40
Lenin, Vladimir Ilyich 52–3, 64, 72, 122, 128, 137
  Development of Capitalism in Russia 122, 137
Leninism 16–17, 129, 192, 198, 232, 254
Lexit 263
liberalism 4, 8, 12, 39, 46, 52–4, 56–7, 60, 62, 66–7, 71–2, 113, 117–19, 124–6, 128, 191, 210
liberté 22, 111, 113–16, 134
life, bare 219–20
Livingston, Ken 132
lizards 165, 243
locust swarms 122
Löwy, Michael 169
longing 82, 103, 112, 130, 188
  unfulfilled communitarian 130
Los Angeles Times 156–7, 160–1, 164, 167, 169–70
Lowenthal, Leo 15–16, 18–19, 25, 43–4, 49, 130, 137, 146–7, 153, 159–60, 170, 172, 205, 227
Lukács, György 175

Maoist-Stalinist 16
Marcuse, Herbert 3, 10, 15–16, 18–19, 25, 205, 212–13, 228
Marx, Karl 3, 7–8, 10, 12, 14, 19, 36–9, 49, 61, 72, 75–6, 78–82, 86, 88–9, 92, 95, 99, 109, 112, 115–16, 122–4, 129, 133–4, 136–7, 139, 149, 158, 163, 170, 172, 179–83, 185, 189, 192, 197, 201, 204, 206, 260–1, 266, 268, 270–2
  critique of political economy 39, 129, 133, 198
  theory of money 88
  'time's carcass,' 82, 180
  value theory 38
  young 30, 266
  'Critique of the Gotha Programme,' 61, 72
  Grundrisse 181
  'On the Jewish Question,' 14, 116, 123, 206, 272
Marx and Engels 60, 112, 123, 134, 189, 204, 224
  Communist Manifesto 112, 118, 122–3, 130, 134, 188, 201, 218, 233, 261
  The German Ideology 122
Marxism 20, 24–5, 30, 60–1, 64, 75, 107, 128–9, 134, 138–9, 169, 179, 184, 193, 229, 260, 270
  Gothic 169, 173
masculine 33, 75, 128, 178, 183
masculinity 97, 100–2, 155, 196
  white 196
Mbembe, Achille 216, 226, 229
McDonnell, John 257, 263, 272–3
Mear One 256, 265–6, 273
mediation 3, 17, 37, 54, 99, 116
  abstract universal 36
  social 37, 92, 119, 264
Meinhof, Ulrike 16, 24, 84
Memmi, Albert 188–90, 201
memory 4, 11, 32, 203, 217, 219, 229, 231
  global 203
memory culture 212, 217
Mendelssohn, Moses 109
migrants 66–7, 216, 222
mimesis 33–4, 270
mimetic behaviour 32–3
MMT (Modern Monetary Theory) 187, 200

modernity 13, 32, 35, 92, 98–9, 100–2, 109, 121, 129–30, 132, 177, 180, 204, 208, 210, 213, 220, 226, 228
  ambiguities of 13
  capitalist 2, 21, 25, 92–3, 97–8, 101, 103, 106, 116–18, 123, 125–6, 129, 131, 134, 212, 265
modernization 13, 35, 96–7, 99, 101
  economic 94
money 7–9, 37–39, 56, 67, 76–85, 87–9, 118–19, 131, 176–80, 182–5, 187, 191–6, 198, 253, 255, 258–9, 264, 266–7
  Jewish 83
  societal mediation by 119
moralistic critique 51
MSI (Movimento Sociale Italiano) 114
multiculture, societal 131
Muslim Brotherhood 127, 132
Muslims 137, 216

nation 2–3, 9, 13, 16–17, 26, 36, 59, 62, 68, 70, 81–3, 85–7, 89, 97, 101, 107, 116–17, 121, 124, 126, 135, 139, 147–9, 175–201, 214, 227, 262
  finite 188, 197
  Jewish 17
  organic 17, 126
national and social revolution, dialectic of 17
nationalism 2, 12–13, 16–17, 19–20, 45, 62, 66, 68–9, 81, 83, 85–7, 91, 94, 108, 114–18, 120, 122, 124–7, 135–6, 147, 153, 217, 238, 240, 251, 256, 263, 267, 270
  and nation-state 114
  civic 125
  economic 262
  imperialist 126
  Israeli 237
  paranoid 125
  pathic 147
  populist 179
  progressive 83, 197
  secular Arab state-centric 128
  socialist 197
  world-wide 13
nationalists 2, 9, 19, 116–17, 123, 130, 134, 176, 187, 194, 235, 241–2, 248, 251

nationality 62, 122–3, 152, 243
national liberation 87, 233
nationals 64, 124
National Socialism (NS, Nazism) 1, 4–8, 11, 15–16, 25, 29, 41, 75, 89, 98, 109, 121–2, 133, 138, 164, 177–8, 187, 203, 205, 208, 214, 223, 226–8, 238, 267, 272
Nationalsozialismus 6–8, 11–12, 25, 138, 163–4, 175, 195, 206, 208, 213, 222, 267, 272
nation and state, unity of 186–7
nation form 117
Nation of Islam 120
nation state 12, 14, 17, 21–2, 51, 70, 86, 88, 114–15, 122–4, 126, 139, 176–7, 179, 186–7, 190, 192, 210, 253, 267
  homogenized territorial 17
  Jewish 13–14, 17, 267
  modern 9, 126, 148
  non-nationalist 20
  Palestinian 267
  redistributive 21
nation-state elites 127
Native American peoples 191
naturalization 92, 96–7, 104
naturalness, supposed 8
negation 9, 13, 106, 122, 151, 182–3, 211
neoliberalism 112, 127, 145, 256, 258–9, 262, 265, 268, 271
neo-Nazi 18, 20, 160, 163–4
Neumann, Franz L. 15, 20, 107, 205, 228
  Behemoth 205
New Age 22, 155–6, 162, 168
New Liberalism 21, 51–73, 128
New World Order 265
Nietzsche, Friedrich 12, 33, 40, 49, 114
Nirenberg, David 122, 137, 210, 266, 272
non-identity 3, 13, 18, 105–7, 123, 209, 220, 225
  ethics and politics of 225
  philosophy of 220
  politics of 21, 106, 225
non-producers, money-grabbing 119
non-whiteness 244
NOP (Narodowe Odrodzenie Polski) 240, 248–9
Nuremburg Laws 219

objectivity, social 38, 78
occidentalism 131
occidentosis 131
Occupy Wall Street 258
Oklahoma City 168
Open Marxism 129, 133, 136
order
  benign economic 259
  social 30–1, 33, 43–6, 119, 203, 209, 214
organic 8, 17, 54–5, 57–61, 63, 126, 155
  composition of capital 193, 199
orientalist 96, 136, 162, 244
OSS (Office of Strategic Services) 205
othering, projective 212, 219
outsider, excluded 186
oversaving 59, 61, 63–5

palingenetic 122, 130
paranoia 44–5, 75, 117, 125, 146, 223, 239
  pathic conspiratorial 22
parasites 25, 51, 55, 57–8, 67, 70, 81–2, 87, 102, 137, 177–8, 207, 253–4, 261, 271
parasitism 53, 55, 57–8, 61, 63, 65
particularism 116, 148
particularity 106, 126, 180, 187, 195, 208, 216, 221, 223
partisans, equating Jews with 222
pathic 45, 144–5, 147, 149, 151, 153
patriarchy 2, 5, 112–13, 117–20, 130
patriarchalism 122
patriotism 13, 114, 124, 126, 190
people, productive 265, 267–8
peripherality neurosis 239
personalities, as systems of scars 41
personifications 9, 37, 41, 76–9, 81–2, 85–6, 102, 148, 207
perversion 42, 44, 56, 65
phantasms 41, 169, 231
pogroms 32, 34–5, 66, 84, 86, 120, 205, 223, 230, 233, 235, 241, 250
Polish United Workers' Party 232
political-economic argument, general 69
political economy 23, 71–2, 76–9, 81, 88–9, 129, 133, 136, 183, 193, 253–73
  classical 56, 60, 260–1, 263
  critique of 77–8, 81, 88, 183, 253, 266, 268, 270
  liberal 59

populism 20, 23, 25, 83, 91, 114–15, 127–8, 135, 137, 143–53, 176, 258
  authoritarian 87, 152–3
  left-wing 151, 153, 199
positivism 38, 62, 102, 106, 118, 123, 163, 158, 170, 262
postcolonial 3, 17, 125
post-fascism 186
postnationalism 19
Postone, Moishe 4–9, 15–17, 20, 24–5, 61, 72, 75–6, 86, 88–9, 92, 98, 109, 116, 125, 127, 133, 138–9, 176–81, 184, 197, 199, 201, 207, 212, 215, 228–9, 253, 257–8, 264, 269, 272–3
  'Anti-Semitism and National Socialism,' 4, 25, 98, 109, 138, 228, 272
power
  abstract 7, 180
  ghostlike 81
  impersonal 268
  infinite 179, 184, 187
  invisible 76, 83
  Jewish 52, 178
  pre-existing societal hierarchies of 149
primitive accumulation, so-called 180, 184, 200
producers of surplus value 78–80, 87
production 1, 8, 12, 21, 33, 36, 39, 47, 56, 58–62, 70, 79, 99, 111–13, 116–19, 121–3, 125, 128–9, 134, 146, 177, 180, 183–4, 189–95, 198, 259–62, 264
productivist analysis 51
progress
  colonizers of 35
  critique of 204
projection 6, 22, 34, 42, 92, 125, 185
  false 34, 185, 207, 217
  paranoid 34
proletariat 2, 30, 60, 122, 130, 188–9, 203–4
  as the Subject of World History 175
protests, right-wing populist 144, 148
Protocols of the (Learned) Elders of Zion 126, 166–8, 171
proto-fascist 125, 128, 131
Proud Boys 153, 168
PSC (Palestine Solidarity Campaign) 255
pseudo-anti-capitalism 124
pseudo-concreteness of immediacy 181
psychoanalysis 1, 3, 40–1, 48–9, 136, 171

Qutb, Sayyid 127–8

race 2–3, 21, 43, 52, 57, 63, 65–6, 68, 89, 93–4, 96, 101, 103, 106–8, 116, 121, 135, 139, 147–50, 152, 166, 171, 173, 179, 183, 186, 190, 193, 198, 201, 205, 209, 222, 244, 251
   active financial 21, 65, 68
   constructions of 101
   and nation 190
   national 64
   reptilian alien 164–5
   violent hierarchies of 150
racialization 91–3, 179, 186, 191, 243
racism 2, 5–6, 8, 45, 91–3, 108–10, 116, 133, 137, 153, 159, 161–3, 167, 171, 175, 177–80, 203–29, 234, 240, 243–4, 255, 267
   antiblack 181, 183
   anti-immigrant 195
   anti-Slavic colonial 100
   biologizing colonial 92
   and colonialism 218
   constitution of 179
   cultural 92, 135
   in general 5, 180–1, 218
   and nationalism 107, 135
   veiled forms of 244
racist endeavour, Israel is a 267
racists 97, 116, 118, 131, 144, 160, 169, 184, 218, 233, 243, 248, 267
radical centrism 191
rationality 15, 33, 43, 92, 97, 121, 224
   bureaucratic-positivist-capitalist plan- 118
   instrumental 102, 204, 207, 213
reactionary 16, 113, 115, 118, 127, 130, 163, 170, 188–91, 254, 265, 268–9
rebellion 31–2, 82–3, 89, 234
   conformist 42, 83
reforms, social 55, 60, 63, 69, 72–3, 115
religion 3, 77, 79, 82, 96, 122, 128, 159, 169–70, 173, 183
   critique of 77, 170
remembrance 11, 231, 235
representation, critique of 198
reptilians 156, 164–6, 168
resentment 11, 33, 35–6, 82, 120, 131, 144, 146–7, 150

revanchist politics 176, 178, 184–6, 188–9, 191, 194, 196–7
Ricardo, David 60, 260–1
rights 17–18, 21, 36, 53–4, 62, 94, 96, 112–13, 115–17, 120, 135–6, 148–9, 190, 210, 221
   human 94, 144, 149, 151–3, 222
   individual 54, 57
   universal 152
   universal human 148, 226
   universal political 66
right-wing 2–3, 22, 91, 112, 114, 134, 146, 153, 240, 271
ritual murder 32, 165
Röhm, Ernst 114
Roma (people) 195, 200
Roosevelt, Franklin D. 134, 187–88
root races 163–4
Rose, Gillian 198
Rothschild 52, 134, 143, 164–5
Rousseau, Jean-Jacques 55, 114
Ruge, Arnold 163, 172
Ruskin, John 55–6, 67, 72

salafism 127
Schiefheilung 44
Schmitt, Carl 63, 186
self-constitution of personhood 125
self-determination 16, 187, 224
   democratic 145
   national 17, 269
self-identity 196
self-interest 70, 99–100
self-reflection 144, 147, 151
self-valorisation, infinite 198
semi-periphery 239
seriousness, fanatical 161
serpent 166
Serrano, Miguel 163
sex 20, 87, 101, 107, 116–17, 135, 149
sexism 26, 75–6, 89, 108–9, 116, 130, 175, 212, 244
sexuality 93, 105, 135, 149–50, 196
Shariati, Ali 128
Shaw, George Bernard 24, 57, 73
Shoah 11, 203, 217
Shylock 39
Sieyes, Emmanuel Joseph 118–19, 138

slavery 30, 99, 103, 162, 180–1, 185, 201, 220, 265
Smolar, Hersz 236–7
snake 165–6
socialism 17, 51–2, 54, 71, 118–19, 121, 123, 126, 128, 169, 191, 232, 262
  nationalist 121–2
social system 37–8, 47, 61
society, bourgeois 2, 9, 11–12, 14, 75, 94–5, 97, 100, 122, 193
  emancipated 30, 209
  false 87, 224
  feudal 96, 261
  Israeli 149
  late-capitalist 4
  modern bourgeois 11
  modern capitalist 2, 12, 14, 106
  modern industrial 59
  multicultural 132
  pre-capitalist 13
socio-biology 244
soil 8, 83–6, 99, 177, 231
solidarity 2, 6, 22, 26, 48, 91, 104, 117, 130, 143–4, 148, 151–2, 220–1, 235, 249
South Africa 52–3, 64, 67–9, 72
sovereignty 177, 186–7
space lizards, Jewish 170
Spinoza, Baruch 151, 154
spirit 3, 58–59, 80, 102, 115, 143, 186, 200, 220, 266
  inner moral 267
  national 87
Stalin, Joseph 16–17, 24, 134, 216, 229, 232–3
state
  and capitalism 51
  capitalist 13, 136, 183, 186
  colonial-settler 240
  cosmopolitan 20
  imperialist 70
  infinite 186, 188
  infinite mediator 185
  intervention 21, 54–5, 193
  Jewish 18, 25, 70, 126, 217, 219, 254, 267–8
  military-carceral 194, 196
  modern 124, 221
  and nation 9, 179, 185–6
  and nationalism 115

police 194–5
political forms of nation and 9
pre-fascist 214
state-centric 112, 131
state form, critique of capitalist 267
statehood, Jewish 18
state system, modern 124
Steiner, Rudolf 163
Strasser, Gregor and Otto 114, 197
STWC (Stop The War Coalition) 254
subject, automatic 37
subjecthood, autonomous moral 224
substance, concrete natural 85
Suez Crisis 221
Super-Imperialism 187, 200
surplus 61, 78, 129
  social 60–2, 64
  unvalorisable 193
surplus value 39, 59–61, 70, 78, 80, 89, 129
sustainability 134
Syrian refugee crisis 222
system 2, 12, 38–9, 45, 58, 61, 70, 81, 84, 86, 105, 108–9, 119, 122–4, 127, 161, 193, 195, 197, 208–9, 258–9, 264
  caste 164
  global 124
  global financial 258
  global nation-state 124, 127
  of imperialism and capitalism 84
  legal 104
  monetary 83
  political 258
  rigged 257–60, 262–5, 267, 269–70
system theory 76

T4 222
Third Estate 118, 138, 195
ticket thinking 151, 207
torture 22, 200, 203, 209, 213
totalitarian 15, 34, 82–3, 87, 98, 115, 205
totality 12, 54, 70, 100, 124, 126, 132, 178
  antagonistic 38
  complex 265
  dynamic 70, 119, 124
  social 105–6
trade, international 62
transversal politics 91, 103

Treitschke, Heinrich von 124
Trump, Donald 108, 147, 161, 166, 168, 173, 175, 177–8, 188–9, 194–7, 200–1, 258

UFO theorists 165
ultraconservative 112, 115, 120, 130–2, 134, 265
underconsumption 59–61, 63–5, 68
    and imperialism 64
universal 38, 88, 131, 133, 160, 198, 203, 208, 247, 249–50
universalism 14, 19–20, 116, 151, 191, 212
    anti-racist 129
    bad 148
    Enlightenment 19–20
    ethical 217
    false 148
    good 148
    illusory 95
    new kind of 116
    racism as 135
    radical 217
    yet another form of 116
universalist 197, 220
    anti-racism 233
universality 7, 24, 148, 185–7, 209, 221, 225
    abstract 36
    compelling 208
    false 152, 218
    limited 187
    totalitarian and particularistic 36
universal theories 116, 124, 160, 177, 185, 198, 208, 223
unproductive aristocratic class 261
unproductive classes, critique of 269
unreason 20, 25, 49, 109, 229
use-value 7, 86, 176, 182–3, 194–5, 198
usury 39, 67, 118, 147, 184
utilitarianism 55, 73
utility 55, 80
    political 221
    social 53, 55–7, 61
utopia 18, 20, 121, 128, 130, 172, 177–8, 227
    spirit of 169
    theological-political deceitful 130
utopian messianism 19

valorisation 190, 192, 194–5, 199, 204
value 7, 11, 20, 38, 52, 60–1, 78–80, 83, 87–8, 99, 114, 119, 124, 144, 148–9, 160, 170, 180, 182–3, 192–6, 198, 259, 264–5, 272
    law of 11, 20, 80
    national 100
    patriarchal family 120
    political 255
    self-valorising 39, 187
    social 65
    source of 180
    substance 181
    surplus 39
    true Labour 259–60
    unrealizable 194
    and use-value 7
    valorisation of 192–3
values, guardian of national 100
Verharmlosung 121
Vietnam 22, 203, 209, 212–14
violence, gender-based 212

wage-labour 180–1, 184, 189–90
wage-slavery 181
Wagner, Richard 37
Wallerstein, Immanuel 107, 116, 129, 135, 139
war, anti-Soviet colonial 223
wealth 21, 55–6, 61–2, 70, 72, 81–3, 95, 115, 118, 167, 177, 184, 192–3, 195–6, 258–60, 262, 264–5, 268
    disparities of 70
    distribution of 21, 260
    expansion of 184
    foundation of 260
    gap 192
    inequalities in 56, 195, 201
    Jewish 83
    material 189, 193, 264
    national 81, 86
    of nations 81, 89
    of parasites 81
    productive 177
    social 61, 79, 198
    societal redistribution of 115
    source of 260
Weininger, Otto 101–2, 107, 110
welfare state

Bismarckian 114
British 51
West, the 126, 131–2, 136, 210–11, 223, 231–2, 243–4
West Germany 4, 10, 76, 138, 201, 214
Westoxification 131
whiteness; white (people) 62, 156, 162, 180, 184, 191–3, 196, 201, 243–4, 251
White Power 166, 172
woman and nature, ambivalent association of 102
world economy 82, 191, 238
world society, capitalist 82, 124
world system 12–14, 22, 70, 116–17, 124–5, 127–8, 132, 239

xenophobia 133, 166, 240

Yiddish 223, 233, 236–7, 241
Yuval-Davis, Nira 91, 100, 103–7, 110, 117, 132, 135, 138–9

Ziege, Eva-Maria 20, 25–6, 31, 49, 75, 89, 110, 215
Zionism 6, 18–19, 25, 118, 148–50, 167, 220–21, 231, 233–4, 236, 242, 245, 249, 255–6, 267–8, 270, 273
Zivilisationsbruch 10, 14–15, 24–5, 208, 211, 226
Zündel, Ernst 164

www.ingramcontent.com/pod-product-compliance
Lightning Source LLC
Chambersburg PA
CBHW071805300426
44116CB00009B/1212